Philip Eade is the author of *Young Prince Philip* (2011), which was a *Sunday Times* top-ten bestseller and was also picked as one of the newspaper's ten best biographies of the year, as was his first book, *Sylvia, Queen of the Headhunters* (2007). Born in Shropshire, he read History at Bristol University and has worked variously as a criminal barrister, English teacher, financial journalist, and obituarist on the *Daily Telegraph*. He lives in London with his wife and daughter.

'If you like your Waugh fast, furious and funny, there is much to enjoy in Philip Eade's sparkling *Evelyn Waugh: A Life Revisited* . . . Waugh's letters are a joy to read, and Eade's coup is his access to a hitherto unpublished cache of them'
                                                            Paula Byrne, *The Times*

'Anyone with the slightest interest in Evelyn Waugh – and who has not been intrigued by his steady return to favour? – should buy, and keep, Philip Eade's *Evelyn Waugh: A Life Revisited*. Why? Because it is packed with brand new, fascinating information about Waugh, his family, his friends and lovers. As well, it "rebalances" a number of entrenched, skewed perceptions of man and soldier. And it is irresistibly readable. [It is also] entertainingly informative, funny, moving . . . and the epilogue is unforgettable . . . I can only testify, if that is the right word, that I have been researching and writing about Waugh since 1963 and that Eade time and again surprised and delighted me'
                                                   Donat Gallagher, *The Australian*

'[I]t is the force of Waugh's energy – creative, sexual and social – that crackles through the pages of Philip Eade's meticulous and wildly entertaining biography . . . Eade supplies an astonishing wealth of detail . . . and is sympathetic to Waugh's many failings without being sycophantic'
                                                      Martin Townsend, *Daily Express*

'Although there have been several other excellent biographies of Evelyn Waugh, this is perhaps the most penetrating and insightful one to date . . . For all the value of the newly available sources and the good use to which Mr. Eade has put them, in the end it is his biographical skills and crisp way with words and phrase that make this such a valuable tool for understanding the perplexing figure'
                                                   Martin Rubin, *Washington Times*

'*Evelyn Waugh: A Life Revisited* represents a sort of tipping point: Eade's even-handedness gently but firmly nudges Waugh's work centre stage again . . . Eade is excellent on tracing the sources of Waugh's delights and horrors, from his life to his work and back again: the failures, the successes, the disappointments, the endless grist to the authorial mill . . . read this book'
                                                         Ian Sansom, *Literary Review*

'Philip Eade has written a brisk, lively, and wonderfully entertaining account of the life of a strange, tormented, unique creature. Through page after page one finds oneself laughing aloud yet again at stories that have been told and retold many times. While previous biographers have been respectful (Martin Stannard) or compassionate (Selina Hastings), Eade seems genuinely to like his subject, and takes Waugh largely as he presented himself to the world. In his preface he writes that his intention is not to offer us a reassessment of Waugh the writer, but "to paint a fresh portrait of the man by revisiting key episodes throughout his life and focusing on his most meaningful relationships". In this admirably modest aim he has happily succeeded'   John Banville, *New York Review of Books*

'A splendid treat. Eade's exploration of the most significant episodes in the life of this fearless, deeply melancholic comedian is a most worthwhile addition to the bowing shelf of Waughiana'   Christopher Hirst, *iNews*

'Eade isn't a standard literary biographer; he is, by instinct and preference, an entertainer . . . He is an assiduous researcher with a considerable narrative gift. He also, crucially, likes his subject. Waugh never much cared what anyone thought of him, but Eade does, and time and again he finds justification for what previous biographers have considered questionable behaviour. He also has a nice, wry turn of phrase . . . this is an exemplary piece of work'   Marcus Berkmann, *Daily Mail*

'Brisk and entertaining . . . intelligent and illuminating . . . the best single-volume life of the author available. To read *A Life Revisited* is to experience a reckoning with a man whose life, like his work, is both a solace and a stimulus'   Matthew Adams, *Irish Times*

'There have been many biographies of Evelyn Waugh and *A Life Revisited* is up there with the best of them . . . what emerges is a captivating portrait of a man who went out of his way to appear much more cantankerous, cold and intolerant than he really was . . . at heart it's a gloriously entertaining indulgence. There isn't a single dull page in the whole book, and it could easily be twice as long without overstaying its welcome'

Eilis O'Hanlon, *Irish Independent*

'Essential . . . compelling . . . Eade's pacey new biography delivers the raw material of Waugh's life . . . treat the Waugh aficionado in your life'
Sunday Times Books of the Year 2016

'For even more laughs, Philip Eade's *Evelyn Waugh: A Life Revisited* demonstrates that Waugh's life, already done by divers hands, really is worth another visit'   *Guardian* Best Books of 2016

'Will send readers back to the novels in droves'
Financial Times Books of the Year 2016

'Philip Eade makes the case that now is the time to revisit Waugh and see if some of the old charges of cynicism, snobbery and emotional cruelty really hold true. The result is a bright, breezy and sympathetic portrait that stops just the right side of sentimental'   Kathryn Hughes, *Mail on Sunday*

'The chief delight of this biography is the way it foregrounds Waugh's own voice . . . Above all, Eade sends readers back to the books. You'll want to have at least the short stories, *Brideshead*, *A Handful of Dust* and the *Sword of Honour* trilogy to hand after reading this . . . Eade shows just how hard-won his effortless brilliance really was'   Suzi Feay, *Financial Times*

'Peppered with humour . . . Eade's fine biography does a very good job of pinning down the particular puckish charisma that made Waugh so popular'   Violet Hudson, *Times Literary Supplement*

'Vastly entertaining . . . a Perrier-Jouët book, frothy and fun'
Laura Freeman, *Standpoint*

'Eade's biography is crisp, diligent and sympathetic; his fresh material adds texture to this oft-told story'
James Fergusson, *Country Life* Book of the Week

'Eade's thoughtful and thorough re-examination will not affect Waugh's status as a novelist, but it may well raise his reputation as a man'
New Statesman

'Eade has launched into this confounding, crowded, complicated life with brio . . . Sympathetic, well-researched . . . *Evelyn Waugh: A Life Revisited* will whet the appetite of any Wavian'

Mark McGinness, *Sydney Morning Herald*

'Any biography of Waugh is entertaining because he was so witty a man, and Mr. Eade does not fail to entertain. He is not only fair to Waugh, moreover; he evidently likes him. It's good to read an admiring rather than a debunking biography' Alan Massie, *Wall Street Journal*

'This crowded, witty biography follows Waugh from the ancestral home in Somerset ("The only bathroom featured a stuffed monkey that had, improbably, died of sunstroke") to the jungles of Brazil. The supporting characters seem stranger, blunter, and more lovable, or hateable, than their doubles in *Decline and Fall* and *Vile Bodies* – in this case, life exceeded art'

The New Yorker

'Reveals a softer side to his personality, different from the brilliant, acerbic wit that previous biographers have focused on . . . A fascinating read'

Rebecca Wallersteiner, *The Lady*

'[Eade's] new biography deconstructs the monster and reattaches the man to the human race' David Pryce-Jones, *National Review*

'Thoughtful and intimate . . . Drawing on previously unavailable letters, manuscripts and diaries, Eade illuminates connections between Waugh's much-lauded fiction and the author's concealed emotional life . . . A convincing portrait of a flawed but gifted artist' *Booklist* starred review

'Well crafted . . . Eade's treatment reveals a man of astonishing awareness of his gifts and failings, great sincerity, and wit' *Publishers Weekly*

'Eade is a gifted narrator and a master at providing the right quote at the right time at just the right length' *The Washington Free Beacon*

EVELYN WAUGH

A Life Revisited

PHILIP EADE

WEIDENFELD & NICOLSON

First published in Great Britain in 2016
This paperback edition published in 2017 by
Weidenfeld & Nicolson
an imprint of The Orion Publishing Group Ltd
Carmelite House, 50 Victoria Embankment
London EC4Y 0DZ

An Hachette UK Company

1 3 5 7 9 10 8 6 4 2

A CIP catalogue record for this book
is available from the British Library.

ISBN (paperback) 978 1 780 22486 2
ISBN (ebook) 978 0 297 86921 4

For Rita

Contents

Contents

Illustrations

All photographs are courtesy of Alexander Waugh unless otherwise stated. While every effort has been made to trace or contact all copyright holders, the publishers would be pleased to rectify at the earliest opportunity any errors or omissions brought to their attention.

FIRST PLATE SECTION

The Waughs, 1890
The Brute out shooting
Midsomer Norton
The Rabans, *c.* 1892
Kate and Arthur Waugh with their bicycles (Boston University)
Posing after their engagement
Alec, Arthur and Evelyn, *c.* 1906
Evelyn with his nanny at 11 Hillfield Road
Kate, Arthur, Evelyn , Alec and poodle at Midsomer Norton, 1904
Alec, Kate and Arthur in the garden at Underhill, 1909
The Pistol Troop, *c.* 1910
Evelyn, aged eight
Evelyn and Cecil Beaton at Heath Mount
Alec, Evelyn, Kate and poodle, 1912
Lancing school photograph (Lancing College Archives)
Evelyn at Lancing, 1921 (Alexander Waugh and Lancing College
    Archives)
At Oxford, 1923
As a teacher at Aston Clinton, 1926
Richard Pares in the Alps with Cyril Connolly (Deirdre Levi)
Alastair Graham (Duncan Fallowell)

Evelyn between Lady Mary and Lady Dorothy Lygon (Private collection)
At Captain Hance's riding academy (Private collection)
Madresfield (Historic England and Bridgeman Images)
Evelyn with Arthur after winning the Hawthornden Prize, 1936
With Penelope Betjeman and her horse at Faringdon House (Private
collection)

THIRD PLATE SECTION

Laura Waugh, late 1930s
Pixton Park
Laura and Evelyn's wedding, 1936
Piers Court
Three photographs at Piers Court
Evelyn in military uniform, 1940
Bob Laycock, photographed by Yousuf Karsh (Camera Press and Martha
Mlinaric)
Evelyn with Randolph Churchill in Croatia
Anna May Wong, Evelyn, Sir Charles Mendl and Laura
Waugh family and staff, late 1940s
Evelyn and Laura returning to Plymouth in the Île *de France*
Evelyn in his study (Mark Gerson and Bridgeman Images)
With his family and two Italian servants, 1959 (Mark Gerson and
National Portrait Gallery, London)
At the entrance of Combe Florey (Camera Press and Mark Gerson)
With James, Laura and gardener
With Margaret in the Caribbean
At Margaret's wedding, 1962
Interviewed by John Freeman for *Face to Face*, June 1960
The Waughs, *c.* 1965

Family Tree

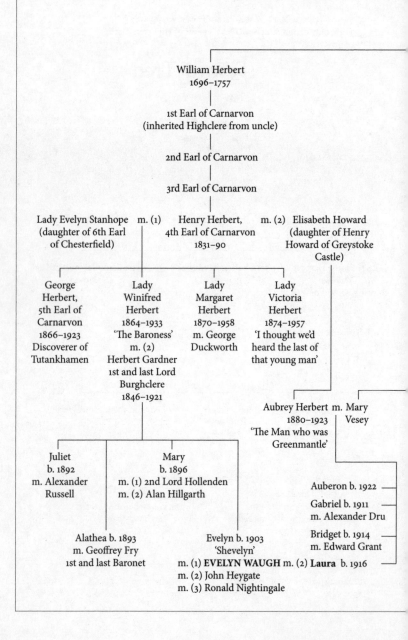

William Herbert
1696–1757

1st Earl of Carnarvon
(inherited Highclere from uncle)

2nd Earl of Carnarvon

3rd Earl of Carnarvon

Lady Evelyn Stanhope   m. (1)   Henry Herbert,   m. (2)   Elisabeth Howard
(daughter of 6th Earl   4th Earl of Carnarvon   (daughter of Henry
of Chesterfield)   1831–90   Howard of Greystoke
                                                                  Castle)

George   Lady   Lady   Lady
Herbert,   Winifred   Margaret   Victoria
5th Earl of   Herbert   Herbert   Herbert
Carnarvon   1864–1933   1870–1958   1874–1957
1866–1923   'The Baroness' m. George   'I thought we'd
Discoverer of   m. (2)   Duckworth   heard the last of
Tutankhamen   Herbert Gardner   that young man'
                  1st and last Lord
                  Burghclere
                  1846–1921

                                                  Aubrey Herbert m. Mary
                                                  1880–1923   Vesey
                                                  'The Man who was
                                                  Greenmantle'

        Juliet   Mary
        b. 1892   b. 1896
        m. Alexander   m. (1) 2nd Lord Hollenden
        Russell   m. (2) Alan Hillgarth
                                                  Auberon b. 1922

                                                  Gabriel b. 1911
                                                  m. Alexander Dru

            Alathea b. 1893   Evelyn b. 1903   Bridget b. 1914
            m. Geoffrey Fry   'Shevelyn'   m. Edward Grant
            1st and last Baronet   m. (1) **EVELYN WAUGH** m. (2) **Laura** b. 1916
                                    m. (2) John Heygate
                                    m. (3) Ronald Nightingale

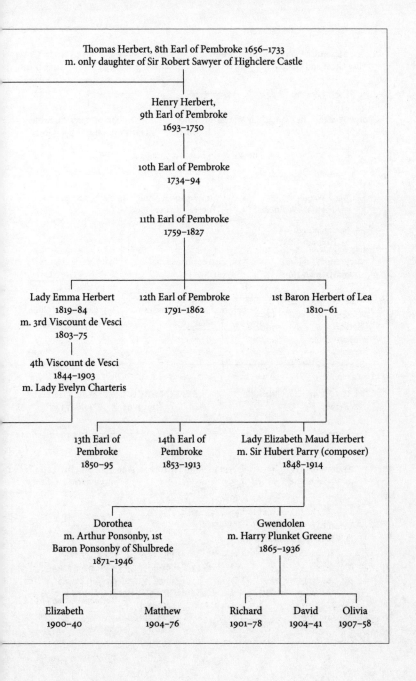

Thomas Herbert, 8th Earl of Pembroke 1656–1733
m. only daughter of Sir Robert Sawyer of Highclere Castle

Henry Herbert,
9th Earl of Pembroke
1693–1750

10th Earl of Pembroke
1734–94

11th Earl of Pembroke
1759–1827

Lady Emma Herbert
1819–84
m. 3rd Viscount de Vesci
1803–75

4th Viscount de Vesci
1844–1903
m. Lady Evelyn Charteris

12th Earl of Pembroke
1791–1862

1st Baron Herbert of Lea
1810–61

13th Earl of
Pembroke
1850–95

14th Earl of
Pembroke
1853–1913

Lady Elizabeth Maud Herbert
m. Sir Hubert Parry (composer)
1848–1914

Dorothea
m. Arthur Ponsonby, 1st
Baron Ponsonby of Shulbrede
1871–1946

Gwendolen
m. Harry Plunket Greene
1865–1936

Elizabeth
1900–40

Matthew
1904–76

Richard
1901–78

David
1904–41

Olivia
1907–58

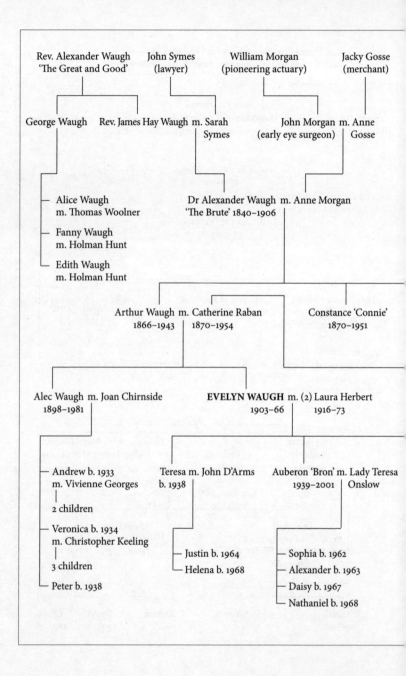

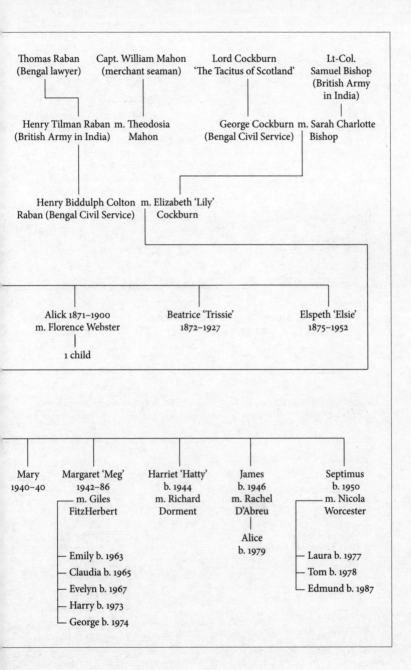

Preface

In one of the funniest scenes in Evelyn Waugh's novel *Brideshead Revisited*, Charles Ryder's father pretends to suppose that his son's very English friend, Jorkins, is an American.

> 'Good evening, good evening. So nice of you to come all this way.'
>   'Oh it wasn't far,' said Jorkins, who lived in Sussex Square.
>   'Science annihilates distance,' said my father disconcertingly. 'You are over here on business?'

Mr Ryder never makes his misapprehension explicit enough to give Jorkins the opportunity of correcting him but he is careful to explain any peculiarly English terms that come up in conversation, 'translating pounds into dollars,' as Waugh writes, 'and courteously deferring to him with such phrases as "Of course, by *your* standards . . ."; "All this must seem very parochial to Mr Jorkins"; "In the vast spaces to which *you* are accustomed . . ."'

Evelyn Waugh played similar games in real life. When a young American fan named Paul Moor wrote to him out of the blue in 1949, he was amazed to be invited by return to stay at Waugh's home in Gloucestershire. Moor later described to Martin Stannard his reception by Waugh's butler and, almost immediately, being confronted by his 'idol', who was wearing a dinner jacket and greeted him with a show of astonishment: 'But I thought you'd be black! . . . What a disappointment! My wife and I had both counted on dining out for months to come on our story of the great, hulking American coon who came to spend the weekend.' Dazed by his host's exaggerated absence of taste, Moor never realised that Waugh was making a joke about his surname.

Later at dinner, when the butler went to fill Moor's wine glass, Waugh waved towards a jug on the sideboard, declaring, 'I'm sure you'd prefer iced water,' as though that was all Americans liked to drink. When Moor bravely declined, Waugh exclaimed, 'But we've gone to so much trouble!' Soon he was off again: 'At breakfast tomorrow I expect you'll want Popsy Toasties or something like that, won't you?' The teasing went on throughout Moor's three-day visit and yet the baffled innocent came away with the impression that his host was 'an essentially kind man'.

A brilliant and extraordinarily clear writer, Evelyn Waugh could hardly have been easier to understand and enjoy on the page; yet the peculiar traits of his character were often harder to fathom, inclined as he was to fantasy, comic elaboration and mischievous disguise. If the imaginative flourishes in his letters were intended to entertain the recipients, the eccentric and sometimes frightening façades he adopted in person were more often designed as defences against the boredom and despair of everyday life.

Moor was right about Waugh's kindness and one only has to read his novels to find the deep humanity behind the forbidding front. One of his more sympathetic American obituarists accurately described him as 'a man of charity, personal generosity and above all understanding', however it is also true that he rarely went out of his way to advertise the benevolent side of his nature. 'I know you have a great heart,' his close friend Diana Cooper wrote to him, 'but you hate to put it on your sleeve – rightly up to a point – but rather than sometimes letting it fly there, by its own dear volition, you pin a grinning stinking mask on the site.'

* * *

This is not a 'critical' biography in the sense that it does not seek to reassess Evelyn Waugh's achievements as a writer, but aims to paint a fresh portrait of the man by revisiting key episodes throughout his life and focusing on his most meaningful relationships. Drawing on a wide variety of sources – published and unpublished – it also seeks to re-examine and rebalance some of the distortions and misconceptions that have come to surround this famously complex and much mythologised character.

My biggest thank you is to Alexander Waugh, who suggested the idea of a new biography to mark the half-centenary of his grandfather's death and gave me unfettered access to his archive which has supplied a great deal of the unpublished material in the book. In the course of researching his own richly entertaining *Fathers and Sons: The Autobiography of a Family* (2005) and more recently as editor-in-chief of the first *Complete Works of Evelyn Waugh* (Oxford University Press; the first of forty-three volumes is due in 2017), he has assembled the most comprehensive Waugh study archive in the world, comprising original manuscripts, rare transcripts, photographs, rare editions, memorabilia, professional records and copies of the vast majority of the existing primary and secondary material.

Among the numerous unpublished letters that cast fresh light on Evelyn Waugh's life there are more than eighty written to Teresa 'Baby' Jungman, with whom he fell hopelessly in love in the 1930s, and who he later claimed formed the basis for every character – male and female – in his masterpiece *A Handful of Dust*. These letters have long been regarded as the holy grail of Waugh biography and while charting the course of this unrequited affair they show a deeply romantic and tender side to his character that counters the popularly-held view of his heartlessness.

No less significant is the brief unpublished memoir written by Evelyn Waugh's first wife, Evelyn Gardner, describing the short-lived marriage that is thought to have unleashed a bitter and capricious side to his character and propelled him towards the Roman Catholic Church.

Evelyn Nightingale, as she became by her third marriage, has had a harsh press and was understandably wary of Waugh's biographers, declining most requests for interviews. She was however forthcoming with Michael Davie, editor of *The Diaries of Evelyn Waugh* (1976), who interviewed her and corresponded with her regularly. In her 1994 obituary in *The Independent* he described her as 'a much more substantial person as well as a much nicer one than the propaganda spread by Waugh's circle had led me to expect'. After his own death in 2005, Davie's extensive collection of Evelyn Waugh papers (including his interview transcripts and copious correspondence with Evelyn Nightingale) were acquired by Alexander Waugh. These records constitute another significant cache of untapped primary sources in his archive.

In the course of editing Evelyn Waugh's diaries Davie had undertaken intensive background research, interviewing several key figures in Waugh's circle besides his first wife, in several cases shortly before they died. Some of them Davie had sought out; others contacted him to correct false impressions – or, as they believed, the outrageous fictions – in the diaries as they first appeared in *The Observer Magazine*. His interviewees included Sir John Heygate, for whom Evelyn Gardner had deserted Waugh, who died shortly after meeting him. Alastair Graham, Evelyn Waugh's intimate Oxford friend, who had become a recluse on the west coast of Wales, was another of those who did not co-operate with any other Waugh biographer to the same extent again, although a few years before Graham's death in 1982 the writer Duncan Fallowell chanced to discover him in a New Quay pub, which began a quest entertainingly related in Fallowell's book *How to Disappear: A Memoir for Misfits* (2011).

Alexander Waugh's archive also holds a significant collection of material donated by Selina Hastings, derived from researches in the 1980s for her own outstanding biography, published in 1994. I am profoundly grateful to her for the resulting access to her numerous interview transcripts and for her great generosity in volunteering several additional stories that she had omitted from her book.

Another part of Waugh's life which the discovery of 'new' material renders ripe for revision is his army career in the Second World War. Here I owe a large debt to Professor Donat Gallagher, who for decades has been scouring military archives across the world for evidence to challenge many of the entrenched myths surrounding Waugh's military service – including Antony Beevor's widely adopted thesis concerning the supposed wrongdoing of Waugh and his commanding officer, Robert Laycock, during the Allied evacuation from Crete in 1941.

I am also grateful to Bob Laycock's son Ben and daughters Emma Temple and Martha Mlinaric for their help with my own research into this complex cause célèbre and for allowing me to quote from their father's unpublished memoir which sets out his version of events on the fateful night in question. I am equally indebted to Richard Mead, whose full and fascinating biography of Laycock – making full use of the memoir – is due to be published in the autumn; he could not have been more open-handed in sharing information and insights.

This book owes a considerable amount to the various scholars, editors, biographers, critics, filmmakers and bloggers who have done so much over the years to illuminate Evelyn Waugh's life and work. In addition to those already mentioned I am greatly indebted to the work of Mark Amory, Martin Stannard, the late Christopher Sykes, Robert Murray Davis, Artemis Cooper, Ann Pasternak Slater, Nicholas Shakespeare, the late John

Howard Wilson, Douglas Lane Patey, Charlotte Mosley, Paula Byrne and Duncan McLaren – whose various books are listed in the bibliography.

For access to various primary sources relating to Evelyn Waugh I am grateful to the Bodleian Library, Oxford; Boston University Libraries; Brasenose College, Oxford; the British Library; Christ Church, Oxford; Columbia University, New York; Georgetown University, Washington D. C.; the Harry Ransom Center, University of Texas, Austin; Hertford College, Oxford; the Huntington Library, San Marino, California; the Imperial War Museum, London; the Liddell Hart Centre, London; the National Archives, Kew; and the New York Public Library. I have sought to obtain permission from all relevant copyright holders and greatly regret it if I have inadvertently missed anyone; any omissions can be rectified in future editions.

I am enormously grateful as ever to my agent Caroline Dawnay and her assistant Sophie Scard; to the endlessly helpful staff of the London Library, where much of this book was written; to Mrs Drue Heinz for a very comfortable and productive four-week fellowship at Hawthornden Castle; and to my preternaturally patient publishers, Alan Samson at Weidenfeld & Nicolson in the UK and John Sterling at Holt in the US. Many thanks too to everyone else who worked on the book at Weidenfeld – Simon Wright, Lucinda McNeile, Leanne Oliver, Elizabeth Allen, Helen Ewing, Craig Fraser and Hannah Cox; and also to Linden Lawson for her excellent copy-editing; Kate Murray-Browne for her painstaking proofreading; and to Christopher Phipps for compiling yet another model index.

Grateful thanks also to the estate of Harold Acton (c/o Artellus Ltd, London), Johnny Acton, the Dowager Countess of Avon, Theo Barclay, Matthew Bell, David Belton, Caroline Blakiston, Rachel Blakiston, Michael Bloch, Tessa Boase, Nina Campbell, Raymond Carr, Matthew Connolly, Barbara Cooke, Richard Davenport-Hines, Maria Dawson, Jill and Tommy Eade, Jo Eade, Duncan Fallowell, Hugo de Ferranti, Claudia FitzHerbert, Giles FitzHerbert, the late John Freeman, Derek Granger, Robert Gray, Jasmine Guinness, Nicky Haslam, Lord Head, Bevis Hillier, James Holland-Hibbert, Kate Hubbard, Luke Ingram, Kathryn Ireland, Paul Johnson, Rosanna Kelly, David Landau, Jeremy Lewis, Imogen Lycett Green, Euan and Fiona McAlpine, Patrick and Belinda Macaskie, Giles Milton, Harry Mount, Rosalind Morrison, Benedict Nightingale,

Michael Olizar, James Owen, Thomas Pakenham, Henrietta Phipps, Saffron Rainey, Alex Renton, Hamish Robinson, Jonathan Ross, Charlotte Scott, Nicola Shulman, Christopher Silvester, Rick Stroud, Michael Sissons, Charles Sturridge, Christopher Simon Sykes, Inigo Thomas, Blanche Vaughan, Rupert Walters, Eliza Waugh, Hatty Waugh, James Waugh, Septimus Waugh, Teresa Waugh, A. N. Wilson, Sebastian Yorke and Sofka Zinovieff. And finally, my love and most profound thanks to my wife Rita and daughter Margot.

1

Second Son

In *A Little Learning*, the autobiography published two years before he died, Evelyn Waugh maintained that his childhood memories were suffused with 'an even glow of pure happiness'.[1] This was possibly designed to thwart what he called the 'psychological speculations' and 'naive curiosity' of nosy interviewers and biographers, who seemed to be always 'eager to disinter some hidden disaster or sorrow'.[2] In any event, there is plenty of contrary evidence that from an early age he occasionally felt both alienated and unloved, excluded above all from the extraordinarily gooey bond between his father, the publisher and critic Arthur Waugh, and his elder brother Alec – the 'popular novelist' as Evelyn later disparaged him. Nothing approaching an equivalent relationship existed between the father and his more exceptional younger son, who remembered that 'at the height of the day's pleasure his [father's] key would turn in the front door and his voice would rise from the hall: "Kay! Where's my wife?"'.[3] The arrival of this intruder would mark the end of his mother's company for the day and confine him to the nursery. 'The latch-key which admitted him imprisoned me. He always made a visit to the nursery and always sought to be amusing there, but I would sooner have done without him.'[4]

Alec remained very obviously his father's favourite throughout Evelyn's childhood. 'Daddy loves Alec more than me,' Evelyn once said to his mother. 'So do you love me more than Alec?' 'No,' she tactfully replied. 'I love you both the same.' 'In which case,' concluded Evelyn, 'I am lacking in love.'[5] 'I was not rejected or misprized,' he later told his friend and biographer Christopher Sykes, 'but Alec was their firstling and their darling lamb.'[6]

When Alec returned home from school for the holidays, a notice would be hung over the face of the grandfather clock in the hall, declaring 'Welcome Home to the Heir of Underhill!' – eventually prompting Evelyn to ask his father: 'When Alec has the house and all that's in it, what will be left for me?'[7]

Underhill was the house that Arthur had built for his family at North End, Hampstead, in 1907, when Evelyn was four. Its construction was paid for by a small inheritance from Arthur's father, Dr Alexander Waugh (1840–1906), an exceptionally gifted country doctor who had won all the major student prizes at Bristol and Barts and invented Waugh's Long Fine Dissecting Forceps – still used by obstetricians today. Publicly jovial and popular with his patients in Somerset, Dr Waugh nonetheless came to be known by his family as 'the Brute'[8] because of his tyrannical behaviour at home. Geneticists might wonder whether certain of his foibles explain the more demonic traits of his grandson Evelyn, who was only three when he died.

Barely a hint of the doctor's less wholesome characteristics found their way into his son Arthur's cloying memoir *One Man's Road*, however family tradition has it that when the word 'sadist' was first explained to him, Arthur responded: 'Ah yes, I believe that is what my father must have been.'[9] Subsequent Waugh memoirists, notably Evelyn and his grandson Alexander Waugh, have been less reticent, hence we learn that Arthur's rowdier younger brother Alick* was regularly thrashed by his father while timid Arthur was deliberately frightened – ostensibly to toughen him up – by being sent downstairs to kiss his father's gun-case in the dark (the Brute was mad about shooting but Arthur, although a good shot, was never keen), or violently swung on five-bar gates, or mounted on a rocking-horse while it reared on its back rockers, or left on high branches for hours on end and then surprised by the blast of his father's shotgun just behind him.[10] After a bad day, Dr Waugh was apt to lash out at the drawing-room ornaments with a poker, or fly into a ludicrously disproportionate rage, as when he came home to find his family using his sacred whist cards to play snap.[11]

---

* Alick left home as soon as he could, enrolling as a naval cadet at the age of twelve in 1883. Six years later he married a Tasmanian girl, Florence Webster, and brought her back to Midsomer Norton, where their son Eric was born in 1900. Later that year Alick died from malaria, whereupon the Brute promptly evicted his widow and child from the house he had lent them, ordered them to pay Alick's funeral expenses and other outstanding bills and packed them back off to Hobart.

Despite the ordeals of his childhood, Arthur made no mention of these explosions in his autobiography, partly, it seems, out of some residual filial piety and partly out of deference to his sisters, who despite being badly bullied themselves remained curiously loyal to their father's memory. He merely recorded that 'the great lesson of our childhood was undoubtedly discipline ... day after day, week after week, discipline, discipline and discipline'.[12]

Evelyn, though, already knew all about the Brute from his mother, who hated her father-in-law with a passion after witnessing his tantrum over the game of snap and eagerly disseminated many of the least flattering stories about him. Later in life Evelyn would entertain his own children with cartoons depicting the Brute's misdeeds and, as his grandson Alexander records, 'the arresting images he produced – snorting nostrils, flaming devil's eyes, lascivious mouth and snapping black-dog teeth – never failed to set their imaginations aflame'.[13]

Arthur grew up asthmatic – a condition often associated with 'nerves' – and a worrier. His mother Annie, a talented watercolourist, was a great worrier too; as her grandson Alec recalled, she was 'infinitely apprehensive ... her imagination pictured dangers everywhere'.[14] Yet however watchful, she could not escape her husband's extraordinary and unpredictable cruelty. Evelyn recorded how one day when his grandmother was sitting opposite his grandfather in a carriage and a wasp settled on her forehead, he 'leant forward and with the ivory top of his cane carefully crushed it there, so that she was stung'.[15]

The Brute derived his nickname partly from stories such as this, and partly to distinguish him from his grandfather, known in the Waugh family as 'Alexander the Great and Good'.[16] Born in 1754 at East Gordon in Berwickshire, where the Waughs had been yeoman farmers for several generations, this Alexander Waugh was ordained a minister of the Secession Church of Scotland before moving south to London – thereby anglicising the family – where he became one of the most celebrated Nonconformist preachers of his day, a vigorous campaigner for the abolition of slavery and founder of the London Missionary Society. His popularity was never more evident than during the remarkable scenes at his funeral in 1827, when his horse-drawn hearse was followed from Trafalgar Square to Bunhill Fields cemetery by more than fifty carriages and a vast crowd of people stretching over half a mile – according to Arthur Waugh 'one of the longest processions that had ever attended a private citizen through the streets of London to his last resting-place'.[17]

Alexander the Great and Good had ten children, among them Evelyn's great-grandfather James, who with his brother George used his inheritance (they each inherited £30,000 from their mother's brother, John Neill, who had made a fortune trading corn during the Peninsular War) to establish a smart chemist's in Regent Street, with exclusive rights to import the mineral waters of Vichy, Seltzer, Marienbad and Kissingen. Still more lucratively, they invented Waugh's Curry Powder – which is still made today – Waugh's Lavender Spike, an ointment for aches and pains, and Waugh's Family Antibilious Pills, which Queen Victoria was known to favour as a palliative.[18] After experiencing a religious calling, James eventually sold his share to George, who further acquired a large house in Kensington, a country villa at Leatherhead and blocks of property in and around Regent Street. Of George's eight beautiful daughters, Alice married the Pre-Raphaelite sculptor and poet Thomas Woolner, and Fanny married his friend Holman Hunt. Ten years after Fanny died in childbirth, Holman Hunt flouted convention and the law as it then stood to marry her younger sister Edith. Evelyn rarely spoke about his heredity but he often expressed fascination with his connections with the Pre-Raphaelites,[19] which helped inspire the choice of subject for his first book, a biography of Dante Gabriel Rossetti.

James meanwhile became an Anglican clergyman and at his own expense built a large vicarage at Cerne Abbas in Dorset, which he later bequeathed to the parish when the Marquess of Bath offered him the living of Corsley in Somerset – near to where most of Evelyn's other forebears had by then somehow converged. There the Rev. James Waugh, a tall, striking figure with a long white beard, 'lived well in mid-Victorian style,' Evelyn recorded, 'with long, abundant meals and an ample installation of servants and horses'. His theatricality would be inherited by subsequent Waugh generations, however his apparent joylessness and high regard for his own dignity and reputation[20] were such that his less reverential descendant Auberon deemed him 'mildly ridiculous'.[21] By Evelyn's reckoning he was fundamentally benevolent, but the same could scarcely be said for his son Alexander.

* * *

Born in 1840, Alexander 'the Brute' Waugh was sent to Radley, where he excelled at almost everything – academic, sporting and theatrical. His subsequent successes as a medical student promised a glittering career in London, however the lure of country life with its endless possibilities for shooting and fishing took him instead to the then remote village of Midsomer Norton, near Bath, where at the age of twenty-four and already sporting fashionable Dundreary whiskers he set up as a GP. He remained there for the rest of his life, tending to patients as far afield as his dog-cart would carry him – including Downside Abbey and school, whose monks later recalled him as always smartly turned out, 'with a button-hole and a jolly word of greeting'.[22] He married Annie Morgan, descended from an ancient but impoverished family of Welsh gentry, 'unambiguously armigerous' according to Evelyn,[23] and granddaughter of William Morgan (1750–1833), the clever, club-footed and acerbic associate of Thomas Paine who later earned a small fortune as a pioneering actuary to the Equitable Life Assurance Company. Annie's father, John Morgan, one of the earliest eye surgeons, died when she was six, and she was brought up by her mother Anne, one of the Gosse family of fundamental Christian Plymouth Brethren movingly if unreliably portrayed by her cousin Edmund Gosse in his classic memoir, *Father and Son* (1907).* Years later Evelyn's grandmother would recall 'with a recurring shiver, the sound of Philip Henry Gosse's [Edmund's father] knock at the door, his austere appearance at the portal, and his solemn but confident question, as he unwound an interminable worsted scarf from his neck: "Well, Cousin Anne, still looking daily for the coming of dear Lord Jesus?"'[24]

Annie doubtless saw marriage as a way of escaping the oppressive solemnity of her childhood, however she quickly found herself bound by a new set of constraints, her well-being according to Evelyn 'entirely subject to [her new husband's] will and his moods'.[25] While pregnant with their first child, Evelyn's father Arthur, she became terrified lest his

---

* In *A Little Learning*, Evelyn Waugh writes that one of his great-great-grandfathers was Thomas Gosse, an itinerant portrait painter. In fact he descends from Thomas's youngest brother John (Jacky) Gosse, who prospered as a merchant in Newfoundland before returning to Poole around 1820. Jacky Gosse's daughter Anne (Evelyn's great-grandmother) was thus first cousin of the naturalist Philip Henry Gosse (Thomas Gosse's son), chief protagonist of his son Edmund's memoir *Father and Son*. And Edmund Gosse was second cousin of Evelyn's grandmother Annie Waugh (née Morgan). See Ann Thwaite, *Glimpses of the Wonderful: The Life of Philip Henry Gosse* (Faber & Faber, 2002).

arrival interfere with her husband's first day of partridge-shooting. To the relief of everyone, he was born a week before the start of the season, on 24 August 1866.[26] After Arthur came his ill-fated younger brother Alick and three girls, Connie, Trissie and Elsie, who were never properly educated and were regularly reduced to tears by their father's outbursts. It is possible that they were all put off men for life and Evelyn later hazarded that 'so far as there can be any certainty in a question which so often reveals surprising anomalies, I can assert that my aunts were maidens'.[27] Though not without suitors, none of them married, Evelyn later explaining that within 'the stratified society of North Somerset they were part of a very thin layer, superior to farmers and tradesmen, inferior to the county families'.[28] After their parents died, the sisters all stayed on at the family home at Midsomer Norton, where Evelyn spent many of his childhood summer holidays, about two months a year. Save for decay, the house had hardly changed since his father's childhood and Evelyn relished its dark hidden corners and assorted interesting smells. Behind the creeper-clad façade lay a rambling interior in which the only bathroom featured a stuffed monkey that had, improbably, died of sunstroke after being brought to England from Africa by a great-uncle. Its grinning teeth were all that could be seen when the room filled with steam. Other curiosities included a collection of fossils in the library that the local coalminers used to bring Evelyn's grandfather, and a glass phial of 'white blood' that he had morbidly preserved from a patient dying of acute anaemia. Evelyn would always be fascinated by the macabre, and when the last of his aunts died in 1952 and he came to oversee the disposal of their property he 'sought vainly for this delight of my childhood'.[29]

For Evelyn the house at Midsomer Norton 'captivated my imagination as my true home never did'. As a boy he explained his preference to his parents on the basis that 'people had died there' – a pointed contrast to the sterile newness of Underhill where he grew up.[30] 'The bric-a-brac in the cabinets, the Sheffield plate, the portraits by nameless artists quickened my childish aesthetic appetite as keenly as would have done any world-famous collection and the narrow corridors stretched before me like ancient galleries. I am sure I loved my aunts' house because I was instinctively drawn to the ethos I now recognise as mid-Victorian; not, as perhaps psychologists would claim, that I now relish things of that period because they remind me of my aunts.'[31]

For Arthur, childhood at Midsomer Norton had held less happy memories. He recalled being 'perpetually haunted by vague apprehensions, fermented by the mysterious talk of the younger servants' – favoured topics included the brutal murder of a local cripple and the wicked activities of a cross-dressing highwayman.[32] Aged eight he was sent to board at a 'dame-school' in Bath, from where he wrote plaintively to his mother: 'Dear Muz, I will try to be a dutiful son and put cold cream on my lips at night.'[33] He later went to Sherborne, where he was teased for being swotty and unathletic. The nightly expeditions to kiss his father's gun-case had failed to arouse any enthusiasm for field sports and the only interests they ultimately shared were amateur theatricals and cricket, which Arthur adored despite being regularly outplayed by his sisters – he eventually scraped into the Sherborne second eleven.[34] To the added disappointment of his father, he showed no desire to enter the medical profession, and instead began to incline towards a literary career, editing the school magazine and winning the Senior Poetry Prize. At New College, Oxford he managed only a double Third in Mods and Greats[35] but won the prestigious Newdigate Prize (past winners of which included John Ruskin, Matthew Arnold and Oscar Wilde) for his poem on 'Gordon in Africa'. A great surprise to everybody, this triumph laid the foundations of what was to be a remarkable literary dynasty, Arthur's descendants having since produced some 180 books between them.[36]

By now resigned to his son's calling, the Brute told Arthur that he had 'nearly cried with joy' when he heard the news. 'You have made us very very happy and it is such a good thing for you in connection with any literary career you may take up & I am so glad because you have had disappointments and have borne them so nobly and now you have gained this great distinction – & one I know you will prize . . . God bless you my own darling son & make your career worthy of your best endeavours & then I know it will be a glorious one.'[37] If subsequently irked by the 'self-satisfied atmosphere of puffed success' surrounding Arthur, the Brute affected equal magnanimity when he learned about Arthur's third-class degree: 'Do you imagine that I look upon my sons as machines for the gratification of my self-esteem? You did your best and that is more than enough.'[38]

After he came down from Oxford, Annie Waugh sent her son's prize-winning poem to her cousin Edmund Gosse, the family's only literary contact, hoping he might open doors. Edwardian England's pre-eminent man of letters, whom Evelyn later shuddered to recall as the worst of the 'numerous, patronising literary elders who frequented our table',[39] Gosse began asking his young cousin to his Sunday literary soirées, where a star-struck Arthur met the likes of Henry James, Thomas Hardy, Bram Stoker, J. M. Barrie, Arnold Bennett and others. He also introduced him to Wolcott Balestier, the dazzling if slightly shambolic American publisher who had recently arrived from New York to woo English authors on behalf of John W. Lovell & Co.*

Balestier asked Arthur to come and work for him but then died suddenly of typhoid in 1891 while on a business trip to Germany, whereupon Arthur found himself placed in sole charge of Lovell's London office. Shortly afterwards, he began writing what turned out to be a very timely first biography of Alfred Tennyson, his idol, which Heinemann managed to publish eight days after the poet died in October 1892. The reviews were glowing – 'Mr Waugh's discriminating judgments have evidently cost time and thought,' said *The Times*, 'and proceed from a critical faculty of no mean order'[40] – and the book soon ran to six editions. It might well have made the twenty-six-year-old Arthur financially independent from his father at last, however in February 1893 Lovell's went bankrupt in New York and Arthur nobly took it upon himself to divert all his book royalties to his staff in lieu of their unpaid salaries. His personal sacrifice was all the greater since he now had to postpone his planned marriage to the girl he had been assiduously courting since his final year at Sherborne.

* * *

Arthur had met Catherine Raban (generally known as Kate, or to Arthur simply as K) eight years previously when her family moved into a village near Midsomer Norton. He remembered one day reading in the library window and seeing their dog-cart hurtling up the drive behind a high-stepping chestnut, the elder brother driving, Kate 'in a tam-o'-shanter cap and long, flowing locks, the apparition, as it seemed to me, of one of the jolliest-looking girls I had ever seen'.[41]

---

* Balestier was followed by his sister Carrie, who came to keep house for him in Kensington but shortly became the 'hated' wife of Rudyard Kipling, the most famous of her brother's new recruits.

Kate Raban had been born in India, where her father served as a magistrate. According to Evelyn, Henry Raban* was regarded with a mixture of admiration and bemusement for his 'familiarity with all the insalubrious purlieus' of his postings, and he eventually succumbed to one of the endemic diseases when Kate was just a year old.

Evelyn thus knew neither of his grandfathers, however the sketch of Henry Raban in his autobiography includes the haunting story of how as a little boy he had been removed from his teenage mother after she remarried and converted to Roman Catholicism (thereby becoming the only Roman Catholic beside Evelyn in the lower branches of Evelyn's family tree), to be looked after by his aunts. Years later they found a rosary that the boy had hidden and slept with as a memento of his lost mother.[42]

Kate's mother was Elizabeth 'Lily' Cockburn, granddaughter of the famous Scots judge Lord Cockburn (1779–1854)[†] whose *Memorials of His Time* is easily the best-written book by any of Evelyn's ancestors. Evelyn professed no particular pride in this illustrious predecessor, once telling a friend that he would have far sooner have been descended from a 'useless Lord', by which he meant a hereditary peer, than from one 'ennobled for practical reasons'.[43] For all his much talked-about snobbery, Evelyn never made any attempt to aggrandise his own antecedents and his position as a member of the hardworking, professional middle classes. He was in fact descended from plenty of useless lords, however he was never an especially diligent genealogist and seems to have been entirely unaware of his various historic links to the nobility via Lord Cockburn and his wife Elizabeth Macdowall, who between them descended from several of Scotland's oldest and grandest aristocratic families. Henry Cockburn could count John of Gaunt and King Edward III among his forebears, as well as the Earls of Buchan, Erroll, Huntly, Marischal and Morton, while Elizabeth descended from the Earls of Calendar, Gowrie, Linlithgow and

---

* Henry Charles Biddulph Colton Raban, born 1837, son of Henry Tilman Raban (born 1799) and Theodosia Mahon (born 1821).

† A friend of Walter Scott and other Edinburgh luminaries at a time when the city was 'the Athens of the North', Henry Cockburn was an engaging figure whose 'rather melancholy eyes, when roused by energy or wit, sparked like a hawk's'. A dash of eccentricity manifested itself in his attire that 'set the graces of fashionable dress at defiance. His hat was always the worst and his shoes, constructed after a cherished pattern of his own, the clumsiest in Edinburgh.' (See *Edinburgh Review*, January 1857.)

Southesk, the first Marquess of Montrose, the first Duke of Lennox and, further back, King Henry I.

* * *

After Henry Raban's death, Lily had married a Raban cousin of his, an army chaplain in India with whom she had two more children. At an early age Kate and her sister were sent to England to be looked after by two maiden great-aunts and a bachelor great-uncle just outside Bristol. According to Evelyn, Kate was 'entirely happy' at their house, 'the Priory' in the village of Shirehampton, and 'all her life she looked back on that elderly *ménage* as the ideal of home'⁴⁴ – an unconscious echo of his own feelings towards his aunts' house at Midsomer Norton. The chaotic houses Kate's family lived in during her adolescence fell far short of this paragon, her stepfather having retired his Indian army chaplaincy to fill short-term vacancies at various West Country churches without a regular vicar.

By the time the Rabans came to live near Midsomer Norton Kate was fifteen, Arthur eighteen and about to start his last term at Sherborne. Smitten at first sight, he began asking her to tennis, picnics and dancing, and as he coyly recorded they soon became 'something more than friends'.⁴⁵ The Rabans were far from bookish – when Kate's half-brother Basset first saw Arthur's library, he cried: 'All these books! And not one a feller could read!'⁴⁶ – but Kate read everything that Arthur lent her and in later life read a book a fortnight, 'always a good one', according to Evelyn.⁴⁷ She did not much like writing letters and, in the estimation of her great-grandson Alexander, though 'shrewd and prudent' she was 'not particularly bright'.⁴⁸ However her calm and reticent nature proved an excellent foil for Arthur's nervous insecurity and impulsive, garrulous theatricality. Their courtship progressed over the next eight years, after which their parents raised no objections to their getting married.⁴⁹

In a typically intimate letter to his elder son Alec, Arthur later confided that 'when I became engaged to your mother, I was able to tell her that I had never had anything to do with any woman in the world. And the chief reason why I had that inestimable gift to give her (for man's innocence is the finest of all marriage gifts) was largely that as a boy I broke myself early of the habit which is worrying you.'⁵⁰ The habit he referred to was masturbation, or 'self-abuse' as he called it.

Yet Arthur evidently found it a struggle to rein himself in. In July 1893 he wrote to Kate: 'I long for you so much, but after being away from you for so long, I can't promise I should be good. So for the sake of your peace of mind, Old Chum, it's just as well we can't meet ... don't long for me to come to you for you know I am a brute and it's better for you that I stay away.'[51] Their great-grandson Alexander deduces from their long engagement that Kate was reluctant to commit, perhaps disconcerted by Arthur's 'immodest and demonstrative gropings'.[52] They were eventually married by her stepfather in October 1893, by which time Arthur had gone some way towards repairing his battered income with freelance literary journalism. After honeymooning at the spa town of Malvern in Worcestershire they began married life in West Hampstead, in a small flat above a dairy off the tree-lined Finchley Road. This was then much closer to the open fields than it soon became and was chosen partly because Kate would have far preferred to live in the country. They also hoped that, being higher than smoky central London, the fresh air would be good for Arthur's asthma.

In the five years before their first son was born, Kate relished her role as homemaker. Having been surrounded by servants in India, her mother was a lousy housekeeper and to Kate's mind lived in a state of continual, avoidable discomfort. Kate decided that her best strategy in any given domestic situation was to think what her mother would do – and then do the opposite.[53] Evelyn later remembered his mother as 'always busy with her hands, sewing, making jam, bathing and clipping her poodle ... and with hammer and screwdriver hanging shelves and building rabbit hutches from packing cases'.[54]

Arthur, meanwhile, concentrated on his career, attending Gosse's Sunday literary gatherings, reviewing books and writing for newspapers and journals. His essays included an appeal for 'Reticence in Literature', published in the first issue of *The Yellow Book*, an avant-garde magazine in which Arthur's piece was hailed by the stuffier *Academy* as 'sane and manly' unlike the rest of the 'worthless, silly' articles. According to Arthur, the essay had an 'immediate, recuperative and permanent influence on my chances of getting literary work', and by the time he came to write his memoirs almost forty years later he had reviewed some 6,000 books.[55] His anxious temperament did not suit the fluctuating fortunes of a freelance, however, and in 1896 he took a job as literary adviser to the board of Kegan Paul, Tennyson's former publishers, in Charing Cross Road, with a salary of £600 a year,[56] while writing reviews when he returned home each evening.

By this time, intending to start a family, he and Kate had moved to 11 Hillfield Road, a Victorian terraced house not far west of their old flat, backing onto a narrow back garden with a lawn, borders, an apple tree and a willow, and a patch where Kate could grow vegetables. The sound of owls at night added to the rural illusion. They had no telephone or electric light but lived comfortably enough, waited on at table by their maid Agnes in a cap and apron,[57] with a man coming two days a week to do the heavier work in the garden. When they returned from holidays, a bare-footed porter would follow their horse-drawn cab all the way from Paddington in order to earn a shilling by carrying down their luggage.[58]

Their street was a cul-de-sac, which made it ideal for learning to ride the bicycles they had bought as part of the cycling craze sparked by the recent development of the 'safety' bicycle, whose inflatable rubber tyres made it far more comfortable than the previous boneshakers and pennyfarthings. Arthur could draw additional reassurance from George Bernard Shaw's pronouncement that bicycling was 'a capital thing for a literary man!'[59] and he and Kate were soon going off on long bike rides to explore the lanes of Buckinghamshire, pursued by their poodle Marquis,* Arthur in tweed jacket and plus-fours, Kate in long skirt and balloon sleeves.

These expeditions continued for several years until Kate fell pregnant with their first child. He was born on 8 July 1898 and christened Alexander, though this was later shortened to Alec, in memory of Arthur's brother Alick, who died in 1900.[60] An indulged child from the start, Alec was given the sunniest room in the house for his nursery, with a south-facing bow window from which the Surrey hills could be glimpsed on a clear day. Almost all his earliest memories revolved around his father, his mother and nurse barely featuring.[61] At five o'clock each day, when Arthur arrived home from work, Alec awaited him with his sketchbook and demanded he draw elaborate gory scenes from history or literature or spectacular disasters that might befall the Waugh household.

---

* Marquis was the first of a succession of spirited poodles owned by the Waughs. Terence Greenidge recalled one of his successors in the 1920s, Beau, having 'an extraordinary habit of eating papers' which he thought appropriate to a publisher's dog.

After Arthur became managing director of the publishers Chapman & Hall in 1902, he would get home slightly later but still found time to read poetry to his son, who loved the sound of it even if he rarely understood what it meant: 'Noble words,' young Alec would murmur when Arthur had finished. 'Noble words.'[62] Arthur also taught Alec to love cricket, and when he was five he gave him a cricket bat and they began playing single-wicket matches on the lawn. When Arthur announced Evelyn's birth that autumn, Alec's immediate reaction was, 'Oh good, now we'll have a wicket keeper.' It proved to be a vain hope, cricket being one of the chief annoyances of Evelyn's early life, the netting over his cot constantly pounded during his elder brother's endless indoor Test matches.[63] Alec admitted that any attempts on his part to teach his little brother its joys only served to reinforce his 'permanent repugnance for the game'.[64]

Evelyn was born at 10.30 on the evening of 28 October 1903, quite suddenly, so Kate recorded in her diary, before the doctor could get there. Despite the speed of the birth, she had lost a lot of blood and needed extensive stitching. For the next few weeks she remained frail, suffering painful headaches and post-natal depression – possibly deepened by the fact that she and Arthur had both been hoping for a girl. She stayed in bed until at least the middle of December, when a wheelchair was brought to the house so that a maid could push her up and down the road outside,[65] and she was only just beginning to regain her strength by the time of Evelyn's christening early in the new year.

On 7 January 1904, at St Augustine's Church in Kilburn, he was christened Arthur Evelyn St John. In later years he grew to dislike both Evelyn, by which he was always known, largely because of the confusion it gave rise as to his sex,* and St John, which he thought gave him an air of absurd affectation.[66]

Unlike Alec, Evelyn remembered very little about his father from his infancy beyond the sound of his coughing and the smell of his pipe tobacco mingled with the menthol preparation he burned for his asthma.

---

* Chosen 'on a whim' by his mother, so he recorded, perhaps as consolation for not having had a daughter, the name was usefully distinctive for his future career as a writer, however his arrival in Abyssinia in 1935 was awaited by an Italian press officer 'in a high state of amorous excitement' holding a bouquet of red roses. 'The trousered and unshaven figure which finally greeted him must have been a hideous blow, but with true Roman courtesy he betrayed nothing . . . and it was only some days later, when we had become more intimate, that he admitted his broken hopes.' *Waugh in Abyssinia* (1936) p. 164.

Although Arthur continued coming to the nursery each evening after work, Evelyn saw his appearance as an unwanted interruption in the day's fun. Of far more interest to him were his mother and his young nurse, Lucy Hodges, the daughter of a Somerset smallholder who had come to look after Alec but formed a far stronger bond with his younger brother. Evelyn remembered Lucy with great affection and her influence could be detected in his early interest in religion – she read the Bible all the way through every six months – in his scrupulous truthfulness (when he wasn't indulging in fantasy) as an adult and in the fact that the nurses in his fiction seemed to be the only characters to escape parody.

* * *

In the autumn of 1906, when Evelyn turned three, his only surviving grandfather, the bad-tempered Alexander Waugh, died from pneumonia after falling ill while out shooting. Evelyn's grandmother did not long survive him, dying fifteen months later. Between them they left enough money – the remnants of John Neill's Peninsular War corn-trading fortune plus income from a coal mine on one of the Morgans' Welsh properties – to enable Evelyn's aunts to remain living quite comfortably at Midsomer Norton, while Arthur decided to use his legacy to build a new house.

The family had long since outgrown their home on Hillfield Road, where Alec's non-stop cricket was getting on everyone's nerves, and one day early in 1907 Arthur set off with Kate to explore the area being developed two miles away, just beyond Hampstead Heath, on what was then the north-western edge of London. From the top of the Heath they came down the steep wooded cutting to the village of North End, passing the bow-fronted Old Bull & Bush pub – soon to feature in Florrie Forde's popular music-hall song – and the carriage entrance of North End Manor, one of the principal houses in what was then still a relatively rural community. Next to this was a small paddock where a character called Gypsy Joe kept his pony and trap and where, with characteristic impulsiveness, Arthur decided he would build his house.

The Sadism of Youth

The chosen plot for their new home was on the North End Road, then still a quiet, dusty lane with low white rails bordering its grassy footpaths, bypassed to the east and west by trunk routes for carters and coachmen. Within a year it would get a lot busier with the opening of the Tube line from Charing Cross to Golders Green, which set in motion a frenetic burst of housebuilding that quickly engulfed the dairy farms and market gardens to the north.

The terminus of the new line was at the junction of Golders Green Road and Finchley Road, a quarter of a mile downhill from where the Waughs built their house. A postcard of this crossroads from 1904 shows a lonely farmstead surrounded by open fields with a wooden signpost pointing to London, Finchley and Hendon[1] – 'such a place,' wrote Evelyn, 'as where "The Woman in White" was encountered'.[2] By the middle of 1907, though, estate agents' pavilions had begun to appear in the fields and by 1914 the entire area had been built over. Evelyn later pronounced his father 'the first of its spoliators'[3] and he spent much of his childhood living beside a vast, sprawling building site.

Nowadays a publisher of Arthur's standing would have to spend well over ten times his salary for an equivalent London house, but in 1907 it cost Arthur barely what he earned in a year to build his new home – 'little more than £1,000' by Evelyn's reckoning.[4] By the standards of those days it was a very ordinary suburban villa, a typical middle-class professional's home, although for a time it had the distinction of being the only new house in the village and its relative isolation made it look far more desirable than it now appears, next to a drive-in car wash.

Arthur involved himself in every aspect of the plans, stepping out all the rooms and stipulating sufficient windows to make it light and airy, although the effect was offset by his penchant for gloomy interior oak panelling, wainscoting and floorboards. The finished house – which Arthur named Underhill after the leafy lane where he and Kate had trysted at Midsomer Norton – was no architectural gem and Evelyn later deemed his father's sentimental attachment to its actual structure 'slightly absurd'. The only two times he could remember being beaten by him was when he had done 'wilful injuries to its fabric; once by paring the corners of a chimney-piece with a new knife, once by excavating a tunnel through a boot-cupboard into the foundations where, until detected, I was able to crawl about under the floor joists'.[5]

Arthur's devotion to his new home was intense, however, particularly since his asthma and slight deafness made him increasingly reluctant to go out in the evening. He was almost certainly the only person in North End at that time who went to work in London, but when he got back home each evening he retreated to his 'book-room' to dash off book reviews for *The Daily Telegraph* (his reviews were written, so Evelyn recorded, 'as he did everything, at deleterious speed'),[6] poems and other writings.

Several evenings a week in the same room after dinner he would read aloud from his literary favourites. Sometimes he also read the popular plays of his youth, 'stepping about the room,' as Evelyn recalled in *A Little Learning*, 'and portraying the characters as he had seen them on the stage'. Evelyn described how Arthur held his family rapt 'with precision of tone, authority and variety that I have heard excelled only by Sir John Gielgud'.[7] 'In these recitations of English prose and verse,' Evelyn wrote, 'the incomparable variety of English vocabulary, the cadences and rhythms of the language, saturated my young mind, so that I never thought of English Literature as a school subject, as matter for analysis and historical arrangement, but as a source of natural joy.'[8] However, as an adolescent Evelyn was frequently embarrassed by these readings and was scathing of them in his diary, describing one of Arthur's typical performances as 'a good lecture but incorrigibly theatrical as usual'. The diary was later bound and left on the shelves at Underhill and after Arthur nosily read what Evelyn had written, he never read aloud again. Alec later begged Michael Davie to omit these references from Evelyn's published diaries, arguing that it was not what he would have wanted.[9]

* * *

French windows led out from the book-room to the garden and to the north Arthur could gaze out across bucolic meadows until they too were sold to developers and houses sprouted up beside them. Kate had a small sitting room directly above on the first floor where Evelyn sometimes sat with her and the boys had a day nursery alongside, to which Arthur eventually added a balcony overlooking the garden. Their night nursery was on the floor above facing the road and the large Victorian villa opposite where the thirty-one-year-old ballerina Anna Pavlova came to live in 1912 in wooded seclusion until her once extensive grounds were built over too. There was one spare bedroom, which was often occupied by some guest or relation from the country,[10] and a solitary bathroom, although the resulting inconvenience, compounded by the fact that it doubled as Arthur's dressing room, was not unusual for a house of its kind at the time.

For Evelyn and his mother, neither of whom were especially enthusiastic city dwellers, the chief attraction of Underhill was the garden where Kate happily spent hours potting, planting, weeding and dead-heading while Evelyn drew countless complaints by climbing over the wall into the neighbouring North End Manor's kitchen garden in search of lost balls. In his autobiography he portrayed the complainant, a maiden lady, as 'an aged misanthrope',[11] however he scarcely went out of his way to endear himself to her. On one occasion he led his friend Mac Fleming into her garden and began lopping cabbages off their stalks, shouting, 'Here we come, the Cabbage Chopping Clan!'[12]

When the manor house eventually came to be sold, Arthur took the precaution of buying this bit of ground, after which it became for Evelyn 'the only part of my home to fascinate me' on account of its tall jungle of weeds and the dark steps leading down to a derelict furnace-house. 'This cellar and this wilderness I took as my special province, thus early falling victim to the common English confusion of the antiquated with the sublime, which has remained with me; all my life I have sought dark and musty seclusions, like an animal preparing to whelp.'[13]

On his frequent childhood visits to his aunts' house at Midsomer Norton, Evelyn thus relished 'the still airs of gas and oil and mould and fruit', the fact that some rooms smelled 'like a neglected church, others like a populous bazaar'. He would always remember their fierce cockatoo with its peculiarly pungent tray and the smell of leather and horses in the stables, even though the coachman had long since decommissioned the old brougham and kept only a solitary pony and trap, making up his hours by cleaning boots and pottering about the garden. To Evelyn's young eyes, the Midsomer Norton household 'belonged to another age which I instinctively, even then, recognized as superior to my own'.[14]

* * *

Almost as soon as they had moved into Underhill, Alec was sent away to board at Fernden, a prep school in Surrey, creating yet more distance between the brothers: the few postcards that he sent to Evelyn from there tended to begin 'Dear It'. Meanwhile Kate began to give four-year-old Evelyn his first lessons at home, shared with a local girl called Stella, the red-headed daughter of their friend Ernest Rhys, the Welsh poet and founder of the *Everyman's Library*. Stella found Kate Waugh 'a dear – everybody was very fond of her' and Evelyn 'so self-reliant, cocky, outgoing and enthusiastic'. He was also 'stronger and more clever than I was, but he did not rub this in'.[15]

But Evelyn's most constant companion at this time was his nurse Lucy, with whom he regularly went shopping in Hampstead, where he was excited less by the merchandise than by 'the dexterity of the shop-keepers . . . with butter-hands weights and scales, shovels and canisters, paper and string . . . I delighted in watching things being well done'.[16] Three times a year they would also go to Hampstead Fair, where Evelyn exulted in the jostling crowds with their 'pentecostal exuberance which communicated nothing but goodwill', the monkeys capering on hand organs and, once again, the smells – 'orange peel, sweat, beer, coconut, trampled grass, horses'.[17] According to Evelyn's autobiography, written some sixty years later, Lucy entirely reciprocated his love for her and was 'never cross or neglectful',[18] however Stella Rhys recalled Lucy once telling them both off and Evelyn countering that she had 'no business to speak to us like that' because 'we're of a much better class she is!'.[19]

It was on one of his regular outings with Lucy that Evelyn came across three children playing on a mound of clay and was invited to join them. They were Jean, Philippa and Maxwell ('Mac') Fleming, who lived on the former farm that was now the estate office of the new Hampstead

Garden Suburb. Their father (Edward Vandermere Fleming) worked at the War Office and to Evelyn's fascination kept a revolver for his family's protection and an Airedale watch-dog called Warder. The Flemings soon became Evelyn's regular holiday playmates and the first of the surrogate families that he adopted during his early life, compensating for what he saw as the shortcomings of his own family and his rather isolated place within it.

Infected by Mr Fleming's defence measures as well as the prevailing unease in the years shortly before the First World War, the children convinced themselves that a German invasion was imminent and set about fortifying the clay heap, storing provisions in anticipation of a siege and preparing poison soup for the enemy. Quickly having established himself as leader of their little band, Evelyn dubbed them 'The Pistol Troop' and rallied them each morning from the field by their house with the cry of 'Hoik! Oy-oik!', his right arm bent across his chest in salute.[20] They agreed a strict code of laws and various initiation tests, such as walking bare-legged through stinging nettles, climbing tall trees and signing their names in blood. Never having been mollycoddled or discouraged by warnings of physical danger,[21] Evelyn was a fearless participant in all these rituals, displaying the same bravery that he would later show when swimming in the sea, which he preferred 'toppingly rough', and as a commando during the Second World War.*

His physical courage and combative nature meant that he liked nothing better than a good fight and relished the regular skirmishes with other 'roaming bands who attempted to enter our fort, whom we repelled with fists, clay-balls and sticks,' he recalled. One regular adversary called Felix aroused particular indignation among the Pistol Troopers by enlisting the support of a far larger band of 'gutter children', as Evelyn contemptuously recorded in his diary at the time. At the height of hostilities, Felix 'came again at a fierce charge but a voley of clay pelits combined with a stick charge drove him back again'. Felix charged once more, repelled this time by a 'smashing blow in the face' from Philippa, 'our best fighter' (she was awarded a medal for bravery that night); and again, now beaten

---

* Arthur Waugh was also curiously brave. He insisted on having all his teeth drawn without gas, refused to take cover from air raids and when warned one night – falsely as it transpired – that there was an intruder in the garden, he strode about it alone with a walking stick calling: 'Come out you ruffian, I can see you.' (*A Little Learning*, p. 67.)

back by 'such a blow in the ribs', delivered by Evelyn to one of Felix's recruits, 'that he fell flat on his face'.[22] Despite his evident satisfaction at this, Evelyn maintained that the conflicts were rarely started by the Pistol Troopers, who as Evelyn later admitted were a self-righteous lot, forever going on about honour, and in any case they needed to save their strength for the Prussian Guard.[23]

* * *

In September 1910, just short of his seventh birthday, Evelyn donned green tweed knickerbockers for his first day at Heath Mount School, twenty minutes' walk away up in Hampstead. The idea had been for him to spend two terms there before following his brother to Fernden, an alarming prospect given Alec's reports about his despotic headmaster, who bade Alec 'finish up!' after he had disgorged his revolting sago pudding, dipped his fingers in 'brown bitter liquid' when he bit his nails and appeared in his bad dreams long after he had left the school.[24] In the event, Kate's wish to keep her younger son at home* combined with Evelyn's evident happiness at Heath Mount meant that he stayed there for six years.

A month after Evelyn's arrival, the headmaster, J. S. Granville Grenfell, told Kate he was 'very pleased indeed with your young man. He is a smart boy, decidedly so, and promises extremely well. I do not know who has been teaching him, but he is better prepared than any boy of his age I have had for a long time. You will I am sure get an excellent report of his work and conduct generally at the end of term.'[25]

'Granny' Grenfell had been a few years senior to Arthur at Sherborne and was by then a forty-six-year-old widower. An admiral's son, he had a naval air with his tall, slim figure, neat, pointy beard and tight-buttoned serge suit, his demeanour alternating 'wrath [with] explosions of bluff geniality, in a way which might be supposed to derive from the quarter deck', as Evelyn recalled.[26] Already strongly attracted to fantasy, Evelyn was particularly intrigued by furtive talk among the boys of his wife's 'death-chamber' somewhere in his lodgings, which he was rumoured to

---

* According to Alec, she also thought that at that age at least Evelyn had 'too gentle a nature' for the Spartan discipline of Fernden (Alec Waugh, *My Brother Evelyn*, p. 168).

have locked and never re-entered and which Evelyn liked to imagine as 'Miss Havisham's bridal room, heavy with dust, festooned in cobwebs and rotting picturesquely'.[27]

Each morning began with roll-call and prayers in the gym, a sentry boy yelling '*Cave!*' at the approach of the headmaster and the room falling silent as he leaped up the steps and entered with a lusty 'Good morning, gentlemen!' Like Dr Fagan's charges in *Decline and Fall*, the boys chorused 'Good morning, sir!' in reply.

Saturdays were more nerve-wracking, when the headmaster drew everyone's attention to the boys who had done well that week and then publicly denounced those who had not: 'What is this I find? *Fletcher.* Fletcher has been idle. Stand out, Fletcher . . . We had better understand each other, young man . . . Any idling, Fletcher, and' – banging his fist hard on the table – 'I'll be down on you like a ton of bricks!' Only later did Evelyn realise that Grenfell's fury was mostly feigned and in any case he never suffered it in its fiercest form as he did well in his lessons and was one of the headmaster's favourites.

Evelyn usually walked to school with Arthur on his way to Chapman & Hall. He remembered these morning walks as the first time he really got to know his father and enjoy his company.[28] Still, Evelyn considered his office 'a offely dull plase',[29] as he recorded in his earliest surviving diary entry shortly before his eighth birthday, and was ashamed of Arthur's 'sedentary and cerebral occupations'. He would have 'better respected a soldier or a sailor like my uncles, or a man with some constructive hobby such as carpentry, a handyman; a man, even, who shaved with a cut-throat razor'. He always saw his father as rather 'old, indeed as decrepit', although he had been only thirty-seven when he was born.[30]

In his first year at school, Evelyn had lessons with a governess until 12.30, when the youngest boys were collected by their nannies. From his second year he stayed until 'middle-day dinner' and was taught by masters whom he recalled stoically as 'mild enough'. None of them were married and they included one who chalked his ruler to ensure consistency of aim when carrying out a multiple beating[31] and another who slobbered over his favourites[32] and bade troublemakers bend over a footstool while he kicked their backsides – he was eventually dismissed for pinching boys' bottoms.[33] 'Some liked little boys too little and some too much,' reflected the adult Evelyn. 'According to their tastes they mildly mauled us in the

English scholastic way, fondling us in a manner just short of indecency, smacking us and pulling our hair in a manner well short of cruelty.'[34]

Cruelty was more likely to come from other boys – not least Evelyn. In 1912, the pretty and transparently timid eight-year-old Cecil Beaton arrived at Heath Mount. Beaton later recalled elevenses in the asphalt playground on his first day when 'suddenly, out of nowhere, the bullies arrived'. Their leader was 'half the size of the others' and ran at full tilt towards Beaton before abruptly stopping just in front of him with a 'wild, diabolical stare'. Standing on his toes, the boy deliberately moved his face closer to Beaton's, 'ever closer until the eyes converged into one enormous Cyclops nightmare'.[35] Several times, according to Beaton, the boy withdrew and thrust himself forward, and then 'stood baring his teeth at me'. In an earlier version of the same story they were black pitted teeth. 'By the time the physical onslaught began, fright had mercifully made me only half conscious.'

Beaton's vivid account of his terrifying introduction to Evelyn Waugh was written almost fifty years after the event. The next year he told the interviewer John Freeman on the television programme *Face to Face*: 'Evelyn Waugh is my enemy. We dislike each other intensely. He thinks I'm a nasty piece of goods, and, oh brother! do I feel the same way about him.'[36] Given their long-standing mutual loathing, it is conceivable that Beaton exaggerated his playground reminiscences. However Evelyn refuted none of them when he reviewed Beaton's book in *The Spectator* in 1961, confessing 'with shame' that 'the spectacle of his [Beaton's] long eyelashes wet with tears was one to provoke the sadism of youth', and that far from it having been an isolated incident, as the photographer suggested, 'the bullying of little Beaton' had been repeated many times. The flimsy excuse for all this, Evelyn recalled, was that 'he was reputed to enjoy his music lessons and hold in sentimental regard the lady who taught him. I am sure he was innocent of these charges.'[37]

The persecution also included greeting Beaton with a loud 'Hullo Cecil!'. The boys generally called each other by their surnames and Evelyn explained to his friend Stella Rhys that it was an 'awful score to a chap to find out his Christian name!'.[38] He and his accomplices also bent Beaton's arms back and stuck pins into him. Evelyn recalled that the harassment stopped only when 'my companion in this abomination and I were caught out and soundly beaten for it by a master'.[39]

Evelyn's cruel streak remained evident throughout his life. Clues to it might lie in the more diabolical characteristics of his paternal grandfather, however if a tendency towards sadism was passed down from grandfather to grandson, it happened without them ever meeting each other. More likely Evelyn's propensity was prompted by the circumstances of his upbringing.

There appears little doubt that at this age he felt entirely loved by his mother, who oversaw his homework each evening and listened to his prayers at bedtime. Their closeness was evidenced by the secret code in which he finished his notes to her: 'Evoggles Goggles Moggles' for 'Evelyn Loves Mother'. If threatened with discipline by his father or Alec – who was given limited powers in this regard when he was eight – Evelyn would throw himself into the back of his mother's high-backed chair in the dining room and shout 'Sanctuary, sanctuary!' Everyone understood that he could not be touched there.[40]

His sense of love and security underpinned the self-confidence and sunny nature for which he was known as a boy – albeit with the occasional fits of 'life weariness and despair' that his friend Stella Rhys noticed. However at the same time he had inherited Arthur's emotionalism, which probably explains why he was later so scathing of this trait in his father, and Alec recalled that as a small boy he was apt to dissolve into tears at the slightest provocation.

Meanwhile, there was plenty of reason for Evelyn to feel left out by his father's blatant favouritism towards his elder brother.[41] In spite of their morning walks to school, Arthur was never entirely at ease with his younger son, and Evelyn could hardly fail to notice that he preferred Alec: in the school holidays they would disappear for long walks arm in arm over the Heath, or to cricket matches or the cinema. Years later, in 1933, Arthur wrote to Alec's elder son on his christening: 'The three great things in my life have been my Mother, my Wife, & my son – your father. Nothing else has mattered much to me but their love.'[42] It was as if Evelyn had never existed.

Alec subsequently admitted that he had 'remained an only child to all practical purposes right through my childhood, my brother Evelyn being in those early days no more than an encumbrance in a corner'.[43] From an early age Evelyn would have been conscious that his elder brother saw him as such. The few surviving postcards that Alec sent to Evelyn from

Fernden were occasionally affectionate, asking 'How is your thumb?' or 'Has your cold quite gone? I hope it has.'[44] However Alec later conceded that he had possibly been 'not very kind' to Evelyn when they were young and that he could 'still visualize the occasion when my mother lectured me on this point'. He confessed that as an indulged child he had grown up with a superiority complex, confident that he was 'going to make a considerable mark in the world', while 'Evelyn may well have felt himself relegated to a second place'.

In all the circumstances Alec ventured that Evelyn might have felt 'challenged to assert himself'[45] – which is presumably what he was attempting with the unfortunate Cecil Beaton in the playground, free at last from the yoke of his father and elder brother. Alec went on to observe that in spite of his later fearsome reputation, Evelyn had 'a very tender heart' as a young boy. 'The toughness was superimposed, in self-defence. Beneath it he was highly vulnerable.'[46]

Evelyn's short stature was possibly a contributory factor in this regard, rendering him more anxious to make his presence felt and thus more aggressive and domineering. He also had to contend with his effeminate name, although he later claimed to have successfully countered derision at school by reference to Field-Marshal Sir Evelyn Wood, who had won a VC during the Indian Mutiny and later commanded the army which defeated the Zulus.*

* * *

Looking back half a century later, Evelyn recalled that he had been 'happy enough' at Heath Mount but that the school was 'merely an interruption of the hobbies and affections of home'.[47] His school career was itself interrupted in the summer of 1912 when he fell ill with acute appendicitis and required an operation at home on the kitchen table. An appendectomy was then far riskier than it is today and not long previously the King's

---

* Leaving aside his gallantry and splendidly mustachioed appearance, Wood was perhaps not the ultimate embodiment of manliness. He was also known for his hypochondria, his vanity – it was said that he had his medal ribbons edged with a black border to accentuate their effect – and for being comically accident-prone, once managing to get his nose smashed by a giraffe that he tried to ride at a private zoo in India. See the *Oxford Dictionary of National Biography*.

surgeon had watched his own daughter die during the same procedure. Eight-year-old Evelyn was thus not told the diagnosis and later recalled a strange man appearing at his bedside inviting him to 'smell this delicious scent', before being put to sleep with chloroform. When he came round after the operation* he felt sick and found his legs strapped to the bed to protect his stitches. His next three nights were successively 'bad', 'good' and 'splendid', so Kate recorded in her diary,[48] but it wasn't until three weeks later that he was able to get out of bed, by which time the strapping had left him so weak that he could barely walk.[49]

To cure his lameness Kate took him off to stay on the Thames estuary near Southend, where they paddled on the mudflats and a nurse came regularly with an electric battery to massage Evelyn's feet and ankles. After three weeks of this regime they returned home but Evelyn's feet had still not recovered, so in late August back they went.[50]

This time Kate left Evelyn there on his own and for the next month he was billeted in a girls' boarding school which had long since been deserted for the summer holidays. His only companion was a little girl named Daffodil whose father was away serving in India and who was punished for wetting her bed by having her hands bandaged for a day. Never having been separated from his family before, Evelyn felt utterly abandoned. The only bright spot was the appearance three times a week of the cheerful masseuse, Nurse Talbot, who after several weeks of seeing how miserable Evelyn was suggested to Kate and Arthur that he lodge with her family instead, which he did for the next five weeks. Her husband was an old soldier who became merry with drink most evenings, singing songs and showering Evelyn with praise. Their daughter Muriel was slightly older than Evelyn and, as he recalled from time to time, she obligingly 'exposed her private parts to me, and I mine to her'.[51] So content was he in this Dickensian household that he forgot to write home, prompting a pious letter from Arthur deploring his ingratitude – which Evelyn later recalled moved him 'not to penitence, but intense resentment'.[52] When he did eventually return home, Kate decided that he should do lessons with the Fleming children under a governess rather than go back to school for the autumn term. Mrs Fleming was for some time under the impression that

---

* This was Evelyn's second operation, the first having been when he was circumcised as a baby.

he was an only child. 'Oh but he isn't,' one of her children corrected her. 'He has a brother at school whom he hates.'[53]

An agreeable consequence of this extended convalescence was extra time spent with the Pistol Troop, which that year began producing a magazine that was typed by Arthur's secretary and bound in full morocco, the first issue beginning with Evelyn's short story 'Multa Pecunia'. Arthur later conceded that while Evelyn had been inclined to take the routine of school 'in a sort of negligent stride' – in stark contrast to Alec – away from school he 'displayed at the earliest age a precocious capacity for organising'.[54] Besides the Pistol Troop and its magazine, he arranged shadow plays and theatricals in the nursery, writing the plays, making the costumes and scenery and directing the Fleming children who were themselves promising actors.[55] More unusually, around this time Evelyn also proved himself 'an irrepressible advocate of female suffrage' according to Arthur. While visiting Boscastle he placarded the harbour with signs he had made demanding the vote for women, and during a garden party at Underhill, when half the guests disappeared from the lawn, they were found crowded into the boys' playroom upstairs listening to an impassioned address by Evelyn on the 'imperative necessity' of the franchise being extended before the next general election.[56]

As a boy Evelyn was rarely lost for something to do. His father remembered him as 'bubbling with ideas'.[57] He spent much of his time either rearranging the nursery furniture and pictures or drawing and painting, committing vivid images to his diary – including a gory picture of his appendix operation in which he is held down by his mother as the surgeon gleefully waves scissors and a knife in the air while a man (possibly Arthur) hammers a chisel into his groin. Battle scenes were another favourite subject, in styles derived from various magazines and comic books, as were inscriptions copied at the British Museum.

He produced illustrated stories, also modelled on comics such as *Chums* and *The Boy's Friend* rather than the classics that Arthur was constantly trying to press on him. He was an intermittent diarist, often in verse, and an eclectic collector – 'coins, stamps, fossils, butterflies, beetles, seaweed, wild flowers, "curiosities" generally'.[58] He possessed a microscope and an air gun, and aged twelve went through a chemistry phase 'when with a spirit lamp and test tubes and assorted bottles, I conducted entirely unregulated and rather dangerous "experiments" in a garden shed'.[59] An obsession with conjuring meanwhile took him often to a shop near Leicester Square, where the staff of expert conjurors soon tired of performing illusions at his request. 'I must have proved [equally] tedious to the audiences I was constantly attempting to mystify,' he later wrote, 'particularly as I composed a facetious patter in imitation of the professionals I sometimes saw at children's parties.'[60]

His imagination and enthusiasm were quickly and broadly aroused, and so when his mother read him an article called 'How to Join the Navy', he promptly resolved to become a 'Merry Jack tar'. 'If I should be a sailor bold / I'd stand up on the deck / I'd lock my prisoners in the hold / And make their ship a wreck'.[61]

Such imaginings were common enough among boys of his age – although his seem to have been more inventive than most. More striking was the interest he began to take in Anglo-Catholicism when he was eleven.[62] At first religion was 'a hobby like the birds' eggs and model trains of my schoolfellows,' he recalled, the appeal 'part hereditary and part aesthetic'.[63] When he went to stay with his aunts at Midsomer Norton he relished the frequent churchgoing and especially Sunday evensong.[64] The High Church curate there taught him to serve at the altar and Evelyn recalled revelling 'in my nearness to the sacred symbols and in the bright early-morning stillness and in the sense of intimacy with what was being enacted'.[65] Back at Underhill, Evelyn began to worry his mother by drawing angels rather than soldiers, and at the age of twelve he made a shrine by his bed with candlesticks and incense and white plaster statues of saints bought from a religious emporium in Golders Green.[66]

As a small boy he had gone with Lucy to the Low Church matins in the village and he later accompanied his parents and Alec to the newly consecrated St Jude's in Hampstead Garden Suburb. One of Lutyens's finest churches, the building was designed to dominate surrounding houses with its tall, pointed spire and sweeping, barn-like roofs;[67] however a far bigger draw for Arthur was the hammy vicar Basil Bourchier, a cousin of the actor-manager Arthur Bourchier and himself an incorrigible performer in the pulpit. Evelyn would later portray him without embellishment in *Charles Ryder's Schooldays* as 'the very remarkable freak named Father Wimperis' who drew great congregations to his church in a northern suburb and 'alternately fluted and boomed from the pulpit, wrestled with the reading-stand and summoned the country to industrial peace. At the end he performed a little ceremony of his own invention, advancing to the church steps in cope and biretta with what proved to be a huge salt cellar in his hands. "My people," he said simply, scattering salt before him, "you are the salt of the earth."[68]

Bourchier's own sung Eucharist was full of incense and the same improvised ritual with the salt. During the actual Communion a large electric red cross was switched on over the altar.[69] His vestments were more than conventionally ornate and his sermons, according to Evelyn, 'dramatic, topical, irrational and quite without theological content'. Arthur maintained they would have served perfectly well as leading articles in the *Daily Mail* and thanks to his friendship with its proprietor, Lord Northcliffe, Bourchier's pronouncements often did appear in that paper, variously demanding the lash for men who attacked women and fines for people who coughed in church, inveighing against vivisection and any clothes that entailed suffering to animals. People flocked from all over London to attend his services.

In his autobiography Evelyn deemed Bourchier 'a totally preposterous parson',[70] however according to his teacher at Heath Mount, Aubrey Ensor, this was a case of him 'taking an after look', whereas as a boy he 'took St Jude's and the Rev. Basil very seriously'. Ensor recalled going to see the medieval morality play *Everyman*, with Bourchier playing the Voice of God (and forgetting some of the Almighty's lines) and Evelyn walking in front of him carrying a large open prayer book.[71] Perhaps because of Evelyn's subsequent loss of faith, the role of St Jude's and Bourchier in his early religious formation has often been understated, not least by Evelyn himself; yet even he conceded that, in spite of the vicar's histrionics, he gained 'some glimpse of higher mysteries' during his services.[72] In any event, Evelyn was confirmed at St Jude's by the Bishop of Willesden on 29 June 1916 and the next week received instruction from Bourchier before his first Communion.[73]

Evelyn's precocious holiness put him at variance with the rest of the family, especially Alec, who 'accepted religion without belief' and saw his confirmation as 'something to be taken in my stride ... the next thing on the list'.[74] Arthur, meanwhile, had undergone a spell of Darwinian doubts in the 1890s but was passing through an Anglo-Catholic phase by the time of Evelyn's birth. After they moved to Underhill, at Evelyn's request Arthur led the family and servants in prayers before breakfast but stopped in 1914, saying it was 'no longer any good'.[75] He served as a sides-man for many years at St Jude's and apparently adhered to the Christian moral code, yet Evelyn doubted whether he had 'a genuine intellectual conviction about any element of his creed'. Arthur seems to have been far more interested in the theatricality of Bourchier's services than in any of the doctrines the vicar purported to teach there, and he was equally entertained by the various goings-on among members of the congre-gation – at another church he attended previously he particularly enjoyed the story of a solicitor of his acquaintance who had allowed himself to be caned by the curate as a means of showing penitence.

Even if the adult Evelyn later came to question the depth of Arthur's theological thinking, as a boy his interest in religion almost certainly helped him to feel closer to his father. For Arthur's fiftieth birthday in 1916 he wrote him a poem, 'The World to Come', describing a soul's journey to heaven, in the metre of Hiawatha. Evelyn later dismissed it as a 'deplor-able' and 'shameful' effort, although at the time he was proud enough to have it bound in leather. Arthur was proud of it too, describing it to his friend Kenneth McMaster his 'most wonderful' present. 'Not bad for a twelve-year-old,' he crowed.[76]

Evelyn's religion brought him into occasional conflict with his other-wise doting mother. One Lent, Kate told him that he should be on his guard against his 'besetting sin', his 'quick and unkind tongue'. He seemed at first to accept this but then rejoined: 'You know, Mother, what is your besetting sin?' 'No, Evelyn,' she replied, 'what is it?' 'A lack of faith in Catholic doctrine.' Recounting the incident afterwards to Alec, Kate admitted: 'And of course, he was completely right. I do lack faith.'[77]

She was thus all the more alarmed when, around the age of twelve, Evelyn announced that he wanted to become a clergyman and 'began to recite long devotions from a pious book'. As a young girl she had grown distinctly disenchanted with her stepfather's clerical life and the last thing she wanted was for her son to follow the same path. From then on, she decided it might be best if she declined to hear Evelyn's evening prayers.[78]

Serving Lord Kitchener

Although he was happy enough at Heath Mount, Evelyn was still due to go and board at Fernden in 1914 in order to prepare him for public school two years later. However the outbreak of the First World War that July caused *The Daily Telegraph* to dispense with all its freelance book reviewers and Arthur promptly lost half his income. Besides 'saving every penny against the winter & giving up at once our nice parlourmaid',[1] as he wrote to a friend, Arthur decided that it would now be quite out of the question to pay for boarding school for Evelyn and he wrote to Grenfell to warn him that even Heath Mount's fees might prove beyond him. According to Evelyn the headmaster replied that if necessary he would keep the boy on for free; another master* recalled that Grenfell discreetly sent a bill without a total – allowing Arthur to fill in whatever sum he saw fit before signing his cheque.[2] Afterwards Arthur solemnly told Evelyn that he was now 'honour bound to be an exemplary pupil' – an exhortation that Evelyn did not remember having yielded to.[3] In any event, Arthur's fears of financial disaster proved exaggerated and he never had to take advantage of Grenfell's generosity.

Evelyn was excited by the outbreak of war and when the family took the train down to Midsomer Norton that August he eagerly counted the signal boxes and sentries guarding the mainline bridges. 'I followed the retreat from Mons to the Marne,' he later recalled, 'and drew countless pictures of German cavalry plunging among English infantry with much blood and gunpowder about.'[4] The Pistol Troop had disbanded before seeing any of their longed-for action, but he and the Fleming children

---

* Aubrey Ensor; see pp. 28, 32.

did their bit by selling empty jam jars for the Red Cross and cut up lino-
leum to sole slippers for wounded soldiers. Their Christmas show, a series
of topical sketches performed before a crowded house in the Underhill
nursery, raised 3/6 for the Belgian Relief Fund.[5] The next summer, 1915,
Mr Fleming arranged for Mac and Evelyn to work as messengers at the
War Office, sitting 'in a smoky den inhabited by an old soldier' while
waiting to take files from one room to another. Evelyn, then eleven,
was determined to 'serve Lord Kitchener', as he recalled, but though
he often passed his door he was 'never summoned to his presence'. He
was nonetheless thrilled by the whole experience.[6] At Underhill nights
were occasionally enlivened for Evelyn by the Zeppelin alarm going off,
whereupon he would be 'brought down from bed and regaled with an
uncovenanted picnic'. Evelyn felt no sense of danger, which was in any
case fairly remote in that part of London – no bombs fell within a mile of
them. On summer nights, however, they would sometimes see 'the thin
silver rod of the enemy caught in the converging search-lights' and 'on
one splendid occasion' he saw a German plane brought down, 'sinking
very slowly in brilliant flame', and hurried out to join those who were
cheering by the roadside.[7]

At school Evelyn raised more war funds by 'making boats, Zeppelins,
etc' and 'selling 'em to other chaps', as he recorded in his diary.[8] He joined
the Boy Scouts and raised a Heath Mount patrol in one of the local troops,
parading on Saturday afternoons in the basement of a shop and marching
to the Heath to play various war games. However, their activities seemed
very dull compared with those of the Pistol Troop. More invigorating were
the many fights he continued to pick at school and describe in his diary.
When a boy called Fletcher accused Evelyn of being a 'silly old thing' and,
behind his back, of being small and a fool, Evelyn declared his intention
to 'slay him'. Spotting him outside the school changing room, he 'called
him and jumped at him and knocked him down and immediately he said
he had never called me a fool'.[9]

Another outlet for his pugnaciousness was afforded by the wave of anti-
German feeling then sweeping the country, as a result of which anyone or
anything vaguely Teutonic – dachshunds included – was liable to come
under attack. Quickly infected by this hysteria, Evelyn described a game
of footer in the autumn term of 1914 as 'grand' apart from the poor posi-
tional play of a boy called Pappenheimer – 'I suppose it comes from being

a subject of that miserable German nation,' he wrote in his diary.[10] Long before the royal family changed its name from Saxe-Coburg-Gotha to Windsor, several boys turned up at Heath Mount with names suddenly anglicised – one called 'Kaiser' reappeared less conspicuously as 'Kingsley'. Evelyn's claim that 'we did nothing to persecute them' is as hard to believe as it is to verify,[11] but in any event the next year he recorded that he and Pappenheimer had decided to settle their quarrels 'with the gloves'.[12]

The enlistment of several masters prompted tearful send-offs at morning prayers during which Evelyn noted that 'there were many chaps who hid behind each other so as not to be caught blubbing'.[13] Among their replacements, the handsome and theatrically inclined Aubrey Ensor made the most favourable impression on him. Alec later maintained that Ensor saw his time at Heath Mount merely as 'a prelude to a substantial career as a dramatist'[14] – an ambition he scarcely realised although he did write and direct a handful of plays and revues on the London stage from the 1920s through the 1940s, occasionally impressing critics with his ear for dialogue and 'neat pen for character sketch'.[15] 'Man' (as Evelyn called him) Ensor's greatest talents lay in the classroom, however, where he was an animated and inspiring teacher, apt to dance around the room while crooning the popular songs of the day.[16] By contrast, Ensor complained that all the headmaster really cared about was the Common Entrance exams, and thus he was forever being told to 'stick to facts' rather than do anything so exotic as to 'try to interest the boys in their work'.[17]

A distant cousin by marriage through the Cockburns, Ensor soon made friends with the whole Waugh family and was often at Underhill. He particularly liked Kate – who was by then nursing hospitalised soldiers in Highgate – 'a lovely person with a quick glint of humour in her eyes'. Evelyn may have inherited the glint, yet Ensor noticed that 'neither of the boys seemed to have reproduced the warmth that lay behind her slight Scots reserve'.[18] He clearly detected something worth nurturing, however, and although Evelyn did not mention him by name in his autobiography, Alec later identified Ensor as a key formative influence in his brother's artistic development, responsible for broadening his horizons and 'opening windows on new landscapes', and in particular for introducing Evelyn to Saki Munro, whose short stories he would always admire. Ensor was a little taken aback when the eleven-year-old boy remarked, 'Terrible man, my father. He likes Kipling.'[19]

As their rapport grew, Evelyn confided to Ensor how whenever he wanted the day off school he would wiggle the end of the thermometer with his tongue to obtain a temperature. And he shocked him by his persecution of a wretched master known to the boys as Uncle Water Rat, and his defiance of the headmaster's request for clemency whenever a master 'more than normally unsuitable was engaged'.[20] Evelyn and Ensor's friendship survived long after both had left the school, and years later, when Ensor was working as stage manager at the Everyman Theatre in Hampstead, he would contrive to get Evelyn tickets for matinees as close to the stage as possible. However he was po-faced when Evelyn sent him scurrilous postcards about the other Heath Mount masters,* and when he received a bundle of caricatures he admitted that he 'felt it better to get rid of them'.[21] Ensor was further reminded of Evelyn's belligerence at the final matinee of an Old Vic season. The only available seats were in a box and Evelyn seemed so to resent the other people in it that he kept referring to Ensor's recent chickenpox. He only stopped when Lilian Baylis entered the box in mortar and gown, which rendered Evelyn speechless.[22]

Despite their ups and downs, they were still sufficiently in touch by the time Evelyn wrote *A Little Learning* for him to send Ensor an uncorrected proof copy, which Ensor annotated, even though he was very friendly with Evelyn's arch enemy Cecil Beaton, to whom Ensor sent samples from his vast collection of theatrical postcards to help Beaton with his work as a costume designer in Hollywood in the 1960s. Evelyn and Beaton had several other friends in common at Heath Mount, including their fellow theatre fan Dudley Brown, Evelyn's regular accomplice in persecuting vulnerable masters and 'business manager' of his private detective agency, Messrs Wuffles† and Co.[23] The son of a prosperous surgeon who lived at one of Hampstead's smarter addresses, the Mount, Brown was a

---

* Ensor recalled: 'In the holidays the following conversation took place:

Me: "Evelyn if you send me another postcard like that I will send a copy to your Head Master and one to your father."

Evelyn: "Man, you wouldn't do that."

Me: "Send me another p.c. and see."

I did not get another.'

† One of Evelyn's nicknames, although he did not permit its universal use, recording in his diary one day: 'Rostail entered [the boot room] and squatting temptingly on the edge of a basin proceeded to call me "Wuffles". I informed him that unless he refrain from using my names in a corrupted form I would have to chastise him. He, knowing he was larger than me, continued with the name whereupon I fulfilled my promise one hundredfold.' (Easter Term, 1916; *EWD*, pp. 8–9.)

good deal richer and more sophisticated than Evelyn and gave him an early taste for the high life. Evelyn was particularly impressed by the fact that while playing football Brown was attended by a nanny 'to refresh him at half time with lemon squash from a thermos flask'. He later greatly disappointed Evelyn, however, by asking him to lunch followed by a matinee and then casually announcing when Evelyn eagerly arrived at his house that there was really nothing good on that he had not already seen.[24] Besides keeping an album of theatre programmes, Brown seemed to know an awful lot about the private lives of actresses and was revered by the other boys for his extensive knowledge of sex. Beaton remembered Brown whispering that children were produced by the man 'mixing his "stuff" with the woman's',[25] and Evelyn, though prudishly shocked when Brown taught him a scatological limerick, recalled being equally fascinated by his theories of reproduction – albeit not the sexual act itself, which he seems to have remained determinedly ignorant of despite the stripping sessions with Muriel Talbot. Whether or not Evelyn succeeded in his reciprocal attempts to interest his friend in Anglo-Catholicism is not clear. In any event, the adult Brown was ultimately drawn to the low life, which he took to 'like a duck to a pond' according to Beaton, and at the age of twenty-two he committed suicide by throwing himself from a window in the rue Jacob in Paris.[26] According to Evelyn the property belonged to 'a notorious pederast and drug dealer'.[27]

Another close friend of Evelyn's at Heath Mount was Ernest Hooper, with whom Evelyn edited (and illustrated) an alternative to the official school magazine. 'By George when the term begins things will hum,' Evelyn told his diary just after New Year 1916. 'I think it's my last so I'm going to raise hell. Our first shell to smash the ramparts of convention is *The Cynic*, the most gorgeous paper out.'[28] Subtitled 'Cynical without being cheaply so. Piquant in moderation. Racy in Excess', the paper was typed and duplicated by Arthur's secretary and in its editorial volunteered 'helpful' observations about the masters' efforts in the rival publication, predicting loftily that 'when they have had a little more experience [they] will be able to produce quite a presentable little paper'. One of these masters, Mr Hynchcliffe, forbade them from selling *The Cynic*, but as Evelyn gleefully recorded they nevertheless sold out of the first issue, covering their printing costs and leaving half a crown over for their war fund.[29] Four more issues followed over the next few months, providing further evidence of the impulses propelling Evelyn towards an eventual literary career – which at that stage largely involved poking fun at masters and fellow pupils, chief among them the unfortunate Cecil Beaton. (The adult Evelyn dismissed it as 'flippant rather than cynical' and conceded that 'the few jokes that are intelligible seem very feeble'.[30])

Despite these various endeavours, it was clear to Evelyn that his father was never going to be as interested in them as he was in the activities of his elder brother Alec, whose exploits at Sherborne (since 1911) Arthur had followed with an eagerness bordering on obsession, awaiting his letters, as Alexander Waugh puts it, 'in the palpitating manner of a teenage paramour'.[31] To his friend Kenneth McMaster Arthur admitted that he had 'built my earthly hopes on him, and one must have something to keep one's ambition young and fresh'. 'Alec's career has, no doubt, in consequence grown too large in my imagination. But I do want to see him doing some of the things that I have had to give up hope of doing.'[32]

Arthur was thrilled when Alec won the school's senior poetry prize, just as he had done, but he derived far greater satisfaction from his sporting successes, Arthur's own shameful inadequacies as a games player having been compounded by a weak chest and poor eyesight. Seizing the opportunity now to relive his inglorious Sherborne career through that of his more athletic and gregarious son, Arthur took about with him a copy of the school roll, annotated with Alec's latest achievements, and with the names of those masters and boys that Alec liked underlined.

These characters and their various peculiarities soon became as familiar to Evelyn as the boys at Heath Mount,[33] and the conspicuous celebration at Underhill of everyone and everything to do with Alec only intensified his feeling of being left out. Indeed at the time he claimed to have felt more than merely excluded; he also felt despised, or so he told Mrs Fleming when in 1914, aged eleven, he went round to her house wearing a bowler hat. 'It belonged to my father first,' he explained. 'Then it descended to Alec: now to me. In fact it has come down to me from generation to generation of them that hate me.' When he was told this, Arthur deemed it yet another demonstration of Evelyn's 'sharp tongue', and his irritation was magnified by Mrs Fleming 'cordially' adding that he had never been a good father to Evelyn, who she said was afraid of him and at his worst in his presence. 'Cheery news!!' wrote Arthur when he reported all this to Alec.

The extraordinary bond between Arthur and Alec was demonstrated the same year when Alec's housemaster told Arthur that his son was worried about masturbating too much – his passions inflamed, so Alec later recorded, by a novel containing nothing racier than 'two luscious descriptions of embraces upon a sofa'.* 'My Own Dear Boy,' wrote Arthur. 'I know from experience that there is nothing that eats into and corrodes the soul more than a secret. Now that you know that *I* know, you can feel there are two of us to fight this trouble – two of us absolutely as one.' Continuing in similar vein for several pages, he warned Alec that persistent 'self-abuse' would lead to 'weakness both of body and mind ... paralysis and softening of the brain' and the risk of his fathering 'feeble and rickety children' – if indeed he was capable of having any at all. 'Say it is Saturday night and the idea attacks you,' Arthur suggested. 'Put it from you at once. Think of cricket or the day's game, of the probable team next week.' As to his reading, Alec should avoid Swinburne, 'who was a victim of self-abuse (as I once told you)' and therefore 'not a very wholesome companion'. 'Nothing inflames the mind like a lascivious picture or a suggestive line of poetry. Try to concentrate on more manly poets and give as much of your mind as you like to games, out of school. You won't get your firsts [colours] unless your body is in subjection. Train the body, by this perpetual effort of putting off temptation, to be the handmaid of the soul, and not its cruel mistress.' He reassured him that 'in all your efforts, your struggles, your failures, your beginnings again, in all that makes life one perpetual battlefield, you have at any rate one fellow soldier by your side; one who has fought all your battles before you and knows every inch of the way'.[34]

Arthur's infatuation with his elder son did not go unnoticed by Alec's headmaster, who accused him of spoiling the boy and making him self-centred. At Chapman & Hall the staff would enquire, slightly tongue-in-cheek, 'And how is Master Alec this morning, sir?'

Arthur's paternal devotion was accompanied by a newfound love for Sherborne, far exceeding any feelings he had had for the place as an unhappy schoolboy. 'More [often] than was wise,' Arthur later admitted, he would catch the train down to Sherborne on Friday evenings after work and install himself for the weekend at the Digby Hotel (later converted into a schoolhouse), entertaining Alec and his friends, watching the

---

* The novel was *Joseph in Jeopardy* by Frank Danby (Methuen, 1912).

school matches on Saturday afternoon and attending chapel on Sunday morning.[35] Kate often went with him and her surviving letters suggest that she became almost as obsessed as Arthur was with the school career of their eldest son.[36] When Alec won his cricket colours in 1915, Kate wrote to him: 'A thousand congratulations! It is almost too good to be true. How we longed to see you wearing that blue and gold ribbon, and now you will do so . . . I am so happy.'[37]

Having listened to the rest of his family going on about what a wonderful time Alec was having at Sherborne, Evelyn was naturally keen to go there too, and one evening in October 1916 he said to his father: 'Oh, look here, Hooper is going to Sherborne in the summer term. Can't you buck up & do some articles in the Fortnightly so as to be able to afford to send me also?' As Arthur told Alec: 'Seeing that I had had an assessment that morning for £142 income-tax to be paid in January, with more to follow in July: & had worked just on 8 hours at my desk – reviewing a book on Germany & the East & making notes for my next Book of the Week – The Soul of Russia & reading Mais* as well, & was dead tired, I felt this insult was about the last straw!'[38]

However, it was not Arthur's annoyance or money worries that stood in the way of Evelyn following his brother to Sherborne but rather a scandal (about which Evelyn claimed to know nothing until he read Alec's account years later)[39] concerning Alec's romantic entanglements with several younger boys at the school – and the novel he subsequently wrote about his experiences, *The Loom of Youth*.

In the throes of one of these affairs, in early 1915, Alec had written to a friend: 'I shall never get tired of kissing Davies† – he is a darling. As he now works in his study in hall, I see an awful lot of him. But he is leaving this term, *O lacrymarum fons*, it will be very lonely without him.'[40] Sometime later he reflected: 'These loves are great passions while they last. They are mad and short and burn themselves with their own fire. I doubt that I shall ever feel again the same ecstasy that I knew three years ago

---

* S. P. B. Mais (1885–1975) was Alec Waugh's inspirational English teacher at Sherborne and featured as 'Ferrers' in *The Loom of Youth*, whose writing and publication he did much to assist. Mais was a prolific author himself, eventually notching up 200 books, and a well-known early broadcaster, his astonishing work rate fuelled by bipolar disorder that went undiagnosed until he was almost eighty. Late in life he was reduced to asking Alex to help him out with bills, pointedly reminding him that he was 'NOT the author of *The Loom of Youth*'.
† William Wookey Northam Davies, known at Sherborne as Davies mi because he had an elder brother at the school.

when I discovered I was in love with Simonds . . . The love of boy for boy is in my mind one of the most beautiful things in life.'[41] The affair with Davies continued well into the summer of 1915 and although Alec claimed to have been devoted exclusively to him, a few weeks before the end of term he was caught in some unspecified but evidently compromising situation with another boy, Mervyn Renton. The headmaster wrote to Arthur, sparing him the 'exact particulars' of what they had been doing but telling him that Alec could not now come back to Sherborne for his final year. Shattered by this letter, Arthur urged Alec to keep the circumstances of his disgrace 'sacredly to yourself. It is the first time to my knowledge that such a thing has happened to a Waugh. I want no one to know of it, except the Chief [the Sherborne headmaster], Mother, you and I. It is enough that we should have to bear it.'[42]

Needless to say, Arthur glossed over all this in his autobiography, yet at the time, far from straining their relations, Alec's humiliation seemed to bring father and son even closer than they had been before. 'Dear Boy,' wrote Arthur, 'I am sure there is some spiritual relation between you and me which transcends the merely material world.' In a subsequent letter, after it emerged that Alec had been shunned by many of the masters and boys, Arthur wrote to him: 'The nails that pierce the hands of the Son are still driven through the hands of the Father also.'

Kate, too, now seemed to worship Alec even more than before. When he ended his Sherborne career in triumph by playing a match-winning innings in the final of the house cricket cup, she could barely contain herself. 'Happy, Happy, Happy! Hurrah! Hurrah! Hurrah! It was some beating that! & your 77, some score that! I am so awfully pleased at your winning that Cup. I nearly went mad with joy . . . My joy is unspeakable. I did want you to finish up like that and you've been and done it!! Thank you ever so much Ally boy for the pride and pleasure you have given me. May you always play the game where ever you are and always come out strong in an emergency.'[43]

When Alec left Sherborne, he was destined for officers' training and ultimately the trenches – whose obvious dangers were soon brought cruelly home to the Waughs by the death of Kate's younger brother, Basset Raban, who was killed when a shell burst in the mouth of the dugout where he had been conferring with his staff. Conscious that his life too might soon be cut short, Alec somehow found time that winter to write a novel, *The*

Loom of Youth. Beginning it just after Christmas 1915, he completed it in a remarkable seven and a half weeks, getting up at 4.30 each morning and returning to his manuscript at night after the day's parades, and then posting each finished section to Arthur.

Halfway through, Arthur pronounced himself 'astonished at the skill which your narrative shows' yet he doubted the wisdom of its publication, given that it was so obviously autobiographical and contained candid descriptions of Alec's contemporaries and masters at Sherborne and references to schoolboy homosexuality which were then considered shocking. Arthur feared that the book would 'make enemies everywhere' and 'neither you or I could ever go to Sherborne again, and all idea of sending Evelyn would be at an end'.[44]

When Alec nevertheless secured a publisher, in January 1917, Arthur applauded his son's 'great achievement' of having a novel accepted at eighteen but admitted he was 'filled with conflicting emotions'. 'Of course this means the end of Evelyn as a Shirburnian,' he wrote. 'I don't know what to do next, but after you have actually got an agreement I shall write to Chief, & perhaps he will advise me. I feel rather lost for the moment: but I must remind myself that I have always been very uncertain about the advisability of Evelyn going to Sherborne, and I shall hope and trust that we may come to a wise decision which will make for the good of us all.'[45]

As publication of *The Loom* loomed that spring, Arthur arranged to have lunch with the Chief at which, according to his autobiography, they agreed that he would have to find an alternative school for Evelyn. Overriding Kate's preference for sending him to a London school such as Westminster or St Paul's, Arthur chose Lancing in Sussex, 'a small public school of ecclesiastical temper on the South Downs' as Evelyn later rendered it in *Decline and Fall*.

As so often with Arthur, the decision was reached with 'a minimum of deliberation', so Evelyn recalled, his tone betraying resentment at his father's snap choice. Arthur could claim no family connections with the school and had never even visited it. However he thought Lancing's High Church tradition would be ideally suited to his self-proclaimed 'church-loving' boy' who, by his own account, aspired to become a parson.[46] Arthur reckoned that the organised liturgical duties entailed by Lancing's twice-daily compulsory chapel services would afford the 'best test' of his religious conviction.[47]

A Lesser Place than Eton

Arthur had started at Sherborne in the summer term so knew perfectly well how difficult it was to go to a new school in the middle of the academic year. Yet his customary impatience to get the job done meant that he set his younger son on precisely the same path – one that Evelyn later reflected resulted in the 'bitter, avoidable loneliness of my first terms at Lancing'.[1] Evelyn was taken there for the first time on a dull and damp morning in May, travelling by train from London to Shoreham on the south coast and then by taxi the last mile up to a cluster of austere flint buildings set on a bleak spur of the South Downs, looking out over the grey English Channel. He later claimed to have parted from his father 'without a pang', excited to be embarking on a new phase of his life;[2] an alternative indication of how he saw his plight at the time was the black border of chains he drew around the relevant page of his pocket calendar.

Founded in 1848, Lancing was the first of the schools built by the Tractarian clergyman Nathaniel Woodard, who had set himself the task of establishing a group of public schools to provide a sound Church of England education for what he saw as the country's neglected middle classes. Each school was rather crudely graded to reflect the peculiarities of the British class system, with the idea that the richer schools would help to subsidise the poorer ones.

Woodard conceived Lancing as the richest and most socially elevated of them all, intended in his mind to cater for the sons of impoverished noblemen as well as those of clergy and other gentry of limited means. Hurstpierpoint, another of Woodard's earlier foundations, was aimed more at the sons of tradesmen, farmers and clerks, while Ardingly was supposedly for smaller farmers, mechanics and shopkeepers.

Lancing was certainly impressive to look at. Though still unfinished, its magnificent chapel was already the fourth tallest ecclesiastical structure in England and to Evelyn's mind the most spectacular post-Reformation church in the country – it was known locally as the Cathedral of the Downs. Furthermore, the school's fixture list boasted matches against Eton, Winchester and Westminster, and its old boys were eligible for the newly founded Public School's Club, evidence that the older schools were beginning to regard it as one of their own.[3]

However, it was still far from comfortable, one of Evelyn's contemporaries recalling that the boys 'slept in stone dormitories with the windows open, a minimum of bed-clothes, and then a cold-bath when we got up at 6.30'.[4] And it had never achieved the social cachet that its founder envisaged. The school roll hardly abounded with sons of the nobility and Evelyn clearly felt that Lancing did not measure up to Sherborne, either socially or academically. His sense of its inferiority was reinforced not only by the endless talk at home about Sherborne but also, rather unhelpfully, by the Lancing headmaster, the Rev. Henry Bowlby, who, as Evelyn recalled, 'never dissembled the opinion, to which we all assented, that Lancing was a less important place than Eton'.[5]

A former contemporary of Arthur's at Oxford, Bowlby had been a scholar at Charterhouse and worked as a housemaster at Eton before arriving at Lancing in 1909. Evelyn's friend Roger Fulford rated Bowlby 'a great Headmaster',[6] and it is true that before the war he had carried out an impressive series of changes, additions and improvements, completing the building of the college, doubling the number of boys and firmly establishing Lancing in the second rank of English public schools. Moreover, his reputation as a successful housemaster at Eton meant that quite a lot of second sons who might otherwise have gone to Eton came to his house at Lancing instead.

By the time Evelyn arrived at Lancing, however, Bowlby had become a rather remote figure. According to the school historian he was by then 'a tired and sick man', worn down by the anxieties of running the school during a war in which his own sons were fighting as well as so many of his old pupils.[7] His wife, meanwhile, was a 'kind, silly woman', Evelyn recalled, 'with a peculiar proclivity for gaffes'.[8] Once, when passing the photographs hung in the chapel of old boys who had been killed in action, she remarked: 'Oh, isn't it nice to see a second row go up!'[9]

Evelyn's descriptions of the headmaster in his autobiography are not especially generous, recording for example that he had got his hurdling Blue at Oxford 'in a bad year' – whereas in fact he had hurdled for Oxford four years in succession and was president of the Oxford Union Athletic Club.[10] Though Bowlby now walked with a limp, he was still tall, lean and 'distinctly handsome,' Evelyn conceded, 'except when the keen winds of the place caught and encrimsoned his narrow nose'. According to Evelyn, his headmaster had more interest in becoming a bishop, like his father, than in schoolmastering, but his ambitions had been thwarted due to his having 'made himself rather ridiculous [at Eton] by his courtship of the more illustrious fathers and by flirtations with the prettier mothers and sisters'.[11]

A possibly greater obstacle was Bowlby's widely-reported acquittal years later, in 1929, while Canon of Chichester, on a charge of molesting four small girls on a train, after, by his own account, feeling their bare legs and 'asking them if they were cold'.[12] While the trial was being reported in the newspapers, one of Evelyn's old school friends came to lunch at Underhill and was in the middle of denouncing their former headmaster when Arthur suddenly interjected: 'There, but for the grace of God, goes Arthur Waugh!'[13] This puzzling – and to Evelyn possibly rather embarrassing – remark was presumably Arthur's way of candidly acknowledging that he too felt vulnerable to temptation at times. Two years previously he had confessed to a clergyman friend that a 'dark-eyed, curly-headed, dainty, smiling little fairy of about 23 *fair springs*' had been massaging his 'hinder parts' to treat his rheumatism. After asking him to remove his trousers, the girl 'waved her delicate fingers mystically & began taking the most reprehensible liberties with my body . . . It was the deepest enchantment I have ever undergone, but my conscience has tortured me ever since.'[14]*

At Lancing, meanwhile, Evelyn had been placed in Bowlby's house, Head's, which was considered the most prestigious in the school. Occasionally the headmaster hobbled round the dormitories addressing dutiful small talk to his charges.† The day-to-day running of the house

---

* Arthur's masseuse was Mollie Udale-Smith. Later in life, after divorcing Sir Ian Abercromby, 10th Bart, she lived on Tenerife, where the local paper described her as 'a liberal and eccentric Englishwoman who changed her husband as she did her shirt'.

† Waiting for a bath one evening, sixteen-year-old Evelyn endured 'seven solid minutes of Head's conversation. He is a bore, though rather an old dear, I'm beginning to think.' (27 September 1919; *EWD*, p. 21.)

was left to the house tutor, Dick Harris, a warm-hearted young man who was especially kind to new boys and, as Evelyn remembered, 'entirely' responsible for 'such vestiges of happiness' that he experienced during his first term.[15] Otherwise it was a painfully lonely time during which the only boy in Head's with whom he was permitted to associate was the other 'new man', Roger Fulford, with whom he was obliged to sit at the 'new man's table', pointedly ignored by the rest of the boys in the House Room.

For their first three weeks, another junior boy was assigned to instruct them in Lancing's strange rules and rituals: who was permitted to walk on which plot of grass; who could link arms with whom; when boys could put their hands in their trouser pockets (in their second year – though with the jacket raised, not drawn back); and so on.

On the third Sunday of term, new boys were required to stand on a table and sing a song. Arthur had suggested 'My wife's gone to the country, hurrah! hurrah!', which Evelyn performed well enough to spare him the usual pelting with books and money boxes.[16] However, in general he was not well liked, and in his first two terms he tended to be written off as an 'awful little tick'.[17] His first experience of the Ascension Day holiday was particularly miserable, when the whole school dispersed but Evelyn found that he had no friends to go with and so spent the day wandering about the empty school grounds alone. 'Evelyn is a misfit, I'm afraid,' Alec wrote to a friend at the time. '[He] hates Lancing. He shouldn't. A boy ought to like his school.'[18]

Evelyn's friend Fulford later recalled that he was 'too independent, too prone to notice oddities and comment on them'[19] – none of which qualities was welcomed in a new boy. Evelyn felt the hostility towards him all the more acutely because, as he recalled, previously he had met 'only people who seemed disposed to like me'. 'Experience has taught me that not everyone takes to me at first sight (or on closer acquaintance),' he wrote, 'but I am still mildly surprised by rebuffs, such is the confidence which a happy childhood founds.'[20]

His isolation at Lancing was exacerbated by his fastidiousness. He was especially revolted by Lancing's doorless, open-drained latrines, 'the Groves', where most boys went in pairs after breakfast but which Evelyn elected to visit alone during school hours at the cost of writing twenty-five lines. He was similarly repelled by the shared tepid, muddy baths after games ('Clubs') and the abysmal wartime food, as a result of which he experienced real hunger for the first time in his life.

His refusal to help less clever boys with their prep on the grounds that it was dishonest won him no friends, nor did his general abrasiveness: 'Poor Evelyn has been getting into trouble at school again and all through that unwise tongue of his,' Kate told Alec. 'Perhaps some day he will learn.'[21] His letters from Arthur were flung towards him by the head of the House Room with a contemptuous sigh – 'Another one for Waugh!' – eventually prompting Evelyn to ask Arthur to write less often, even though the letters were a great solace to him.[22] Lancing's respect for religion meant that he was rarely ridiculed for kneeling, in defiance of convention, at the *incarnatus* in the Creed at Holy Communion, however his habit of remaining 'plunged in prayer' by his bedside long after everyone else had finished was considered strange.

His conspicuous eccentricities suggest a desire to set himself apart from the other boys. Yet he later maintained that this was not always the case. 'I did not admire the other boys,' he wrote in his autobiography. 'I did not want to be like them. But in contradiction, I wanted to be one of them. I had no aspirations to excel, still less to lead; I simply longed to remain myself and yet be accepted as one of this distasteful mob.'[23]

Sunday afternoons were especially desolate, with the House Room out of bounds for two hours and the boys despatched to the Downs in their straw hats and black coats. 'I often found myself walking alone or obliged to make a rendezvous with some equally unpopular boy in another House.'[24] He sought refuge from his loneliness in the classroom, the school library, where he could only go on Sunday evenings until he was awarded his 'library privileges', and in chapel. Services were held every morning and evening and three times on Sunday, when the names of old boys killed in action that week were read out, a sombre ritual that became especially affecting for Evelyn after Alec was posted to the Western Front that summer.

The first summer holidays could not come soon enough as far as Evelyn was concerned and as they approached he eagerly marked off the days in the calendar he kept in his pocket. But just as the boys' trunks appeared in the dormitories and he was on the point of going home, he caught mumps and was told that he had to spend the first two weeks of the holidays in the school sanatorium – an injunction that came as 'an insupportable blow', he recalled.[25]

More homesick now than ever, he spent his quarantine reading a copy of *The Loom of Youth*, which he refused to let his fellow invalids see.[26] By the time he was eventually allowed back to Underhill, his parents were far more preoccupied with the welfare of Alec, who was on the point of being sent to France (in late July) – and then straight into the Battle of Passchendaele, where three out of seven of the line officers in his company would be killed.

While that battle was still raging, glowing reviews of *The Loom of Youth* appeared in the press and it quickly became a bestseller, as talked about as *Tom Brown's School Days* had been sixty years previously. Arthur was delighted by its success yet dismayed that the book was seen as an attack on his old school. Alec wrote from the trenches denying this but the school magazine declined to print his letter. When Alec in turn refused to resign from the Old Boys' Society, his name was summarily removed from the school roll, whereupon Arthur felt he had no choice but to 'stand by my son, and follow him into exile'.[27] Evelyn, meanwhile, was sent to Midsomer Norton to stay with his aunts, who found him 'greatly improved' after his first term at public school. 'He couldn't be nicer,' wrote Aunt Connie, 'so pleasant and ready to do anything we want him to do and pleased with any little joy we try to arrange. I don't think he is nearly so satirical as he used to be. We are all very happy together.'

After a miserably cold and wet autumn term back at Lancing, during which Evelyn begged Arthur to remove him, the next holidays he arrived home to find a new member of the household, Barbara Jacobs, to whom Alec had become engaged after an intermittent two-year courtship. She was the daughter of Arthur's friend W. W. Jacobs, the famously grumpy humorist and author of *The Monkey's Paw*, who was said to have earned more than any other English writer of the time except Rudyard Kipling. Barbara was staying with the Waughs while attending a course of lectures at Bedford College in Regent's Park, and although she was nearly three years older than Evelyn they took to each other immediately. Over the next two years she and her family would replace the Flemings as Evelyn's favourite holiday companions, and he went often to their home at Berkhamsted, where Barbara's brother attended the school of which Graham Greene's father was headmaster.

Evelyn's most vivid memories of Berkhamsted were of the games the children used to play in the Jacobses' galleried music room, during which he and Barbara's younger sister Luned would seek each other out 'grapple, and, while the younger players squealed in the excitement of arrest and escape, would silently cling and roll together. We maintained a pretence of conflict. There was no kissing, merely rapturous minutes of close embrace. No mention of our intimacy was ever made between us. But after the game, when the lights came on, we would exchange glances of complicity and it was always either she or I who proposed "the dark game".'[28] Their attachment did not go unnoticed by Alec, who in January 1919 told his friend Hugh Mackintosh that 'Evelyn has become quite amorous, I regret to say. [He] loves Barbara's sister, a comely wench, and at odd periods of the day they are observed holding hands.'[29]

The attraction to Barbara meanwhile was purely platonic – or so Evelyn maintained. He was intrigued by her upbringing and rebellious and agnostic beliefs which were so different to his. 'Until I met her, maiden-aunts and Anglican clergy had been in the ascendant; in Barbara I met the new age. I did not surrender to it without reserve, but I was stimulated by the encounter.'[30]

She was equally entranced by her new young friend and years later remembered him as 'a perfectly darling boy, the nicest youngster you can imagine'.[31] They spent entire days exploring London together randomly by bus, or, to Arthur's dismay, daubing the walls of the old nursery – which Evelyn had redesignated 'the studio' – with their experiments in Cubism. Her enthusiasms rubbed off to the extent that Evelyn pretended to be a socialist at various times over the next few years[32] and his form master cautioned him against approving 'merely those things that are ultra-modern'.[33] However Arthur discerned that his son was 'not yet so wedded to what is new that you seem likely to despise what is old. You may copy the Cubist in your living room, but an Old Master hangs above your bed.'[34]

Evelyn's next school holidays were once again overshadowed by the family's fears for Alec, who was reported missing after straying behind enemy lines during the 1918 German spring offensive. Arthur's anxiety this time was mixed with irritation at Evelyn and Barbara's apparent indifference. 'Their loud laughter rings through the house,' he wrote to Jean Fleming. 'I sit alone and think of the other boy, lonely, cold, hungry, even if he is alive; and I wonder *what* their hearts are made of.'[35] Arthur spent ten fretful days replying to letters of sympathy before he eventually received a telegram from the Red Cross at Geneva to say that Alec was being held as a prisoner of war.

* * *

Evelyn had been miserable at Lancing during wartime, however life there perked up considerably after the Armistice of 11 November 1918. Alec was home by Christmas and Evelyn recalled that holiday as 'the most joyous of my life'.[36] Back at school, food was at last plentiful and the tuck shop, which in wartime had stocked only occasional oatcakes and tired bits of fruit, now brimmed with such long-forgotten delicacies as buns and chocolates and walnut whips.[37]

The House Room's eight most senior boys, 'the Settle',* vied with one another to throw the finest tea party, with piles of crumpets, cakes, pastries and in summer strawberries and cream. Those with private studies ('pits') procured the odd pot of caviar and *foie gras* from London, and various varieties of China tea from a shop in Piccadilly, brewing them 'as nicely as a circle of maiden ladies,' Evelyn recalled, and 'discoursing on their qualities as later we were to talk of wine'.[38]

Socially, Evelyn had also begun to feel more assured. Within Head's House he had grown steadily more respected and even feared for his strong will and determined independence. By the age of fifteen, he and Roger Fulford and Rupert Fremlin[†] fancied themselves leaders of the self-styled 'Bolshies', a group of boys who Evelyn later maintained were benevolent towards their juniors but hunted 'as a small pack to bring down our equals and immediate superiors'.[39] He and his friends 'practically controlled the founts of popularity,' Evelyn recalled, 'and capriciously stopped or let them flow'.

Victims of their persecution included one Desmond O'Connor,

---

* So named because among their privileges was to be allowed to sit on the settle by the fire in the House Room.

† Waugh described Fremlin as 'a delightful mercurial fellow, whose father we wrongly believed to have a been eaten by a tiger'. His alternations of exuberance and depression were known as 'Fremlin's states'. He was later with Evelyn at Oxford, but died young of blackwater fever, a complication of malaria, in Nigeria (*A Little Learning*, p. 125 and *Mallowan's Memoirs*, p. 27).

nicknamed 'Dungy', who had unwisely antagonised Evelyn when Alec went missing by suggesting that he had deserted or was a traitor. When O'Connor was promoted above Evelyn and his cronies onto the house 'Settle' and as head of the dormitory, they 'exercised every ingenuity' to humiliate him. As an adult the wretched Dungy apparently shot himself while in India – as Evelyn recorded with neither relish nor remorse.[40]

Another casualty was Emlyn Bevan, later a prosperous City man and fellow of Evelyn's at White's but known at Lancing for obvious reasons as 'Buttocks'. Evelyn recalled how he and Fulford composed a song which 'celebrated his large posterior, his gluttony, his affectation for shaving before he need'.[41] Cruel as the jibes often were, Evelyn did at least admit that 'in all these nasty manoeuvres there lay the hidden fear that I myself might at any moment fall from favour and become, as I had been in my first year, the object of contempt'.[42]

The Bolshies also directed mockery at their new house tutor, E. B. 'Gordo' Gordon, who replaced the popular Dick Harris in September 1919. To begin with the rheumatic Gordo appeared duplicitous and sneaky, prowling about the house unheard in his gym shoes, for which he was dubbed 'Pussy-foot' and 'Super-spy'.[43] Yet Evelyn soon realised that he was essentially a good sort who moreover helped foster his artistic interests.

Evelyn was at that time particularly passionate about lettering and illumination, recently inspired by having visited with his parents the Arts and Crafts community at Ditchling and met the famous calligrapher Edward Johnston. The great scribe had shown him how to cut a turkey quill and demonstrated his 'foundational' hand, taking the fourteen-year-old boy's breath away with the sweep and precision of his strokes, which as Evelyn later remembered were 'as virile as a bullfighter's'.[44]

In 1919, aged sixteen, Evelyn won the Lancing art prize (judged by the architect Detmar Blow) for an illuminated collect, and one teatime after a characteristically unsuccessful boxing match Gordo summoned him to his study so that he could show his prize prayer to another local scribe called Francis Crease. Evelyn had noticed this peculiar-looking man on Sundays in the school chapel, 'an incongruously elegant figure in the side aisle' who would sit through most of the service in meditation and then, after the sermon, suddenly wrap his cape around him and disappear onto the Downs.[45] Dressed foppishly in soft tweeds and a silk shirt and cravat, the man had 'a pink and white complexion often found in nuns', a high-pitched voice and a 'delicate, almost mincing' gait.

Evelyn maintained that Mr Crease was 'without immoral proclivities', although he conceded that he 'showed a distinct interest in the better-looking boys'.[46] With his ginger hair, big ears and bright, staring eyes it is debatable whether the young Evelyn came within that category. In any event Crease went into raptures about Evelyn's border decoration, declaring it far better than anything he could hope to do. He also said he thought the script shamefully unworthy of it and offered to teach him how it should be done.

So with the permission of his house tutor one afternoon in January 1920 Evelyn walked over to Crease's 'cloister', an isolated farm four miles away across the Downs at Lychpole. On this first visit he lost his way in the mist and on his second he was caught in a heavy hailstorm and arrived sopping-wet. 'Crease met me at the door and led me to his bedroom where he lent me dry socks, trousers and shoes,' Evelyn's diary records, although he tactfully omitted such details in his letter the same day to his father, whom he reassured that besides being 'rather effeminate, rather affected', Crease was 'very refined and artistic, well bred and charming . . . the truest dilettante I have ever seen'.[47]

Though never especially keen on Crease's elaborate Celtic-style script or decorations, Evelyn quickly fell under his spell, confiding to his diary within a few months that 'I owe anything at Lancing worth remembering to him'.[48] He later admitted to having enjoyed the actual lessons far less than the 'hot scones, [handleless] Crown Derby cups and conversation' that followed.

Crease was reticent about his past but hinted vaguely that he had previously been attached to an Anglican fraternity and once held a distinguished academic post at Corpus, Oxford – although Evelyn later thought it more likely that Crease had come to know the university through his friendship with a rich American fellow there. He did not name the American in his autobiography,[49] but Evelyn may have been referring to the flamboyant art and pornography collector Edward Perry ('Ned') Warren, an extremely wealthy Bostonian who ran an all-male establishment at nearby Lewes House, wrote A *Defence of Uranian Love*, which has been described as 'the premier pederastic apologia in the language',[50] and would have a pervasive influence on Evelyn's generation of English aesthetes at Oxford in the 1920s.

The extent to which Crease followed his friend's credo is hard to ascertain at this distance, but most other Lancing housemasters warned their boys against going to visit him. There is no evidence that he ever behaved improperly towards his new pupil, however, and so intensely did Evelyn enjoy the visits that Thursday soon became his favourite day of the week. 'It is such a relief to get into refined surroundings, if only for an afternoon,' he recorded at the time.[51] Sometimes Crease would accompany him halfway on the walk back to school, 'I eagerly questioning him about architecture or aesthetics or Limoges or Maiolica,' recalled Evelyn, 'he trying to turn me to the beauty of the evening and the downs'.[52]

Crease's letters to Evelyn that spring term reveal a growing familiarity, one of them telling him that 'I can be as direct as you sometimes & you don't like it so much in others as in yourself – but it is good for you. You want a Friend who is a thorn in the flesh not an Echo!'[53] Their rapport did not go unnoticed by Gordo and in March 1920 Evelyn recorded that his house tutor had become 'very jealous of Crease's influence' and had 'been subtly trying to put me off him'. More awkwardly, Dick Harris subsequently forbade Evelyn's friend Dudley Carew from going over to tea with Crease, apparently on the basis that he had 'heard scandal of him'. Evelyn evidently passed the whispers on to Crease, who shrieked that he would send his landlord to the headmaster to vouch for his innocence.[54]

As if to demonstrate his own devotion, meanwhile, Evelyn had invited Crease to stay at Underhill for ten days during the Easter holidays – never having asked any of his Lancing contemporaries home – an invitation that was then repeated in a letter from Kate Waugh. Crease felt exceedingly apprehensive at the prospect, the more so having read Arthur's description of the visits to Underhill of the ill-fated young poet Ian Mackenzie, a friend of Alec's at Sandhurst who had stayed there several times before dying of pneumonia on Armistice Day. Arthur described how their first evening had been spent 'under the red lamps by the book-room fire, taking down one book after another, and each reading favourite passages in turn'. Even more alarming to the pathologically shy and reclusive Crease was Arthur's recollection of how Mackenzie liked to start the day by singing and how 'we made him roar with laughter at the breakfast-table as we imitated the strains that accompanied the process of his dressing'.[55]

Before Crease could be persuaded to come, Evelyn had to reassure him that his family was nothing like as hearty as Arthur had made out, and also that his father would cover all his expenses. When eventually he did come, Crease spent much of each day in his bed and at other times cowered in the book-room with his hands over his eyes.[56] It was evidently more enjoyable than he had feared, however, and proved to be the first of several visits.

Most significantly as far as Evelyn's development was concerned, Crease's first visit to Underhill changed the way he saw his father, the scribe having perceptively observed that he thought Arthur Waugh 'charming, entirely charming, and acting all the time' – an assessment with which Evelyn's mother agreed. 'My eyes were opened,' wrote Evelyn, 'and I saw him, whom I had grown up to accept in complete simplicity, as he must always have appeared to others.'[57] From that moment on, his attitude to Arthur would grow progressively more dismissive.

What Arthur made of Crease is unclear – he doesn't get a mention in his autobiography *One Man's Road* – although after Alec's troubles at Sherborne he may have been a little apprehensive about the relationship between this old-maidish man and his younger son, as much as he was offended by Evelyn's observation that until he met Mr Crease, he had 'lived among philistines'.[58] In any event, Arthur treated their guest 'kindly if somewhat derisively', so Evelyn recalled.[59] Kate was far more indulgent and continued asking Crease to Underhill for years to come, even after his arrest on a charge of sexual misconduct – a case of mistaken identity according to Evelyn.

Evelyn's attachment to Crease grew during the summer term of 1920 to the extent that his going away for a month in May made Evelyn 'very depressed and unhappy . . . he is the only real friend I have here. I do believe that I am getting homesick again after three years.'[60] In his mentor's absence, Evelyn continued going over to Lychpole to practise his illuminated script, and one afternoon he broke the blade of one of his quill-cutting knives. He thought little of it at the time but Crease was far more annoyed than he had expected and wrote to tell him that the knife was very old and quite irreplaceable. In any case, it was in a drawer and Evelyn had no right to be using it at all; he had betrayed his trust. The next post brought another letter from Crease apologising for sounding so cross and their sessions resumed as before when he came back. But their friendship was never the same again.

Crease went away again that October, this time for nine months, and when he returned in July 1921 Evelyn recorded in his diary: 'The spell is broken. His influence has quite gone. I see just a rather silly perhaps casually interesting little man.'[61] As Evelyn later recalled, he had already transferred his allegiance to 'the more forceful and flamboyant' figure of J. F. Roxburgh, an outgoing and agnostic man of the world, in many ways the exact opposite of the monastic aesthete Crease.[62]

5

············

Watertight Compartments

Later renowned as the first headmaster of Stowe and universally known
by his initials 'J. F.', John Fergusson Roxburgh was a brilliant classicist
who had taken a First at Cambridge and been recruited to the Lancing
teaching staff before the war to boost the school's academic standing. Tall
and slightly stooped, he cut a dash with his flamboyant wardrobe – the
boys counted fourteen suits – and the various idiosyncratic mannerisms
he had cultivated as an undergraduate. With his sonorous voice and
precise diction he was especially effective at inspiring the boys to read
poetry and plays. His popularity was boosted by his religious scepticism
and his liberal approach to discipline. His biographer recounts how one
boy who was returning with a 'cricket-bag stuffed with bottles of beer and
cider for an end-of-term party had the misfortune to be offered a lift by
J. F. who heaved the bag into his car. He said nothing as the bottles clinked
but when he dropped him off handed him a packet of fifty cigarettes and
said, "Perhaps these will come in useful."'[1]

When Roxburgh came back to Lancing after the war (during which he
had been recommended for an MC and his younger brother was killed)
Evelyn quickly became a devotee, delighting in his sarcastic asides about
the headmaster's 'profound classical witticisms', as Roxburgh described
them, and finding his French lessons 'really a joy. It is almost worth doing
the wretched subject.'[2] 'Every hour in his form room was exhilarating,'
Evelyn later recalled.[3] Just as the younger and more reclusive Evelyn had
been drawn to the hermit-like Crease, the more convivial Roxburgh now
appealed to his growing gregariousness.

It was in Roxburgh's modern play-reading society in October 1920 that
he first studied George Bernard Shaw's *Candida*,[4] which gave him further

unflattering insight into the character of his father. Evelyn evidently associated Arthur with the Rev. James Mavor Morell, the sermonising husband of the play's heroine. The next April, Evelyn recorded in his diary: 'Father has been ineffably silly the whole holidays. The extraordinary thing is that the more I see through my father, the more I appreciate Mother. She has been like Candida and went to Father, whom she must have despised, because he needed her most. I always think I am discovering some new trait in his character and find that she knew it long ago.'[5]

Meanwhile Evelyn so revered Roxburgh that for a time he even adopted his way of speaking as if he had a hot potato in his mouth.[6] More permanently influential were his stipulations on the precise use of grammar and his hatred of clichés. Besides the French lessons, Evelyn had Roxburgh for 'general' subjects in the Upper Sixth from September 1920, studying anything that caught the master's fancy. Each week the boys wrote 250 words on a chosen subject, which Roxburgh would then read and hand back with verbal comments of praise or debate or, more disconcertingly, no comment at all – a sure sign that the piece had bored him rigid. For Evelyn, most disparaging of all was the remark, 'Excellent journalism, my dear fellow,' which he interpreted as 'trite in thought, colloquial in expression and aiming for effect by smartness and overstatement'.[7]

Evelyn never doubted that Roxburgh was homosexual: 'Most good schoolmasters are,' he reasoned. 'How else could they endure their work?' In his autobiography he professed to think it unlikely that Roxburgh would have given his desires 'physical release' with his pupils, yet shortly before leaving Lancing he had recorded in his diary how Tom Driberg had entered Roxburgh's darkened room one day and found him in a chair with a boy called MacDonald, looking very embarrassed.[8]* But Evelyn was not Roxburgh's type. 'I was small and quite pretty in a cherubic way. His tastes were more classical than rococo.'[9] Roxburgh's particular favourite was his head of house, Eddie Capel Cure, a 'golden-haired Hyancinthus' to whom J. F. gave a motorcycle which the boy soon crashed, ruining his handsome looks.† With Evelyn, meanwhile, Roxburgh merely discerned 'potentialities worth cultivating'.[10]

---

* Driberg was never an especially reliable witness, however he later vehemently denied this particular story (Francis Wheen, *Tom Driberg*, pp. 28–9).

† W. E. Capel Cure later modelled his career on Roxburgh, becoming a master at Stowe after graduating from Cambridge and J. F.'s closest personal confidant. Like J. F. he remained a bachelor. He died of cancer in 1953. See Annan, *Roxburgh of Stowe*, pp. 50, 196–7.

Evelyn's ambitions at this time were more obviously directed towards a career as a draughtsman than as a writer. However, as Roxburgh noticed, for someone of his age he was exceptionally well read and discerning about literature, and he had by no means ruled out the idea of following in the Waugh family literary tradition. In the autumn term of 1920 he made his first proper stab at a novel, the transparently autobiographical 'study of a man with two characters by his brother'.[11]

In the surviving ten-page fragment, the hero Peter Audley is at public school in Sussex in 1918 and contemplating the possibility of going off to the trenches the next year: 'He had learnt much of what it was like over there from his brother, but Ralf saw everything so abstractedly and with such imperturbable cynicism. Peter flattered himself that he was far more sensitive and temperamental. He was sure that he would not be able to stand it.'[12] However, Peter clearly admires Ralf's 'awfully clever' idea of living his life in 'watertight compartments'[13] – recalling a suggestion of Alec's that Evelyn seemed to see as a means of giving the freest possible rein to the Jekyll and Hyde sides of his own character.

The war was by then a fading memory for Alec. Bored at Chapman & Hall and wretched in his marriage, he was also suffering a crisis of confidence in his writing career. So when his seventeen-year-old brother – a year younger than Alec had been when he wrote *The Loom of Youth* – breezed home for the Christmas holidays announcing that he had started a novel, Alec naturally appeared 'apprehensive of a rival',[14] as Evelyn noted in his diary, his unease deepened by Evelyn's choice of subject. Although Evelyn thought his novel 'fairly good' and 'pretty sure' to get published, his family's disapproval combined with 'my own innate sloth' soon caused him to abandon it – though not before he had written a revealing dedication to himself, bemoaning the lot of an aspiring writer brought up in such an entirely literary family:

> Many of your relatives and most of your father's friends are more or less directly interested in paper and print. Ever since you first left the nursery for meals with your parents downstairs, the conversation, to which you were an insatiable listener, has been of books, their writers and producers; ever since, as a sleepy but triumphantly emancipated school boy, you were allowed to sit up with your elders in the 'bookroom' after dinner, you have heard little but discussion about books . . .

By the end of March 1921 Roxburgh was sufficiently impressed by Evelyn to ask him to tea in his small study, an honour only accorded to a select few. 'How delightful,' declared Roxburgh when Evelyn arrived. 'We have nothing to do until chapel but eat eclairs and talk about poetry.'[15] Six months later, following the publication of the first issue of the school magazine under Evelyn's editorship, J. F. wrote to tell him: 'If you use what the Gods have given you, you will do as much as anyone I know to shape the course of your generation.'[16]

Roxburgh's tribute to Evelyn followed a string of accolades in his final year at Lancing, during which he became editor of the Lancing magazine and president of the debating society, and won both the poetry and English literature prizes. After the literature prize in June he wrote blithely to Arthur: 'I've got the Scarlyn, all right ... I am a little cheered. Of course it is no testament to my brain – there was no serious competition – but I think it shows a certain capacity for work.'[17] He was also offered house captaincy in the spring of 1921 as a way of curbing his ongoing campaign of ridiculing the school Corps.[18] His choice was to either accept or leave the school. Knowing how much it would mean to his father (whom, despite all his scornful thoughts, Evelyn was still keen to please) and that it was a precondition of the other positions he wanted, he reluctantly accepted.[19]

But his new responsibility made him feel miserably lonely and disloyal to those who had looked to him for leadership in their troublemaking. He dreaded being thought of as self-important, officious or patronising, and his gloom was compounded by his loss of religious faith. He took to going for long walks after lights-out with with another senior boy called James Hill, during which they consoled each other about the 'loneliness of leadership' and talked about suicide, Evelyn going so far as to compose 'last letters' in which he admitted his deep fear of failure: 'I know I have something in me,' he wrote to his friend Dudley Carew, 'but I am desperately afraid it may never come to anything.'[20]

Just as he was about to embark on one such excursion a frantic letter arrived from Arthur, who had somehow heard about his nocturnal visits to the seashore. 'It is years since we have heard anything that has so distressed us,' wrote Arthur. 'That you, a House Captain, in the confidence of your leaders, should play such a rotten & contemptible game. It is unworthy of the name of Waugh, and doubly unworthy of yourself, of whom I have always been so proud ... When Alec told me this sort of thing was going on at Sherborne, I asked him for his word of honour that he would never do it ... I appeal to you to send me by the first post your honourable assurance that never again will you break bounds, never go out at night, never do anything so fatuously foolish to endanger your whole future.'[21] Still ignorant of the circumstances surrounding Alec's earlier expulsion from Sherborne, Evelyn thought the letter 'unconvincingly rhetorical', a product of his father's habitual theatricality which made him wince. But he wrote in his diary: 'I am at least glad he has taken a strong line about something at last.'[22]

Arthur admired even if he did not much like the play that Evelyn had written that term called *Conversion*, a satire of public-school life in three burlesques: 'As maiden aunts think it is'; 'As modern authors say it is', a skit on *The Loom of Youth*; and 'As we all know it is'. In the final act Evelyn's hero is blackmailed out of his troublemaking in chapel just as Evelyn had recently been persuaded out of ragging the Corps. 'Now look here,' says the prefect, 'we shall be needing another House Captain next term and I shall recommend you ... Now, will you be sensible?'[23] 'Congratulations on your wit and cynicism,' Arthur wrote after he had read it. 'With such promise I feel you are bound to come off at Oxford. You have at 17 what we laboured to get, and couldn't, at 23. Go on and prosper and my heart goes with you.'[24] After it had been performed to great applause before the whole school, Roxburgh told Evelyn the epilogue showed 'a touch of genius'.[25]

* * *

Among Evelyn's contemporaries, his friend Roger Fulford later recalled his 'immense, uncanny power over his schoolfellows'.[26] Another boy, Christopher Chamberlin, thought him 'the first subversive person I've met who was obviously thinking for himself'.[27] However, Max Mallowan, the future archaeologist husband of Agatha Christie and one of Evelyn's main intellectual rivals while at Lancing (after beating Evelyn in his Roman history essay, Mallowan crowed to his parents, 'That is a triumph!'),[28] recalled that he was 'popular among the boys for he was amusing and always ready to lead us into mischief, but he had a way of getting others into trouble and himself invariably escaping. He was courageous and witty and

clever but was also an exhibitionist with a cruel nature that cared nothing about humiliating his companions as long as he could expose them
to ridicule.'[29] But just as Evelyn admitted to hiding the fear that he might
at any moment suddenly fall from favour, his truculent and domineering
demeanour did not preclude the occasional influence of other boys. One
who made a significant impact on him was the future politician Hugh
Molson, who later recalled that he and Evelyn had been 'close friends
without really liking each other',[30] while Evelyn ultimately deemed
Molson 'a pompous ass'.[31] However, when Molson had first arrived at
Lancing in October 1919, sixteen-year-old Evelyn thought him 'amazing'
and 'undoubtedly clever', with 'the true aristocrat's capacity for being
perfectly at home in anyone's company'.[32]

If not quite aristocratic, the amazing Molson was the scion of a prosperous Canadian brewing family who now lived near Lancing at Goring
Hall, which Hugh's father, a Unionist MP, rented from the Bowes-Lyons.
Though born in Montreal, Major Molson had been educated at public
school in England and was scarcely distinguishable from the local gentry,
listing his recreations in *Who's Who* as 'shooting, motoring, golf'. Evelyn
paid several visits to the Molsons at Goring, designed by Charles Barry
and frequented for a time by the young Lady Elizabeth Bowes-Lyon, the
future Queen and later Queen Mother. It seems likely that this was his
first experience of staying in a large English country house and he noted
approvingly how comfortably the Molsons lived and that dinner was 'excellent and beautifully served'.[33]

Molson went equally often to the more modest Underhill, where Arthur
Waugh struck him as 'a caricature of a Victorian' with a rhetorical, sentimental, canting way of speaking. The adolescent Evelyn, meanwhile,
'couldn't bear it, or him,' noted Molson, 'and made no bones about expressing it at table or in the presence of his parent'. This was all rather
embarrassing for Molson, especially given Arthur's tendency to appeal
to him for sympathy and wonder aloud what he had done to deserve this
treatment from his son.[34]

Evidence of what Evelyn later saw as Molson's self-importance came
soon after his arrival at Lancing, when he edged Evelyn into one of the
bays in the school library and confided that he had written a book on education which he meant to publish.[35] The same term, when asked whether
he was interested in politics, Molson replied 'preternaturally so' – thus

acquiring the nickname 'Preters', which stuck for the rest of his Lancing career.

Destined to follow his father into politics and at one time touted as a future leader of the Conservative Party, at school Molson espoused a curious combination of socialism, atheism, pacifism and hedonism.[36] Among his other precocious endeavours was a series of essays, some of which he pressed on Arthur Waugh for criticism, others he persuaded periodicals to publish. Evelyn deplored his friend's long-winded prose,[37] yet the mere fact of publication served as an important spur. After Molson boasted to him that he had had an article accepted, Evelyn told his diary: 'I must try and write one next holidays.'[38]

Another activity in which Molson led the way was drinking. Before he had taken to alcohol in earnest himself, Evelyn marvelled at his friend's consumption during a drive out from school on Ascension Day, 1921. Molson had borrowed a car and at lunch in Chichester managed to get through: 'a neat whisky, a whisky and water, a gin and bitters, two whisky sodas, two liqueurs, a double whisky almost neat, two bottles of cider, two glasses of port, one neat whisky'. On the drive back he was 'a trifle risky' and 'drove round and round the market cross shouting to passers-by that we were looking for the alms houses'.[39]

Evelyn did not approve of all of Molson's excesses. In February 1921 he recorded after a morning's walk together: 'He is very much all over himself as he has just stolen more cocaine from the doctor. I see myself having a fairly hectic time with him . . .'[40] And after they spent a reading fortnight together in preparation for their Oxford scholarship exams, he primly dissuaded his friend from letting off steam with a night of 'whoring' – not that Evelyn would prove completely averse to such recreations in his later bachelor life.

Back in 1919, it was also Molson who had come up with the idea of a cultural society for the Upper Fifths, frustrated with not being allowed to air his important views at the school debating society. He recruited Evelyn and Fulford and together they founded the Dilettanti Society (the name suggested by Evelyn) for poetry readings, art lectures and political debate. Applicants poured in, among them Tom Driberg, the future journalist and Labour MP who recalled an unsettling interview in which Evelyn strode up to him one day in Great School and barked: 'Who's your favourite artist?' According to Driberg's biographer, he was so 'flustered by the unblinking stare of Waugh's eyes' that he 'suddenly forgot every artist who ever lived. Eventually, in a panic, he managed to pluck a random name from some distant recess of his brain – "Sir John Lavery". It was a ridiculous reply. But, to his surprise, he was elected forthwith.'[41] Another boy who said that his favourite painter was Landseer was promptly rejected.[42]

A bespectacled scholar eighteen months Evelyn's junior, Driberg would become a lifelong friend and credited Evelyn with providing much of the literary and artistic stimulus during his time at Lancing. Like Evelyn, he was very unpopular at the school to begin with, alienating other boys with his showy intelligence and unashamed aestheticism, his extravagant High Church religiosity and his camp renditions of Roxburgh's fruity diction. Despite his hatred of Driberg's politics, which by the age of fifteen veered towards Communism, Evelyn soon warmed to him, particularly after both became sacristans in the school chapel, serving at the Eucharist and changing the altar frontal.

It was to Driberg that Evelyn eventually confided that he had lost his faith, a bombshell delivered in the summer of 1921 in the midst of arranging the altar for the Sunday service. According to Evelyn, Driberg said that if he no longer believed in God, he had no business handling the altar cloth.[43] Driberg's slightly different memory of the incident was that he had rebuked Evelyn for not hanging the altar cloth straight, to which Evelyn retorted: 'Nonsense! If it's good enough for me it's good enough for God!' – a remark that Driberg later deemed 'mildly blasphemous [but] not a proclamation of atheism'.[44]

In his diary, Evelyn recorded that he had been an atheist for the past two terms without the courage to admit it to himself. He felt sure it was only a phase, however, and the only thing that really worried him was the possibility that it might cut him off from a devout boy named John Longe, whom he liked better than any other Lancing contemporary at the time. 'If I thought it would I would believe anything,' he wrote. 'He has been one of the few things that make school worthwhile.'[45]

In later life Driberg was a famously reckless homosexual* and while

---

* Driberg (later Lord Bradwell) was the first person in public life to be described as a homosexual in a *Times* obituary. His entry in the *Oxford Dictionary of National Biography* records that as an adult he 'had a consuming passion for fellating handsome, lean, intelligent working-class toughs . . . his sexual prowling never abated'.

at Lancing he wore make-up during the holidays and in term-time harboured several unrequited crushes. He more or less controlled himself
until his last year, however, when as deputy head of school he made unwelcome advances to a boy in his dormitory.[46] Perhaps keen to welcome
his friend to the fold, Driberg maintained that the schoolboy Evelyn, too,
had had similar inclinations but that he repressed them. 'I certainly never
heard of him as a practising homosexual until later, at Oxford,' Driberg
wrote. He saw Evelyn's subsequent marriages and outspoken intolerance
of homosexuality as a 'suppression of his true nature' and ventured that
the pressure of denying his bisexuality may even have helped precipitate
the eventual mental breakdown related in *The Ordeal of Gilbert Pinfold*.[47]
Despite subjecting some of the characters in his fiction to archly homo-
phobic contempt, Evelyn admitted in his autobiography to having been
'susceptible to the prettiness of some fifteen-year-olds' (in 1920 he gave
'library privileges' to a boy called Lowther 'just because he is pretty')[48]
yet maintained that he 'never fell victim to the grand passions which
inflamed and tortured most of my friends'.[49] In his last year at Lancing
he wrote disapprovingly in his diary of 'keennesses' and congratulated
himself for suppressing such emotions, preferring to act as censorious
confidant to his more besotted friends.

Evelyn's reserve may have partly reflected his immaturity and prudish-
ness – references to sex in his diaries tended to be couched in terms such
as 'filth', 'lust' and 'depravity'. But in any case he was less restrained with
girls and at the age of fifteen he appeared to be keen on several. Besides the
'comely wench' Luned Jacobs, who admitted to having adored Evelyn,[50]
Alec discerned him to be 'somewhat enamoured' of Hugh's sister Moira
and 'a little affected' towards Philla Fleming – he wrote home before the
holidays urging his parents to arrange some theatricals and 'choose a play
in which I kiss her passionately'.[51]

Philla, though, was a waning flame, as in due course would be poor
Luned. In the autumn of 1919 Evelyn wrote brutally in his diary: 'I trust
she [Luned] realizes the ridiculous affair is at an end' and 'if she does
open the subject again I think I shall have to snub her. She is really not
worth it.'[52] Evidently he had second thoughts and the next Christmas
holidays they again held hands and frolicked by the fire. Evelyn hazarded
at the time that she 'would have let me kiss her had I wanted to', and later
that year it did develop into a fully fledged kissing romance. However, in

January 1921 he wrote to her telling her that it was finally over.⁵³ Luned responded with a pathetic letter: 'What a fool is a fond wench,' wrote Evelyn in his diary – a line from *The Beggar's Opera* which he saw six times that year. Nevertheless, she later recalled his letter ending their affair as 'the kindest' and acknowledged that in any case she was 'too young [and] a boy of Evelyn's age was not going to be tied down to a little schoolgirl'. Besides 'he was streets ahead of me intellectually'.⁵⁴

Evelyn's attraction to Luned had dwindled that summer ('She has coarsened out a lot')⁵⁵ and he had found himself drawn to others, among them the 'divine' Betty Bulleid, whom he met with his aunts at Midsomer Norton, 'sweetly pretty,' he recorded, 'much better than Luned'.⁵⁶ More recently he had fallen for the 'remarkably pretty'⁵⁷ Ursula Kendall, daughter of an Old Etonian headmaster friend of Arthur's in Hampstead, 'beautiful and gracious and womanly,' seventeen-year-old Evelyn wrote wistfully in his diary, 'but I am afraid that others, better than I, have seen this too'.⁵⁸ A flirtation followed – at any rate a friend later described Ursula as an 'old love of Evelyn's'⁵⁹ – however after accompanying her to one or two dances that spring he discovered that Ursula was madly in love with a slightly older boy, a likeable but as Evelyn saw it 'quite brainless and slow' Old Wykehamist called Bobby Shaw. Around the same time, he also took a shine to the more boyish-looking Joan Laking, sister of the rakish Sir Francis Laking, Bt, but she turned out to be a lesbian.

Joan Laking was a first cousin of Dudley Carew, Evelyn's slavish disciple at Lancing, a fellow habitué of the school library and co-founder of the Dilettanti, of which Evelyn was the elected chairman, Carew the secretary. Their friendship had developed along similarly unequal lines, with Evelyn the condescending master, Carew the doting pupil: 'If only I can hold his affection I shall be alright,' Carew anxiously told his diary.⁶⁰

Like Evelyn, Carew was an aspiring writer and he later published a couple of novels – 'justly forgotten' as one Waugh scholar brutally puts it – before joining *The Times*. Virtually everything he wrote at Lancing he passed to Evelyn for criticism. When in June 1920 Carew sent a poem that began: 'You have broken all my idols / Given me fresh creeds to keep', Evelyn reflected that it was 'rather embarrassing to have so large an influence which works out in such a bad poem'.⁶¹

Carew later accepted Evelyn's description of him as a 'natural hero-worshipper', yet he saw himself as Evelyn's Boswell and hung on his every word. He is often seen as a risible figure, and certainly his conversations with Michael Davie while he was editing Evelyn's diaries suggest a rather pathetic character: 'Oh Evelyn, dear, Oh . . . He was so wonderful, and he makes himself out so dreadful . . . He was perfection as a boy.' But to give Carew his due, he was among the first to recognise Evelyn's extraordinary talent. 'Oh but he's great,' he wrote in 1921. 'I have got unwavering faith in his genius.' Accordingly he kept every scrap that Evelyn wrote to him, all of which he ultimately sold to the University of Texas in a rage after reading Evelyn's unkind portrayal of their friendship in *A Little Learning*. Carew contended that what had latterly damned him in Evelyn's eyes was not so much his obsequiousness – he claimed unconvincingly that he 'always stood up to him'[62] – as the fact that he had introduced Evelyn to his disastrous first wife, having earlier become too close for comfort to Evelyn's parents.

Carew was a frequent visitor to Underhill and his diary affords revealing glimpses of the Waugh household just as Evelyn was about to become an adult. In August 1921, he recorded that the normally jovial Alec was 'an extraordinary chilling and repressing influence. Directly he comes in Arthur stops making jokes. Evelyn stops being clever, I stop talking and only Mrs W is left undisturbed. He has gimlet eyes, a baleful glare . . .'[63] unbeknown to Carew, Alec was wretchedly unhappy at the time, hating his job reading 'tenth-rate' manuscripts at Chapman & Hall[64] and even more miserable in his marriage with Barbara, whom he had wed under pressure from her parents in July 1919.

At first the couple had lived at Underhill, before eventually building a wooden bungalow on a small plot at Ditchling bought with Alec's earnings from *The Loom of Youth*.[65] Throughout this time the marriage remained unconsummated, however, a situation for which Alec gallantly claimed full responsibility, attributing their difficulties to his ignorance of 'the physiology of sex' and of 'the amount of tact and skilful patience that is required to initiate an inexperienced girl'.[66] Alec and Barbara eventually separated in January 1922 and a year later divorced. Alec's humiliation was completed by the judge who, struggling to grasp his explanation as to what had gone wrong, peered over his spectacles and said: 'I think I understand, young man, you couldn't get it in.'[67] The non-consummation became the subject of endless ribald speculation in the Waugh family, Evelyn's son Auberon suggesting 'a malfunction of erectile tissue due to invisible emanations from a silver cup inscribed from W. W. Jacobs, which was kept, for some unclear reason, next to the newly-weds' bed'.[68] There also lurked a suspicion that Alec, despite his subsequent reputation as a compulsive womaniser, remained essentially homosexual. One of his sons recalled him in old age sitting outside a café in Tangier, watching some handsome young Arab go by and sighing: 'Just think of the firm dusky limbs quivering beneath that fella's djellaba.'[69] Privately, meanwhile, Alec indelicately let slip that the real obstacle was Barbara's hymen, which he claimed was 'built like a concrete portcullis'.[70]

* * *

By the autumn term of 1921 Evelyn was well and truly tired of Lancing, yet typically he used his low spirits creatively, filling the school magazine with what he later described as 'preposterous manifestos of disillusionment'[71] and founding the Corpse Club 'for people who are bored stiff'.[72] Members were required to wear black silk tassels in their buttonholes, wrote to each other on mourning notepaper and whenever a new one was elected, Evelyn as self-appointed 'Undertaker' would announce that 'The Undertaker finds a mournful pleasure in announcing the interment of the late Mr . . .'[73]

The one bright spot was the prospect of going to Oxford, so besides his various official jobs Evelyn was busy cramming 'like hell' for a history scholarship. He took the precaution of writing to Arthur to tell him how 'very repugnant' he found the idea of staying on another term at Lancing and that in case he failed to get a scholarship he was prepared to go up to Oxford 'on a minimum wage'. Mindful of the trouble his son might cause if he stood in his way, Arthur promptly consented to his leaving that term and either going straight to Oxford or to France.[74] Evelyn was greatly relieved. 'I should have only stagnated and fallen in love with some underschool if I had stayed on,'[75] he wrote in his diary. A week later, however, he was still fretting that he was 'open to fall in love with someone', that 'people like Onslow and Kimmerling interest me too much' and that 'I shall have to take care if I want to leave with credit and self-respect'.[76]

In early December Evelyn travelled to Oxford to sit the scholarship exams, accompanied by his friend Preters Molson, who sought to galvanise himself with a dash of strychnine but to no avail. The other candidates struck Evelyn as 'absolute oiks but monstrously intellectual',[77] nonetheless it proved to be 'a week of pure euphoria', staying in a hotel for the first time on his own and being well looked after by Lancing old boys who had gone up to Oxford before them. The general paper, in particular, he 'simply loved', writing at length about the Pre-Raphaelites and Arthur Symons's *Life of Beardsley*, and afterwards he felt confident that he had done well. The next week two letters arrived at Lancing, one to say that he had won the £100 Hertford College open history scholarship, another from his prospective tutor C. R. M. F. Cruttwell congratulating him on his 'extremely promising' work, saying he had been especially impressed by his general paper, his question on the Reformation in English history, and above all by his English prose style which was 'about the best of any of the candidates in the group'.[78]

The next day, after saying his goodbyes and arranging for his successors to take on the school magazine, debating society and library, Evelyn caught the late train to Ditchling, leaving Lancing for good. 'I am sure I have left at the right time,' he wrote in his diary, 'as early as possible and with success.'[79]

6

....

All That One Dreams

Arthur was delighted with his son's achievement and brazenly basked in the glory that he felt reflected on himself. 'Thank you, my dear Boy,' he wrote as Evelyn made his way back to Underhill, 'for the honour & happiness you have brought to your home. May the future be worthy of this beginning.' With possibly unintended condescension, he added that next to New College (his old college), whose scholarships Evelyn had thought unduly competitive, he too would have chosen Hertford. 'It is a small but thoroughly good college, and the emoluments are the best on the list.'[1] The £100-a-year emoluments provided by Evelyn's scholarship were especially welcome for Arthur who, like most British publishers, was far worse off than he had been ten years previously and had been worrying even more than usual since the expiry of the Dickens copyright in 1920, which left a large hole in Chapman & Hall's income.[2]

Evelyn's headmaster, meanwhile, was relieved no longer to have to deal with the boy's restlessness at school. 'He had begun to grate at his surroundings,' wrote Bowlby in his final report, 'and the friction was bad for him & threw out sparks which made little fires in some of the characters about him, partly no doubt kindling, but partly destructive! For all his brilliance he is curiously young and out of touch with reality. But he is looking for it and if he will search diligently & humbly & be content with some beaten tracks, instead of wanting to make a new road every time, he will find it – and himself.' If Evelyn found that patronising, Roxburgh's report was more straightforwardly favourable: 'His work has great merit and is sometimes really brilliant. I think he has quite unusual ability and a real gift for writing. We shall hear of him again.'[3]

Privately, Roxburgh rebuked him for having spread the 'contagion of disillusionment'[4] in his last term at school, however Evelyn assured Dudley Carew that he was now 'pretty full of beans'[5] at the prospect of going to Oxford so soon. Whereas at Lancing he had felt apprehensive and resentful to be starting in the middle of the academic year, this time he was excited to be going to university as 'a lone explorer'.[6]

When he arrived in January 1922, Hertford's best rooms had all been taken by the Michaelmas freshers, so for his first two terms he made do with a poky set over the JCR buttery from where the smell of anchovy toast wafted up each afternoon.[7] Here he lived not unlike Paul Pennyfeather or Charles Ryder before he met Sebastian Flyte, in a typical freshman's tangle of emotions. 'I am very shy and a little lonely still but gradually settling down,' he wrote to Carew a few weeks into his first term. 'I wish I could find some congenial friends.'[8]

To begin with he saw a lot of his old Lancing cronies: Max Mallowan, Rupert Fremlin, James Hill and Preters Molson – who was not yet up but being coached for another attempt at a New College scholarship, which he eventually achieved at the third go. It was with the pleasure-seeking Preters (and Hill) that Evelyn got drunk for the first time, polishing off three-quarters of a bottle of Madeira, a glass of port and two tumblers of cider and then loudly reciting Newbolt in the quad – all 'very pleasant', he told Tom Driberg afterwards. 'I don't feel the least ill after it.'[9]

For Evelyn, the effect of drink mattered far more than the taste of it. Besides being another way of going against the grain at a time when the political mood in Britain seemed to favour introducing Prohibition, getting drunk offered the perfect means of conquering his shyness and broadening his social range. According to a friend at Hertford, 'he drank to get into a world that was not his world'.[10] By Evelyn's own account most of his Oxford friendships were forged while drunk and he was fervent in preaching the benefits of intoxication.[11] 'Do let me seriously advise you to take to drink,' he urged Driberg. 'There is nothing like the aesthetic pleasure of being drunk and if you do it in the right way you can avoid being ill the next day. That is the greatest thing Oxford has to teach.'[12]

Driberg was still at Lancing and, despite Evelyn's avowed euphoria at having left, at lonelier moments during his first Oxford term his thoughts still drifted back to his old school. To Dudley Carew, who also remained there, he affected disdain at the idea of keeping up with the past yet admitted that he was 'vain enough' to want to know what was said of him now that he had left: 'I imagine I am pretty well disliked now as good God I deserved to be. [But] I am changing pretty hard and I think for the better . . .'[13] He also could not resist writing the odd piece for the school magazine, including a robust reply (under the pseudonym Lavernia Scargill) to a conceited critic of the Corpse Club.

At Oxford, for the time being at least, he remained relatively unobtrusive. He learned to smoke a pipe and to ride a bicycle and went for long walks around the surrounding villages, bounding along with his stubby oak walking stick. He bought a cigarette box engraved with the Hertford College arms and a printed panorama of Oxford, and even played the odd game of hockey, relishing its 'pleasant old world violence'. More ominously, he had begun to spend money with reckless abandon and later explained to his cousin Claud Cockburn that he 'kept the creditors quiet in the traditional Oxonian manner of the day by simply ordering more and more goods'.[14] He never went to chapel, did not frequent the lecture room and read almost no history despite his tutor's exasperated demands: 'Damn you, you're a scholar!'[15]

Evelyn found ample time for other books, however, among which he particularly admired Lewis Carroll's *Alice's Adventures in Wonderland*, which he famously alludes to in *Brideshead* when Charles Ryder sets off for lunch with Sebastian for the first time: 'I was in search of love in those days, and I went full of curiosity and the faint, unrecognized apprehension that here, at last, I should find that low door in the wall which opened on an enclosed and enchanted garden, which was somewhere, not overlooked by any window, in the heart of that grey city.'

Equivalent glimpses of Wonderland had beckoned for Evelyn when, as a timid fresher feeling cut off from the best of what Oxford had to offer, he began to make friends with a wild, dishevelled 'second-year man' at Hertford called Terence Greenidge. In the prevailing Oxford parlance, Greenidge was 'a zany'[16] or, as Harold Acton described him, 'a dear, charming loony'.[17] His foibles included a mania for picking litter off Oxford pavements and stuffing it in his pockets, and a habit of pinching small items belonging to others – hairbrushes, nail scissors, keys and so forth – and hiding them behind books in the library.

Yet it was in Greenidge's rooms that Evelyn met the president of the Union and the editor of *The Isis*, introductions which in turn quickly led to his speaking at the Union and contributing to the magazine. Given the

The Waughs in 1890. From left: Elsie, Connie, Dr Alexander Waugh ('the Brute'), Alick, Annie (Mrs Waugh), Arthur and Trissie.

The Brute: Annie was terrified lest Arthur's birth interfere with his first day of partridge-shooting.

Their house at Midsomer Norton: Evelyn relished its dark hidden corners and assorted interesting smells.

The Raban family circa 1892, with Arthur and Kate top left.

Kate and Arthur about to explore the lanes of Buckinghamshire, and (*below*) posing after their engagement; as Evelyn later saw it, his father was 'acting all the time'.

Left to right: Alec, Arthur and Evelyn, circa 1906.

Evelyn on the steps of 11 Hillfield Road with his nanny, Lucy Hodges.

Kate, Arthur, Evelyn, Alec (with cricket bat) and their poodle on holiday at Midsomer Norton, 1904.

Alec, Kate and Arthur in the garden of the newly built Underhill, 1909.

Evelyn (second from right) with the Pistol Troop, circa 1910.

Evelyn, aged eight.

Evelyn (second top row, third from left) at Heath Mount, with his bête noire Cecil Beaton (same row, third from right).

Alec, Evelyn, Kate and their poodle in 1912.

Head's House during Evelyn's desolate first year at Lancing, 1917. Evelyn is sitting second from the left on the ground, next to the other 'new man', Roger Fulford, far left. The Rev. Bowlby is behind the cup in a dog collar.

From top to bottom: Evelyn at Lancing in 1921, at Oxford in 1923 and teaching at Aston Clinton in 1926.

Evelyn's first love at Oxford, Richard Pares, seen here in the Alps with Cyril Connolly (wearing beret); Evelyn complained of having been 'cuckolded by Connolly'.

Evelyn's next 'friend of my heart' was Alastair Graham (*below*), pictured here shortly before they met at Oxford. *Right*: the photo he sent beckoning Evelyn to 'come and drink with me somewhere'.

Lundy Island, Easter 1925: (left to right) Richard, Olivia, Gwen and David Plunket Greene, Terence Greenidge and Elizabeth Russell. Evelyn is seated in foreground.

On the same Lundy holiday: Olivia Plunket Greene, Patrick Balfour, David Plunket Greene and Matthew Ponsonby.

Evelyn on his Francis-Barnett motor-bicycle at Aston Clinton in February 1926.

zeal with which he had taken to drinking, it was apt that Evelyn's maiden Union speech in early February 1922[18] should oppose a motion calling for Prohibition, although with characteristic contrariness within a few months he spoke in favour of it, saying he was a Conservative and that Prohibition ought to be a Conservative principle.* *Oxford Magazine* recorded the 'good impression' he made in his first debate,[19] however Evelyn readily conceded that he had no talent for oratory and was quite unable to assume the appropriately grave tone for the debates, besides which he was far too ignorant of the politics and current affairs that were routinely discussed.†

Perhaps more influentially, Greenidge launched Evelyn's Oxford social life and accelerated his descent into drunkenness by introducing him to the Hypocrites' Club (motto: 'water is best'), the much-mythologised dive on St Aldate's which was then in the process of being taken over by a band of hedonistic Old Etonians. Evelyn found the riotous and self-consciously childish atmosphere there immediately congenial and later described the Hypocrites' as 'the stamping ground of half my Oxford life and the source of friendships still warm today'.[20]

Many of these friendships had a pronounced homosexual flavour, not that there was anything especially unusual about that at that time. As John Betjeman later remembered, 'Everyone was queer at Oxford in those days!'[21] According to Terence Greenidge, himself an active homosexual, 'the attraction of man for man' was apparent well beyond the Aesthete set that Evelyn befriended at the Hypocrites'. Greenidge claimed to have witnessed 'many a hearty "blind"', even in Athletic Magdalen, where the behaviour of the most unlikely people showed evidence of tender feeling'. The cox 'of a very sporting college' also told him stories about the private lives 'of the crews whom he used to steer so well, and they were remarkable stories'.[22]

If Evelyn had been sexually repressed at Lancing, here at Oxford he at last felt able to shed his inhibitions, emboldened as much by the overtly camp and licentious atmosphere as he was by the drink. When Anthony

---

* Douglas Woodruff, later editor of *The Tablet*, had recruited Evelyn to the debating chamber as one of the Conservatives, at that time outnumbered by the Liberal contingent. 'I proclaimed myself a Tory but could not have defined Tory policy on any current topic.' (*A Little Learning*, p. 183.) He belonged to the Oxford Carlton Club and the smaller Chatham.
† Evelyn did however enter himself for the Union elections in June 1923, coming last with twenty-five votes. His friend Christopher Hollis was elected president with 309.

Powell first saw him at the Hypocrites' he was sitting on Christopher Hollis's knee, and when Tom Driberg came for his scholarship exam he and Evelyn enjoyed 'some lively and drunken revels ("orgies" were they?), mainly homosexual in character: I remember dancing with John F, while Evelyn and another rolled on the sofa with (as one of them said later) their "tongues licking each other's tonsils"'.[23] (Perhaps not surprisingly, Driberg was unsuccessful in that scholarship attempt.) His friend and biographer Christopher Sykes averred that Evelyn frankly admitted to having passed through 'an extreme homosexual phase' while at Oxford, which 'for the short time it lasted, was unrestrained, emotionally and physically'.[24]

* * *

Towards the end of his first term, Evelyn wrote to tell Carew that Oxford was 'all that one dreams'.[25] In the summer term it got even better. 'Life here is very beautiful,' he wrote to Driberg in May. 'Mayonnaise and punts and cider cup all day long. One loses all ambition to be an intellectual.'[26]

A week before the holidays began, Evelyn again wrote to Driberg asking him to be kind to the brother 'of a friend of mine here called Pares' who was due to start at Lancing the next term. 'As far as I can gather he is a fragile & sensitive flower. If he is anything like his brother, he is also abnormally clever.'[27]

The friend was Richard Pares, widely admired among Oxford undergraduates for his bright blue eyes, flax-gold hair and, as A. L. Rowse wistfully remembered, 'red kissable lips'. Rowse admitted to having fallen victim himself to Pares's 'charm and desperation',[28] while Evelyn's later rival for Pares's affections, Cyril Connolly, beheld 'the look of a Rossetti angel with a touch of Mick Jagger'.[29]

According to Christopher Hollis, who remained a lifelong friend, Evelyn's homosexuality at Oxford represented a passing phase at a time when girls were in short supply and strictly chaperoned. Yet while the phase lasted there were at least two intense relationships, and the first of these was with Pares, 'my first homosexual love', as Evelyn later described him to Nancy Mitford.[30] A year older than Evelyn, Pares had come up to Oxford from Winchester the term before him, in the autumn of 1921. A history scholar at Balliol and a future Fellow of All Souls, he was certainly abnormally clever, however he was also strangely submissive. Years later

Hollis recalled that Pares had 'become a complete prostitute more from obligingness than anything else';[31] or as Harold Acton observed, 'My de-ar, he lends his body.'[32] His timid acquiescence was possibly a legacy of his troubled relationship with his father, the celebrated but emotionally wintery Russian expert, Sir Bernard Pares, who was 'responsible for much family unhappiness' according to Rowse. In any event, Richard was a nervous, delicate child.

Much of the attention he attracted at Winchester had been unwelcome – he 'hated being pursued by buggers', as Rowse robustly recorded[33] – however there was apparently at least one love interest before Evelyn. 'I have been inwardly faithful to one boy for more than two years,' he told Evelyn, 'and he is only dispossest this morning and by you, so I think I shall be constant to you for three years and then turn Papist. How much I shall have to confess depends on you.'[34]

Having begun sometime during Evelyn's first year – possibly during his first term – their affair seems to have peaked around Christmas 1922.* In a letter to Evelyn written during that vacation from his home in Surbiton, Pares declared himself 'tired of pretending not to be in love with you, which I have done intermittently since the fourth week of last term'. It was 'impossible not to be level-headed after receiving a letter from you, for the bare receipt of it plunges me precipitously into sentimentality which increases in geometrical progression the first five times I read the letter through . . . Thoughts of me in bed? O Come.'[35]

In the same letter, Pares wrote that his 'only fear of writing love-letters to you is that they might come to be read out in court like those of Mrs Thompson, and the counsel for the defence would say it was one of the greatest love-affairs of history – which it is – and the Judge would say it was a guilty passion – which also it is'. Edith Thompson was a young Essex housewife who was then awaiting execution for conspiring with her young lover to murder her husband. The allusion adds to the impression that Evelyn and Pares's love affair was more momentous than is often suggested.

Rowse, a notoriously inaccurate gossip, later described it as 'a very intense adolescent affair' and hazarded that Evelyn would have been the more active, masculine partner, Pares more passive and feminine. Pares

---

* '. . . my few romances have always culminated in Christmas week, Luned [Jacobs], Richard [Pares], Alastair [Graham]' (Christmas Day 1924; *EWD*, p. 194).

himself confided to Rowse that he had never before experienced anything like it. It was, wrote Rowse, 'Pares's great love affair' and 'they were inseparable in Evelyn's first year'.[36] Pares was passionate about *Alice's Adventures in Wonderland*, which may help to explain why it became such a favourite narrative template for Evelyn in his future fiction.

Theirs was an attraction of opposites. Besides his intellect – far more academic than Evelyn's – Pares was renowned for his puritanical self-discipline, yet according to another great friend, Isaiah Berlin, who regarded Pares as 'the best and most admirable man I have ever known', he 'needed, and was sustained by, the greater vitality of others, and re-warded it with grateful and lasting affection'.[37] But if he was attracted by Evelyn's fizzing energy, Pares was equally repelled by his heavy drinking. 'I loved him dearly,' wrote Evelyn, 'but an excess of wine nauseated him and this made an insurmountable barrier between us. When I felt most intimate, he felt queasy.'[38]

Evelyn demanded complete dedication from those to whom he gave affection – as with his lopsided friendship with his Lancing disciple Dudley Carew – and for a time he expected Pares to accompany him on his regular benders at the Hypocrites' and elsewhere. To begin with Pares meekly complied, even going so far as to speak at the Union in favour of drunkenness, but it soon became evident that he had neither the inclination nor the constitution for it. Moreover, despite his 'gift for absurdity and frivolity', as an article in *The Isis* recorded,[39] Pares was always far more studious than Evelyn. Eventually, as Evelyn recalled, he was 'rescued from bohemia and preserved for a life of scholarship'. He subsequently took a First, became a don and wrote a series of books on the eighteenth-century West Indian sugar trade as impenetrable as they were magisterial.

His saviour from Evelyn was the Dean of Balliol, F. F. 'Sligger' Urquhart, who lured him into his more sober salon, thereby earning Evelyn's lasting contempt. Towards the end of the spring term of 1923, another member of Sligger's circle, Cyril Connolly, admitted to being 'rather gone' on Pares. Despite Pares's promise to Evelyn that he would be 'yours for three years or ad nauseam'[40] he and Connolly were soon to be seen walking around the colleges together arm in arm. Evelyn felt sufficiently betrayed to complain later of having been 'cuckolded by Connolly'.[41]

The nature of Evelyn's love affair with Pares is difficult to define at this distance, although Evelyn's Hertford friend Tony Bushell was adamant that Evelyn's fastidiousness would have precluded a physical affair. 'The idea is preposterous,' Bushell scoffed in a television interview. 'Absolutely not possible, and I know.'[42] Christopher Hollis remembered Evelyn telling him that his affections at that time were 'much more romantic than carnal'.[43] Harold Acton also tended to the view that the relationship was 'idyllically platonic',[44] although he may have preferred to think that given his own unrequited crush on Evelyn.

If there really was no physical element, it might seem odd that Evelyn himself should have referred to the affair as homosexual to Nancy Mitford – unless he was trying to impress her with what an intrepid young libertine he had been. In letters to Carew at the time Evelyn admitted that he had been 'incredibly depraved morally' and also that 'my diary for the period is destroyed'.[45] This seems to be the only evidence that he kept a diary during his time at Oxford, however in his future life Evelyn habitually destroyed his diary covering times of greatest emotional upheaval. All the indications are that Pares's abandonment of him was more wounding than Evelyn was prepared to let on, and the painful end of the affair can be said to have given rise to the theme of faithlessness that would recur throughout his young life and again and again in his fiction.

* * *

In his third term at Oxford, Evelyn had moved to larger rooms on the ground floor of Hertford's front quad. In *Brideshead*, Charles Ryder's priggish cousin Jasper warns him: 'I've seen many a man ruined through having ground-floor rooms in the front quad. People start dropping in . . . you start giving them sherry. Before you know where you are, you've opened a free bar for all the undesirables of the college.'[46]

This certainly reflected Evelyn's own experience, just as Charles's first encounter with Sebastian recalled an evening when members of the Bullingdon came roaring out of Terence Greenidge's rooms and rushed across the quad to get back to Christ Church before the Great Bell stopped ringing. 'But there was a straggler,' remembered Bushell, 'and about the middle of the quad he turned away from the rest of them and staggered over towards Evelyn's room where he was sick through the window.'[47]

His new rooms soon became the epicentre of the self-elected 'Hertford underworld', whose chief protagonists were Evelyn, Greenidge, Tony

Bushell, the budding actor who had come second to Evelyn in Hertford's history scholarship exam, and Evelyn's Lancing friend Philip Machin. Most days at lunchtime they gathered in Evelyn's rooms for bread and cheese and plenty of beer. When his old Lancing friend Preters Molson was invited he sniffed, 'I usually prefer to have a hot lunch,' thereby lumbering himself with a new nickname.

'Hot Lunch' Molson later remembered being shocked at Evelyn's wild and irresponsible behaviour at these lunches. Tony Bushell recalled that Evelyn 'always drank a good deal' at these events, 'a good deal'. Starting with a glass or two of Sandeman's Brown Bang, a heavy, glutinous sherry, he would then go on to beer and in the afternoon, while Bushell and the other athletes went off to play games, he 'just went on drinking'. By five o'clock, when the games players had returned and were eating their anchovy toast in the JCR, Evelyn would often be completely sozzled, 'purple in the face with blotches on the backs of his hands'. Not infrequently he would then carry on drinking throughout the evening.

Bushell recalled him as 'a wonderful drunk ... a marvellous drunk. Wonderful company, witty, funny, wildly funny'.[48] Others, though, had less wonderful experiences. Tamara Abelson, the daughter of an émigré former official in the Tsar's treasury and one of very few girls at the university in those days, made friends with Evelyn during long walks across the meadows with her Alsatian dog, Ghost. One day Evelyn turned up 'unpleasantly drunk,' Tamara recalled, 'rude and violent', and she threatened to cut him off for ever if he went to see her like that again. He never did, although with others his roistering continued unabated and he often became objectionable.

Even at the Hypocrites', never noted for its sobriety, Evelyn's behaviour occasionally went too far. On Anthony Powell's first visit there in the autumn of 1923, towards the end of Evelyn's second year, he learned that Evelyn had been banned 'for having smashed up a good deal of the Club's furniture with the heavy stick he always carried'.[49]

By this time, Evelyn had introduced another new friend to the Hypocrites', Harold Acton, whom he had met at the Newman Society, listening to a talk by G. K. Chesterton (evidence, incidentally, that Evelyn remained intellectually interested in religion even if he no longer went to chapel). By some distance the most significant influence on Evelyn's social and artistic development at Oxford – as he later acknowledged by dedicating

Decline and Fall 'in homage and affection' to him – Acton was considered by far the most striking and promising student of their era,* although his renown has not lasted anything like as well as that of Evelyn and several other protégés.

The son of an Italianized English father and an immensely rich American mother (Acton himself left $500 million when he died in 1994), Acton had grown up at a magnificent Florentine villa before being packed off to prep school in Berkshire, where he founded a precocious magazine on art and fashion and regarded standing on chairs and reciting poetry as a perfectly normal way of making new friends.[50]

At Eton he fell in with another unashamedly camp and rich half-American, Brian Howard, with whom he collaborated to produce the *Eton Candle* magazine with shocking pink wrappers, yellow endpapers and contributions from Max Beerbohm, Aldous Huxley (then a young beak at the school) and the Sitwells. Their Eton Society of Arts numbered several of Evelyn's future Oxford cronies, among them Hugh Lygon, who Anthony Powell assumed owed his membership to an unrequited 'tendresse' felt for him by either Brian Howard or Robert Byron rather than to his intellect, which was far from remarkable.[51]

When Acton arrived at Christ Church in the Michaelmas term of 1922, he painted his gloomy Gothic rooms bright yellow and festooned them with artificial flowers and wax fruit. Tall, plumpish, with a domed forehead, long black side-whiskers and oriental-looking eyes, he was an easily recognisable figure 'shouldering and mincing his way' about Oxford. Familiar accoutrements included grey bowler hat, black stock, pleated mauve trousers as wide as a skirt (the so-called Oxford bags which he popularised)† and tightly rolled umbrella.[52] Their near-contemporary John Rothenstein, later director of the Tate Gallery, recalled a near-collision with Evelyn and Acton on an Oxford street corner, 'two figures with scarves flying in the wind, one fair, shortish, with fanatical eyes set wide apart [Evelyn]; the other tall, dark, with an expression of pride oddly blended with courtliness'.[53]

---

* A. L. Rowse wrote: 'Never can there have been *such* undergraduate reclame, such publicity, such a peculiar ascendancy as that exerted by Harold Acton in his day at Oxford.' (*A Cornishman at Oxford*, p. 23.)

† Lord Boothby claimed to have started this fashion some years earlier. (*My Oxford*, ed. by Ann Thwaite, p. 32.)

Like Anthony Blanche in *Brideshead*, whose creation ('part Gallic, part Yankee, part, perhaps, Jew; wholly exotic') owed an equal amount to Brian Howard, Acton declaimed Eliot's *The Waste Land* through a megaphone from his balcony to puzzled passers-by; and when confronted by a gang of hearty rugger players, he exclaimed to a fellow aesthete: 'Oh my de-ah, we are so dec-a-dent and they are so in-no-cent.' After coming down with a cold, he wailed: 'Oh, my de-ah, I've been so mis-er-able a-all the day.'⁵⁴

Acton's affectations – he later described his recreations in *Who's Who* as 'hunting – Philistines' – attracted occasional hostility, most notably when, in the summer of 1923, a band of 'big ruff animal louts', as he described them, smashed his window with a poker. 'I, tucked up in bed and contemplating the reflection of Luna on my walls, was immersed under showers of myriad particles of split glass, my head powdered glass-dust and my possessions vitrified.'⁵⁵ But by the time he left Oxford, when he was recognised as the pre-eminent figure in the artistic life of the university, he had won over even the athletes.

He and Evelyn were unlikely soulmates, but Evelyn was fascinated by Acton's exotic background and enthusiasms and relished their shared 'zest for the variety and absurdity of life opening to us; a veneration for (not the same) artists, a scorn for the bogus'. It was Acton who steered him away from the fusty Francis Crease, 'that nice old maid' as Acton called him,⁵⁶ whom Evelyn had continued to see during the holidays, and towards such prophets of modernism as T. S. Eliot and Gertrude Stein. In June 1923 he took him to the bizarre, under-rehearsed yet to Evelyn captivating first public showing of Edith Sitwell's *Façade* at the Aeolian Hall in London, where one uncomprehending critic complained of the poet reciting 'drivel through a megaphone'. Later that evening, at an after-party at Osbert Sitwell's house in Carlyle Square, Evelyn met Lytton Strachey and Clive Bell; however it was the Sitwells whom he really aspired to know, seeing them as torchbearers of the avant-garde and an inspiration to all those wishing to blaze a new artistic trail. They 'radiated an aura of high spirits, elegance, impudence, unpredictability, above all sheer enjoyment,' he later wrote. 'They declared war on dullness.'⁵⁷

For his part, Acton was drawn to what he called Evelyn's 'friskiness'. More awkwardly, he also appears to have found him physically attractive – he described him achingly in his memoir as 'a prancing faun, thinly disguised by conventional apparel. His wide-apart eyes, always ready to be startled under raised eyebrows, the curved sensual lips, the hyacinthe locks of hair . . . So demure and yet so wild!'[58] In the same book, Acton painted himself as a young Casanova, proudly recalling numerous 'bygone loves' at Oxford and of having 'kindled flames in Elgin marble breasts' and enjoyed 'ecstacies on the Thames and at Thame . . . I have not forgotten a single kiss . . .'[59] Yet if he ever did make overtures to Evelyn the signs are that he was rejected, one letter from that time hinting at jealousy of Evelyn's more passionate friendships: 'Please forgive me if I said that about "R. I. P." [Richard Pares] last night,' wrote Acton. 'Truth will out, I suppose, in spite of the fact that I had tried hard not to hurt your feelings or to "sneer" . . . You are, as I have said before, a faun, but I had never credited you with the fantastic whimsies of a faun, nor with the enigmas of one; now I do. Besides it is rather elegant to have an unhappy love affair . . .'[60]

According to Evelyn, Acton harboured similarly unrequited feelings for the 'strikingly handsome hearty'[61] – presumably Tony Bushell – who unwittingly drew him almost daily to Evelyn's offal lunches in his rooms at Hertford. While everyone else drank beer, Acton 'would sip water and gaze ardently at the inaccessible young athlete'.[62]* In return Acton gave many lunch parties of his own in his rooms at Christ Church where Evelyn made several long-lasting friendships.

Among these were three who had been at prep school with Acton as well as Eton – Mark Ogilvie-Grant, the 'reckless roof-climber' Billy Clonmore, who as an undergraduate held a supper party on the roof of an Oxford church and later became a priest, and the 'secretly studious' David Talbot Rice who, almost uniquely among their peer group at Oxford, went out with a student of the opposite sex, Evelyn's friend Tamara Abelson, whom he later married.

With the new Michaelmas intake of 1923, Evelyn's circle expanded to include several more of what was an exceptionally talented generation of Etonians – Anthony Powell, Oliver Messel, Henry Yorke (the novelist Henry Green), Robert Byron, who belied his future calling by yelling 'Down with abroad!' whenever travel was mentioned, and Brian Howard,

---

* ·Evelyn and Tony Bushell were not the only ones who spurned his advances. James Lees-Milne later recorded how during the Second World War he half-heartedly agreed to go to bed with Acton, who was then in uniform, but 'next morning he rebuked me for icy-cold unresponsiveness'. (James Lees-Milne, *Diaries 1984–1997*, ed. by Michael Bloch, p. 373.)

who even his close school friend and collaborator Harold Acton admitted was 'completely amoral'.[63] Later immortalised as Ambrose Silk in *Put Out More Flags* as well as Anthony Blanche in *Brideshead*, Howard was one of those whom Evelyn 'did not greatly like' but 'in my innocence, I was proud to know'.

He felt much the same way about two other Oxford contemporaries, both at Balliol, the raffish yet tediously didactic Peter Rodd, who later married Nancy Mitford, and Nancy's more wayward cousin 'Baz' Murray, whom Evelyn deemed 'a satanic young man'.[64] Evelyn later fused several of their least appealing traits in the character of Basil Seal, his Balliol-educated anti-hero in *Black Mischief* and *Put Out More Flags*. Murray was renowned at Oxford for his intellectual brilliance (he was the son of a well-known Classics don and himself a scholar), but equally for his casual approach to sex, money and personal hygiene. Like Basil Seal he later covered the Spanish Civil War as a journalist (Evelyn added 'gun-runner')[65] on the Republican side and died there in the kind of bizarre circumstances that might easily have featured in an early Waugh novel – having caught a deadly virus from a female ape he had bought in Valencia docks and reportedly cavorted with in his hotel room in a state of drunken disillusionment after a series of failed love affairs.[66]

Fifteen years previously, at Oxford, it was Murray who had helped F. A. Philbrick (later a chemistry beak at Rugby) to rough up Evelyn in retaliation for a campaign of teasing after Philbrick admitted to having rather enjoyed beating smaller boys at school – the persecution culminated when a film was shown with a scene of a man being flogged and the whole cinema erupted in a loud chant of Philbrick's name. Evelyn later took his revenge by attaching Philbrick's name to a series of disreputable characters in his early fiction.

Yet none of these enmities came close to that which Evelyn felt towards his Hertford history tutor, C. R. M. F. Cruttwell, for whom he developed a dislike that was, as his brother Alec recalled, 'mutual, instinctive and irrational as love'.[67] Seen by his fellow dons as a rather sad and lonely bachelor, Cruttwell disguised his painful shyness behind a gruff and uncompromising manner.[68] Even Evelyn later conceded that he was probably a 'wreck of the war', yet he could not resist mocking his 'petulant baby' face, his pipe 'usually attached to his blubber-lips by a thread of slime'. 'As he removed the stem,' Evelyn went on, 'waving it to emphasise his indistinct speech, this glittering connection extended until finally it broke leaving a dribble on his chin. When he spoke to me I found myself so distracted by the speculation of how far this line could be attenuated that I was often inattentive to his words.'

At Oxford Evelyn mercilessly caricatured 'Crutters' in student magazines and told anyone who would listen about the perversions he supposedly got up to with his dog. 'Now he's raping the poor brute,' he whispered to his cousin Claud Cockburn as they listened to the strange sounds coming from the rooms above Evelyn's, 'and at this hour in the morning!'[69]

Evelyn's initial gripe with Cruttwell was the don's frenzied insistence that Evelyn fulfil his obligations as Hertford's first history scholar, a demand which Evelyn early made clear his intention to ignore, seeing his scholarship as a 'reward for work done, not as the earnest of work to come',[70] and maintaining later that while he knew all about his Oxford friends' political and religious opinions, love affairs, finances, etcetera, he would have 'thought it indelicate to inquire what school they were reading'.[71] However he also affected to take against Cruttwell's undisguised misogyny (he called female dons 'drabs' or, if they were emotional, 'breastheavers') and his propensity to bully those weaker than himself.

Evelyn famously attached Cruttwell's name to an unsavoury character in each of his first five novels and seems to have resolved to pursue the feud indefinitely after Cruttwell's 'gratuitously derogatory' letters to Evelyn's first mother-in-law, Lady Burghclere, shortly before his marriage in 1930.

Long after both Cruttwell and Evelyn were dead, Evelyn's son Auberon cheerfully seized any opportunity to revive the vendetta. When the *Oxford Dictionary of National Biography* published an entry on Cruttwell which recorded, besides his various achievements as a historian, his 'passion for flowers and for country life', Auberon rebuked the publishers for omitting to mention 'the peculiarity for which he was much more widely suspected'. (Their solution was simply to remove the reference to flowers from subsequent editions.) In 2003, at an Evelyn Waugh centenary dinner at Hertford, Auberon's son Alexander surprised the assembled scholars by calling on them to raise their glasses to Cruttwell, 'that he may forever be remembered as a dog sodomist and a total shit'.[72]

7

....

His Poor Dead Heart

After living so uproariously during term time, Evelyn inevitably found the holidays at Underhill rather dull by comparison. In the spring of 1922 he told Driberg that north London suburbia was 'quite indescribably dreary'.[1] His relations with his father, whose stagy readings in the book-room he found increasingly excruciating as he grew older, were further strained by disagreements over his refusal to do any work and his persistent overspending. To supplement Evelyn's scholarship, Arthur had allowed him a further £220 annually, which with birthday presents and various other demands to meet unpaid debts took up more than a quarter of his earnings, then around £1,000.[2] Yet despite this generosity, friends Evelyn took home were often horrified by the way he spoke to his father. One of them shuddered to recall Arthur asking Evelyn how he could be so charming to his friends and yet so unkind to his father. 'Because I can choose my friends,' said Evelyn, 'but I cannot choose my father.'[3]

Evelyn could be equally cruel to Alec, as when he suggested that their cousin, Claud Cockburn, who was in need of £200 to pay some debts, ask him for a loan. By his own account Alec was by then making around £800 a year from his writing[4] yet nevertheless politely refused the request. Incensed that Alec should spurn his 'more deserving and artistic' cousin in this way, Evelyn muttered sternly: 'That bald-headed lecher needs a lesson in how a gentleman should comport himself' – Evelyn had conceived the theory that excessive sexual activity since the end of his marriage had caused his brother's hair to fall out. He then led several sorties from Oxford to London, during which he and his friends would burst out from hiding places and surprise Alec and his latest girlfriend, yelling 'Boo to

Alec the bald-headed lecher!'. He assured Cockburn that Alec's women were 'apt to be rendered frigid by anything unconventional'.[5]

Alec seems to have been remarkably good-natured about all this – at least he later recalled only the good times they had during this period, introducing Evelyn to his Bohemian friends in London, taking him to parties and generally feeling proud of his 'witty, lively, hopeful' younger brother.[6] For his part, in later years Evelyn paid tribute to his brother's generosity – 'a host who introduced me to the best restaurants of London, on whom I sponged, bringing my friends to his flat and when short of money, sleeping on his floor, until the tubes opened when I would at dawn sway home to Hampstead, in crumpled evening dress among the navvies setting out for their day's work'.[7]

* * *

Arthur Waugh may have worried that his younger son was frittering away his time and money at Oxford, yet amid all the drinking binges he was in fact remarkably busy across a range of activities, albeit none that bore the slightest relevance to his history degree. At that time, Evelyn still had more confidence in his talents in illustration and design than he did in his Union debating skills or indeed his writing. He later admitted that drawing made him more 'entirely happy' than he ever felt when reading or writing and, ever ambitious to get better, he took lessons during the holidays in wood-engraving and during term time went with Peter Quennell to draw the 'remarkably unalluring' nude models who sat for life classes at the Ruskin School of Art.

Throughout his time at Oxford he designed bookplates for friends and dust-jackets for Chapman & Hall, contributed woodcuts to the *London Mercury* and *Golden Hind*, and was much in demand to design headpieces and covers for various university magazines and programmes. His distinctive and frequently macabre woodcuts were particularly admired by the university art critics.[8] At a time when his reserves of filial piety were running particularly low, one of these depicted 'That grim act parricide', in which a deranged young man with a pistol advances towards an older man looking not unlike Arthur Waugh, somewhat alarmed and vulnerable in an armchair. The cartoon was part of a ghoulish series portraying Evelyn's own version of 'The Seven Deadly Sins' and appeared in

Cherwell, the most subversive of the Oxford magazines of that time and the mouthpiece for the aesthetes and intellectuals, who tended to disparage the more athletically orientated *Isis*.

The Isis paid its contributors, however, so the perpetually improvident Evelyn was more than happy to work for that magazine too, supplying numerous cartoons and other illustrations as well as light verse, short stories, film reviews and Union reports, all written under the nom de plume 'Scaramel'. On the first page of the magazine there appeared 'Isis Idol', generally a profile of a sporting hero or leading light of the Union, although Evelyn neatly turned the slot on its head by contributing a paean to Harold Acton, the mincing non-athlete *par excellence*, as well as a rather less fulsome portrait of his 'badger-like' history tutor.

References to Cruttwell were also discernible in two short stories that Evelyn published in *Cherwell* in 1923, 'Edward of Unique Achievement' in which an undergraduate develops such 'an absorbing and immeasurable hatred' for his tutor that he decides to murder him; and 'Conspiracy to Murder', in which a young man is driven mad by the 'ill-dressed and rather dirty' don who lives in the room opposite and 'snarls like a beast' whenever they pass on the stairs.

Of more biographical interest, however, were two other stories that appeared in different Oxford magazines the same year. In the first of these, the intriguing yet often overlooked 'Portrait of Young Man With Career', published in *The Isis* in May 1923, a pushy student named Jeremy visits 'Evelyn' in his rooms and asks for an introduction to Richard Pares, explaining 'I feel he is a man to know.' Evelyn calls Pares 'an amiable rogue' and protests that he hardly knows him. If this was an ambiguous dig at the lover who had recently forsaken him, the story made far more unsettling reading for his friend Hugh Molson, who immediately recognised himself in the character of Jeremy, whose deep appreciation of the sound of his own voice and tiresome ambition extend to an intention to become president of the Union, a goal Molson achieved two years later.

In the story, Jeremy fails to take Evelyn's hint about hardly knowing Pares and continues:

> 'Nonsense, I'm always seeing you about together. I am not doing anything 'fore lunch on Tuesday. How about then? Or Friday I could manage, but I should prefer Tuesday.'

So it was arranged.

There was a pause; I looked at my watch; Jeremy took no notice; I looked again.

'What is the time,' he said, 'Twenty-three to. Oh, good! – hours yet.'

'Before a fool's opinion of himself the gods are silent – aye and envious too,' I thought.

'I'm speaking "on the paper" on Thursday.'

'Good.'

'About the Near East. Macedonia. Oil, you know.'

'Ah.'

'I think it ought to be rather a good speech.'

'Yes.'

'Evelyn, you aren't listening; now seriously, what do you really think is wrong with my speaking. What I feel about the Union is . . .'

A blind fury, a mist of fire. We struggled together on the carpet. He was surprisingly weak for his size. The first blow with the poker he dodged and took on his shoulder; the second and third caved his forehead in . . .

The latter scene is a wish-fulfilling daydream that Evelyn has lapsed into while his visitor drones on. When Jeremy does eventually get up to leave, he parts with a final annoying request: 'Oh and Evelyn, if you know the man who reports the Union for the *Isis*, you might ask him to give me a decent notice this time.'

In so ruthlessly skewering Molson as a self-important bore, 'Portrait of Young Man With Career' effectively ended their friendship. When Molson was later asked why he and Evelyn had fallen out, he recalled that they had been on 'one of our usual long walks and I suppose I am inclined to be long-winded. I got to talking about oil and when *Isis* came out next week there was a repetition of much of what I had said . . . After that I never felt like going out for a long walk with him and telling him what was going on in my mind.'[9] Molson professed to dislike what he called Evelyn's 'intellectual cruelty', as well he might, yet in truth the friendship became unviable after he discovered what Evelyn really thought of him.

Doubtless having Molson's youthful excesses as much in mind as his overweening ambition, Evelyn could never take him anything like as seriously as he appeared to take himself. When Molson ultimately became a life peer as a Unionist politician (he is remembered now chiefly for the soundbite 'I will look at any additional evidence to confirm the opinion to which I have already come'), Evelyn could only ever bring himself to refer to him with the 'Lord' between quotation marks.

* * *

Evelyn's other noteworthy short story from 1923 was 'Antony, Who Sought Things That Were Lost', which appeared in Harold Acton's short-lived arts journal *The Oxford Broom*, for which Evelyn had already designed covers and produced two 'Cubist' cartoons. A macabre tale of two imprisoned lovers, Count Antony and Lady Elizabeth, who ruthlessly betrays her husband with their pockmarked turnkey, it was influenced by James Branch Cabell's mannered fantasy novel *Jurgen* (1919), as Evelyn later wincingly admitted, 'that preposterously spurious artefact which quite captivated me at the age of nineteen'. Even Acton later conceded that the story had 'seemed rather better than it was in fact' as he had been under Evelyn's 'elvish fascination' at the time. Yet however flawed it might have been in stylistic terms, with hindsight it can now be seen to contain the seeds of Evelyn's later masterpiece *A Handful of Dust* (1934), with Antony the forerunner of Tony Last, the chivalrous husband whose bored wife (Lady Elizabeth / Brenda Last) betrays him with a worthless bounder (the turnkey / John Beaver).[10] Just as *A Handful of Dust* reflected Evelyn's bitter sense of betrayal over the ending of his first marriage, 'Antony' was written while he was suffering 'the pangs of neglected love' for Richard Pares, as Terence Greenidge later maintained.[11] Both works also drew on Evelyn's nostalgia for a romantic past and his cynical belief that romantic expectations will never be fulfilled.

* * *

If Richard Pares's desertion destroyed nineteen-year-old Evelyn's hopes in the spring of 1923, he wasted little time before taking up with the next 'friend of my heart', as he described him, a handsome eighteen-year-old* at Brasenose called Alastair Graham, who was later disguised in *A Little*

---

* Alastair Hugh Graham was born on 27 June 1904 (see *Burke's Peerage*, Graham, Bt, of Netherby), and so would have turned nineteen in the summer of 1923.

Learning as 'Hamish Lennox'.[12] Eight months younger than Evelyn, well-born, rich and dreamy, Graham became one of the great loves of Evelyn's early life. As a muse, he made the most obvious contribution to the composite character of Sebastian Flyte in *Brideshead*, which in manuscript twice has 'Alastair' in place of 'Sebastian'.

Like Pares, Graham was seen by Evelyn's contemporaries as a catch. Anthony Powell remembered him as 'frightfully good-looking, with rather Dresden china shepherdess sort of looks ... a lot of people were undoubtedly in love with him'.[13] Among the queue of admirers was Harold Acton, who in the midst of Graham's affair with Evelyn gushed in a letter jointly addressed to the two of them: 'I had erections to think of you two angels in an atmosphere salinated with choir boys and sacerdotal sensuality!'[14] He later described Graham as a Pre-Raphaelite beauty but 'a cock-teaser',[15] and told Duncan Fallowell that he had 'the same sort of features as Evelyn liked in girls – the pixie look'. He was not a hearty, Acton added, 'but he dressed like a hearty, in the country style, plus-fours and *tweeds*'.[16]

Evelyn was fond of tweed breeches too, yet there were other more significant similarities. Unlike Pares, Graham had 'no repugnance of the bottle', as Evelyn put it, or as Harold Acton preferred, he 'drank like a fish'. Intellectually and artistically curious, he read widely throughout his life yet he was by nature also profoundly lazy. Having refused to go back to Wellington at the age of fifteen, at Oxford he was even more neglectful of his history studies than Evelyn. 'I could not have fallen under an influence better designed to encourage my natural frivolity, dilettantism and dissipation,' Evelyn later wrote, 'or to expose as vulgar and futile any promptings I may have felt to worldly ambition.'[17]

The gap in Evelyn's diaries makes it hard to say how or when their friendship began – as Graham ruefully told the diaries' eventual editor, 'a lot of his happier experiences are not recorded'[18] – however it must have been before the end of the summer term 1923, when Alastair failed his Mods and on the advice of the principal of Brasenose was removed from the university by his mother.

Mrs Graham's decision threw Evelyn into 'a momentary restlessness', as he later downplayed it, and at the beginning of the Michaelmas term he asked his father if he too might be taken away from Oxford and sent to Paris to live as a bohemian artist. Not surprisingly, Arthur did not like this idea.[19] 'I want to go down for good but I cannot explain and my parents are obdurate,' Evelyn wrote to Carew.[20] What was it that he could not explain to his parents? His love for Alastair perhaps?

Alastair meanwhile was 'settling down and writing,' his mother told the Brasenose bursar, 'so far hard'. She said he would soon be 'taking up Architecture at London University', an endeavour that was to prove even less enduring than his Oxford career.[21] But though Alastair had left the university, he and Evelyn remained 'inseparable', so Evelyn later recalled, 'or, if separated, in almost daily communication'.[22] Alastair 'continued to haunt Oxford', driving down regularly from his home in Warwickshire in his two-seater motor car, whereupon he and Evelyn would zoom off into the Oxfordshire countryside, sometimes with a third passenger squeezed in the dicky, more often just the two of them. 'We hardly saw anything of Evelyn at that time,' Acton lamented. 'He [Graham] and Evelyn were always together. An infatuation. Oh definitely an infatuation.'

In advance of one such visit, Alastair wrote a letter enclosing a photograph of himself naked, posing like some alluring wood nymph beneath an overhanging rock face, his backside pointing seductively towards the camera:*

My dear Evelyn,

I'm sending this down by David [Plunket Greene] or the Bastard John [Greenidge, elder brother of Terence], whom I'm seeing this evening. I am sad that you wouldn't come up for this party. I am afraid it will be bloody. One can always drink but it is rather a cheap path to heaven. I've found the ideal way to drink Burgundy. You must take a peach and peal [*sic*] it, and put it in a finger bowl, and pour Burgundy over it. The flavour is exquisite. And the peach seems to exaggerate that delightful happy Seraglio contentedness that old wine evokes. An old French lady taught it to me, who has a wonderful cellar at Lavalles. I've been in bed with pains in my ears for the last two days. May I go and call on your parents one day, or would they hate it? I do not know whether I ought to come to Oxford next week or not next week. It depends on money and other little complications. If I come, will you come and drink with me somewhere

---

* Auberon Waugh told Duncan Fallowell that whether Graham enclosed the photograph or whether Evelyn put it in the envelope later was uncertain.

on Saturday? If it is a nice day we might carry some bottles into a wood or some bucolic place, and drink like Horace. I'm afraid this is a poor wandering letter. But I cannot write letters. It was only meant to express my sorrow at your absence from this party. I wish you felt merrier, and were not so serious.

With love from Alastair, and his poor dead heart.

It seems safe to assume that Evelyn had this letter somewhere in mind when he wrote the passage in *Brideshead* in which Sebastian beckons Charles: 'You're to come away at once, out of danger. I've got a motor-car and a basket of strawberries and a bottle of Château Peyraguey* – which isn't a wine you've ever tasted, so don't pretend. It's heaven with strawberries.'[23]

Though undated, Alastair's letter was most likely written in 1924, as he would presumably not have suggested calling on Evelyn's parents before he had met them, which according to Kate Waugh's diary happened in December 1923, when Evelyn took him for supper at Underhill.[24] Evelyn later indicated that the affair had 'culminated' that Christmas.†

Evelyn went far more often to Alastair's home, Barford House, near Stratford-upon-Avon, which was by then presided over by Alastair's widowed mother Jessie, Alastair's father having died the year before he went to Oxford. 'Mrs G', as both Alastair and Evelyn called her (or alternatively 'the Queen Mother'), had been as mad about hunting as her husband – the excellent surrounding country had been the reason they had bought the house in the first place – but she no longer kept horses. Instead she 'gardened with all the fury of the chase', Evelyn recalled, although her vigour failed to rub off on her languid son, who was forever being exhorted to 'get out of the house and do something!'.

Barford is nothing like the size of Brideshead or its television alter ego, Castle Howard, which Evelyn visited only once in 1937, yet was far more akin to the stately pile he described in the novel. Nonetheless beneath Barford's handsome, peeling, white-stucco façade can be glimpsed the

---

* Peyraguey is a sweet Sauternes and remained one of Evelyn's favourite wines. He always preferred it unchilled and referred to it as 'White Claret'. (See Alec Waugh, *A Year to Remember*, p. 107.)

† '... my few romances have always culminated in Christmas week, Luned, Richard, Alastair [Graham] (Christmas Day 1924; *EWD*, p. 194). Given that Graham was abroad over Christmas 1924, it seems Evelyn was referring to the previous year.

same gold-coloured ashlar that Charles Ryder sees on his first visit to Brideshead; its front is embellished with a similar, albeit far less grand, row of Ionic half-columns; and there is even a dome and lantern on the roof, though again on a considerably more modest scale than in the book. When Charles Ryder remembers, 'I had been there [to Brideshead] before, first with Sebastian more than twenty years ago on a cloudless day in June . . .' it is perfectly conceivable that Evelyn is recalling his own first visit to Barford. He is explicit (in Chapter Four) that the June day Charles remembers is in 1923, the same summer that Evelyn's own love affair with Alastair Graham had begun. The first mention in Kate Waugh's diary of Evelyn visiting Barford is admittedly not until 3 January 1924, however all the other evidence points to her son having been there the previous summer – without perhaps telling his mother.

If Evelyn had sampled country-house life with the Molsons at Goring Hall, at Barford he gained a far fuller appreciation. Alastair Graham was far closer to a 'true aristocrat' than Hugh Molson. His mother was a South-ern belle – her American family's cotton fortune being the main source of Alastair's substantial private income – his father a bona fide scion of the British landed aristocracy. The younger son of a baronet and grandson of the 12th Duke of Somerset, Hugh Graham had grown up at Netherby Hall in Cumberland and devoted his life to hunting, shooting and fishing. His sisters, Alastair's aunts, were the Duchess of Montrose, the Marchioness of Crewe, the Countess of Verulam and Lady Wittenham. Alastair was the last person to name-drop his grand relations so Evelyn may not have picked up on all this, yet while staying at Barford (which he was to do on countless occasions, occasionally for several weeks at a stretch) he gained his first meaningful entrée into the upper class world that he eventually came to inhabit.

For Alastair, who had not inherited his father's passion for field sports, Barford was a place of refuge. A natural recluse ('rather quiet', said Acton; 'buttoned-up', according to Powell), he craved undisturbed solitude, and in a later letter to Evelyn wrote: 'All the beautiful things that I have seen, heard or thought of, grow like bright flowers and musky flowers in a garden where I can enjoy their presence, and where I can sit in perfect peace and banish the unpleasant things in life. A kind of fortified retreat that no one can enter except myself.'[25]

As Evelyn fell in with Alastair's wish to shut himself off from the outside world, during his final year his Oxford friends saw less and less of him, as did the History School. A late burst of cramming in the summer of 1924 proved insufficient and he was uncomfortably aware as he left the exam room that the questions had been 'rather inconvenient'. His chances would hardly have been improved by his behaviour at a dinner party held by Cruttwell for the history candidates, 'at which I arrived tipsy and further alienated their sympathies by attempting, later, to sing a Negro spiritual'.[26] At the end of July he returned to Oxford for his viva, dressed in dark coat, scholar's gown and white tie and fortified by a whisky from his favourite wine merchant. He sensed that it was 'purely formal', however, and telegraphed his parents to warn them of 'my certain third', confirmation of which duly came the next day.

Pure as Driven Slush

Evelyn confided to his recently resumed diary that he was 'much dispirited' by his Third, although on the day he got his results he deferred the gloom with a lengthy drinking spree, eventually winding up at the Abingdon Arms in Beckley, a village just north of Oxford where he and Alastair had rented a leaky caravan ('sans horse', as Evelyn described it)[1] to escape from Mrs Graham.[2]

The next week he and Alastair set off for Dublin, 'a most unattractive place,' thought Evelyn, 'full of barbed wire and ruins and soldiers and unemployed' – and pubs that closed at 9 p.m. Their two-week Irish jaunt was further blighted by dingy hotels, 'ghastly' fizzy beer and towns that all reminded him of Shoreham. It was in Ireland that Cruttwell's valedictory letter caught up with him: 'I cannot say that your 3rd does you anything but discredit; especially as it was not even a good one; and it is always at least foolish to allow oneself to be given an inappropriate intellectual label ... I hope that you will soon settle in some sphere where you will give your intellect a better chance than in the History School.'[3]

Back at Barford things scarcely improved during a week in the company of an 'extremely quarrelsome' Mrs G, and when Evelyn eventually got back to Underhill he was irked by the presence of 'a horrible wireless apparatus' which Arthur had recently acquired; 'contrary to modern domestic conventions,' Evelyn later wrote, 'it was he who always wished to hear it, I to turn it off.'[4]

The onset of autumn deepened his despondency about the future, exacerbated by the prospect of Alastair's imminent departure for Africa to spend the winter with his sister in Kenya.[5] No less depressing was the thought that he would then have been beginning his last term at Oxford

– the ninth he needed to complete his degree having come up in a by-term – had not the certainty of his Third and Cruttwell's subsequent withdrawal of his scholarship persuaded Arthur that this would be a complete waste of money.

Prior to that Evelyn had been keenly anticipating a term of 'pure pleasure', for which he had reserved digs on Merton Street to share with his old Hypocrite friend Hugh Lygon, whom he recalled in his autobiography as 'always just missing the happiness he sought, without ambition, unhappy in love, a man of great sweetness'. Dubbed 'lascivious Mr Lygon' by Evelyn, Hughie was one of the more promiscuously homosexual Hypocrites and it has often been suggested that he and Evelyn were lovers. The timing of this supposed liaison has never been convincingly established, however, and in any case the evidence that they ever went to bed together – while perfectly possible – is far flimsier than one might imagine, comprising a mixture of hearsay and reading between the lines. Selina Hastings evidently had reservations about her three informants and accordingly played down the possibility of an affair. More recently Paula Byrne has been more emphatic about the matter, writing that Tamara Talbot Rice 'reported that John Fothergill let Evelyn have rooms at the Spread Eagle at Thame at a special mid-week rate so that he and Hugh could meet in private'.[6] That appears to clinch it, but did Tamara Talbot Rice really say that? No date or source is given for the assertion, however it appears to come from the brief note of Selina Hastings's interview with her in 1991, which is in Alexander Waugh's archive. According to the note, Mrs Talbot Rice said in that conversation that 'everyone knew' they had an affair and she also mentioned Evelyn getting a good rate at the pub. But she said nothing about them using it as a trysting place.[7]

Whatever the nature of Evelyn and Hugh Lygon's relationship, it has long been recognised that Hugh's father, the 7th Earl Beauchamp, was the main inspiration for Lord Marchmain, just as Hugh's elder brother Viscount Elmley (president of the Hypocrites' when Evelyn joined) provided the model for Bridey (the characteristics he supplied included Bridey's distaste for fox-hunting), and Hugh himself shared many of the characteristics of Sebastian – his restlessness, his self-destructive drinking, his ever-present teddy bear[8] and his ethereal beauty, described by Anthony Powell as that of 'a Giotto angel living in a narcissistic dream'.[9] Yet nowhere in the various mentions of Hugh in Evelyn's surviving diaries and letters – which contain several references to Hugh's love affairs with others – is there a hint of sexual intimacy between them.

* * *

With his Oxford plans thwarted and his finances so precarious that he had stooped to writing begging letters to friends, Evelyn now faced the bleak prospect of having to remain at Underhill indefinitely, longer at any rate than he had lived there since he first went to Lancing. By way of distraction, he spent long afternoons at the cinema and otherwise strove to make headway with a novel called *The Temple at Thatch* (about a young man dabbling in black magic at his ancestral folly) which he had started in June but already sensed would never be finished. Lacking conviction that he could make it as a writer and in search of a more definite purpose, he enrolled at Heatherley Art School, whose term began fortuitously on the same day as Alastair's embarkation, 18 September.

Then located on Newman Street, just behind Tottenham Court Road, Heatherley boasted an array of illustrious alumni – among them Burne Jones, Rossetti, Millais, Henry Moore, E. H. Shepard and Walter Sickert – however when Evelyn went there most of the students appeared to be 'respectable girls who, like myself, were believed at home to be "artistic"', while the few men seemed 'bent upon making commercial careers'.[10]

On his first day, when he was set to draw 'a thin man with no clothes but a bag about his genitalia', he recognised no kindred spirits, and from then on lunched either by himself or with his old Oxford friend Tony Bushell, who was training to be an actor at the nearby Royal Academy of Dramatic Art. Most days they made do with a pub on Tottenham Court Road where they could get a large ham roll and a half a pint of beer for sixpence,[11] but occasionally they treated themselves at Previtali's restaurant, where they celebrated Evelyn's twenty-first birthday on 28 October. Arthur took the opportunity of his son's coming of age to remit the money he had lent him during his Irish trip and gave him a further £5 besides, 'most like a gentleman', thought Evelyn.[12]

Throughout this time, in order to escape the tedium of Underhill, Evelyn relied greatly on his brother Alec, who was by then enjoying his post-divorce freedom as a bohemian bachelor about town. He had rented an elegant first-floor flat on Earl's Terrace in Kensington, with a bedroom that served as an extra sitting room for parties, separated by a curtain in stylish emulation of the Algonquin Hotel in New York. He painted the high ceilings primrose-yellow and the walls pale blue and the whole place was 'pleasantly suffused with the smell of a luxurious Russian Leather soap he used', a friend remembered.[13]

Besides the cocktail parties and suppers he held there, Alec took his brother along to soirées staged by notable 1920s hostesses such as the 'inexhaustibly hospitable'[14] Gwen Otter and the avant-garde writer Mary Butts, who had earlier studied magic with Aleister Crowley and would soon become an opium-smoking intimate of Jean Cocteau. Mary Butts held a memorable 'super-party' for Alec at her large house in Belsize Park promising 'unlimited drink, dancing, female attractions, secluded corners',[15] although it only really got going after Evelyn began lacing the claret-cup with brandy.

Among those caught up in the resulting maelstrom was the young writer Rebecca West, who later became a staunch fan and supporter of Evelyn's work and remained so until the 1950s, when they fell out irreparably over a libel suit. At similar gatherings Evelyn met luminaries such as Tallulah Bankhead and her then girlfriend Gwen Farrar: 'My family warned me about men,' the former quipped, 'but they never mentioned women!' On another occasion she boasted, 'I am as pure as driven slush.'[16] No less licentious was her lisping secretary, Sir Francis Laking (brother of Evelyn's friend Joan), whom Evelyn witnessed pouncing on Alec – much to his brother's gratification, he could not help noticing.[17] Another evening, casting himself in the role of spectator as so often, Evelyn watched as Alec 'turned up late and a little drunk and after his fashion, fixed upon the ugliest woman in the room, bore her off and lechered with her'.[18]

It was a constant source of vexation for Evelyn that his lecherous brother was always so much more successful with women than he was, especially as Alec seemed to boast no obvious physical advantages, being as one contemporary recalled 'very unattractive, tiny and stout'. His appeal seemed to lie mainly in the fact that he was so persistently keen. He was also more obviously charming and approachable than Evelyn, and according to one contemporary, perhaps crucially, he seemed to be 'very very interested in bores – the more boring the person, the more fascinated Alec became. So he was every hostess's dream guest.'[19]

It was Alec who in early 1924 first introduced Evelyn to Elsa Lanchester, one of Mary Butts's numerous lodgers. At the age of just twenty-two she had recently established a popular cabaret club, the Cave of Harmony, which soon became Evelyn's favourite nightspot. By the summer he had developed a crush on her and persuaded her to take a part in a silent film he had written with Terence Greenidge called *The Scarlet Woman*,* much of which they shot in the garden at Underhill; he later referred to it as 'the Elsa film', and when she subsequently went on to become a well-known actress and the wife of Charles Laughton, Evelyn liked to claim that it was he who had 'invented' her.

In Alastair's absence, meanwhile, Evelyn continued to visit Barford, although whenever he went into Leamington with Mrs Graham he felt 'a little sad to pass all the public houses where Alastair and I have drunk'.[20] In early November he was lured back to Oxford by John Sutro's invitation to a luncheon at which his attendance was kept a secret from the other guests – Harold Acton, Mark Ogilvie-Grant, Hugh Lygon, Robert Byron, Arden Hilliard and Richard Pares (recently elected a Fellow of All Souls) – who 'feted me spontaneously in a way to rekindle all my love of Oxford'.[21] An epic lunch of 'hot lobster, partridges and plum pudding, sherry, mulled claret and a strange rum-like liqueur' was followed by beer at the New Reform Club, dinner at Merton, more beer in the rooms of 'a charming hunting man called Reynolds', a further session at the Nag's Head pub, then on to the old Hypocrites' to drink whisky and watch *The Scarlet Woman*.

'After about this stage of the evening my recollections become somewhat blurred,' Evelyn's diary continues. 'I got a sword from somewhere and got into Balliol somehow and was let out of a window at some time having mocked Arden and Tony Powell and talked very seriously to Peter Quennell . . .'[22] He returned to Oxford every weekend for the rest of that term, each one consistently more debauched than the last, and adopted the latest Oxford fashion of wearing polo-neck jumpers, 'most convenient for lechery,' according to Evelyn, 'because it dispenses with all unromantic gadgets like studs and ties'.[23]

With his tendency to overdo it whenever he happened to venture out,

---

* They had started filming it at Oxford, including a sequence by the Littlemore Asylum. 'Evelyn had a thing about loonies at the time,' recalled Tony Bushell. 'There were poor loonies looking through the gate and all that.' The negative of that particular sequence was subsequently lost by Terence Greenidge.

Evelyn soon realised that 'it is not possible to lead a gay life and to draw well'.[24] Though he was 'by no means the worst in the class' at Heatherley, the whole business of art school had begun to pall. In December he briefly considered going to live in Sussex as pupil to the printer and bookplate designer James Guthrie, however on a two-day recce he found that, much though he liked his whole family, he was less impressed by their printing press and still less by the discomforts of their 'ugly little house' near Bognor.[25] As a last resort, he turned to the 'one profession open to a man of my qualifications' and took a job as a prep school master in north Wales.

As Evelyn prepared to take up this post in late January 1925, he reflected that he felt more desolate than he had done since Alastair's embarkation for Africa in September – only now the main cause of his unhappiness was a girl.

* * *

His latest infatuation was with eighteen-year-old Olivia Plunket Greene, whose brother (Richard) Evelyn had befriended in his last year at Oxford. Evelyn first met Olivia in early December and was quickly smitten. If not a classic beauty, she was curiously attractive with bobbed hair, 'minute pursed lips and great goo-goo eyes'.[26] Evelyn saw her again two weeks later and again two days after that, when they ended up in his bedroom at Underhill – albeit chaperoned by Alec and Terence Greenidge – before she eventually left at three.

The next day (Christmas Eve) Evelyn sent her a book that Alec had acquired from Oscar Wilde's son called *Irais* – an obscure 'lesbian novel' describing an intense sexual relationship between two girls at a Catholic boarding school.[27] 'I wonder whether I am falling in love with this woman,' Evelyn wrote in his diary that evening,[28] beguiled by the intensity of her enthusiasms, her forthright opinions, her ability to be outrageous without compromising her 'essential delicacy'.[29] That she seemed to enjoy getting drunk as much as he did was an added bonus.

Not everyone was charmed by Olivia – her aunt Dorothea Ponsonby thought her 'a rude, egotistical frivolous vain painted child'[30] – however to certain men she was irresistible, not least due to her reputed 'fastidious but intense appreciation of sexual pleasure',[31] as one forlorn suitor put it.

As various boyfriends discovered to their cost, she was also a notorious tease.

* * *

Doubtless hopeful that the sexy book might spark something between them, Evelyn spent the week after Christmas impatient for a letter from her. At last, on 30 December, she rang up and they went for a pub lunch followed by a magic show. On New Year's Eve she came for lunch at Underhill and afterwards sat by the fire and talked until tea, at which point she abandoned her previous plans and went with Evelyn to the cinema.

On New Year's Day Evelyn went for the first time to her house on Hanover Terrace (now Lansdowne Walk) in Holland Park and took an instant liking to her liberal and indulgent mother Gwen, by then separated from Olivia's father, the singer Harry Plunket Greene. He later wrote of having fallen in love with the entire family and 'focused the sentiment upon the only appropriate member'. He first told Olivia he was in love with her on 4 January in a nightclub, then wrote the next day to assure her that he had meant everything he said. For the avoidance of doubt, he said it all over again the day after that when they ended a long night out at the flat of Audrey Lucas, the daughter of Arthur Waugh's friend E. V. Lucas, who complicated the situation somewhat by telling Evelyn that she was in love with him.

Olivia evidently relished the attention yet she repeatedly resisted his advances. The Plunket Greenes' lodger Harman Grisewood later remembered her telling him that she 'couldn't possibly sleep with anybody so hideous',[32] however he was hardly an impartial witness given that he also loved Olivia 'to the painful point of being entirely consumed by it,' he admitted. 'Destroyed some might say.'[33]

On 11 January Evelyn described a 'desolate tea' with Olivia at Hanover Terrace 'in front of a gas fire quarrelling in a half-hearted sort of way. Most of the time she insisted monotonously "I don't think you love me any more" and then became aloof when I attempted to prove that I did.'[34] A week later Evelyn saw Olivia kissing his friend Tony Bushell at the theatre and reacted by being 'very rude' to her, but she was 'too drunk to mind'. The next day he turned up drunk at her house after midnight with the same Tony Bushell, broke a gramophone record and refused to go until Olivia knelt down and apologised to him, which she refused to do, 'quite rightly', he later conceded. They made up the next day, just before he forlornly departed for Wales, when she told him he was 'a great artist and must not be a schoolmaster'.[35]

* * *

Unlike its lavishly embellished portrayal as the towered and turreted Llanabba Castle in *Decline and Fall*, Arnold House was a bland Victorian property perched above the village of Llanddulas on what Evelyn called the 'highly geological'[36] Denbighshire coast, between Rhyl and Colwyn Bay. He completed the last leg of the 250-mile journey from London by taxi, buried beneath a pile of bags belonging to the thirty boys he had reluctantly chaperoned on the train from Euston, who had then walked up from the station. The headmaster's wife, Mrs Banks,* greeted him sternly. 'The boys know they must carry their own bags. You should not have let them do that to you, Mr Waugh.' She then handed him a message she had taken down on the telephone. 'I hope you can understand it. I certainly cannot.' Sent by Hugh Lygon and John Sutro, it read 'On Evelyn, on.'

The dislike was mutual from then on, alleviated only briefly when Alastair and Mrs Graham came to visit Evelyn a month later and impressed Mrs Banks with their evident social superiority. 'Some *very* nice friends of yours have called for you, Mr Waugh,' she said. 'I am sure Mr Banks will excuse you from all duties while they are in the neighbourhood.'[37]

Evelyn's duties were in any case fairly vague at first. 'It is the most curiously run school that ever I heard of,' he wrote to his mother soon after arriving. 'No time tables nor syllabuses nor nothing. Banks just wanders into the common room & says "There are some boys in that class room. I think they are the first, or perhaps the fourth. Will someone go & teach them Maths or Latin or something."'[38]

Evelyn rated himself 'an obvious dud' as a schoolmaster, as inept at exercising authority as he was at carving the joint in the school dining room. But although he also admitted to finding 'a certain perverse pleasure in making all I teach as dreary to the boys as it is to myself',[39] he

---

* In *A Little Learning* (p. 222) Evelyn called the Bankses Mr and Mrs Vanhomrigh – 'pronounced by some who sought her goodwill "Vanummery"'.

seems to have been quite popular. Derek Verschoyle – later literary editor of *The Spectator*, where he recruited Evelyn as a columnist – remembered being favourably struck by his tweed coat, voluminous plus-fours and high-necked jumper, and by his agreeably laissez-faire attitude in the classroom: 'It could not be said that he made any great formal effort to teach [however] if any child showed curiosity on any specific point he would attempt to satisfy it.'[40] When it was his turn to take prep, Evelyn left his charges to their own devices instead of doing the rounds, while he used the time to write. (If anyone was impertinent enough to ask he would say that he was writing a history of the Eskimos.) Verschoyle also recalled that when Evelyn was in charge of 'communal walks', the boys vied to walk near him as they found his stories so entertaining.

At games, on the other hand, Evelyn was 'so undistinguished a performer that after a few humorous episodes it was thought better that he should not exercise with the senior boys'. Instead he was 'issued with a whistle and allowed to amble harmlessly around the football field with the ten-year olds'.[41] Even more humiliating was Evelyn's first riding lesson at a local livery yard when, having not ridden since childhood, he was put on a leading rein, only to be met 'in this contemptible situation' by the whole school returning from football.[42] Perhaps to bolster whatever was left of his dignity, he began to smoke a pipe and grow a moustache.

Midway through the term, Evelyn told Harold Acton that, while not a bad school, 'it is a sorry waste of time & energy'. Any time and energy left to him tended to be spent pining for Olivia, engraving a bookplate for her and writing letters 'full of sorrow and devotion'[43] which she either ignored or replied to with such lack of emotion as to make him even more miserable. 'All the term I have been allowing her to become a focus for all the decencies of life,' he wrote in his diary, 'which is foolish of me and not very fair to her.'[44] Drinking, as ever, provided a diversion and he enjoyed leading his common-room colleagues ('a rum lot united like defeated soldiers in the recognition of our base fate')[45] astray in the local pubs. But he could hardly wait for the Easter holidays, not least since he had been invited to stay with all the Plunket Greenes for two weeks in a rented lighthouse on the island of Lundy, off the north coast of Devon.

Back in London Evelyn quickly reverted to his bad old ways, and on the second evening he so shocked his besotted friend Audrey Lucas with his drunken behaviour that she wrote begging him never to get drunk

again. Her letter went unanswered, however, having arrived on the morning of his next spectacular misadventure, an episode later recycled as the
late-night carouse involving Charles, Sebastian and 'Boy' Mulcaster in
Brideshead. Evelyn and Olivia had organised a party to celebrate Richard
Plunket Greene and Elizabeth Russell's engagement, but the drink they
ordered failed to turn up. Evelyn accordingly went off to fetch it, persuading Olivia's cousin Matthew Ponsonby to drive him. Having retrieved
it, Evelyn announced he needed to go home to change and suggested a
pub crawl to Underhill, a further seven miles away to the north, to which
Ponsonby again meekly agreed. After two more glasses of beer there they
eventually headed back to the party, with Evelyn insisting on stopping at
yet more pubs on the way.[46]

As their erratic expedition neared its completion they were pulled over
by the police in the Strand after the inebriated Ponsonby drove the wrong
side of a traffic island. Later that night his father Arthur, a member of
Ramsay MacDonald's first Labour government, had to be woken by his
daughter Elizabeth to go and bail his son out of Bow Street police station.
He refused to do anything for Evelyn ('rather ill-naturedly, I thought'),
who was eventually released after four hours in a cell and made it to the
party just as it was breaking up. The next morning he was fined 15/6 for
being 'drunk and incapable', and reportedly 'made a bad impression as
he appeared in court in pink trousers & a green high-necked jumper and
cheeked the police'. When one officer said, 'Come along, my boy,' Evelyn
shot back, 'Don't call me "my boy", my man.'[47] Ponsonby, meanwhile, was
lucky to get away with a fine of 22 guineas – of which Evelyn offered to pay
half – and the loss of his licence for a year. *The Daily Telegraph*'s report
did not name Evelyn, but his friends and family knew perfectly who the
'incapably drunk' passenger was. 'A quantity of liquor found in the car
was afterwards claimed by this man,' the report added.[48]

Evelyn's behaviour shocked even some of his own age group. 'I am all
for a carouse now and again,' Elizabeth Russell's sister Georgiana* primly
confided, 'but I think there is something disgusting about Evelyn.'[49]
Arthur Ponsonby naturally blamed the 'disreputable' Evelyn for leading
his 'good-natured and weak' son astray, telling his wife Dolly (sister of

---

* Later Georgiana Blakiston. Known as 'Giana', later that year she was conspicuously drunk
herself at her sister's wedding. (See 22 December 1925; *EWD*, p. 238.)

Gwen Plunket Greene) that Evelyn had been 'distinctly drunk and therefore drew suspicion on M who was not sober'.[50]

Later in the year, if Evelyn's diary is to be believed, the Ponsonbys' hapless son would be involved in another far more serious motor accident while drunk, 'killing or at any rate seriously injuring a small boy'.[51] However, that Easter, as far as their family was concerned, Evelyn was very much the guilty party, and hence Matthew and Olivia's grandmother, Lady Parry, was 'disgusted' to hear that he was going to stay the next day with the Plunket Greenes 'just as if we didn't care when we are all so upset'. Frantic telephone calls passed between the cousins. Evelyn himself received what he called a 'piteous' letter from Lady Parry and no answer from Dolly Ponsonby after he wrote to her trying to mend fences.[52]

The Lundy house party included Elizabeth Russell, Julia Strachey and Terence Greenidge, who annoyed Evelyn with his 'new and disagreeable mannerism' of licking the backs of his hands, and later claimed apropos Olivia that 'she had fallen a bit for me!'.[53] Another girl there, Anne Talbot, confessed to Evelyn that she did not know what a phallic symbol was but then appeared to be the most enthusiastic participant in an 'amazing orgy' Evelyn walked in on one evening a few days later,[54] seeing her 'almost naked being slapped on the buttocks and enjoying herself ecstatically. Every two minutes she ran to the lavatory and as soon as she was out of the room everyone said, "My dear, the things we are finding out about Anne." It was all rather cruel.'[55]

On the whole it was an enjoyable two weeks for Evelyn, albeit marred by 'the insistent sorrow of unrequited love', of which he felt unable to cure himself even though he realised it was almost as trying for Olivia as it was for him. He was also troubled by the news that his own admirer, Audrey Lucas, was soon to marry Elsa Lanchester's partner at the Cave of Harmony, Harold Scott. 'It seems to be a most improper arrangement,' Evelyn mused, 'and one for which I am largely responsible.'[56] Having failed to respond to Audrey's desperate letter about his drinking, Evelyn feared she was 'marrying this vulgar man out of mockery'.[57] It proved to be an unhappy union.

From Lundy Evelyn went stay at Barford for a few days' heavy drinking with Alastair, who had arrived back from Africa just after New Year. But by that time Evelyn only had eyes for Olivia, and he continued to pursue her fruitlessly for a few days back in London before returning 'in immeasurable gloom' to Arnold House for the summer term. Within a week he was debating the 'paradoxes of suicide and achievement' and bought a revolver from the newly arrived second master, Dick Young, with the idea of killing himself.[58] Young was 'a dapper man of sunny disposition who spoke in the idiom of the army', but as Evelyn soon discovered, he was also 'monotonously pederastic and talks only of the beauty of sleeping boys';[59] as Evelyn later admitted, he provided 'certain features' for the character of Captain Grimes, his most memorable creation in *Decline and Fall*: 'When you've been in the soup as often as I have,' Grimes tells Paul Pennyfeather, 'it gives you a sort of feeling that everything's for the best, really . . . The last chap who put me on my feet said I was "singularly in harmony with the primitive promptings of humanity".'[60] In *A Little Learning* Evelyn recalled how, a few weeks into the term, Young surprised his colleagues by saying how much he had enjoyed a school trip to Snowdon in honour of the headmaster's birthday, a singularly tiresome expedition for the other masters. '*Enjoyed* yourself?,' they asked incredulously. 'What did you find to enjoy?' 'Knox minor,' he said with radiant simplicity. 'I felt the games a little too boisterous, so I took Knox minor away behind some rocks. I removed his boot and stocking, opened my trousers, put his dear little foot there and experienced a most satisfying emission.'[61]

Evelyn was fascinated by Young's cheerful recollections of past ignominies: 'expelled from Wellington, sent down from Oxford, and forced to resign his commission in the Army. He had left four schools precipitately, three in the middle of the term through his being taken in sodomy and one through his being drunk six nights in succession. And yet he goes on getting better and better jobs without difficulty.'[62] He admired his 'shining candour' and his unfailing ability to bounce back, and the development of his comic outlook as a novelist undoubtedly owed something to their fellowship. He spent many evenings with him in the pubs at Llanddulas and kept in touch after they ceased to be colleagues.

If Young helped keep Evelyn's spirits up during his second term at Arnold House, so too did his excitement about a new book, which would be published the following year as a short story, 'The Balance'. 'I am making the first chapter a cinema film and have been writing furiously ever since,' he told his diary. 'I honestly think that it is going to be rather good.'[63] He had also heard from Alec that C. K. Scott Moncrieff, the famous translator of Proust, might want him as a secretary. Happily imagining a year in Italy sipping Chianti under olive trees, Evelyn promptly gave his notice to Mr Banks. 'I never give notice,' said Young, when he heard. 'It's always the other way about with me. In fact, this looks like being the first end of term I've seen, old boy, for three schools.'[64]

Evelyn's life briefly seemed full of promise, but then came a letter from Harold Acton with his crushing assessment of *The Temple at Thatch*: 'Too English for my exotic taste. Too much nid-nodding over port. It should be printed in a few elegant copies for the friends who love you such as myself.'[65] Evelyn promptly consigned the manuscript to the school furnace. Next came the news that Scott Moncrieff did not need him after all. 'It looks rather like being the end of the tether,' Evelyn told his diary.[66]

At the end of *A Little Learning*, he described how all this drove him to leave his clothes and an appropriate quotation from Euripides on the beach one night and swim out to sea with thoughts of drowning, only to be turned back by jellyfish. 'As earnest of my attempt, I had brought no towel. With some difficulty I dressed and tore into small pieces my pretentious classical tag . . . Then I climbed the sharp hill that led to all the years ahead.'[67]

9

Becoming a Man of Letters

There is no corroboration for the drowning attempt in Evelyn's diary or letters and it may very well have been an imaginative flourish to lend a dramatic and slightly farcical finale to his account of his early years. Yet this was undoubtedly a low point. Sent on his way from Arnold House with a few 'valedictory discourtesies' from the headmaster, back in London he became acutely aware of the gulf between his own situation and that of his close friends: Harold Acton was at the height of his Oxford popularity and esteem; Tony Bushell, when Evelyn visited him in his dressing room at the Adelphi Theatre, seemed 'superbly important nowadays with Cabinet ministers waiting on him with their cars and amorous Jewesses offering him their beds';[1] Robert Byron was about to set off on the adventure to Greece that would lead to his first book; Peter Quennell was already a published poet, the most 'poetical' since Swinburne according to Evelyn's bête noire Edmund Gosse;[2] even Evelyn's school sidekick Dudley Carew had published a novel and was assistant editor on a weekly newspaper. Only Alastair Graham remained as determinedly idle and dissolute as ever.

Evelyn and Alastair were together a lot that August and a resumption of romance is hinted at in Evelyn's recollection of their having 'dined in high-necked jumpers' at Barford and done 'much that could not have been done if Mrs Graham had been here'.[3] After that visit Alastair wrote to him: 'I feel very lonely now. But you have made me so happy. Please come back again soon. Write to me a lot, because I am all by myself, and I want to know what you are doing . . . My love to you, Evelyn; I want you back again so much.'[4] There is a sense here of Alastair beginning to lose his hold over Evelyn, and more palpably so in his next letter. 'Thank you for your letter,' he wrote a few days later. 'Evelyn, it was very serious for a poor careless, happy person like me. Of course I want you to treat me as your nature wishes to. I don't understand how one could treat anyone otherwise without being insincere.'[5] Evelyn's pulling away doubtless had to do with his crush on Olivia, with whom he had gone to stay on the Norfolk coast for a week in September 1925, taking with him a kitten as a present. But in any case he appears to have been turning his attention more towards girls in general, and had confided to certain friends that he wanted to find a wife.[6] The same month he recorded going to 'a party given by one of the homosexual painters I had met at Mary Butts. He wanted to dance with me and Bobbie [Cecil A. Roberts] but it seemed too repulsive and I am afraid we were rude.'[7]

In a bid to find more congenial work, meanwhile, he had applied to all the London art galleries and art magazines, but to no avail.[8] So in late September he reluctantly began a new teaching job at Aston Clinton in Buckinghamshire, an Italianate pile formerly owned by the Rothschilds where backward public schoolboys were crammed for university entrance. With only thirty 'mad boys' (or 'lunatics'), as Evelyn called them, in the whole school, he had more free time here, besides which the proximity to the fleshpots of London and Oxford, as well as his entertaining Cockburn cousins just four miles away at Tring, made life far more agreeable than at Arnold House. So too did the presence in the common room of his great friend Richard Plunket Greene, to whom Evelyn acted as best man when he married Liza Russell that December, another event marred for him by his jealously over Olivia.

When some of Richard and Elizabeth's wedding party eventually ended up at the Berkeley, Evelyn looked on as Olivia did 'that disgusting dance of hers'[9] – her version of the Charleston, which was so much the rage then among the Bright Young People.[10] Much of his heartache about her stemmed from the fact that she made such a show of being sexually available to everyone. Everyone, that is, except Evelyn, who was barely allowed to touch her. A month earlier, at Matthew Ponsonby's party, Evelyn observed that 'Olivia as usual behaved like a whore and was embraced on a bed by various people'.[11] Harman Grisewood later insisted that she 'would never have accepted these physical caresses from anyone to whom she was herself attracted'.

She was not greatly attracted to Grisewood either, however during his four years as the Greenes' lodger, he sometimes put her to bed when she was too drunk to undress. On such occasions, he recalled, 'I was allowed – encouraged indeed – to make love to her a little . . . a macabre and an agonising experience for a man who was consumed by love for her and enthralled by her.' When it stopped, 'well before the natural outcome of such pleasures', she would say to him, 'If you live in the furnace, sometimes you are allowed a glass of water.'[12]

More regular boyfriends experienced similar frustrations. Some years later, after having become a Catholic and taken a vow of chastity, Olivia wrote to Augustus John's highly sexed son Henry, himself a recent fugitive from the Jesuits: 'If I let you hold me in your arms, it is for a variety of reasons . . . Your embraces are lessons, but most enjoyable, like a lesson in eating ice-cream or treacle.' In the summer of 1935 they had been due to go to Cornwall together when he received a six-page letter outlining various reasons why she could not have sex with him. He drove on down to Cornwall as planned but she did not follow. He was last seen on a desolate stretch of cliffs, 'walking along,' Michael Holroyd writes, 'swinging a towel, his aunt's Irish terrier at his heels'. His body was washed up on a beach two weeks later, dressed only in a pair of shorts.[13]

* * *

For Evelyn, meanwhile, any distraction from Olivia was welcome, and after a 'dreary' Christmas with the whole Waugh family crammed into Alec's flat for two nights, he agreed to go to Paris – his first time abroad – with a heavy-drinking actor-manager called Bill Silk, an ardent admirer of Tony Bushell's, who promptly took him to a male brothel.* There Evelyn was kissed by a nineteen-year-old youth whom he found 'attractive but [I] had better uses for the 300 francs which the patron – a most agreeable young man in evening dress – demanded for his enjoyment'. While Bill haggled in bad French over the price, Evelyn then arranged 'a tableau by which my boy should be enjoyed by a large negro who was there but at the last minute, after we had ascended to a squalid divan at the top of the house and he was lying waiting for the negro's advances, the price proved

---

* Unlike in Britain, where they would remain illegal until the 1960s, homosexual acts had been legal in France since the Revolution.

prohibitive and, losing patience with Bill's protracted argument with the patron, I took a taxi home and to bed in chastity. I think I do not regret it.'[14] For the rest of the trip, leaving his companion to his nightlife, Evelyn concentrated on sightseeing.

Back in London, another diversion was provided by Elizabeth Ponsonby, Matthew's fashionable elder sister, one of the first girls to have her hair shingled. Later the model for Agatha Runcible in *Vile Bodies*, Elizabeth was the fabled leader of the Bright Young People and gave the impression at least that she would sleep with anyone who wanted to sleep with her.[15] Evelyn had met her the previous autumn without being especially bowled over – 'two years ago, or less even, I suppose I should have been rather thrilled by her,' he wrote in his diary.[16] But in January 1926, at one of Alec's dinner parties, she 'made vigorous love' to Evelyn which flattered him, and on reflection he was sorry not to have accepted. 'She has furry arms,' he noticed. When he met her again the next evening, however, she seemed 'entirely to have overcome her attraction to me'.[17] She was still on his mind a month later when, on a brief dash to London, he sent 'Liz' a card asking her to come for cocktails at the Ritz 'but she did not'.[18] When Alec invited her to a cocktail party in March, she again failed to show up.[19]

The prospect of the Lent term meanwhile was made bleaker by Richard Plunket Greene's departure for a new job at Lancing. As a parting gift for his best man he had bought him a Douglas motor-bicycle, whose inaugural run 'shook off 12/6 worth of its lamp,' Evelyn recorded, 'broke its front brake and stand and number-plate' but otherwise went 'creditably'.[20] Heading back to Aston Clinton in the rain a few days later for the start of term, it went less well 'and finally outside Tring made me wheel it a long way and buy it a new tyre'.[21] Undaunted, shortly after that Evelyn set off for Oxford, more than thirty miles away, returning after dinner 'beastly wet and windy and no light on my bicycle', once falling over and 'all the time sliding all over the road'.[22] The next day he made for Barford, a 'dolorous' sixty-mile journey, again in the dark and rain, during which his bike required a lengthy repair en route when a nut came off the clutch. Three miles short of his destination he again came to a halt with the engine 'refusing to grapple with the wheel'; later he learned it had '"sheared off a key", whatever that may be'.[23]

Evelyn was soon persuaded to swap his Douglas for a smaller but more reliable Francis-Barnett, on which he proceeded to undertake even more hair-raising journeys, often in the dark, his lights usually not working, the roads wet or icy, and with plenty of alcoholic refreshments taken en route. When Dick Young, 'the lecher from Denbighshire', came to visit him in March Evelyn could not help but cast an envious glance at his 'marvellous' Sunbeam, perhaps mindful of the effect his more substantial Douglas had had on his credibility with the boys, making him, unlikely as it sounds, 'the idol of the school'.[24] The Francis-Barnett was not entirely unimpressive, however, as can be seen from the famous motorcycling photograph of Evelyn which, as Duncan McLaren has now established, shows him outside Aston Clinton astride his new machine in February 1926.

With no Richard Greene to drink with, Evelyn tolerated the odd glass with an officious cavalry officer on the staff with the suitably Wavian name of Captain Hyde-Upward, whose one redeeming feature so far as Evelyn was concerned was his habit of thoughtfully polishing and cleaning out his pipe while standing naked at his bedroom window.[25] But generally he preferred the company of the boys, especially his two favourites, Edmund and Charles, who kept house for him in the sitting room the headmaster had allowed him over the stables, while he repaid them with tea and strawberries, went for walks with them, sat with them on the golf course and read aloud from *The Wind in the Willows*. He did not entirely shirk his disciplinary responsibilities and in March recorded that 'the children have begun to be a little naughty so I have started being strict with them, which is a bore'.[26] In the summer term he 'found Edmund out of bounds and beat him with mixed feelings and an ash plant. He was very sweet and brave about it all. I have given him a Sulka tie as recompense.'[27]

Evelyn's friendship with Edmund and Charles would doubtless raise eyebrows today, especially since he seemed to think nothing of inviting Dick Young to visit him at the school, taking him to 'see the children at football', whereupon he promptly 'fell in love with Richard Hollins'. After a subsequent visit, Evelyn recorded: 'Young of Denbighshire came down and was rather a bore – drunk all the time. He seduced a garage boy in the hedge.'[28] In his autobiography Evelyn maintained that he envied Young 'his unclouded happiness but not his exploits',[29] and there is nothing in his diaries to contradict this. His own romantic sights remained firmly fixed on Olivia, and with her proving so elusive there was always still

Alastair, with whom he had been reading T. S. Eliot's poems in January, 'marvellously good but very hard to understand',[30] and went to a dance – 'only it is called a "ball" because it is in the country' – after which Alastair drove the car up the bank on the way home.

A natural drifter, Alastair was prone to disappear without warning, as when he vanished for ten days in April before being discovered drunk in the Lotti Hotel in Paris.[31] In his absence on another longer trip to Constantinople, Evelyn reflected, 'I have missed him more than I would have thought.'[32] But in all probability by this stage they were just friends, so for instance when returning in July from a jaunt to London at dawn Evelyn recorded that 'Tony [Bushell] slept in my room in the stables, Alastair in his car'.[33]

Yet they were still close enough for Evelyn to invite himself to accompany Alastair and his mother to Scotland for three weeks in the summer. Mrs G had been less warmly disposed towards Evelyn since discovering that her son was guaranteeing his overdraft and, as Alastair recalled, his 'deplorable manners' during the course of the trip 'did nothing to clear the atmosphere'.[34] The two of them then went on to France, where Evelyn reflected, 'I think I have seen too much of Alastair lately.'[35]

Alastair would in any case soon be off to take up a diplomatic post in Athens; however before leaving he wanted Evelyn to write a pamphlet for the printing press he had brought home from Turkey. Evelyn had made some notes on the Pre-Raphaelite Brotherhood the previous November at Underhill after spraining his ankle climbing out of a window, and he rattled off *PRB: An Essay on the Pre-Raphaelite Brotherhood 1847–54* in four and a half days. If it now seems rather whimsical and patronising in tone, it was a bold effort given that the Pre-Raphaelites were so out of fashion at the time. Six decades later the young Evelyn Waugh would be hailed as having been 'a lone voice crying in the modernist wilderness' and 'one of the most distinguished pioneers of the Victorian revival'.[36]

The original publication of *PRB* came a month after that of Evelyn's short story 'The Balance', which he had written the previous summer. At thirty-eight pages, Evelyn had hoped it might make a short book, but the manuscript he sent to Chatto & Windus was politely returned, as was the copy Evelyn sent to Leonard Woolf – whose rejection letter chanced to arrive the day after Evelyn recorded in his diary that he had been lent 'a novel [*Mrs Dalloway*] by Virginia Woolf which I refuse to believe is good'.[37] After yet another refusal, Alec eventually came to its rescue and included it in the volume he edited in Chapman & Hall's series of *Georgian Stories*, published in October 1926, along with contributions from Aldous Huxley, Somerset Maugham, Liam O'Flaherty and others.

As Alec said, Evelyn's was 'an *avant-garde* piece',[38] an experimental collage with abrupt shifts in form and tone, and characters and situations closely drawn from his life. Subtitled 'A Yarn of the Good Old Days of Broad Trousers and High Necked Jumpers', it features an art student recently down from Oxford called Adam Doure who tries to poison himself when the fashionable Imogen Quest blithely ends their affair, blaming her mother. If the experimental narrative techniques did not quite come off in this instance, it was nonetheless an extraordinary piece of writing for a twenty-one-year-old, and the use of cinematic descriptions to achieve greater objectivity, the one-sided telephone conversations and skilfully handled passages of sustained, unattributed dialogue all prefigured devices used to great effect in his later fiction. The *Manchester Guardian* pronounced it 'brilliant',[39] albeit 'for all the most futile reasons'[40] in Evelyn's view. The American writer Conrad Aiken came closer to the mark, acclaiming it as an 'astonishingly rich portrait of a mind' and predicting that the author might 'do something very remarkable [providing] he is not too clever'.[41]

Despite the encouraging reviews, Evelyn still lagged behind some of his contemporaries, most obviously Henry Yorke, who had begun his first novel *Blindness* while still at Eton and published it, under the pseudonym Henry Green, just before leaving Oxford that autumn. Evelyn felt 'impelled' to write and tell him 'how very much I like it. It is extraordinary to me that anyone of our generation could have written so fine a book.'[42] Two years younger than Evelyn, Yorke was now about to embark on a stint on the factory floor of the family engineering works in Birmingham, an experience that would lead to his second novel, *Living* (1929), whereas Evelyn remained glumly stranded at Aston Clinton, attempting a life of 'sobriety, chastity, and obedience' after his mother had paid off his debts yet again.[43] As he passed his twenty-third birthday, for which Arthur gave him 'some very expensive underclothes, and a pound to buy some dinner with', he was growing increasingly frustrated with schoolmastering, irritated by the boys' 'prattle'[44] yet at the same time ashamed of how rude he could be to them. At the end of term, the headmaster grudgingly gave him a £10 pay rise. 'I think next term will be my last,' Evelyn wrote in his diary.[45]

A trip that Christmas holidays to Athens, where Alastair had been posted as honorary attaché to the British Minister, Sir Percy Loraine, did little to cheer him. Alastair had been fascinated by ancient Greece since childhood, brought up on tales of his great-grandfather, the 14th Duke of Somerset, who had travelled throughout the Levant in the 1840s 'with a shotgun under one arm and a copy of Homer under the other'.[46] An additional draw was that the Mediterranean was then seen as 'the place for Anglo-Saxon gay men to escape to', as Duncan Fallowell puts it, a place where 'misfits of all kinds' could 'breathe more easily and be themselves'.[47] Alastair was a cousin of Lady Loraine, which doubtless eased his appointment; however there were whispers about Sir Percy which, if true, would also have made Alastair an appealing recruit. An ostensibly strait-laced Northumbrian landowner and able diplomat with what his friend Harold Nicolson called 'a weakness for the processional', Sir Percy was also rumoured to have a 'liking for young men and low life' and to have had an affair with the young Francis Bacon, his distant kinsman by marriage, thus helping to extend the painter's 'experience and observation'.[48]*

Whether Loraine helped extend Alastair's horizons in the same way is a matter for conjecture, but in any event Alastair seemed to be seizing every opportunity to explore his sexuality away from the restrictive laws of England; as Evelyn recorded, the modern flat he shared with another diplomat was 'usually full of dreadful Dago youths called by heroic names such as Miltiades and Agamemnon with blue chins and greasy clothes who sleep with the English colony for 25 drachmas a night'.[49]

Unimpressed by Alastair's new friends and by Athenian cafés, which he said reminded him of potting sheds, Evelyn eventually struck out alone for Olympia, where he saw the Hermes of Praxiteles that had been found by archaeologists only fifty years previously, 'quite marvellous and well worth all the trouble I have taken to see it'.[50] Yet despite his conscientious and adventurous sightseeing, he was nagged by a feeling of having

---

* Roger Mortimer recalled that in retirement Sir Percy Loraine lived in the flat below his parents at 76 Sloane Street and that he used to go abroad for the winter, during which time his butler used the flat as a brothel. 'My mother could not understand the weird noises that could be heard from 2 p.m. onwards. I think my father rather enjoyed them.' (*Dear Lumpy*, p. 126.)

inherited his father's 'homely sentiments': 'The truth is that I do not really like being abroad much. I want to see as much as I can this holiday and from February shut myself up for the rest of my life in the British Isles.'[51]

Home was eventually regained in late January 1927 via Corfu, Brindisi, Rome and Paris, after almost a month away, and he was soon back at Aston Clinton, busily corrupting a new master called Attwell, who seemed to have led 'the dullest life imaginable' at Oxford and been a virtual teetotaller before being cajoled into drunken binges by Evelyn. Returning from one of their sprees they came across another new member of staff, a matron who had recently given Evelyn a ham and struck him as an 'admirable' sort. What happened next is not clear, although Evelyn later told friends that as a joke he had said some suggestive things to her in French as she came out of the bathroom in her dressing-gown.[52] The following day, while Evelyn and Attwell were sitting by the fire laughing about the night before, the headmaster came in and sacked them both. From then on, Evelyn recorded, it became 'rather a harrassing day'. The next morning Evelyn 'slipped away feeling rather like a housemaid who has been caught stealing gloves'.[53] He warned his parents in advance by telephone that he would be coming, explaining tactfully that he had been dismissed for drunkenness, and when he got there 'dined in a very sorrowful household'.[54] The next day, feeling 'tired and discouraged' after 'trying to do something about getting a job', he wrote his diary: 'It seems to me the time has arrived to set about being a man of letters.'[55]

The same day he wrote to say goodbye to Edmund and Charles, his letter crossing with one from Edmund enclosing two photographs of himself:

Dear Evelyn,

  I cannot tell you how sorry I am that you have left and that I never came to say good bye but I was too shy as you had your friend, Cecil Roberts, with you. I am writing this in bed instead of going to call you, I shall miss doing that awfully. Every one is very upset at your leaving. Watkinson asked me especially to remember him to you when I wrote. I do not know what Pig [Charles] & I will do now without your room to go up & tidy or wash up (in cold water). I went up there yesterday to see what you had done with all your things & it looked so bare without your books & candle sticks & the Ikon (I cannot spell it).[56]

* * *

Back in London following his dismissal, Evelyn had a discouraging interview with a Father Underhill to explore the idea of his becoming a clergyman before accepting a temporary job at a dismal school in Notting Hill, where 'all the masters drop their aitches and spit in the fire and scratch their genitals' and the boys 'pick their noses and scream at each other in a cockney accent'.[57]

Prior to taking up that post he 'spent two days writing a story about a Duke'[58] for the well-regarded *New Decameron* short story series. 'A House of Gentlefolks' reintroduces Ernest Vaughan, Adam Doure's dissolute friend (and Evelyn's alter ego) in 'The Balance', who has now been sent down from Oxford and befriends the Duke of Vanburgh's supposedly backward grandson and heir after being asked to take him around Europe. More straightforwardly readable if less ambitious than 'The Balance', it appeared later that year alongside stories by Michael Sadleir, G. B. Stern, L. A. G. Strong and others.

As he usually did when in London, he saw a lot of the Plunket Greenes, and after lunching with them one day he complained to his diary that 'Olivia could talk of nothing except black men'.[59] Since the opening of the Blackbirds revue the previous autumn it had become chic for Bright Young People to entertain black people at their parties, to the extent that when issuing an invitation promising no such adornment Evelyn took to saying, 'It's not a party, there won't be a black man.'[60] Evelyn had in fact seen the Blackbirds shortly after it opened and he went again several times with Olivia after leaving Aston Clinton, recording on one occasion that they 'called on Florence Mills and other niggers and negresses in their dressing-rooms. Then to a night club called Victor's to see another nigger – [the American cabaret star] Leslie Hutchinson.'[61]* It is a commonplace to accuse Evelyn of being racist in such diary entries, just as it is to describe various other pronouncements as anti-Semitic or snobbish.

---

* Known as 'Hutch', Hutchinson's romantic entanglements were a source of particular fascination to Evelyn. Despite being married with a baby, Hutch was at the time openly living with a girl called Zena Naylor (the illegitimate daughter of the art critic Langton Douglas), who soon complained of his sleeping with Olivia's sister-in-law, Babe Plunket Greene. To complicate matters further, Zena soon became the girlfriend of Alec Waugh, who had to plead with Evelyn to change a brothel sign that read 'Chez Zena' in one of his illustrations for *Decline and Fall*.

But his apparent prejudices almost invariably contained elements of self-parody or mischievous provocation, or stemmed from a compulsion to say the unsayable. Regarding his descriptions of the Blackbirds, it is worth bearing in mind that language and attitudes were very different then, and in any case the hostesses who courted and patronised black artists, treating them as fashionable and amusing accessories rather as Mrs Beste-Chetwynde does with 'Chokey' in *Decline and Fall*, were if anything more amusing to him than the black performers themselves.

In Evelyn's case there may also have been jealousy over Olivia's outspoken fascination with black men and her rumoured affair with Paul Robeson. By now Evelyn knew all too well the depressive, self-obsessed flipside of Olivia's character after witnessing such scenes as her 'packing bottles in a bedroom littered with stockings and newspaper. Fatter and larger generally, unable to talk of much except herself and that in an impersonal and incoherent way.'[62] Yet according to Harman Grisewood he remained desperately in love with her and one day, when the message finally got through that she would never sleep with him, he took hold of her hand and very deliberately burnt the back of her wrist with his cigarette. Olivia found this sadistic act strangely moving, and when she showed the scar to Grisewood she confided that she felt very sorry for Evelyn, 'sorry', as Grisewood later recalled, 'that she could feel no physical attraction for him and sorry that this knowledge should have so frightful an effect, driving him to a sort of frenzy'.[63]

For Evelyn, meanwhile, the only way of getting over his obsession with Olivia was for him to find someone else, and on 7 April 1927 he recorded in his diary: 'I have met such a nice girl called Evelyn Gardner.'

10

....

Shevelyn

There has been a certain amount of debate about when or where the two Evelyns met, Dudley Carew recalling that it was he who introduced them at his flat (and that was why Evelyn was so horrid to him in later years)* and others suggesting that it happened at the lodgings that Evelyn Gardner shared with her best friend Pansy Pakenham on Ebury Street in Belgravia. Evelyn certainly went to the girls' Ebury Street party, describing it in his diary as 'a pleasing little one',[1] however that took place in late May 1927, more than six weeks after the Evelyns' first meeting. According to Evelyn Gardner, whose written account of their relationship has not been seen by any previous biographer,† they had first met at an earlier party given by Sylvia Brooke, Ranee of Sarawak, self-styled 'Queen of the Headhunters', at her large house on Portland Place, introduced by their mutual friend Bobbie Roberts.

Recalling this first meeting, 'Shevelyn', as Evelyn's friends soon took to calling her, wrote: 'I saw a young man, short, sturdy, good-looking, given to little gestures, the shrugging of a hand which held a drink, the tossing of a head as he made some witty, somewhat malicious remark. He was easy to talk to and amusing.'[2] Besides thinking her 'a lovely girl', Evelyn never recorded his initial impressions of Shevelyn, although she later presumed 'he was interested in me because I was gay, boyish looking with an Eton crop and very slim'. A possible additional draw, she hazarded, was 'that I

---

* This is impossible as by his own account Carew did not meet Evelyn Gardner until they were fellow passengers on the Rajah of Sarawak's hired bus to the Epsom Derby, won by Call Boy, in June 1927. (See *Fragment of Friendship*, pp. 77–8.)

† Written in 1975 and running to nineteen pages, this was described by Shevelyn as 'a full account which the children can dispose of as they like after I am dead'. (Evelyn Gardner to Michael Davie, 8 December 1975, AWA.)

belonged – so he thought – to the society to which he not only wished to belong but of which he wished to become an undoubted member'.

Her father, Lord Burghclere, illegitimate eldest son of the 3rd Lord Gardner and the actress Julia Fortescue, had been a Liberal MP and President of the Board of Agriculture under Gladstone then Rosebery. Her mother, Lady Winifred, eldest daughter of the 4th Earl of Carnarvon, and a distant kinswoman of Gwen Plunket Greene, was the scholarly biographer of James, 1st Duke of Ormonde and George Villiers, 2nd Duke of Buckingham. Winifred's brother sponsored Howard Carter's Egyptian archaeological expeditions and participated in the discovery of Tutankhamen's tomb in 1922. But Shevelyn longed to escape her illustrious background. Born in 1903 (a month before Evelyn Waugh), the youngest by seven years of four daughters, she never went to school and was brought up by a nanny and governesses, her sister Mary, the next youngest, having been married off when Shevelyn was eleven, after which, as she recalled, 'the servants became my greatest friends'. She remembered the sensation of being 'as it were in a cage with no knowledge of the world or the real behaviour of others. One was enclosed and the bursting out when freedom came was not good.'

Of her parents Shevelyn far preferred her father, 'whose sunny disposition and ever-kindly wit,' according to *The Times*, 'together with his fame as an amateur actor are perhaps better remembered than his services to Liberalism'.[3] However he was fifty-seven by the time Shevelyn was born and she saw very little of him as a child, although she fondly recalled his winking at her across the table during boring lunch parties. He died in 1921, when she was barely eighteen. Her mother, on the other hand, was 'formidable' and 'absolutely terrifying' as far as Shevelyn was concerned – notwithstanding her dainty figure, tiny waist and mice-like feet.

Lady Burghclere's starchiness may have stemmed from having had to sacrifice her own adolescence. Her mother died when she was eleven, leaving it to her to entertain her father's guests at Highclere Castle (the 'real' Downton Abbey) as if she were a grown-up. Her father eventually remarried and when he began crawling around playing bears with his baby son on the drawing room floor, she was horrified that he could be so undignified. When she came to have Shevelyn, her daughter remembered no affection at all. 'One could never explain one's presumed misdemeanours,' wrote Shevelyn, 'because words froze in one's mouth or didn't even get as far as freezing. Neither my sister Mary nor I remember her ever coming into the nursery or schoolroom. There were no goodnights, loving or otherwise, or prayers being heard at bedtime.'

On the face of it the three elder Gardner daughters had all married well,* although none of the marriages was especially happy and by the time Shevelyn was grown-up two of them had already failed and there were whispers of 'bad blood' in the family, which Shevelyn presumed referred to her actress grandmother, some of whose warmth and demonstrativeness she herself exhibited in her role as the archetypal Modern Girl, calling friends 'angel-face' and 'sweetie-pie', and referring to Proust, whom she once declared herself 'buried in', as 'dear old Prousty-wousty'.[4]

Shevelyn's longing to 'burst out' was allied to a natural flirtatiousness, a slim figure, pert little nose and, like her distant cousin Olivia Plunket Greene, round 'goo-goo' eyes that men found highly attractive. By the time she was twenty-three she had been engaged nine times, often simultaneously, her assorted fiancés including a ship's purser whom she had met on a trip to Australia, where her mother had sent her to break up another unsuitable entanglement. When she met Evelyn Waugh at Sylvia Brooke's party she had recently accepted a proposal from the Ranee's handsome ADC and former boyfriend Barry Gifford, whom shellshock had transformed from dashing First World War hero to hopeless soak and 'frightful bounder' in several people's estimation. Shevelyn knew he was an alcoholic, but 'in my immature way I imagined I could cure him'; however they had to hold fire for the time being because he was still technically married.

* * *

Aside from finding Evelyn Waugh attractive and fun, the fact that he was a writer was also very appealing, given that she had recently quit her job as a *vendeuse* at the Maison Arthur fashion store on Dover Street in order to write a play, and was keen for an entrée into the literary world. When they met he had just begun a trial stint on the *Daily Express*, and

---

* In 1914 Mary married Geoffrey Hope-Morley (Morley's underwear); they divorced in 1928. In 1915 Alathea married Geoffrey Fry (Fry's chocolate); the marriage lasted but was very strained. In 1916 Juliet married Alexander Cumming-Russell of Clochan; they separated within twenty-four hours and divorced in 1922.

after their first lunch à deux at the Green Park Hotel in late May he went straight off to cover a fire in Soho, where 'an Italian girl was supposed to have been brave but had actually done nothing at all'.[5] He was sacked shortly afterwards, perhaps not surprisingly if the advice he subsequently offered budding journalists was any reflection of the attitude he displayed at work. When assigned a story, 'the correct procedure is to jump to your feet, seize your hat and umbrella and dart out of the office with every appearance of haste to the nearest cinema'.[6] There the probationer was advised to sit and smoke a pipe and imagine what any relevant witnesses might say. It was perhaps Evelyn's good fortune that in his seven weeks on the paper, not one of the pieces he filed was published.

Shortly before being let go by the *Express*, after toying with the idea of writing a book about the Mormons, he had in any case been commissioned by Duckworth's, where his friend Anthony Powell worked, to write a biography of Rossetti in time for the centenary of the painter's birth the next year. Arthur Waugh gloomily predicted that the book would never be finished and that he would have to make good the publisher's advance of £20 which Evelyn, who invariably lurched towards largesse when in funds, had spent in a week. However, after two weeks with his parents and Alec in the South of France (during which Evelyn and Alec visited the Marseilles red-light district, which may have occasioned Evelyn's first sexual encounter with a woman), he knuckled down, and after three weeks he had completed 12,000 words. A month later he was up to 40,000, helped by a stint at the Abingdon Arms in Beckley (where he and Alastair had rented their horseless caravan three years earlier), from where he went most days to Oxford to write in the Union library, which Rossetti and other Pre-Raphaelites had decorated with murals in the 1850s. Next he decided to patch up his quarrel with Mrs Graham and move on to Barford, where he could work undisturbed in a room under the roof called the cock-loft, formerly a lady's maid's 'cutting-out room', furnished with only a table and, as Alastair recalled, 'one of those headless, armless, legless dummies representing the ideal Victorian lady's figure'.[7]

Despite doing all the research as he went along – including interviewing Rossetti's former secretary Hall Caine in bed and looking 'like a Carthusian abbott', and visiting Kelmscott Manor, where Rossetti had shared a lease with William Morris, whose daughter Evelyn found to be 'a detestable woman' – he managed to complete *Rossetti: His Life and Works* within seven months. By today's standards the eventual 227 pages includes a lot of long direct quotations – comprising as much as a third of the text in some chapters – however considering that he was barely twenty-four, and that the book is studded with strikingly trenchant and at the time unfashionable opinions, it was a highly impressive achievement.

Did the thought of enhancing his eligibility in the eyes of Evelyn Gardner give an extra spur to his writing? Almost certainly it did. After their lunch date in May there had been a long weekend over Whitsun when they both stayed in Wiltshire with Shevelyn's sister Mary Hope-Morley, who was by then estranged from her first husband and entertaining his replacement, Alan Hillgarth, 'very sure of himself', noted Evelyn in his diary, 'writes shockers, ex-sailor'. There was then a long interval while Evelyn got on with Rossetti before he again began to pursue her in earnest in mid-September. In late November – by which time he had taken a leaf out of the Pre-Raphaelites' book and was learning to be a cabinet-maker at the Academy of Carpentry – he told his diary that he was seeing Shevelyn 'a lot', and she had recently been to dinner at Underhill to meet his parents, after which she told a friend: 'Old Mr Waugh is a complete Pinkle-Wonk. He wears a blue velvet coat at dinner, just like Papa did, and talks about actresses who were the toasts of his young days. I like that kind of thing.'[8]

A little wiser perhaps after his forlorn pursuit of Olivia, Evelyn seems to have blundered only once with Shevelyn when, 'a little too tight' one evening, as she told a friend, he was furious when she wouldn't let him take her home. 'When I got back about 1.30 the telephone rang, & a small precise voice said, "Is that Miss Gardner?" "Yes." "What I want to say is, Hell to you!" Clang went the receiver. I did laugh so much. Evelyn apologised profusely the next day, he is so sweet.'[9] 'Sweet' is a word that crops up a lot in her descriptions of him at this time.

Evelyn had been vaguely on the lookout for a wife for the past two years, and it had evidently already crossed his mind that Evelyn Gardner might be the one. When one day she let slip out of the blue that she was thinking of going to Canada, he realised he could afford to dither no longer. Three days later, on 12 December, Evelyn took her out to dinner at the Ritz Grill and proposed. 'Let's get married and see how it goes,'[10] is how he phrased it, according to Shevelyn, who recalled there being no mention of love. She asked for time to think about it but the next day rang up to accept.

She later admitted that, much though she 'liked Evelyn and admired him sincerely', she 'should have considered it far longer than I did. But I was anxious to get married and settle down.' Her sense of urgency had been heightened by two recent developments. Her closest sister Mary, whom she idolised to an extent unfathomable to her friends, had announced that she was going to marry the cocksure shocker writer Alan Hillgarth (to whom Hevelyn had taken a virulent dislike, as had her flatmate Pansy Pakenham) and follow him to South America. And Pansy had also just got engaged to the painter Henry Lamb. 'Suddenly there was the danger of my having to return home,' recalled Shevelyn. 'I did not think that my mother would allow me to live alone [and was afraid she] might cut off my allowance.'

To give her her due, besides the sheer convenience of marriage at this time she also felt that Evelyn would be far more stimulating company than the 'solid 100% he-men' with whom she had previously consorted, whose appeal, she told a friend, lay 'in their directness and sex-appeal' yet whose charms tended to wear off to the point when they became 'hum-drum'.[11] Her acceptance of him was encouraged by Pansy, who told a friend at the time that 'after all these toughs & cavemen that make up her usual clientele, E. Waugh seems like claret after whisky [and] seems to be kind and bracing at the same time'.[12] Pansy had been equally instrumental in persuading Evelyn to take the plunge when he did. 'I was <u>greatly</u> in favour of this,' she wrote to a friend just after the engagement, 'as I thought E. Gardner had lost her nerve about marriage & that if she didn't do it at once she would let it peter out out of sheer funk.'[13]

Evelyn's proposal does not sound all that romantic, it is true, and is often adduced as proof that he was not especially in love with her. Equally plausible, however, is that he was nervous and unsure of her response and anxious to protect himself against her possible rejection, which would have been perfectly understandable with Barry Gifford still lurking about, and given all the knocks his confidence had suffered at the hands of Olivia. In any case, Shevelyn later implied that his breezy suggestion was far less threatening and more appealing to her than a passionate declaration of love, telling Michael Davie that she interpreted it as meaning that absolute faithfulness was not required by her. 'I had been brought up to believe everything that people said. I believed him. I was a ninny.'[14]*

Whatever the depth of his feelings for her, Evelyn was also keen to get away from home. 'How I detest this house [Underhill],' he had reflected earlier that autumn, 'and how ill I feel in it. The whole place volleys and thunders with traffic. I can't sleep or work . . . The telephone bell is continually ringing, my father scampering up and down stairs, Gaspard [the dog] barking, the gardener rolling the gravel under the window and all the time the traffic. Another week of this will drive me mad.'[15]

It was nonetheless there that Evelyn asked his fiancée to spend five days over Christmas, after which Shevelyn wrote to Kate thanking her 'for the happiest Christmas I have ever had. I loved being at Hampstead & wish I were with you still. I have never thanked you properly for the letter you wrote me, when I got engaged to Evelyn. It was so much the nicest letter I have ever had. Somehow, I thought that you wouldn't be pleased, because Evelyn is such an exceptional person, and I know how fond you are of him. I hope I shall be able to make him happy. I think when one loves someone, as much as I love Evelyn, one is terrified of disappointing them.'[16]

Shevelyn was to go to Underhill many times after that, giving her ample opportunity to observe the Waugh household. When talking to her, Alec Waugh referred to Underhill as 'the little house', hinting that she might find it rather humble compared to what she was used to, however it struck her as far more of a home than the various places in which she had grown up. She was occasionally taken aback by the tensions between the two brothers and also by Evelyn's ill-concealed aversion to his father's sentimentality. But overall she found the Waugh parents far easier to get along with than her own mother, of whom she had recently observed that 'unless you agree with her every word she is furious. The great thing is to say "quite" to every remark she makes.'[17]

Lady Burghclere – known unaffectionately as 'the Baroness' by her daughter's friends – had already made it plain that she was not remotely in favour of her daughter marrying an 'impoverished, suburban trainee carpenter', as Evelyn's grandson later put it.[18] How much snobbery there

---

* In his obituary of Evelyn Gardner in the *Independent*, Davie wrote that the casual nature of the proposal 'gave Evelyn Gardner the impression, she explained later, that Waugh was not wholly committed to the marriage'. However the notes of his interview with her say nothing about Waugh's implied lack of commitment, but rather: 'Implication seemed to be that absolute loyalty not required of her, she thought.' (Michael Davie interview with Evelyn Gardner, 24 February 1973; AWA.)

was on her part and how much subsequent embroidery by Evelyn is any-one's guess, although years later he told Nancy Mitford that 'it never occurred to me to think I wasn't a gentleman until Lady Burghclere pointed it out'.[19] One thing was made perfectly clear from the start: she was never going to give her consent to their marriage while Evelyn was without a job. However, when he subsequently sought one at the BBC, she used her connections (her one remaining son-in-law Geoffrey Fry wrote to Evelyn's interviewer, Lance Sieveking, who happened to be a friend of his*) to make sure he did not get it.[20]

Lady Burghclere meanwhile began gathering all the evidence she could of Evelyn's unsuitability, even visiting Cruttwell at Oxford to grill him about Evelyn's career there. As Shevelyn reported, the embittered don was 'palpitating with perverse vices' and assured Lady Burghclere that Evelyn drank copious amounts of vodka and absinthe, went about with disrep-utable people, lived off his parents, ill-treated his father, had no moral backbone or character, would soon cease to love Shevelyn and would drag her 'down into the abysmal depths of Sodom and Gomorrah'.[21]

After listening to this lurid list Lady Burghclere made a last desperate attempt to reclaim her daughter, asking her to stay for a fortnight in early May with the inducement of publicly announcing the engagement. It had been eighteen months since Shevelyn last spent the night under her mother's roof, however she was worried about money and anxious not to lose her mother's support, so accepted. On arrival she was confronted with Cruttwell's charge sheet and an ultimatum that the marriage could not possibly take place for two years. Evelyn was then summoned and, according to Pansy's account, 'behaved with admirable firmness, threat-ening to get married in a week', whereupon Lady Burghclere tearfully collapsed and agreed to consent to a wedding providing Evelyn found a job first.[22] 'Victory to the Evelyns!' declared Shevelyn.[23]

* * *

Lady Burghclere's demand that Evelyn get a job was not surprising, al-though hindsight renders it slightly absurd, and Pansy and her fiancé

---

* Lance Sieveking had met Evelyn a few times at parties and liked him and he later recalled going 'conscientiously through the motions for half an hour, discussing and assessing his abilities and ending up with a voice test. I was really sorry to turn him down.'

Henry Lamb, who had recently painted Evelyn's portrait (since lost) with pipe in one hand, pen in the other, hovering over the manuscript of *Decline and Fall*, were among those who felt that way at the time, accusing her of 'gross materialism' and predicting that Evelyn was 'obviously going to be a successful author in a few years' time', that the couple could scrape along till then, and that in the meantime 'a job' would only waste his energies.[24] As a writer herself, Lady Burghclere cannot have been blind to his potential, having received an advance copy of *Rossetti* (inscribed 'with kind regards' as opposed to 'with love') in April, and then presumably seen the favourable reviews, most prominently in *The Observer*, where J. C. Squire paid tribute to Evelyn's 'terse elegance and unobtrusive wit', and the *Nation & Athenaeum*, which called it 'both lively and reliable'. Almost equal admiration was elicited a month later by Evelyn's sublime rebuke to *The Times Literary Supplement* for referring to him throughout its far less enthusiastic notice as 'Miss Waugh'. 'My Christian name, I know is occasionally regarded by people of limited social experience as belonging exclusively to one or other sex,' Evelyn wrote; 'but it is unnecessary to go further into my book than the paragraph charitably placed inside the wrapper for the guidance of unleisured critics, to find my name with its correct prefix of "Mr". Surely some such investigation might in merest courtesy have been taken before your reviewer tumbled into print with phrases such as "a Miss of the sixties".'[25] Rebecca West considered this 'a model of how one might behave to that swollen-headed parish magazine' and expressed the hope that 'you will go on being so much more intelligent and amusing than most people in such a useful form'.[26] What Lady Burghclere made of all this is not recorded.

Unbeknown to her, meanwhile, throughout the spring of 1928, Evelyn had also been working hard on *Decline and Fall*, the novel that would make his name. He had first mentioned it to Duckworth's the previous September, and read the first 10,000 words – which were scarcely altered later – to Anthony Powell towards the end of that year. Powell recalled thinking it 'extremely funny', although when he subsequently asked about the novel's progress Evelyn replied disconcertingly, 'I've burnt it.'[27]

Dudley Carew then remembered being regaled with 'the first fifty pages or so' in January 1928 at Underhill, with Evelyn sitting in the chair from which Arthur used to declaim after dinner. 'A happiness, a hilarity sustained him that night, and I was back giving him my unstinted admiration as I did at Lancing. It was marvellously funny and he knew that it was. As was his habit in those old, innocent days, he roared with laughter at his own comic invention and both of us at times were in hysterics.'[28]

Buoyed by the prospect of marriage and the growing realisation that he was finally creating something that would do justice to his extraordinary talent as a writer, Evelyn was probably as happy that spring as he had ever been, and his exuberance comes through clearly in the book. A stint writing at The Bell at Aston Clinton was followed by several weeks in March and April in Dorset at the Barley Mow pub in Colehill, two miles from where Shevelyn and Pansy were lodging in a boarding house at Wimborne, also writing novels – Pansy's would be published a month after *Decline and Fall* as *The Old Expedient*. Henry Lamb had rented a house at Poole, seven miles away on the coast, in which to paint while he waited for his divorce from his first wife to come through.

Shevelyn was struggling with her own novel – which concerned 'the thoughts of a man and a girl during twelve hours [going] back through their lives, looking at the same situations from different points of view'[29] – but was proudly delighted with Evelyn's. 'It is really screamingly funny and I think there is a good chance of its being a success, if not a bestseller,' she told a friend, 'but I don't think our mothers will approve of it, certainly mine won't!'[30] During their stay in Dorset Pansy thought Shevelyn seemed 'really much better than I have seen her in a long time'. 'I don't think she is wildly in love with E. W.,' she continued, 'but I doubt if she is capable of sustained passion. However she is very fond of him & looks up to his brains & respects his strength of character. At any rate she will not be able to despise him when the first raptures are past which would have inevitably happened with Barry & his like. She has to work hard for him which is the best thing for her.'[31]

In mid-May they all moved back to London, Evelyn initially to Underhill and the girls to new lodgings at 7 Upper Montagu Street, kept by a charming if rather slatternly Irishwoman. 'I suppose this will be the last abode that Evelyn and I will share together,' wrote Pansy:

It has been a strange little partnership and I am afraid I have been no help to her in her struggles. Perhaps she never does struggle, only drifts with the tide & that is why she gets into such difficulties. Her marriage still seems remote & it is hard to imagine how much she cares for the other Evelyn.

Not enough to follow him barefoot through the world, certainly, but on the other hand she is happier with him & since their engagement than she has been for a long time. The absence of Mary & the necessity to share & intrigue with her is also a great relief ... Now the only issue is whether they are to raise a little money & elope or wait until the maternal sanction wafts them to St Margaret's Westminster. Evelyn Waugh is for the former course, EG for the latter. That's why I don't consider her passion for him can be illimitable, or has she prematurely exhausted her capacity for passion? I wonder if the emotions can be worn out from too much use? I don't see why not.[32]

Two weeks later Evelyn recorded in his diary: 'Evelyn and I were married at St. Paul's [*sic*]* Portman Square, at 12 o'clock. A woman was typewriting on the altar. Harold best man. Robert Byron gave away the bride, Alec and Pansy the witnesses. Evelyn wore a new black and yellow jumper suit with scarf. Went to the 500 Club and drank champagne cocktails under the suspicious eyes of Winifred Mackintosh and Prince George of Russia. From there to luncheon at Boulestin. Very good luncheon. Then to Paddington and by train to Oxford and taxi to Beckley.'[33]

---

* More correctly St Paul (no 's) Portman Square, built in 1779 as a proprietary chapel for the Portman Estate.

A Common Experience, I'm Told

Like so much in Evelyn's diaries, his account of the wedding service was a mix of fact and fantasy. According to Shevelyn, no one was typing on the altar, although she did remember the sound of a typewriter coming from the vestry as they went in and being a little disconcerted by the mustachioed clergyman who married them, with his Cockney accent and heavy black boots.[1] Harold Acton recalled her being so overcome by the whole occasion that she could barely bring herself to say the words 'I do'.[2] Her jitters beforehand had been sufficiently advertised for Robert Byron to complain to his mother of having 'to *fetch* Evelyn Gardner to the church and I know she won't come'.[3] However after honeymooning at Beckley, of all places, where Evelyn and Alastair had shared their caravan, she declared herself happy with married life. The Waugh parents were holidaying in France at the time of the wedding but were telegraphed on the day and took the news in their stride. 'Arthur well again, Evelyns married,' Kate noted nonchalantly in her diary.[4] Lady Burghclere, though, was furious, 'quite inexpressibly pained', she told Evelyn after Geoffrey Fry[5] eventually broke it to her in mid-July, although years later Nancy Mitford could clearly recall her saying how pleased she was that her daughter should marry into 'such a good literary family'.[6] In any event, she immediately announced it in *The Times* 'to avoid scandal and misconstruction', as she charmingly told Shevelyn.[7]

Inconveniently for Evelyn's writing career, meanwhile, Lady Burghclere's sister was married to Sir George Duckworth, the brother of Evelyn's publisher Gerald Duckworth,* who had thus known all about Lady

---

* The Duckworth brothers were also, incidentally, the elder half-brothers of Virginia Woolf, who later accused them of having molested her during her childhood and adolescence.

Burghclere's disapproval of her prospective son-in-law. When Evelyn had submitted the manuscript of *Decline and Fall* in May, 'Uncle Gerald'[8] (as Evelyn dubbed him) personally intervened to demand the omission of many of the more indelicate scenes, whereupon Evelyn promptly took it down the street to Chapman & Hall, figuring that with his father abroad it would be easier for them to accept it, which they did, albeit ultimately with alterations only slightly less extensive than those that had been insisted on by Duckworth's. Soon after his return from honeymoon Evelyn set about designing the wrapper and going through the proofs and noted testily in his diary that 'Chapman's <u>not</u> an easy firm to deal with'.[9] At that point he and his new wife were briefly occupying dingy rooms at 25 Robert Adam Street, just off Baker Street, which Evelyn had taken shortly before their wedding to enable them to marry at the nearby church of St Paul. For the rest of the summer they lived at Underhill, before renting a flat in September on a handsome if then slightly dilapidated Georgian square in Islington.

The move to 17a Canonbury Square, their first proper marital home, coincided with the publication of *Decline and Fall*, an event that very quickly and profoundly changed Evelyn's life. The first review to appear, in *The Observer*, pronounced it 'richly and roaringly funny' and praised the author's 'exquisite ingenuousness of manner combined with a searching ingenuity of method; he is a critic of life, whose weapon is the joke disguised as a simple statement; he is an important addition to the ranks of those dear and necessary creatures – the writers who can make us laugh'.[10] The verdict that really mattered, however, came two weeks later, when England's grandest and highest-paid literary journalist Arnold Bennett, whose weekly column in the *Evening Standard* was splashed along the sides of London omnibuses, hailed the arrival of 'a genuinely new humorist' and 'an uncompromisingly and brilliant malicious satire, which in my opinion comes near to being quite first-rate'.[11]

Besides the universal acclaim in the press, Evelyn was congratulated equally effusively by his new friend Rebecca West, for whom it was 'one of the few funny books that have really made me laugh', and perhaps more surprisingly by the left-leaning Naomi Mitchison, who wrote to tell him she thought it 'perfectly plumb'. 'The really odd thing about it is the unity; you've kept it up all the time, so that at the end one is laughing in the same tone (and with the same violence) as at the beginning. And it's so ridiculously intelligent. I adore funny books, but when one looks for them one never finds anything but P. G. Wodehouse, and after all one is a high-brow.'[12] John Betjeman, whom Evelyn had befriended while both were schoolmasters, later recalled that to many of Evelyn's friends *Decline and Fall* seemed 'so rockingly funny, there could never be anything quite so funny again'.[13]

Gratifying as all this was, Evelyn was embarrassed a month later when J. B. Priestley and Cyril Connolly both drew attention to the enormous gulf in quality between his brilliant novel and Harold Acton's aptly named *Humdrum*, which had come out shortly after. Evelyn had dedicated *Decline and Fall* to Acton 'in homage and affection', however Priestley was adamant that 'Mr Waugh owes no homage to Mr Acton as a novelist, for the latter's story is a poor thing, showing us nothing but a vast social superiority to everybody and everything. I have always heard that Mr Acton is one of our brightest young wits, but "Humdrum" seems to me to be really tedious. Perhaps his title was too much for him.'[14] Connolly was scarcely less damning, observing that whereas *Humdrum* 'falls rather flat', *Decline and Fall* 'seems to possess every virtue which it lacks'.[15]*

The friendship between Evelyn and Acton thus entered a decidedly awkward phase, with Evelyn's star now clearly in the ascendant and Acton's reputation equally obviously in decline, a state of affairs to which the former mentor evidently found it hard to adjust. 'I don't know what to say to Harold,' Evelyn confided to a mutual Oxford friend around that time. 'If I tell him that I am going to lunch at the Ritz, he says "Of course you're a famous author but you can't expect a nonentity like me to join you there." If I suggest that we should go to a pub, he says, "My dear, what affectation – a popular novelist going to a pub."'[16]

Others were upset by *Decline and Fall* for different reasons. Eddie Gathorne-Hardy and Paddy Brodie (the latter a notably wild and drunken man about town who once mistook the bar at the Ritz for a *pissoir*)[17] had flown into 'a furious rage',[18] so Acton told Evelyn, after their names were borrowed for the extravagantly camp character Martin Gaythorn-Brodie – it was changed to the Hon. Miles Malpractice in the second edition in November for fear of libel. Similarly, Robert Byron wrote to say how 'very

---

* While praising *Decline and Fall* in a letter to Arthur Waugh, Charles Scott Moncrieff also referred to *Humdrum*: 'It seems that only a very rich young man can afford to write as badly as this.' (25 October 1928; AWA.)

cross'[19] he was about the character of Kevin Saunderson (subsequently renamed Lord Parakeet), who arrives late and drunk to Mrs Beste-Chetwynde's weekend party and walks around 'birdlike and gay, pointing his thin white nose and making rude little jokes at everyone in turn in a shrill, emasculate voice'.[20] This was too obviously Gavin Henderson, an equally mincing friend of Byron and Brian Howard's, whom Evelyn confided to his diary he found 'most trying'.[21] Though briefly married, Henderson was, as one contemporary put it, 'a roaring pansy', and after succeeding his grandfather as the 2nd Lord Faringdon famously began a speech in the Upper House, 'My dears . . .'[22] Just as recognisable was Cecil Beaton, whom Evelyn had bullied so mercilessly as a schoolboy in Hampstead and who now found himself caricatured as the photographer David Lennox who accompanies Gaythorn-Brodie/Malpractice to King's Thursday: 'They emerged with little shrieks from an Edwardian brougham and made straight for the nearest looking-glass.'[23]

Evelyn shrugged off the offence his book caused. 'I am threatened with four civil actions and a horse whipping,' he wrote cheerfully to his publisher.[24] In any case the shedding of uncongenial acquaintances was offset by the new friendships he was beginning to make through his marriage and the more strategic contacts he had begun to cultivate following his establishment as the newest of London's literary lions, entertaining Arnold Bennett to dinner one night at Canonbury Square, and the next day having Cyril Connolly to lunch, an occasion that left Connolly with a lasting memory of the two Evelyns as 'this fantastic thing of the happily married young couple whom success had just touched with its wand'.[25]

Connolly was equally struck by their 'very small spick and span bandbox of a house', filled with odd bits and pieces lent by friends or bought from local junk shops and altered by Evelyn or made by a local carpenter. Portraits of each of them by Henry Lamb hung in the tiny dining room. When Harold Acton visited he found Evelyn crouched on the floor, sticking postage stamps onto a coal scuttle then applying a coat of varnish, 'endowing it with a patina of Sir Joshua Reynolds'. 'The atmosphere was that of a sparkling nursery,' recalled Acton. 'One hoped to see cradles full of little Evelyns in the near future, baby fauns blowing through reeds, falling off rocking-horses, pulling each other's pointed ears and piddling on the rug.'[26] But that was not to be.

Throughout that autumn and winter, Shevelyn was plagued by

ill-health. According to her written account of their marriage, she suffered severe period pains for which she underwent an operation – without which, her surgeon then discovered, she would never have been able to have children, although she recalled that she and Evelyn had no immediate plans in that regard, having 'decided to wait until we were better off'.[27] Sometime after that, in early October, Evelyn came home one day to find her feverish – 'a touch of influenza', he noted nonchalantly in his diary;[28] the next day she became delirious as her temperature soared to 104. A few days later her mottled face led their doctor ('a cross between a butcher and vet in appearance', Evelyn recorded)[29] to diagnose German measles. Her sister Alathea and brother-in-law Geoffrey Fry suggested she go and convalesce at their house at Oare in Wiltshire; but it was two weeks before she was strong enough to travel down there.

They stayed at Oare for the best part of a fortnight while she recuperated and Evelyn got on with the various newspaper assignments organised by A.D. Peters, the then up-and-coming literary agent Alec had introduced him to in order to capitalise on the success of *Decline and Fall*. 'Please fix up anything that will earn me anything,' Evelyn wrote to Peters after he was taken on, 'even cricket criticism or mothers' welfare notes.'[30] Several were written from the standpoint of the nation's youth but providing he was well paid, he was happy to write about anything, so when the *Evening Standard* misunderstood his proposal to write about 'The Manners of the Younger Generation' and asked for a piece on 'The Mothers of the Younger Generation', he promptly dashed off 1,000 words on mothers instead. In June the next year he was similarly unhesitant when asked for a piece by *The Birth Control Review* of New York.

A handsome country house spectacularly situated beneath the Downs, Oare is nonetheless described by Pevsner as 'townish' and Evelyn found there 'an epicene preciosity or nicety about everything that goes better with cigarettes and London clothes than my tweeds and pipe'.[31] Originally Georgian and more or less square, the house had recently been enlarged and modernised by Clough Williams-Ellis, whose scheme had been written up in *Country Life* in March 1928 while Evelyn was still working on *Decline and Fall*. As Duncan McLaren suggests, the featured revamp may conceivably have prompted Margot Beste-Chetwynde's request to her architect Professor Silenus to replace her Tudor country house King's Thursday with 'something clean and square'. Equally, Alathea Fry, who struck Evelyn as 'extraordinarily ingenuous with a fluttery eagerness', may have contributed something to the creation of Margot herself, who arrives at the Llanabba sports 'like the first breath of spring in the Champs Élysées'. Like Margot and Paul Pennyfeather, Alathea was ten years older than Evelyn, and she had been photographed by Curtis Moffat in mannered poses not entirely dissimilar to the photographs taken by David Lennox of the back of Margot's head and the reflection of her hands in a bowl of ink.[32]

Alathea was arguably the most beautiful of all the Gardner sisters, although her looks were apparently wasted on her husband Geoffrey, who was far more interested in the various young men he had to stay at Oare, one of whom Evelyn described on the first weekend of their stay: 'Young Mr. Wayman [an accountant] appeared first in riding clothes and rode, then in white flannels and played tennis, then in tweeds and went out shooting – "having a smack at the longtails" as someone described it to Geoffrey – then in evening clothes and talked about architecture.'[33] Oblivious of Geoffrey's previous deviousness over the BBC job, Evelyn seemed equally unaware that he and Shevelyn were still under the scrutiny of this outwardly graceful and witty yet essentially rather cruel and calculating man. At the end of November, when Shevelyn was well enough, the Evelyns threw a house-warming cocktail party at Canonbury Square, cramming their flat full of guests cheerfully celebrating what most assumed to be the start of a long and happy marriage. However Mary Pakenham later recalled that as she left with Geoffrey, who gave her a lift home, he remarked: 'And when they buried her the little town had never seen a merrier funeral'[34] – presumably an intimation of his forebodings about Shevelyn's health and/or their marriage, neither of which was set to prosper over the course of the next year.

After spending Christmas in Wiltshire with Henry and Pansy Lamb, whose wedding they had gone to shortly after their own, in February 1929 the Evelyns set off for a cruise around the Mediterranean, a trip conceived as a kind of belated honeymoon and an opportunity for Shevelyn to recuperate properly while Evelyn earnt some money by writing articles and a book. *The Daily Express* marvelled that *Decline and Fall* had been so successful that the young author was able to afford this luxurious expedition out of his royalties,[35] whereas in fact Evelyn's enterprising new agent had managed to obtain free passages in return for favourable publicity.

Evelyn's eventual travel book, published in 1930 as *Labels*, accordingly devoted several pages to extolling the *Stella Polaris*'s 'quite remarkable' comfort, 'almost glacial cleanliness' and 'Jeeves-like standard of courtesy and efficiency'.[36]

But what had looked set to be a delightful adventure quickly became a nightmare for Shevelyn, who began to feel feverish as soon as they reached Paris. A dose of crème de menthe (unhelpfully suggested by a friend of Evelyn's) did no good at all and by the time they were in the train heading south she was 'beginning to feel very ill indeed', she later recalled.[37] In *Labels*, Evelyn disguised himself and his wife as 'Geoffrey and Juliet', the author's intermittent travelling companions, 'a rather sweet-looking young English couple – presumably, from the endearments of their conversation, and marked solicitude for each other's comfort, on their honeymoon, or at any rate recently married. The young man was small and pleasantly dressed and wore a slight, curly moustache [Evelyn had recently grown one in line with his original idea to call his travel book 'Quest of a Moustache'];[38] he was reading a particularly good detective story with apparent intelligence. His wife was huddled in a fur coat in the corner, clearly far from well . . . Every quarter of an hour or so they said to each other, "Are you quite sure you're alright darling?" And replied, "Perfectly, really I am. Are *you* my precious?" But Juliet was far from being all right.'[39]

As Shevelyn's condition worsened they eventually moved to a more comfortable carriage – though Evelyn fretted about the expense – and on arrival at Monte Carlo she 'trudged miserably beside Evelyn through falling snow from hotel to hotel until we found one that would take us in'. Two days later, an English doctor consented to her going aboard the *Stella Polaris* providing she remained in her bunk, however as soon as the ship slipped out of port she began to cough up blood. By now suffering from double pneumonia and pleurisy (as it was later diagnosed) and unable to sleep because of her cough, it was 'a horrible voyage', she recalled, 'imprisoned in that little cabin with its closed port-hole and dark walls at which I looked for so long'. At Haifa they hired a nurse, 'a pallid, skinny Israeli who cannot have had much training for all she did was to insist on scraping my tongue with a spoon'. When they reached Port Said she was taken ashore by stretcher 'looking distressingly like a corpse',[40] and rushed to the British Hospital.

At first it was feared that she might not survive and Evelyn sent a postcard to Pansy Lamb saying that by the time she got it, Shevelyn would probably be dead.[41] She did eventually pull through, however, and after ten days she was 'sitting up in bed knitting and reading and falling deeply in love with her doctor', Evelyn reported.[42]

Evelyn visited the hospital every day to read aloud from P. G. Wodehouse but otherwise wrote articles to help defray their escalating expenses, pondered a new novel and disconsolately loitered about the 'intolerably dull'[43] Port Said: 'This is not the town I should have chosen for a month's visit,' he wrote to Henry Yorke. 'There is one expensive hotel with a jazz band and bugs, innumerable bars where the P & O stewards may be seen getting mildly drunk on Guinness at 2/6 bottle, two brothels, one European one Arab ... and this [Union] club where the shipping office clerks attempt to create an Ethel M. Dell garrison life.'[44] Occasionally he was entertained by the consul and his 'harlot' wife, who led the women guests away after dinner saying, 'Goodbye darling men. Keep your naughtiest stories for us.' On another evening at a dance, Evelyn reported, 'she opened her mouth and invited me to throw sugar into it'.[45]

Alastair Graham briefly visited from Athens and took Evelyn to Cairo for some 'varied and vigorous nightlife'; he also gave them £50 so they could 'struggle along for another week or two'.[46] Of the Cairo trip Shevelyn recalled that she 'didn't grudge Evelyn the invitation or its acceptance' but also remarked: 'I don't think he would have done that if he'd really loved me, would he?'[47]*

At the end of March they travelled south to the Pyramids and a two-week stay at the Mena House Hotel, 'very enormous & hideously expensive but sunny & I think a good place for Evelyn's recuperation', Evelyn told Harold Acton. It was a chance too to see the Tutankhamen discoveries, 'real works of art – of exquisite grace,' Evelyn reported, 'just as fine as anything which has survived of Athenian Art'.[48]

From there they headed to Malta to rejoin the *Stella Polaris*, Shevelyn by now well enough to organise the ship's fancy-dress ball, while Evelyn, unlikely as it sounds, joined the onboard Sports Committee, 'which is

---

* The demonic voices who accuse Pinfold of being 'queer' in *The Ordeal of Gilbert Pinfold* (1957) later demand: 'I want the truth, Pinfold. *What were you doing* in Egypt in 1929?' If this hints at an illicit dalliance with his former lover, the voices' naming of the Mena House Hotel where Evelyn stayed with his wife seems to suggest otherwise.

very serious indeed'.[49] At Athens they saw Alastair Graham and Mark Ogilvie-Grant, and at Constantinople they joined the Sitwells for 'a brief & rather uneasy luncheon party at the Embassy'.[50]

Approaching Venice in early May, Evelyn told Harold Acton that it was at last turning into a delightful voyage. 'Evelyn is growing stronger every day. There is plenty of sun and a calm sea and a very good background of ludicrous fellow travellers to amuse us in between ports. In the Bosporus a Greek tried to seduce first Evelyn & then me & then the bar-steward. Evelyn & I were flattered & delighted but the bar steward furious & the Greek had to leave the ship.'[51] As they headed for home (via Barcelona – where Evelyn was dazzled by the buildings of Gaudí – and Lisbon), he reported that they were thinking of 'taking a minute house & settling somewhere in the country for the summer', partly on account of being so 'hideously' broke but also so that he could get on with writing his new novel, *Vile Bodies*.[52]

Although she sequestered herself in the country in later life, Shevelyn cared little for rural seclusion at that time and so was perhaps never especially keen on that idea. The voyage had evidently also gone on too long as far as she was concerned, and towards the end she told a friend that 'we are getting a little fed-up and shall be glad to get home'.[53] In *Labels*, written after the devastating events of the coming summer, Evelyn described being woken several times in the night by the ship's foghorn as they neared Harwich, 'a very dismal sound, premonitory, perhaps, of coming trouble, for Fortune is the least capricious of deities, and arranges things on the just and rigid system that no one shall be happy for very long'.[54]

When they reached London at the end of May Evelyn's publisher at Duckworth's, Tom Balston, confided to Anthony Powell that he thought the Waughs' marriage seemed strained, although Shevelyn declared herself 'frightfully well – really much better than before I caught that beastly pneumonia'.[55] Having already missed so many parties in the three months they were away, she was loath to go and sequester herself in the country just as the most vibrant London season since the war was reaching its peak.

Thus, as Evelyn soon reported to Henry Yorke, they came to a fateful arrangement whereby she went to live at Canonbury Square, accompanied by her old friend Nancy Mitford, while he went off to write his book in a pub.[56] In the meantime they stayed a few days at Underhill and on

5 June Kate Waugh noted innocently in her diary: 'Evelyns lunched with J Heygate.'

John Heygate had been a friend of both Evelyns since the previous autumn, introduced coincidentally by the same Bobbie Roberts who had brought the Evelyns together at the Ranee's party. For a time they made 'such a happy trio', Heygate later recalled. The slightly louche son of an uncompromisingly conventional Eton housemaster, and heir via his equally strait-laced uncle to an Irish baronetcy and some 5,000 acres in County Londonderry, Heygate also descended through his mother from the diarist John Evelyn, and had very nearly been named Evelyn himself after his distinguished ancestor, which, as his friend Anthony Powell drily remarked would have added an extra layer of confusion to future events.[57]

Tall, reasonably good-looking, with 'an easy rather lounging carriage', as Powell described it, he was reputed to be 'agreeably successful with women', albeit 'well short of being anything like a professional woman-izer'.[58] He used to say that his chief misfortune was that stupid people thought him intelligent and intelligent people thought him stupid. After Oxford he had gone to Heidelberg to learn German and formed a lasting romantic attachment to that country, but after failing to get into the Diplomatic Service he had suffered a breakdown, possibly exacerbated by his heavy drinking, and began hallucinating that everyone around him in a London club was talking German. By the time he met the Evelyns his troubles were reasonably well hidden – although they would re-emerge later – and he was working as an assistant news editor at the BBC. Evelyn would later describe Heygate as 'radically contemptible', however according to Powell he 'was very much taken' with him when he first got to know him.[59] Shevelyn maintained that she had initially thought Heygate 'a nice young man but nothing more'.[60]

While Evelyn took himself off to the Abingdon Arms to write, Heygate was among those entrusted with chaperoning Shevelyn and Nancy Mitford, who recalled a succession of costume balls so endless that 'we hardly ever saw the light of day, except at dawn'.[61] The summer of 1929 was a particularly hectic one for the well-connected partygoers known as the Bright Young People who were about to be definitively satirised in Evelyn's new novel:

'Oh Nina, *what a lot of parties*' (... Masked parties, Savage parties, Victorian parties, Greek parties, Wild West parties, Russian parties, Circus parties, parties where one had to dress as somebody else, almost naked parties in St John's Wood, parties in flats and studios and houses and ships and hotels and night clubs, in windmills and swimming-baths, tea parties at school where one ate muffins and meringues and tinned crab, parties at Oxford where one drank brown sherry and smoked Turkish cigarettes, dull dances in London and comic dances in Scotland and disgusting dances in Paris – all that succession and repetition of massed humanity... Those vile bodies...)

For a time Evelyn's writing regime worked well, and on 12 June 'Dragoman' (his friend Tom Driberg) reported in the *Daily Express* that he had telegrammed his wife: 'Novel started splendidly. All characters horribly seasick.'[62] By 20 June Evelyn reckoned he had written 25,000 words in ten days. 'It is rather like P. G. Wodehouse all about bright young people,' he told Henry Yorke. With Evelyn 'chained hand and foot' to his novel, Shevelyn and Heygate came to Beckley to see him and they all went for lunch at the Trout Inn just north of Oxford with Heygate's girlfriend Eleanor Watts, a twenty-year-old undergraduate at the university. Shortly afterwards Heygate proposed to Eleanor but she was unsure, and when they subsequently went to a party in London – she later recalled that it had been held by Bobbie Roberts, a curiously catalytic figure in the whole Shevelyn story – Heygate got so drunk that Eleanor left without him. Shevelyn was also there and ended up going home with Heygate; they were found together at his basement flat in Cornwall Gardens the next morning by a manservant.[63] Shevelyn later recalled that the realisation that she was 'very seriously in love' with Heygate came as an 'emotional thunderbolt'.[64]

Oblivious of all this and happy with the progress of his novel, Evelyn told Henry Yorke that he was toying with the idea of coming up to London for Bryan and Diana Guinness's 1860s party on 25 June 'if I thought there would be anyone who wouldn't be too much like the characters in my new book'.[65] He did not go in the end, but afterwards the indubitably safe Harold Acton thoughtfully reassured him that he had 'danced blissfully' with Shevelyn. Later that evening, however, Heygate had taken Shevelyn and Nancy Mitford on to another party aboard the schooner

Friendship, moored off Charing Cross pier, where *The Tatler* inadvertently photographed them lounging on deck in 'a very amiable position', as Heygate later described it.[66] There was another couple in the foreground yet Heygate was clearly recognisable and Shevelyn, with her back to the camera, could also be identified from the costume in which she had been photographed by *Sketch* at the Guinnesses' party.[67]

The next evening, Thursday, 26 June, Shevelyn and Heygate were both among the guests at a small dinner party held by Tom Balston when Heygate, having been up till dawn the previous night, fell asleep between courses. The day after that they went to Anthony Powell and Constant Lambert's cocktail party at Tavistock Square. On that occasion Evelyn did travel up from Beckley, however Powell remembered that he and his wife arrived separately, neither of them seemed to enjoy themselves and they left early, together, after what appeared to be a brief altercation between Shevelyn and Heygate. 'This was the first public occasion when there was a sense of something being wrong between the Waughs,' wrote Powell. 'Quite how wrong I did not even then take in.'

The next day the two Evelyns went to stay at Heygate's parents' house on the Solent. Powell was again a witness and remembered 'no special tensions throughout the visit',[68] although when they went to tea at Beaulieu Elizabeth Montagu observed that 'Waugh seemed bored and monosyllabic, whilst his wife and Heygate tried rather too hard to compensate.'[69]

Shortly after this, on 13 July, Powell and Heygate set off on a motoring trip to Germany and according to Powell spoke little about 'the embroilment in which Heygate now undoubtedly found himself'. (Nor, incidentally, did they talk much about the rise of Hitler, even though Heygate later admitted that on a previous trip to Bavaria he had carried with him a letter that began: 'Dear Hitler, this is to introduce John Heygate, a young Englishman interested in your movement.')[70] After two weeks they reached Munich, where various urgent cables awaited them: 'Instruct Heygate return immediately Waugh.'[71]

The events leading up to this stern missive had begun with the appearance of the incriminating photograph in the 3 July issue of *The Tatler*, which threw Shevelyn into a desperate quandary, knowing that many of their friends would have seen it. Her sister Mary begged her to say nothing, however her flatmate Nancy Mitford advised her to tell Evelyn that she loved him and to say that her attitude in the photograph was not what it appeared. 'But I *don't* love him,' said Shevelyn, explaining that she had never loved her husband and that she had only married him to escape the tyranny of her mother.[72]

By now anxious to come clean, she wrote a letter to Evelyn (which he received on about 9 July and promptly destroyed) saying she was in love with Heygate, and when Evelyn returned to London three days later she confessed that she had already slept with him. Evelyn's subsequent divorce petition stated: 'My wife and I had a long talk upon the subject, and I agreed to forgive her if she would give up Heygate. This she promised to do.'[73]

There followed a miserable fortnight during which Shevelyn told Alec Waugh that Evelyn was drinking far too much and making himself ill, and then accusing her of trying to poison him. When Alec remarked that they had always seemed so happy together she replied: 'Yes I suppose I was,' then after a pause, 'but never as happy as I've been with my sisters,' which struck Alec as a peculiar thing for a wife to say about a husband.[74]

They were photographed looking distinctly gloomy at Vyvyan Holland's 'Tropical' party on the *Friendship* – one caption commenting that the author of *Decline and Fall* appeared 'somewhat scared even though there were no fierce Zulus on board'[75] – and at Henry Yorke's wedding on 25 July the groom's aunt, who had presumably got wind of Shevelyn's predicament, wryly noted her 'outward mood of butter not melting in her mouth'.[76]

The next day Evelyn and Eleanor Watts took the train to Crewe to stay for a few days at Haslington Hall, her family home in Cheshire. Shevelyn was supposed to have gone too but, as Heygate later recalled, 'she changed her mind and returned to me'.[77] This is probably the point at which Evelyn realised once and for all that the reconciliation was not going to work so sent the famous cable summoning Heygate from Germany.

At Haslington, Evelyn and Eleanor sat around miserably drinking Black Velvets, Eleanor by now regretting having turned Heygate down and Evelyn so distraught that he suggested a suicide pact in the rhododendrons. Eleanor later told Selina Hastings that she suspected Evelyn was not so much madly in love with Shevelyn as flattered that such an attractive woman had been prepared to marry him.* She urged him to put her out of his mind, to which he replied, 'I can't, I can't.'[78]

Shevelyn's desertion could hardly have come at a worse time as far as Evelyn's work was concerned, with *Vile Bodies* barely half written and *Labels* not even started although he had promised to deliver it to Duckworth's by the end of July. 'The last few weeks have been a nightmare of very terrible suffering,' Evelyn wrote to his publisher, 'which, if I could explain, you would understand. You shall have the book, unless I go off my head, as soon as I can begin to rearrange my thoughts. At present I can do <u>nothing</u> of any kind.'[79] A few days later he asked Balston to omit the dedication to his wife in all subsequent editions of *Rossetti*.

Evelyn returned home to an empty flat on 1 August and the next day received a letter from Shevelyn saying that she was living with Heygate, at which point he decided to file for a divorce and asked Alec to tell their parents. 'It's going to be a great blow to them,' said Alec, to which Evelyn retorted, 'What about me?'[80] Arthur reacted as predicted. 'Your poor, poor mother,' he said when Alec broke the news, 'your poor, poor mother.' Only Kate seemed to think about her wretched son.[81]

A few days later Evelyn wrote to his parents: 'I asked Alec to tell you the sad & to me radically shocking news that Evelyn has gone to live with a man called Heygate. I am accordingly filing a petition for divorce. I am afraid that this will be a blow to you but I assure you not nearly as severe a blow as it is to me . . . My plans are vague about the flat etc. May I come & live with you sometimes?'[82] He added that 'Evelyn's defection was preceded by no kind of quarrel or estrangement. So far as I knew we were both serenely happy. It must be some hereditary tic. Poor Baroness.'[83]

Clearly the marriage had not been as happy for Shevelyn as Evelyn thought. At the time she was heard to complain that her husband was 'bad in bed',[84] and she later told Michael Davie that she suspected Evelyn of being homosexual. It is true that Evelyn had had very limited sexual experience with women, and the opportunities to make up for this during their marriage were doubtless limited by Shevelyn's various illnesses. Nonetheless it seems just as likely that their incompatibility was due

---

* Mary Pakenham's view was that Evelyn had been 'tremendously gratified when this aristocratic, chic, honeypot consented to be his wife, and naturally when she threw him over it was shattering' (see Note by Lady Mary Clive on Evelyn Gardner [1987], copy in AWA).

to a straightforward lack of chemistry as any deficiencies in his sexual technique or orientation. He would have several passionate affairs with women in years to come and went on to have seven (six surviving) children from his second marriage. While he was always frank about his earlier homosexual experiences and did not go out of his way to deny being to some extent bisexual, the weight of evidence points to his having been predominantly heterosexual by the time he married.*

For his own part, Evelyn told Harold Acton that his reason for seeking a divorce was 'simply that I cannot live with anyone who is avowedly in love with someone else . . . I did not know it was possible to be so miserable & live but I am told that this is a common experience.'[85] Acton was glad Evelyn was 'making a gesture of it for Heygate is too contemptible, and he ought to be made to realize how monstrously he has behaved'. However he was so tactless about the possible reasons for Shevelyn's betrayal ('Are you so very male in your sense of possession?'[86]) that Evelyn complained to Henry Yorke that 'homosexual people however kind & intelligent simply don't understand at all what one feels in this kind of case'.[87]

On 6 August, two days after being told of Evelyn's troubles, Arthur and Kate went to meet Lady Burghclere and Geoffrey Fry to see if anything could be done to save the marriage. They all decided that if Evelyn could be persuaded to hold fire with the divorce proceedings, it might be a good idea for Shevelyn to go to Venice with her sister Alathea, 'in order to think it over once more,' as Shevelyn recalled, 'and perhaps on my return it might be possible for Evelyn to take me back'.

While she was away Heygate went to stay at the Watts's beach house at Selsey where, evidently anxious to keep his options open, he again asked Eleanor to marry him in case Shevelyn did change her mind and went back to her husband. Eleanor 'would not hear of it', she later recalled.[88] Heygate then cabled Shevelyn to let her know that he was waiting for her and she promptly returned to London to be with him. Evelyn's divorce petition was duly served on 9 September.

---

* Anthony Powell recalled having been on a train once with Evelyn later in life when a very good-looking young man entered their compartment pushing a tea trolley. After he had gone, Powell asked Evelyn if he preferred men or women, to which Evelyn replied: 'I suppose I must say I prefer women – but when I see a boy like that I get an awful pang!' Selina Hastings to author, February 2016.

Perversion to Rome

In the months following the break-up several of Shevelyn's closest friends switched their allegiance to the man she had thrown over. Pansy Lamb, whose husband Henry told Evelyn how profoundly he admired his 'magnificently patient & generous'[1] response to the 'catastrophe', was herself not vastly impressed by her former flatmate's justification that 'Waugh was too difficult to live up to & that he secretly hated her when he was ill!' or the fact that 'she really seems to enjoy the publicity her conduct entails'.[2] Shevelyn had been staying at the Lambs' Dorset cottage in mid-August when the first lawyer's letter arrived announcing that Evelyn was suing for divorce, prompting her to exclaim, 'Well, you can't call life dull!'[3]

Nancy Mitford had given Shevelyn a dinner party to celebrate their engagement the previous year and she regarded her as her best friend,[4] yet as soon as she became aware of the affair she moved out of the flat at Canonbury Square. Shevelyn later maintained that Nancy left 'not because of her admiration for Evelyn but because Lord or Lady Redesdale insisted',[5] but in any event the two friends never saw each other again and instead Nancy set about developing a lifelong friendship with Evelyn, someone whom she and her sisters did not yet know well but nevertheless idolised as the author of their favourite book, *Decline and Fall*.[6]

Nancy's twelve-year-old sister Jessica later recalled her excitement when 'Evelyn Waugh, a writer feller and one of the main Swinbrook sewers'[7] promised to immortalise her pet sheep Miranda by substituting the word 'sheepish' for 'divine' in his forthcoming *Vile Bodies*, and duly did so with his description of Edward Throbbing's 'perfectly sheepish house in Hertford St'.

Nancy, meanwhile, began meeting Evelyn regularly for lunch at the Ritz, where he teased her for being 'a dangerous red' and advised her on her doomed love affair with the homosexual Hamish Erskine, explaining to her about 'sexual shyness in men',[8] of which he may have had some experience, but also suggesting she 'dress better & catch a better man'. 'Evelyn is always so full of sound common sense', Nancy wrote to Mark Ogilvie-Grant.[9]

For a time, Nancy's nineteen-year-old sister Diana was even more instrumental in mending Evelyn's broken heart. The most beautiful of the Mitfords, a ravishing blue-eyed blonde described by James Lees-Milne as 'the nearest thing to Botticelli's Venus that I have ever seen',[10] Diana had at her disposal several luxurious houses where Evelyn could lick his wounds and catch up with his writing.

As with Nancy, Evelyn had got to know the Guinnesses through Shevelyn, and in July he had written the introduction to their catalogue of works by 'Bruno Hat', the imaginary German artist whom Bryan claimed to have discovered in a shop in Sussex and whose spoof exhibition was held at their house on 23 July, towards the end of the Evelyns' failed reconciliation fortnight. After his return from Cheshire to find Shevelyn had gone for good, Evelyn miserably took refuge at the Guinnesses' house on the Sussex coast. On separate occasions that month and the next he also stayed with them in Ireland at Knockmaroon, just west of Dublin's Phoenix Park, after which he buried himself away at a pub in Devon in a painful attempt to finish *Vile Bodies*. 'It has been infinitely difficult,' he wrote to Henry Yorke in September, 'and is certainly the last time I shall try to make a book about sophisticated people. It all seems to shrivel up & rot internally and I am relying on a sort of cumulative futility for any effect it may have. As soon as I have enough pages covered to call it a book I shall join Bryan & Diana in Paris.'[11]

In early October, after scrawling 'The End Thank God' across the last page, he duly made his way to the large Guinness flat in the 7th arrondissement. Each morning, with Diana by then pregnant with her first child and resting in bed, Evelyn made a start on his Mediterranean travelogue *Labels* while Nancy worked on her first novel, *Highland Fling* – which she subsequently had to alter 'quite a lot as it is so like Evelyn's [*Vile Bodies*] in little ways,' she told Mark Ogilvie-Grant, *'such* a bore'[12] – and Bryan was busy with *Singing Out of Tune*, a portrait of a failed marriage and also, like *Vile Bodies*, an indictment of a way of life. (It is often said that his idea came from the Waughs' marriage, although by the time the book came out in 1933 Bryan and Diana had themselves separated following her affair with Oswald Mosley, and Bryan begged his wife to tell everyone that it was *not* their story.)

Back in London, Evelyn took to arriving at the Guinnesses' house at 10 Buckingham Street (now Buckingham Place) in the morning and staying all day. Diana was fascinated by dazzlingly clever men and equally capable of fascinating them. Having recently struck up a close rapport with Lytton Strachey, she now found herself similarly taken with Evelyn. They would 'laugh all day long', she remembered. 'You couldn't help loving him. He was so funny and so unlike anyone else.'[13]

During her confinement, with Bryan out most days reading for the Bar, Diana became increasingly dependent on Evelyn for her entertainment and in due course he began to fall in love with her. A decade later, in his unfinished novel *Work Suspended*, Evelyn described the novelist-narrator John Plant's growing infatuation with the pregnant heiress Lucy Simmonds, which he later admitted to Diana was 'to some extent a portrait of me in love with you'.[14]

On his usual morning call, John is greeted by Lucy 'lying in bed in a chaos of newspapers, letters and manicure tools':

> Couched as she was, amid quilted bed-jacket and tumbled sheets – one arm bare to the elbow where the wide sleeve fell back and showed the tender places of wrist and forearm, the other lost in the warm depths of the bed, with her pale skin taking colour against the dead white linen, and her smile of confident, morning welcome; as I had greeted her countless times and always with a keener joy . . . her beauty rang through the room like a peal of bells . . . So another stage was reached in my falling in love with Lucy, while each week she grew heavier and slower and less apt for love, so that I accepted the joy of her companionship without reasoning.

The similarities between fact and fiction extended to the narrator's sense of losing her after the birth of her child, however for the time being Evelyn had Diana all to himself, sitting on her bed during the morning while she dealt with her correspondence, then accompanying her on various excursions in the afternoon – 'carriage exercise' in her chauffeur-driven

Daimler to the zoo and occasional visits to Underhill for tea – before returning for dinner in the evening.

Seeing Evelyn almost every day as she did at this time, and with him doubtless striving to be as cheerful and amusing as he could, Diana became convinced that the break-up of his marriage had not hurt him as severely as many of his old friends supposed and that there was even 'a good deal of relief' stemming from his recognition that he had made a mistake in marrying Shevelyn in the first place. 'But his pride was hurt, naturally, & the very fact that everyone felt so loudly sorry for him was salt in the wound, even if the wound was superficial.' In any case, she added, 'one couldn't have had him constantly in the house if he'd been saddled with the other Evelyn, who though very pretty wasn't much else'.[15]

When *Vile Bodies* was published in January 1930 Evelyn dedicated it to the Guinnesses, whose numerous kind gestures had also included giving him a birthday lunch at the Ritz and sending him a Christmas stocking 'full of lovely things including a gold watch!!' as Kate was thrilled to record.[16] He in turn sent them the leather-bound manuscript of his book as a belated Christmas present with apologies that it 'will never be of the smallest value'. In 1984 it was sold at Christie's for £55,000, enough in those days to buy a small house in west London.[17]

His divorce also came through that month, and in a preface to a later edition Evelyn admitted that the 'sharp disturbance in my private life' had upset the latter part, where the tone shifts dramatically at the beginning of Chapter Seven, the point at which he resumed writing after being abandoned by his wife.

His nominal hero Adam Fenwick-Symes becomes the hard-pressed gossip columnist 'Mr Chatterbox', who resorts to 'snaps and snippets about cocktail parties given in basement flats by spotty announcers at the BBC' – a caustic reference to Heygate, whom Evelyn derided as 'the Basement Boy', presumably because he lived in a basement flat.* When, in the next chapter, Adam takes Nina, whom he hopes to marry, and Ginger Littlejohn, the rival who steals her, to a party on an airship moored in a 'degraded suburb', it is hard not to think of the incriminating photograph of Shevelyn and Heygate taken aboard the *Friendship*: 'There were two

---

* Anthony Powell thought the tag resulted from Evelyn's having met Heygate at Powell's basement flat, however it is a little hard to imagine Evelyn coining it due to Heygate's occasional presence in *someone else*'s basement.

people making love to each other near him . . . reclining on cushions.' The scene also includes clear allusions to Shevelyn's casual attitude to their marriage:

> 'Nina,' said Adam, 'let's get married soon, don't you think?'
>
> 'Yes, it's a bore not being married.'
>
> 'I don't know if this sounds absurd,' said Adam, 'but I do feel that a marriage ought to *go on* – for quite a long time, I mean. D'you feel that too at all?'

Critics once again praised the book's great wit and originality, however the reviews this time were not quite so universally glowing, with Arnold Bennett regretting 'the lack of a well-laid plot' which 'resulted in a large number of pages which demand a certain obstinate and sustained effort for their perusal'.[18] Interviewed by the *Paris Review* more than thirty years later, Evelyn himself called it 'a bad book, I think, not so carefully constructed as the first'.[19]

However, as he also recalled, he had 'popularised a fashionable language like the Beatnik writers today, and the book caught on'.[20] With *Vile Bodies* selling 2,000 copies a week, expressions such as 'shy-making' and 'too too sick-making' soon spread far beyond the Guinnesses' circle of friends where Evelyn had first heard them. Within a month of publication, the *Daily Mirror* reported that black suede shoes (among the various spoof fashions propagated by Adam during his stint as Mr Chatterbox) were being 'much worn up at Oxford just now'.[21]

Evelyn's own stock also rose dramatically. 'My dear Waugh,' his old mentor J. F. Roxburgh wrote to him, 'You are now so eminent that I dare not use your Christian name as I once did!'[22] Sought out by literary lion-hunters such as Sibyl Colefax and Emerald Cunard, he soon became a fixture in fashionable society, his diary routinely recording lunch with Noël Coward ('a simple, friendly nature. No brains.'), tea with the Labour Prime Minister Ramsay MacDonald ('a nasty and inadequate man'), and dinner with the Duke of Marlborough ('such a mundane mind,' whispered the duchess, 'will go to any party for which he is sent a printed invitation'). Not in the least bit shy about capitalising on his fame, he wrote after one evening: 'After dinner I went to the Savoy Theatre and said "I am Evelyn Waugh. Please give me a seat." So they did.'[23]

The huge success of *Vile Bodies* earned Evelyn considerable sums in royalties and simultaneously completely revived the fortunes of Chapman & Hall, whose business had been precarious ever since the lapse of Dickens's copyrights in 1920. It also enabled Evelyn to demand increasingly exorbitant rates for his journalism. 'I will only do <u>feature</u> articles,' he told his agent, '– not side columns like Heygate – with photograph of me and general air of importance.' To editors he was equally forthright. 'I should quite like to broadcast but what will you pay?' he wrote to the BBC. 'It isn't any good my taking up your time with a voice test if at the end, you find my avarice insupportable. Broadcasting is clearly more exacting work than journalism. I get £20 a thousand words' writing. I suggest £25 a thousand for speaking. If that's too much don't answer.'[24] The response on this occasion was 'Too expensive, have a cocktail?',[25] however enough newspapers did meet his demands and in May he was elated to record that his regular annual income had temporarily rocketed to £2,500 a year.

That spring, 1930, he finished writing *Labels* while staying at the Guinnesses' seaside house in Sussex. The book was published in late September and again dedicated to Bryan and Diana, 'without whose encouragement and hospitality this book would not have been finished'. Diana's baby was born at the beginning of March, a boy who was soon christened Jonathan partly due to the fact that Evelyn, who stood godfather, was at the time contemplating a biography of Jonathan Swift.

After recovering from giving birth, with her old nanny engaged to look after the baby, Diana was keen to make up for lost party-going time and although Evelyn continued to see her regularly for a while, with so many other people now vying for her attention he resented the loss of their previous intimacy and in due course started to behave as objectionably as only he knew how. In July he went to stay with them at Pool Place in Sussex: 'Diana and I quarrelled at luncheon,' he recorded in his diary. 'We bathed. Diana and I quarrelled at dinner and after dinner. Next day I decided to leave. Quarrelled with Diana again and left.'[26] At various parties over the next few weeks he went out of his way to avoid her. Eventually he wrote her a note: 'When I got back last night I wrote you two long letters and tore them up. All I tried to say was that I must have seemed unfriendly lately and I am sorry. Please believe it is only because I am puzzled and ill at ease with myself. Much later everything will be all right. Don't bother to answer. E.'[27]

A few weeks later Bryan wrote innocently to say how glad Diana was to receive his letter: 'We had both been very upset by your coldness. If it was due to anything she had done or said perhaps the cause can be explained away. But I daresay it was something too elusive to put into words. Anyway you must remember that we are missing you a great deal; and if you should be able to change your mind and come over for a few days nothing would make us more happy.'[28] But Evelyn kept refusing their invitations, so Diana reluctantly concluded that he no longer wished to be her friend. It was one of the deepest friendships in each of their lives, yet it lasted barely a year. During Diana's pregnancy, Evelyn's visits to her served as a bubble within which he could forget about the trauma of his marriage, and it seems that as soon as Diana began to see other people he felt his humiliation all over again.

It was not until a few weeks before he died that Evelyn attempted to explain: 'You ask why our friendship petered out. The explanation is very discreditable to me. Pure jealousy. You (and Bryan) were immensely kind to me at a time when I greatly needed kindness, after my desertion by my first wife. I was infatuated with you. Not of course that I aspired to your bed but I wanted you to myself as especial confidant and comrade. After Jonathan's birth you began to enlarge your circle. I felt lower in your affections than Harold Acton and Robert Byron and I couldn't compete or take a humbler place. That is the sad and sordid truth.'[29] It was one of the last letters he wrote.

Diana had consoled herself by telling Nancy that his behaviour had latterly become 'so horrid when he did come that one didn't miss him at all'.[30] Yet she remained fiercely loyal to his memory and quick to refute whatever misconceptions she perceived about him. She maintained, for instance, that to call him a snob was nonsense – which is perhaps debatable, although it is certainly true that he was never drawn to grandeur for its own sake and did not choose his friends on account of their rank or worldly position. Neither did he go out of his way to court popularity among aristocrats; indeed his behaviour towards them was often so far from sycophantic as to be downright rude – which is perhaps why so many of them ended up with a grudge of some sort or another against him and a (snobbish) tendency on their own part to accuse him of social climbing. 'He liked people,' wrote Diana, 'as I do, because they amused him, or he was fond of them, or he found them stimulating; sometimes he sought their company because of some oddity which delighted the novelist in him. He disliked those who bored or irritated him, and needless to say they, too, were all sorts of men and women ... there was never any question of him trying to get to know grandees. The boot was on the other foot.'[31]

It is probably true that Evelyn, for his part, did not 'aspire to Diana's bed', although that is not the same thing as saying that he did not find her attractive, which he almost certainly did. As with a lot of men, the more unobtainable the girl, the more attractive she became.

The reverse had been the case with Audrey Lucas, the only daughter of a domineering father whose more submissive demeanour Evelyn evidently found less alluring. But she had remained keen on him, and he began to see a lot of her after his divorce, by which time her marriage to Harold Scott was also going badly (they later divorced and she married the actor Douglas Clarke-Smith). Even if Evelyn knew that he was unlikely to fall in love with Audrey, he may have figured that with his sexual confidence shattered by his wife's desertion, an affair might help to rebuild it. Alec Waugh, whose travel book *Hot Countries* sold 80,000 copies that year, first got wind of their liaison when Evelyn visited him for five days in the South of France at Easter and told him that he was on his way to a romantic rendezvous in Monte Carlo.[32] Arthur Waugh innocently observed that Evelyn returned from that holiday to Underhill 'very tired but well'.[33] A month later Audrey announced she was pregnant. 'I don't much care either way really,' Evelyn noted nonchalantly in his diary, 'so long as it is a boy.'[34] He remained as non-committal as ever and two weeks later he went to bed with another married woman, Dorothy Varda, a noted beauty and renowned man-eater who was by then separated from her husband, the porcelain collector Gerald Reitlinger: 'Went back and slept with Varda,' Evelyn recorded, 'but both of us too drunk to enjoy ourselves.'[35] A week after that Audrey told him she was not pregnant after all, 'so all that is bogus', wrote Evelyn. Audrey was at least shrewd enough not to let him have his way with her whenever he chose, and after a party later that evening Evelyn recorded that he had 'waited for hours to sleep with Audrey but she was too tired'.[36] Their on-off affair continued until the end of the summer.

The fling with Audrey was presumably good for morale, however with the failure of his marriage still very much on his mind Evelyn was inclined to play down the importance of sex within marriage in his journalism. In an article that summer entitled 'Tell the Truth About Marriage', he wrote that to say that you cannot lead a happy life unless your sex life is happy was 'just about as sensible as saying, "You cannot lead a happy life unless your golf life is happy"'. The modern attitude, he added, was that 'the moment a couple's physical interest in each other starts to slacken, it is their duty to look for other mates'. He advocated teaching children that sex 'is not infinitely important or infinitely satisfying'. 'Teach them fully about birth control and encourage them to find out for themselves exactly how much sex is likely to mean in their own lives: they will not then marry out of curiosity or inexperience. Arrange a system of legal marriage, registered, like any other legal contract, by mutual consent. Then leave it to the Church to show the sacramental importance of marriage to her own members.'[37]

The last sentence reflected momentous recent developments in his own spiritual outlook. The previous year, after informing Alec that Shevelyn had left him, he said: 'The trouble about the world today is that there's not enough religion in it. There's nothing to stop young people doing whatever they feel like doing at the moment.'[38] Evelyn later admitted that at the time of writing *Vile Bodies* he himself was 'as near to an atheist as one could be',[39] however Alec was in no doubt that the break-up of his marriage and the ensuing feeling of emptiness hastened his conversion to Roman Catholicism.

Since his divorce Evelyn had seen a lot of Gwen and Olivia Plunket Greene, both recent Catholic converts, and he later told a friend that during their various discussions Olivia 'bullied me into the Church'.[40] However according to Father Martin D'Arcy, the Jesuit priest to whom Olivia recommended Evelyn go for instruction at Farm Street in July 1930, 'no one could have made up that mind of his for him'.[41] Evelyn later explained that the first ten years of his adult life as an atheist had proved to him that life was 'unintelligible and unendurable without God',[42] that he had come to the conclusion that Western civilisation owed its entire existence to Christianity, and that Christianity in turn seemed to exist in its 'most complete and vital form' in the Roman Catholic Church. He realised that 'Catholicism was Christianity, that all other forms of Christianity were only good in so far as they chipped little bits off the main block'; hence it was 'a conversion to

Christianity rather than a conversion to Catholicism as such'.[43]

In Father Martin D'Arcy he could scarcely have found anyone more in tune with his growing revulsion with the 'barbaric' modern world and his hazily conceived romantic nostalgia for the old English Catholic past. Evelyn candidly admitted that he didn't 'feel Christian in the absolute sense',[44] however D'Arcy was so impressed by his unsentimental conviction as to the truth of the Catholic doctrine that he was prepared, as Evelyn later put it, 'just to get the seed in anyhow & hope some of it would come up'. D'Arcy, who remembered it as 'a special pleasure to make contact with so able a brain',[45] received him into the Roman Catholic Church at Farm Street on 29 September. The only witness he asked along was Tom Driberg, who interpreted it as part of his remit to inform his *Express* readers about Evelyn's conversion the next day. His only godparent was a charwoman who happened to be working there that day.

Evelyn had told his parents two days before, whereupon Arthur recorded that Kate was 'very, very sad over news of Evelyn's secession to Rome' (although she was typically reticent about her feelings in her own diary). To Arthur, whose family had for so long been steeped in Anglicanism, it felt like a betrayal and he later referred to Evelyn's 'perversion to Rome'.[46] For both parents, perhaps the saddest aspect of their son's 'going over' was that it seemed to extinguish any hope of his marrying again and giving them grandchildren owing to the fact that the Catholic Church did not recognise divorce. Father D'Arcy was later adamant that at the time Evelyn took his decision, the possibility of having his first marriage annulled had not yet been foreseen, and that by becoming a Catholic he was effectively committing himself to remaining a bachelor for the rest of his life.

Terence Greenidge also remembered Evelyn telling him at the time that he was now 'tied to Evelyn G for life unless [Greenidge] bumped her off(!)' but that Catholicism would at least prevent his 'making a fool of himself again over marriage'.[47] Yet his sacrifice was particularly poignant given that he had spent so much of his adult life yearning to be married and had recently begun to fall for one of the great loves of his life.

13

....

The Dutch Girl

Known then as 'Baby' – a name she never liked and eventually managed to discard – Teresa Jungman was the younger daughter of the prominent London hostess and talent-spotter Mrs Richard Guinness, who was herself generally referred to as 'Gloomy Beatrix' or 'Gloomy Guinness' or just plain 'Gloomy', not so much for her curious habit of closing the curtains during lunch parties as for her very deep voice and doom-laden conversation – she was once overheard demanding of a startled milliner's assistant: 'I want a hat for a middle-aged woman whose husband hates her.'[1]

Baby and her elder sister Zita were from Gloomy's first marriage to Nico Jungman, an impoverished Dutch-born artist 'greatly beloved', according to his obituary, 'for his artless charm of manner and almost childlike simplicity of character'.[2] The obit tactfully left unspecified the 'successive misfortunes, often cruelly undeserved' that befell this naive and generous-hearted man, however they included being abandoned by Baby's mother while he was interned in Germany for four years during the First World War (Baby was barely ten when they divorced in 1918) and she fell in love with the far wealthier Dick Guinness, scion of the banking branch of that family and himself chairman of the Mercantile & General Insurance Company.

The new Mrs Guinness soon became a dedicated salonnière and by the late 1920s their house at 19 Great Cumberland Place was a hub of fashionable London society, where clever young politicians like Bob Boothby mixed with writers and artists such as the Sitwells, Noël Coward, Lord David Cecil, Oliver Messel and Cecil Beaton. Loelia Ponsonby (a close friend of the Jungman sisters whose subsequent marriage to Bendor

Westminster, the 2nd Duke – of whom more later – was memorably described by James Lees-Milne as 'a definition of unadulterated hell') met Evelyn at one of the many gatherings there and thought he looked like a furious cherub, watching with his 'glaring eye', missing nothing and giving the impression with his pungent remarks that he was 'an unhappy man who found in the world much to amuse but little to admire'.[3]

Mrs Guinness's guests tended to find her similarly alarming, however her daughters remained remarkably unfazed by her relentless teasing and their striking beauty and spirited attitude to life soon rendered them among the most dazzling of the Bright Young People. With their equally high-spirited friends Eleanor Smith (Lord Birkenhead's daughter) and Enid Raphael (who once quipped, 'I don't know why they call them private parts – mine aren't private') they initiated the nocturnal treasure hunts and masquerades that came to define high society in the late 1920s. Both sisters were much photographed by Cecil Beaton, who admired Baby's 'Devonshire cream pallor and limpid mauve eyes' and 'her hair, spun of the flimsiest canary-bird silkiness' which fell 'lankly over her eyes' or was 'thrown back with a beguiling shrug of the head'.[4]

Beside her pale beauty, Baby was renowned for her pranks, one of which was to borrow her mother's Rolls-Royce and mink coat and go about pretending to be a widowed Russian émigré who had been forced to sell her jewels to educate her 'poor leedle boy'. In the same guise she attended a garden party with two borzois and approached an old general gushing about how she would never forget the night they had spent together in Paris during the war. The general, who was with his wife, coldly replied that he had only spent one night in Paris during the war. 'Zat was zee night,' said Baby, before melting away into the crowd.[5]

Notwithstanding her mischievousness, Baby also did regular charitable work and was a very strict Catholic, her faith inherited from her mother, whose family had moved to Birmingham as followers of Cardinal Newman. Thus she blended the beauty and zest of Evelyn Gardner with the intelligence and underlying seriousness and unavailability of Olivia Plunket Greene. For Evelyn it was an irresistible combination, as it was for several other disappointed suitors, including Pansy Pakenham's brother Frank (much later Lord Longford), who had 'a tremendous walkout' with Baby after meeting her at the Birkenheads' in 1928,[6] although, as he admitted, 'no one ever got anywhere with her sexually'.[7]

Exactly how or when Evelyn first came across her is unclear, although when he died his prayer book was found to contain a pressed orchid and fern next to which he had written '19 January 1930' – thought by some to be the date in question.[8] After a gap of eighteen months from the time when he and Shevelyn were setting up home together in Islington in November 1928, Evelyn's surviving diary does not resume until the beginning of May 1930. The first mention of Baby Jungman is on the 26th of that month, when they both dined at the Savoy with Frank Pakenham. It was evidently not their first meeting and Evelyn may already have let on that he liked her, given his observation that Baby seemed 'anxious to be friendly and very sweet'. Six days later, however, at lunch with Desmond Parsons (Robert Byron's great unrequited love), Baby arrived very late, left early and 'sat at the other end of the table so I couldn't speak to her'.[9] The following week she accepted an invitation to a lunch party Evelyn was giving at the Ritz but chucked at the last minute, telling him via a friend that she wouldn't be able to come after all as she was going to the country, which provoked a rant by Evelyn in the *Daily Mail* the next week – headlined 'Such Bad Manners!' – against 'incompetent young women who just do not know how to organize their affairs'.[10]

Baby's mother later told Evelyn that Baby was in tears after their resulting 'tiff', and when he went to lunch at their house in July Evelyn 'sat at a side table with Baby who was sweet'. Subsequent encounters were rarely more encouraging than this but they seemed to do nothing to diminish Evelyn's ardour. A consummate if perhaps unintentional heartbreaker, for the next few years Baby Jungman neither surrendered to his advances nor discouraged him from continuing to press his suit, telling him on various occasions that she enjoyed his being in love with her 'too much not to encourage it as much as I can in a subconscious way' and that 'If you weren't married you see it would be different because I might or I might not want to marry you . . .'[11]

* * *

Foreign travel was one way that Evelyn could relieve the torment of unrequited love, and in the six years after the break-up of his first marriage he travelled a great deal. The first of these trips, to Abyssinia, resulted from a conversation he had while staying with the Longfords at Paken-ham Hall (now Tullynally) in Ireland in the early autumn of 1930.

It was his second visit there that year, both times at the invitation of Frank Pakenham (a younger brother of the then earl, Edward Longford), whom he had met through Pansy in 1928 and latterly got to know at Gloomy Guinness's parties in Great Cumberland Place, a few doors along from the Longfords' townhouse where Frank was born. They became closer after Evelyn's marriage ended and, as Frank modestly recalled, 'climbed the slopes of London society together'.[12] It was during this period that Evelyn, keen to spend as much time as possible away from Underhill, 'discovered the delights of the large country house', as Alexander Waugh puts it. That summer, besides the Longfords and Guinnesses, he also went to stay at Sezincote with the Dugdales and at Renishaw with the Sitwells, the latter in Cyril Connolly's assessment 'exactly the sort of aristocrats he longed to be himself'.[13] But to give Evelyn his due, he did not pretend to be anything other than an outsider, affecting an attitude to the upper classes that was more sardonic than sycophantic. 'No-one has a keener appreciation than myself of the high spiritual and moral qualities of the very rich,' he wrote in the *Daily Mail*. 'I delight in their company whenever I get the chance.'[14]

John Betjeman, sometimes bracketed with Evelyn as a fellow social climber from the middle classes, had been at the same house party at Sez-incote and when Evelyn went to Pakenham for ten days in September, he was there too. Not nearly as well known as Evelyn at that time, Betjeman nonetheless seemed far more at ease with himself to the extent that, in Evelyn's eyes at least, he became 'a bore rather',[15] endlessly belting out re-vivalist hymns and joking about eccentric Irish peers. Evelyn by contrast appeared nervous and self-conscious and said very little at mealtimes, although their hostess did remember him coming down to breakfast and demanding 'Who's got any funny letters this morning?'[16]

Evelyn was presumably aware that Frank Pakenham had been as besot-ted as he was with Baby Jungman, which may explain why, after dinner on the last evening, he took it upon himself to whisper to the beautiful girl Frank had invited to stay on this occasion: 'Go after Frank. Go up with him. Follow him. Go on.' The girl was Elizabeth Harman, whom Frank had briefly fallen for at Oxford but then forgotten about for two years while he courted Baby. There may have been an element of self-interest in Evelyn's advice but Elizabeth was not to know that and she obediently followed Frank up into his bedroom, where, as she recalled, 'we conducted an ardent but chaste and anxious conversation about ourselves far into the night'.[17] Evelyn himself recorded in his diary: 'Frank and Harman slept together on Frank's last evening but did not fuck.'[18] They were married the next year.

Evelyn, meanwhile, was assumed by the other guests at Pakenham to have resumed his love affair with Alastair Graham, whom he had brought along with him from Renishaw, where Alastair had irritated Georgia Sitwell by 'boasting' that his mother was the model for Lady Circumference in *Decline and Fall*.[19] The suspicion that they were once again lovers was scarcely allayed by Evelyn's tendency to camp it up and put on a high-pitched voice whenever they were together, which was most of the time.[20]

Alastair was at the time on leave from Cairo, where he and Mark Ogilvie-Grant had followed Sir Percy Loraine when he moved there from Athens in 1929. Loraine's biographer records Cairo society being rather taken aback by 'the sparkling intelligence and decidedly informal air of these young aesthetes'. Known as 'the Embassy girls', they were famous for their laziness and incompetence and it was a mystery to those unaware of the rumours about Sir Percy that such a stickler was prepared to put up with them for so long.

In any event the posting provided Alastair with a fund of good stories, and the richly embellished one he told one evening in the library at Pakenham about the visit of two Abyssinian princes, who declined to take off their bowler hats and silk capes during a stuffy High Commission lunch party, promptly persuaded Evelyn to attend the coronation of the Emperor Haile Selassie in Addis Ababa that November instead of going to China and Japan as he had originally intended.

Soon after returning from Ireland, Evelyn went on his own to stay at Barford as a guest of Mrs Graham. In the ballroom – which she had built onto the house in 1925 in order to throw a party for Alastair's twenty-first, which in the event never took place – there was a large *Times Atlas of the World* from which, in a curiously rash act of vandalism, Evelyn tore a page for use on his forthcoming Abyssinian trip. Mrs Graham was so horrified when she discovered this that she banished him from her house. He returned there a year later, however, when he was trying to start *Black Mischief* but found it impossible to work with Alastair. 'We just sit about sipping sloe gin all day,' he complained. 'I am reading all the case histories in Havelock Ellis and frigging too much.'[21] The last appearance of Evelyn's name in the Barford visitors' book was in 1932, by which time he had stayed there on more than twenty occasions, sometimes for several weeks at a stretch.[22] After that they disappeared from each other's lives. Years later, when Alastair's niece asked him why their friendship had ended, he replied vaguely, 'Oh, you know, Evelyn became such a bore, such a snob.'[23]

By the time he said this, while Evelyn had carried on, as Alastair perhaps saw it, moving in ever grander circles to the point at which he eventually married into the aristocracy and installed himself in a Palladian country house with his coat of arms over the portico, Alastair had completely withdrawn from high society to live in a remote fishing village on the west coast of Wales.

Soon after leaving the diplomatic service in 1933, when Sir Percy Loraine was transferred to Ankara, Alastair had been warned by the police to leave London 'or go to prison'[24] following the discovery of his illicit (the laws of the land being what they then were) affair with the Welsh poet Evan Morgan, soon to be Viscount Tredegar.[25]*

In 1936 he bought a rambling white house just outside New Quay called Wern Newydd, where he lived as a virtual recluse. His mother had died two years previously and he took with him a few old retainers from Barford and had a rumoured £10,000 a year. Occasionally he threw parties for his neighbours, who at various times included Augustus John and Dylan Thomas. The latter described Alastair as 'the thin-vowelled laird',[26] and in *Under Milk Wood* used him as the model for Lord Cut-Glass, who 'lives in a house and a life at siege', and has 'a fish-slimy kitchen', presumably a reference to the pickled herring Alastair served at his parties and the pamphlet he wrote entitled *20 Different Ways To Cook New Quay Mackerel*, a testament to his fondness for sea-fishing as well as cooking.

However, neither Thomas nor anyone else in New Quay seemed to know that Alastair had also been the model for Sebastian Flyte in *Brideshead*. He remained more or less incognito in this respect until the late 1970s, when he was encountered in the Dolau Inn by the writer and critic

---

* Their trysting place was the Cavendish Hotel, whose proprietress Rosa Lewis had begun her career as a kitchen maid for Alastair's uncle, Willie Low, a crony of the future King Edward VII. Rosa was thus generally very well disposed towards Alastair and his friends, however she was so offended by Evelyn's portrayal of her as Lottie Crump in *Vile Bodies* that she banned him from the premises.

Duncan Fallowell. Not knowing who he was, Fallowell chanced to fall into conversation with him about Evelyn Waugh, about how 'well-endowed' he was as a writer and so forth, at which point the well-spoken stranger at the bar suddenly interjected: 'He wasn't well-endowed in the other sense, I'm afraid.'[27]

Fallowell never established whether he was referring to Evelyn's private parts or to the fact that he never had any money and Alastair was always having to bail him out. When the Granada television series of *Brideshead Revisited* went on air in 1981, Fallowell returned to New Quay, knocked on Alastair Graham's door and asked him out to dinner. Alastair replied that he had had a stroke and was 'not fit to be seen!'. He could not remember anything, he said, it was all so long ago, then remarked, somewhat cryptically, 'he was older than me you know'.[28] Alastair Graham died the next year, in 1982, 'taking his secrets with him'.

* * *

The Abyssinian trip that Alastair had inadvertently sparked, and on which Evelyn embarked a month after leaving Pakenham in 1930 armed with press accreditations to the *Graphic*, *Times* and *Express*, lasted five months in all and also took in Zanzibar, Kenya and Cape Town, providing him with material for the travelogue *Remote People* as well as what he promised his parents on leaving Addis would be 'a first rate novel'[29] – *Black Mischief*.

Near the end of his journey, he wrote to Baby: 'I am just going to a lake called Tanganyika where everyone dies of sleeping sickness. I have also caught typhus in a prison, malaria in a place called Hawash, and leprosy in a Catholic church, so I am fairly sure not to come back.'[30] A few weeks after arriving home in the spring of 1931 he fell ill with a temperature of 101 and ulcers on his throat. But rather than having contracted any of the exotic diseases enumerated to Baby, he was found to have been poisoned by some watercress eaten at a hotel by the Thames.

That summer all four Waughs went on holiday to Villefranche in the South of France, only the second time that Evelyn's parents had ventured to 'the palms, the sunlight and the South',[31] as Alec put it, and by Alec's account it was a great success, even though Arthur insisted on wearing the same tweed suit that he wore in England together with scarf, vest and long-legged underpants, maintaining 'I like to feel the wool against my skin.'[32]

Arthur had brought with him the proofs of his soon-to-be published autobiography *One Man's Road*, a sentimental tome which bizarrely contained no reference whatsoever to his younger son's writing career, despite the fact that *Vile Bodies* had already established Evelyn as one of the country's most celebrated young novelists and his books had done much to rescue the fortunes of Arthur's troubled publishing house. Instead Arthur made plain his distaste for what he saw as the kind of vulgar self-publicising that Evelyn had been so conspicuously guilty of each week recently in the press, pointedly bemoaning the fact that 'nobody seems content to do his work nowadays without blowing a horn to call attention to his proficiency'.[33] Arthur's determination to deny his son any further publicity may also have stemmed from recent friction between them after they found themselves living under the same roof again after Evelyn's divorce – although Evelyn kept away whenever he could, borrowing flats from friends or going to stay in the country. Unbeknown to Evelyn, relations had been further strained when Arthur's curiosity got the better of him one day and he began reading the bound volumes of Evelyn's diaries, which he kept on a shelf in the former nursery that Arthur was now using as a study. The diaries contained numerous unflattering references to Arthur which left him 'immensely humiliated and distressed' according to Alec, who recalled: 'My mother told me that he never really got over it, that he kept harking back to it.'[34]

Equally, Arthur may not have appreciated his portrayal in *Vile Bodies* as the dotty Colonel Blount who allows his house, Doubting Hall, to be used as a film location providing he can appear as an extra – just as Arthur had done with Evelyn and Terence Greenidge's student film, *The Scarlet Woman*, in 1924. Nor could he have failed to recognise himself in another of the book's characters, Adam's publisher Mr Rampole, who is based, like Arthur, in Henrietta Street and is described as a 'benign old gentleman' who is nonetheless notoriously stingy in his dealings with young authors. When Arthur looked back on 1931 he wrote in his diary, 'Much kindness at home and abroad. Particularly from K [Kate] and Alec.'[35] There was no mention of Evelyn.

* * *

Besides entertaining their parents, the Waugh brothers saw various others in the South of France, among them Cyril Connolly, Aldous Huxley and Somerset Maugham, the last of whom they visited twice at his villa on nearby Cap Ferrat and Evelyn offended by addressing him as 'Dr' Maugham and feigning ignorance of his literary reputation. Evelyn's rudeness was partly a symptom of his growing restlessness with the family holiday and he soon went himself off to an uncomfortable monastery in the hills in a bid to try and finish *Remote People*, which he took back with him to his publishers in June 1931; it was eventually published that autumn to reviews which mostly reflected the haste in which it had been written. 'I think you have the most important of the young English writers in Evelyn Waugh,' his new American publisher, John Farrar, was informed by a respected littérateur, 'but my God, will you stop him writing travel books!'[36]

When Evelyn returned to the Riviera in mid-July he was accompanied by a very pretty thirty-three-year-old divorcee called Pixie Marix, to whom he had been introduced by his friend Patrick Balfour, and whom he quickly whisked off to a hotel well away from his brother. 'Evelyn has gone wenching down the coast,'[37] Alec told Balfour. Evelyn's paramour was more respectable than Alec made her sound, however she was reputed to enjoy what she called 'brinking', leading men on but stopping short of what Alec delicately termed 'a bestowal of ultimate favours'.[38] Evelyn evidently grew frustrated with this and complained to Balfour: 'That girl has made a fool of me & taken all my money . . . It is all very distressing & humiliating. Apart from anything else she is so boring and so American at heart. I could drown her with pleasure.'[39] Eventually, Pixie realised that unless she gave him what he wanted she would have to make her own way home, so she changed tack and decided to let him have 'so much of it that he would wish he had not brought the matter up'.[40] At night she kept him at it until two or three in the morning and at dawn she would 'bound into his room, eager and voracious'.[41] A week later, Evelyn wrote to Balfour again: 'I said some hard things about Mrs. Marix. Well subsequent events have not justified my first estimate of her character . . . [she] is a nice girl really.'[42]

* * *

It was in France that summer that Evelyn first read in a newspaper about a divorce suit involving an aristocratic Liberal politician whose predicament would later give him the idea for *Brideshead Revisited*. The petition had been filed by Countess Beauchamp, the mother of his Oxford friends Hugh Lygon and William Elmley. Although the newspapers did not say so at the time, her grounds had to do with Earl Beauchamp's homosexuality, evidence of which had been rigorously compiled by the Countess's jealous and vindictive brother, Bendor Westminster, and at the Duke's insistence was set out in unsparingly explicit detail in the petition: 'THAT throughout their married life at 13 Belgrave Square, Madresfield Court, and Walmer Castle, aforesaid, the Respondent habitually committed acts of gross indecency with certain of his male servants, masturbating them with his mouth and hands and compelling them to masturbate him and lying upon them and masturbating between their legs . . .'[43]

Lord Beauchamp's fondness for his footmen, whose faces were routinely powdered, was an open secret, and when Evelyn read about the divorce his first reaction was 'So the story has broken.'[44] But while he had known the sons at Oxford, he had never been to their vast moated manor house in Worcestershire or met their sisters, even though they were great friends of Baby Jungman and the Mitfords. He went to Madresfield Court, the house that would cast such a famously powerful spell over him, for the first time that autumn after obeying Baby's suggestion that he attend Captain Hance's famous riding academy in nearby Malvern and subsequently being invited by Mary Lygon (whom he chanced to meet lunching with Mrs Guinness) to stay with them while he was doing so.

With Lady Beauchamp having recently decamped to a house on the Westminster estate in Cheshire with their youngest brother Richard, and Lord Beauchamp, known as 'Boom' in the family for his resonant voice, driven into exile on the Continent by the threat of criminal prosecution, the three unmarried Lygon girls now had the run of the fully staffed Madresfield and regularly filled it with their friends. The eldest, twenty-four-year-old Lady Sibell, later admitted to finding Evelyn 'rather tiresome and terribly rude',[45] however her two younger sisters, Lady Mary and Lady Dorothy, then aged twenty-one and nineteen, took to him at once, relishing his endlessly entertaining banter and apparent unwillingness to take anything seriously, least of all himself. He was equally entranced by them and quickly adopted them as yet another of his surrogate families. 'I miss you both very much at school and in play time,' he wrote to them after one of his early visits.

Mary had been known since childhood as Maimie and Dorothy as Coote, and to these Evelyn soon added Blondy and Poll respectively, while giving himself the mock-Masonic sobriquet of Boaz (which he later bestowed on the Azanian Minister of the Interior in *Black Mischief*). Certain traits of their friends were incorporated in a secret code, thus 'Dutch' came to denote anyone or anything problematic or uncooperative, a reference to Evelyn's enduring and much-discussed difficulties in wooing Baby Jungman, whom he generally referred to as 'the Dutch girl'; 'Highclere', the Hampshire seat of the Earls of Carnarvon, was used for anything imposing and luxurious; and to laycock (or lacock) meant to chuck a social engagement, coined after a genial but evidently forgetful young cavalry officer called Robert Laycock (later Evelyn's wartime commanding officer in the commandos) whom Evelyn routinely referred to as 'Chucker': 'Very very sorry for lacocking tea,' Evelyn wrote to Maimie.

Evelyn's irreverent mischievousness was such that it was 'like having Puck as a member of the household', Coote recalled.[46] The sundial in the garden at Madresfield was inscribed: 'That day is wasted on which one has not laughed.' Standing by this one day, Maimie said to Evelyn: 'Well, you and I have never wasted a day, have we?'[47]

The laughter helped alleviate the Lygon girls' sadness over the loss of their father, to whom they were devoted despite his extreme love of formality – always referring to his children by their courtesy titles and insisting that liveried footmen stand behind each chair in the dining room – not to mention his notoriety as a prowler, which meant they had to warn any handsome male guests they had staying at Madresfield to lock their doors at night. They were never reconciled meanwhile to what they saw as the treachery of their mother, a pious and unworldly woman who famously declared after failing to grasp the essentials of what her husband was accused of: 'Bendor tells me that Beauchamp is a bugler.' Bendor, meanwhile, charmingly wrote to Beauchamp after his downfall: 'Dear Bugger-in-law, you got what you deserved.'

Soon looked upon by the sisters as an extra brother, Evelyn found the family's plight deeply affecting and told Baby that the Arts and Crafts chapel that Lady Beauchamp had given her husband on their marriage (the only part of Madresfield that Evelyn eventually borrowed for his creation of Brideshead Castle) was 'the saddest thing that ever I saw'.[48] He shared the sisters' concern about their brother Hugh, whose alcoholism and general profligacy led to his going bankrupt in the spring of 1932, which in turn prompted a breakdown and a brief spell in an asylum. And he was at one with their growing antipathy towards their stiff elder brother William, Lord Elmley, the only one of the siblings remaining at Madresfield not to have taken their father's side.

However much he loved being at Madresfield, Evelyn knew that he had to tear himself away from time to time in order to get on with the various articles he had promised as well as the novel that eventually became *Black Mischief*. Towards the end of October he wrote to Patrick Balfour: 'I am having a healthy time riding all day and romping with the bright young Lygons in the evenings but not doing any work or making money – in fact spending pots so must get away quick.'[49] He proposed joining Balfour for a stint at the Eastern Court Hotel near Chagford in Devon, a low-ceilinged, old thatched farmhouse which was to become his favourite writing refuge for years to come. 'I pretend to my London chums that I am going to hunt stags,' he told the Lygons, 'but to you who are intimates and confidantes I don't mind saying that I shall sit in my bedroom writing books, articles, short stories, reviews, plays. Cinema scenarios, etc. etc. until I have got a lot more money.'[50] Within a few days of getting there, he admitted that he had been 'fox catching on Thursday with a pack called [the] South Devon. We galloped like mad for five hours over Dartmoor. My horse fell down once but it wasn't my fault & I made a "plucky re-mount". I pretend I am a farmer & don't pay any money.'[51]

Having previously groaned to Baby Jungman that he was 'lonely and depressed here & the book [*Black Mischief*] is going badly',[52] he felt better after his day's hunting: 'Sweet Tess,' he wrote afterwards, 'I have done only 2 pages of the novel but they are masterly. I don't see how narrative could be finer, of its kind.'[53] His feelings for her remained as unreciprocated as ever, however, which tended to produce quarrels whenever they met. 'If you look on me simply as a pair of trousers for your mother's parties,' he wrote after one painful scene, 'you can't mind if I ask to be released from an engagement to watch your dogs go to the lavatory. If you regard me as a friend of your own you mustn't be disagreeable in quite that way. Isn't that reasonable!'[54]

On this occasion he could at least look forward to seeing her again over

Christmas at Madresfield. But on that occasion Baby proved no more receptive to his endearments than usual and in the new year the same old pangs returned: 'I hope you have every kind of success and amusement and marry a rich marquess,' he wrote in January, 'or a brilliant young novelist or something equally exciting.'[55]

Another regular guest at Madresfield was Stanley Baldwin's younger son Windham, known by Evelyn as 'Frisky' and more widely as 'Bloggs'. In common with Evelyn, the ginger-haired and bespectacled Baldwin had had the occasional dalliance with Pixie Marix while also being hopelessly smitten with Baby Jungman, on the basis of which he and Evelyn had formed a mutually commiserative alliance, bolstered by the fact that neither saw the other as much of a threat in the looks department: 'Mrs Reginald Marix is back in London,' Evelyn informed Frisky in mid-January 1932, 'Theresa is hunting in Leicestershire. Make the best you can from these Words to the Wise.'[56] Their shared lack of success as suitors cemented what proved to be a lasting friendship and in later life Baldwin recalled that Evelyn was 'always wonderfully unrude to me and my wife; I can't think why; and I've always been grateful'.[57]

* * *

In February, staying at the Spread Eagle at Thame where he was working on two short stories (possibly 'Bella Fleace Gave a Party' and 'Cruise'), Evelyn again wrote to Baby, telling her that he had 'thought of you this morning and yesterday and in fact every day since I left London' and that he was 'sorry that I am so consistently tiresome with you'. He would shortly be going abroad, he added, in a bid 'to leave loneliness by being alone for a bit as I used to be able to do'.[58] He was away for barely two weeks, much of the time spent travelling to and from Spain, where he went to look at Gothic cathedrals and from where he inevitably again wrote to Baby, imploring her to 'think of me now and then between telephone calls'.[59] When he returned and she went off to stay with some friends in Ireland, another letter followed her. 'How you must be missing me,' he wrote optimistically, 'but cheer up. These separations are the very manure of love.'[60] He went on to tell her about the recent first night at the Vaudeville Theatre of the stage version of *Vile Bodies*, at which 'everyone laughed very loud and the criticisms this morning seem pretty genial'. Yet as he lamented to Frisky Baldwin: 'Did little Miss Jungman send me a line of good wishes from Ireland? Not on your life.'[61]

He spent Easter at Stonyhurst, the Catholic boys' public school where his old Oxford friend Christopher Hollis was teaching and where he went several times in the early years of his Catholicism. On this occasion he spent much of his time there working on his novel, the delivery of which John Farrar in New York was now beginning to hassle his agent about: 'You can tell these troublesome yanks that the novel will be called BLACK MISCHIEF and will be ready for them in about 3 weeks,' Evelyn wrote Peters in early May. 'It is extremely good.'[62]

Begun in September 1931 and mostly written during his various stays at Madresfield and Chagford, *Black Mischief* had taken him eight months to complete, far longer than his first two novels, partly a measure of how distracting he found life at Madresfield, where he groaned every time he shut himself away in the old nursery to write. 'Oh how I should love to live in your Liberty Hall,' he wrote to Coote in the spring of 1932, 'but the trouble about poor Bo is that he's a lazy bugger and if he was in a house with you lovely girls he would just sit about and chatter and get d.d. [disgustingly drunk] and ride a horse and have a heavenly time but would he write his book? No, and must he? By God he must.'[63] He found it impossible to stay away for long, however, and in May he was back there again – when the girls and their guests posed as models for the drawings he did for *Black Mischief* – as he would be in June, August, October and several times in November and December.

* * *

On 21 May 1932, after putting the final touches to *Black Mischief*, Evelyn caught the early aeroplane to Paris, from where he was to take a train to Rome to be privately confirmed by Cardinal Lépicier.[64] His unlikely travelling companion for this pilgrimage was a singularly undevout Catholic friend called Raymond de Trafford, 'a fine desperado', as Evelyn described him, from a Lancashire landowning family whom he had met the previous year in Kenya. Having supplied several of the characteristics of Basil Seal in *Black Mischief*, de Trafford would later feature in James Fox's *White Mischief* as the wildest of the notorious Happy Valley set. He was particularly renowned for having been shot by his lover Alice de

Janzé at the Gare du Nord in Paris in 1927 (an attempted murder-cum-suicide) and then marrying her five years later, in February 1932, before leaving her again three months after that, his final gesture being to hurl a cocktail in her face at a Parisian café and then burst out laughing.[65] It was very shortly after this that he met up with Evelyn on his way to Italy.

To Evelyn's great relief, Hugh Lygon was due to join them later in Rome. 'My word I am glad Hugh is coming to Italy,' he wrote to Coote, 'because between you and me and the w.c. Raymond de T. is something of a handful. v. nice but so BAD and he fights & fucks and gambles and gets D.D. all the time. But Hugh & I will be quiet & chaste and economical & sober.'[66] For the time being Evelyn was held up in Paris by Raymond's wayward behaviour: 'He arrived at the Ritz in evening dress having not been to bed,' Evelyn reported to Baby. 'He slept all yesterday until ten – I left him tight at four this morning just off for gambling at Le Cercle Haussman. If I don't manage to move him tomorrow I shall go alone.'[67]

When they did eventually reach Rome, they were joined not only by Hugh Lygon but also by his sisters Coote and Maimie. They had all come along in order to see their father, who was renting Lord Berners's opulent apartment overlooking the Forum for the summer. It was there that they all stayed, despite the fact that there was only one bedroom, which was generally occupied by Lord Beauchamp and his handsome young valet Robert Byron, whom he had recruited while wintering in Australia. 'Wasn't it extraordinary that we were all there in one room?' Evelyn wrote years later to Maimie.[68]

This was the first time that Evelyn had met Lord Beauchamp, whom he had heard so much about. They went sightseeing together and by all accounts got on very well, admiring each other's intelligence and interest in art and church architecture. On a trip to join Maimie Lygon in Venice later that summer in August, Evelyn inadvertently gathered more material for future use in *Brideshead*: 'On some days life kept pace with the gondola, as we nosed through the side-canals and the boatman uttered his plaintive musical bird-cry of warning; on other days, with the speedboat bouncing over the lagoon in a stream of sun-lit foam . . .'[69]

In both Rome and Venice that summer Evelyn also hit it off with Lady Diana Cooper, the actress and renowned beauty at whose fortieth birthday party on one of Venice's islands he had witnessed the famous brawl begun by Richard Sykes and Randolph Churchill which inspired a new word in his private vocabulary – to 'sykes', meaning to hit or smash up. Evelyn had first met Lady Diana that spring in London through Hazel Lavery, with whom he had been having a casual on–off affair. He soon became as infatuated with her as he had been with Diana Guinness, yet despite their often ferocious quarrels their friendship proved considerably longer-lasting. Beside the fact that she was bright, beautiful and very grand, Evelyn admired Diana's cleverness, her unusual wit, her sense of adventure and her extraordinary self-confidence – like all his great women friends, she never allowed herself to be bullied. Diana meanwhile was 'enraptured by [Evelyn's] wit, his sensibility, his gusto, his affection for her', yet equally dismayed by his black rages and random cruelty. She was one of the few women who could call him to order. That autumn, when Evelyn joined her in Birmingham while she was touring the provinces in a revival of *The Miracle*, a red-faced man approached them and breathlessly asked if he was going the right way to the railway station. Evelyn replied that indeed he was, knowing full well that the station was in the opposite direction. When it dawned on Diana what he had done she refused to speak to him again until he ran after the man, corrected the mistake and helped him with his heavy suitcase.[70]

It was a measure of how greatly Diana delighted in Evelyn's company that she was prepared to forgive such indefensible badness and welcomed his frequent visits over the next few months as she moved about the theatres of Manchester, Glasgow and Edinburgh. He would sit loyally with her in her dressing room and later take her out to dinner; by day they toured the great houses of the district – Chatsworth, Hardwick, Belton, and her two old family homes, Haddon and Belvoir.

Mindful perhaps of her husband's well-known infidelities, Evelyn was at first not entirely averse to the idea of an affair, however that was the last thing Diana wanted. When she later learned how Evelyn had snorted at the notion of her as a *'grande amoureuse'*, she retorted: 'How the hell can he tell if I am or not? Just because I never responded to his dribbling, dwarfish little amorous *singeries*, he need not be so sure!'[71] If that sounded cruelly dismissive, she could be equally eloquent on the subject of her devotion to him, later recalling that during this time she had 'wanted to bind Evelyn to my heart with hoops of steel'.[72] In a possible reference to Baby Jungman, she wrote to him: 'You know perfectly well that you have no Baby as loyal as this Baby and if you believe anything else you are very foolish.'[73]

Black Mischief was published at the beginning of October, dedicated 'With love to Mary and Dorothy Lygon'. An exuberantly tasteless black comedy about the absurd attempts of Oxford-educated Emperor Seth to modernise the fictional African island of Azania, it met with mixed reviews. The most glowing came from L. A. G. Strong in *The Spectator*, who pronounced it 'a brilliant book', 'exceedingly funny', 'amazingly well-written'. 'No one but Mr Waugh could have written a single page of it.'[74] Eric Linklater in *The Listener* was similarly effusive: 'The manner in which Mr Waugh controls his widely varied matter is admirable. His narrative is swift and picturesque, and his cutting – if one may borrow a Hollywood term – is masterly. "Black Mischief", indeed, shows an all-round growth of strength.'[75] Others, though, were less convinced, among them James Agate in the *Express*, who found the satire 'heavy-handed', while Geoffrey West in *Bookman* complained that 'Mr Waugh still seems to suffer from his early illusion that the vapid fatuities of Ronald Firbank are funny.'[76] None of this greatly bothered Evelyn, not least since it was the Book Society's choice as Book of the Month, the first impression of 15,000 copies sold out before publication, and by early October a third was already in the press.

In matters of the heart, however, Evelyn's situation remained as bleak as ever. The marriage later that month of his brother Alec to an Australian heiress called Joan Chirnside served only to underline his own lack of progress with Baby Jungman, as did the fact that he was unlikely to be able to marry anyone at all now that he was a Catholic divorcee. At the wedding itself Evelyn was seen to behave 'like a malignant demon with a red hot poker' and loudly announced to anyone within earshot that he had now set his sights on the attractive Surrealist painter Eileen Agar, ignoring the fact that she was there with her six-foot-tall Hungarian boyfriend (later husband) Joseph Bard. Evelyn subsequently renewed his acquaintance with Eileen while staying the weekend with Alec and Joan, where Eileen recalled how he tried to 'lure, charm and finally push me into the bushes on our walks through the woods' and later that night boldly called for her outside her bedroom door, which she rewarded only with a chaste kiss on the brow, 'cool as a coconut, but with perhaps a hint of indulgence', as she recorded. She was perfectly happy with her 'calm and steady' existing lover and 'had no desire to rush into a passionate and agitated affair which would leave me no chance to pursue my all-consuming interest – painting'.[77]

Evelyn was evidently neither Baby Jungman nor Eileen Agar's type, however he was then still impishly good looking, as well as affectionate, charming, clever and extremely funny, and there were undoubtedly women who did find him attractive. A year or two later, he had an affair with a married actress in her early twenties called Clare Mackenzie (stage name Clare Brocklebank), whom he took to stay at Chagford and then evidently abandoned: 'That was the unkindest cut of all,' she wrote to him afterwards. 'Was it absolutely necessary to leave me when I needed you so desperately badly? . . . I can't believe you would willingly kick me so hard once I was down. One kind word last night would, I believe, have saved me cracking so badly . . . My hand is so shaky this morning I can hardly hold the pencil steady, but the doctor's given me some soothing medicine which may help. And God do I need it after your note this morning. I shan't stay here long now; what's the use, I should only be miserable without you . . . I still can hardly believe you've really done this . . . Please ignore a telegram in very bad taste if it reaches you I hope it doesn't. I'm afraid I felt so ill I lost all sense of proportion & broke the rules.'[78]

He cast an even more powerful spell on Joyce Gill, two years his senior, whom as Joyce Fagan he had first met via Alec while he was at Oxford, and smuggled into an all-male party with her posing as Terence Greenidge. She was the only guest to dinner at Underhill on his 21st birthday and it was her flat in Canonbury Square that Evelyn rented after his marriage to Shevelyn in 1928. At some point after the marriage ended, Evelyn and Joyce began an affair. To outward appearances she remained devoted to her American husband, Donald Gill, yet throughout her marriage Joyce had wrestled with a side of her nature that was bohemian, flirtatious, impulsive and adventurous, and she later admitted having agonised over a suggestion of Evelyn's that she abandon her family and accompany him on one of his expeditions in the 1930s. In 1938, after Evelyn had remarried and was about to become a father, Joyce wrote him a letter that said much about the intensity of their relationship:

It is too difficult not to write to you now, Evelyn, because things have not been going well, because it's nearly March 13th which was the day you jokingly suggested that we might meet each year until I am 70. And so I suppose that day will be for me a kind of lovely agony for ever and ever . . . I have arranged my life now, as I think best, to give the least trouble to you or to Don. When you were married I found that to drive the children back to their Prep-School I had to pass very near to you. So, to be out of temptation, I arranged to have them living at home. It is better so, anyway . . . And in compensation, I do what you suggested & what in my foolishness I thought almost a crime. I think of you all the time when I am making love, until the word and Evelyn are almost synonymous! And in the darkness each night & in the greyness of each morning when I wake I remember your face & your voice and your body and everything about you so earnestly and intensely that you become almost tangibly beside me. And after that I can forget you for the day (except when I am alone). It is a kind of exercise which, together with being tied hand & foot by the family, keeps me from behaving like the pitiable sort of fool I was 2 years ago. At least I hope it will keep me from it. It is only for the next few years. After I am 40 I won't want to see you. Then it will just be dismal aged despair! Then even the impossible possibility of having your child will be gone. And I suppose that is at the root of this – this – I can't call it infatuation because I know that that is an unworthy word for it; because I know, darling, that love is a juster description. And every night I tell myself that your wife now has your child in her body and I think of it and of you always, so that when I do hear or read about it I shall not be unprepared. I tried to do the same thing about your marriage, but darling, it was the dearest kindest thing of you to write about it, and it is because you are like that – because you are Evelyn, that I shall try most terribly hard to conform to the normal convention of 'decency' (Christ! what a phrase) and not bombard you with love letters. And if I do ever write darling, it is not a 'begging letter' only because I remember that once you said 'write to me if it helps'. I know that was before you were married again – so I shall not write every day . . . Almost I could be contented if every night I could write & say 'Evelyn I love you' & every morning I could say Evelyn God bless you! But what nonsense! Of course I could not be content. I have only to remember your eyes – your mouth and my heart aches as if it were a stone cut by a diamond . . . Goodnight & good morning and good day for always, dearest.[79]

* * *

In the autumn of 1932 travel again seemed to offer Evelyn the best means of distraction from his lovesickness, and after pondering a variety of far-flung destinations – Moscow, Borneo, Peking – he finally settled on the Amazon jungle. When he sent Baby a copy of *Black Mischief* in late September 'simply to show you that I was still thinking of you', he breezily added that he was 'Off to British Guiana quite soon'.[80] However the prospect of leaving appeared only to intensify his feelings for her. In October he told her from Chagford that it seemed 'all make-believe being genial and friendly with you just as much as it was before when I was disagreeable because when the natural relationship is love everything else is a fraud'.[81]

Sometime later, on a final visit to Diana in Glasgow before setting off to South America, he wrote again to Baby: 'I miss you but I won't go on about that.'[82] Two days before he left she joined him for lunch at the Ritz with a Guiana-hand called Lieutenant-Colonel Ivan Davson: 'She sat quiet while he and I spread a map on the table and talked of Guiana,' Evelyn recorded.

On his last evening, 1 December, they dined together at Quaglino's (caviar aux blinis, cold partridge, marrow on toast) and the next morning attended Mass at Spanish Place followed by breakfast over which she presented him with a medal of St Christopher, the patron saint of travelers, to wear round his neck – 'gold, Cartier, very expensive,' he told Diana, 'saved out of her pocket money. Deeply moved.'[83] They motored down to the docks at Tilbury in her mother's car. 'Deadly lonely, cold, and slightly sick at parting,' Evelyn wrote in his diary. 'Teresa drove off to lunch with Lady Astor in London. We sailed at about half-past two. Down the river in heavy rain and twilight. Heart of lead.'

14

....

Off to the Forest

Shortly before leaving for Georgetown Evelyn told Diana Cooper that he
had spent 'a very pious few days going to church with that Dutch girl'.[1]
They had even discussed the possibility of their both 'taking up the religious life', as he recalled in a letter to Baby en route, albeit adding that on
reflection it now seemed very presumptuous to have been talking about it
'as though it were joining a club'. 'Here am I going off to the forest to see
if it would suit me to be a missionary,' he wrote. 'It is just like the people
who used to be continually coming to my father and saying they would
like to be novelists because it was congenial indoor work with no fixed
hours and long holidays.'[2]

As he implied, he was not perhaps obvious missionary material, yet
however seriously he ever viewed that aim, the mordant account he subsequently wrote in *Ninety-Two Days* (the title itself brought to mind a
prison sentence) suggests that he did look upon the journey as a form of
penance – even if the artist in him also hoped that this distant and barbarous place might yield 'experiences vivid enough to demand translation
into literary form'.

His choice of British Guiana (now the independent republic of
Guyana) came from the fact that it had always seemed to him on a
map to be 'absurdly remote'.[3] However, he may have been additionally
prompted by Peter Fleming's recent reports in *The Times* describing
a harebrained expedition to try and find the explorer Colonel Fawcett,
who had vanished seven years earlier in the Brazilian jungle while
searching for the lost city of El Dorado. Two days before leaving
Evelyn had had tea with Fleming 'to talk of equipment for forests'.[4]
The next day he had packed a suitcase and grip: 'A few tropical suits,

camera, books, a pair of field boots and settler shirt and shorts.'[5]

Evelyn's previous travels, including the trip to Abyssinia, had never taken him far from the company of other Europeans or for that matter a hotel, however his expedition to British Guiana was to be of an altogether different order, 'sterner stuff', as Eric Newby later classed it, involving travel 'much more in the manner of a Victorian explorer: with guides who were at best unpredictable, through country in which there was a considerable degree of danger'.[6]

The discomforts began as soon as he boarded the SS *Ingoma* at Tilbury. This sluggish cargo vessel was 'not at all like Highclere',[7] he told Maimie Lygon, but instead resembled 'an Irish packet-boat with the second-class decks removed to leave a clear deck for the accommodation of two prize bulls, a race horse, a couple of fox hounds and some hens'.[8] The heating system did not work – a particularly unfortunate defect in midwinter – and it creaked noisily 'like a pair of new boots'.

For the first week until they were well past the Azores the sea was very rough, however while most of the other thirty passengers were 'being sick or else very sullen & quiet', Evelyn, who was a good sailor, resiliently strode about the boat with a big cigar feeling like 'no end of a swell', as he told Maimie Lygon.[9] Otherwise he lay in the three-berth cabin he had managed to secure for himself, smoking, studying maps of the jungle and reading – histories of Guiana, D'Arcy's *Nature of Belief* and two books of Thomist philosophy.

He thought a lot about Baby and wrote to tell her that he 'could have cried at any moment' as they parted. 'I wanted very much to kiss you goodbye but didn't have the heart to [risk] another escape.'[10] The next day he wrote again: 'Your St Christopher comforts me and gives me a feeling of not being quite alone. Think of me sometimes.'[11] A few days later he told her that she was 'very often in my thoughts – closer and dearer than ever before', and in another letter: 'Don't go falling in love with anyone while I'm away. I thought it would be a good thing but now I know I couldn't bear it ... I'd sooner have your love with all the unhappiness it would probably cause both of us, than anything I can think of at the moment.'[12]

After two weeks at sea they finally reached Antigua and two days after that Barbados. On Trinidad Evelyn was shown around by a man who disconcertingly disclosed that he was Baby Jungman's first cousin, and more awkwardly he was invited to stay by the manager of a hotel that Alec had insulted at length in *The Coloured Countries*. Plied with multiple rum swizzles and lent silk pyjamas and a dressing-gown 'gayer than I should have dared choose for myself', he pronounced all this an 'exemplary manner in which to accept criticism'.[13] Privately, however, he recorded that except for the new bed, 'the hotel had all the defects Alec complained of'.[14] 'General impression of Trinidad,' he concluded, 'that I don't want to see it again.'[15]

His first glimpse of Guiana, on 22 December, was no more uplifting: 'misty palm-fringe through pouring rain and a few factory chimneys . . . dreary wind-swept wharfs; some corrugated iron roofs of warehouses'. On the bright side there was a cable from Baby and an interview with a local paper which produced the headline: 'Handsome and Well-Formed Novelist'.[16] Nonetheless he recorded: 'General impression of Georgetown that I don't mind how soon I leave it.'[17]

Obliged to stay there for ten days while he planned his venture into the interior, he was looked after over Christmas by the Governor, Sir Edward Denham, and his wife, lunching with them on Christmas Eve at Government House, dining there again on Christmas Day – 'Rather a pathetic evening of the Denhams' charming attempts to be homely among childless officials . . . I sat between a black attorney general and a white archdeacon'[18] – and the day after Boxing Day embarking on a three-day trip up the great Essequibo River on their comfortable steam yacht.

At last all was ready for his own expedition and on New Year's Eve he wrote to Baby: 'Unless anything odd happens you won't hear from me for some time as I am just starting on a journey up country and there are no post offices there. I don't quite know where I am going yet.'[19]

His guide was an emaciated eccentric called Mr Haynes (Mr Bain in *Ninety-Two Days*), commissioner for the Rupununi district. 'Half black and more than half crazy',[20] as Evelyn described him to Diana Cooper, Haynes was soon regaling Evelyn with accounts of his horse, which supposedly swam underwater, and how he found his way through the bush with the help of parrots which flew on ahead on reconnaissance.

On 3 January 1933 they caught a slow train down the coast to New Amsterdam and the next day a paddle steamer up the Berbice River with 'monotonous vegetable walls on either bank' to Takama. They continued from there by horse south to Kurukupari ('I had no idea where Kurupukari was, but it sounded as good as anywhere else'),[21] covering the ninety miles in six days, with Mr Haynes constantly discoursing on subjects such as his own extraordinary honesty, courage, efficiency, generosity, horseman-ship, physical prowess and sex appeal. He had a fair amount to say too about the local fauna and in *Ninety-Two Days* Evelyn later recorded a few of the choicest examples of his guide's 'experienced ear':

'Listen,' said Mr Bain one day, 'that is most interesting. It is what we call "the six o'clock beetle", because he always makes that noise at exactly six o'clock.'

'But it is now quarter past four.'

'Yes, that is what is so interesting.'[22]

'Throughout the week's ride,' Evelyn wrote in his diary, 'Haynes did not once stop talking, except at night when he kept me awake with asthma and retching.'[23] By the time they reached Kurukupari – a single wooden house in a clearing on a slight hill – he had had quite enough of his com-panion and left him behind as he pressed on towards the ranch of a man named Christie, a further five days' ride away.

When he eventually arrived there on the afternoon of 20 January after an 'intolerably hot ride' through bush and savannah, a few hours ahead of his two bearers and cook, Evelyn found Mr Christie 'reclining in ham-mock and sipping cold water from the spout of a white enamelled teapot'. Christie had 'a long white moustache and white woolly head; his face was of the same sun-baked, fever-blanched colour as were most faces in the colony but of unmistakeable Negro structure'. When Evelyn greeted him and asked where he could water his horse, Christie smiled at him dream-ily and told him that he had been expecting him:

'I always know the character of any visitors by the visions I have of them. Sometimes I see a pig or a jackal; often a ravening tiger.'

I could not resist asking, 'And how did you see me?'

'As a sweetly-toned harmonium,' said Mr Christie politely.[24]

That night they drank a lot of rum and talked about Christie's preaching and his translation of the scriptures into Macushi. Christie recalled seeing in another vision 'the Love of God' and, as Evelyn recalled, 'pronounced it to be spherical in shape and slightly larger than a football'.[25] Evelyn later wondered if he had dreamt the whole encounter until he read in a mission magazine about a previous visitor to Mr Christie's ranch, a priest who had offered his host one of the medals of Our Lady which he carried for distribution among converts. Christie studied it for a moment before giving it back: 'Why should I require an image of someone I see so frequently?' he said. 'Besides, it is an exceedingly poor likeness.'[26]

The next morning Evelyn was off again at 6.45 a.m. and by eleven he had reached the next ranch on the border with Brazil, where he wolfed down 'a dish of fried eggs, minced tasso fried with herbs, bananas and delicious Brazilian coffee'.[27] At the next ranch, a few more hours on, he gratefully accepted a lift in a motor van to Bon Success, which did the journey in a third of the time it would have taken by horse, albeit rather less comfortably. From Bon Success he then drove on up beside the Takutu River to the Jesuit mission at St Ignatius, 'as lonely an outpost of religion as you could find anywhere'.[28] There he spent a very affecting ten days as a guest of Father Mather, 'the kindest and most generous of all the hosts of the colony', whose skill at carpentry reinforced Evelyn's view of the priest as craftsman, 'a man with a job which he alone was qualified to do'.

Evelyn eventually moved on on 1 February and three days later reached Boa Vista, a town whose name ('lovely view' in Portuguese) combined with Haynes's misleading description had led him to imagine rather more than the ramshackle huddle of squalid buildings that greeted him. Gone in an instant was the mirage he had conjured of 'shady boulevards; kiosks for flowers and cigars and illustrated papers; the hotel terrace and the cafés; the baroque church built by seventeenth-century missionaries . . .'[29] More alarmingly, no one seemed to know anything about the fast motor launches that supposedly plied constantly between there and Manaós and by which Evelyn hoped to be able to return to civilisation via the Amazon River. At the Benedictine mission where Father Mather had arranged for him to stay, the monk told him that it was quite impossible to predict when another boat would leave.[30] During his days of waiting he found little to occupy himself other than to wander desultorily about the town and every so often call in at the wireless office to see if there was any news of the boat. 'Goodness the boredom of Boa Vista,' he wrote to Diana Cooper after he had been stuck there a week, 'I am already nearly crazy. No one here speaks a word of English. The Benedictine priest (Swiss) knows a few sentences of French but for the last four days he has been down with fever. There are no books except an ant-eaten edition of Bous-set's sermons and some back numbers of a German pious periodical for children. One cannot get drunk as the only liquor in the village is some very mild, very warm beer, which I can drink at a table in the store in a cloud of flies stared at by Brazilians in pyjama suits and boaters. There are of course no cars or boats for hire and nowhere to go in them if there were. No roads outside the village at all – bush on one side, pampas on the other, vast shallow river full of sand banks on other sides. No hotel or café or life of any kind. Everyone asleep most of the day . . . I shan't ever again undertake a journey of this kind alone. I am getting homesick and shall return direct as soon as I get to Manaós.'[31]

As so often with Evelyn, boredom eventually gave way to a burst of creativity, and five days later he sent his agent what he described as 'a grade A short story', almost certainly 'The Man Who Liked Dickens', the superbly chilling tale which later served as the penultimate chapter of *A Handful of Dust*, the novel now seen as his greatest masterpiece. Accord-ing to Evelyn's diary the story was written in just two days between 12 and 14 February, although evidently it had been brewing in his imagination ever since he left Mr Christie, who is the clear original in the short story of Mr McMaster (Mr Todd in *A Handful of Dust*), the sinister settler who takes the hapless Paul Henty (Tony Last) captive on his isolated ranch and makes him read Dickens to him day after day for the rest of his life.

'The Man Who Liked Dickens' draws on Evelyn's feelings of being stranded in Boa Vista combined with the remembered sensation of en-trapment he had felt while his father sat in the book-room at Underhill reading aloud from Dickens – a memory doubtless revived by the stash of Dickens novels Father Mather kept at St Ignatius. McMaster, incidentally, was the name of one of Arthur Waugh's closest friends.

Henty has stumbled on McMaster's ranch while on an expedition aimed at winning back his unfaithful wife. When a rescue party of three Englishmen does finally arrive, Henty misses them because he has been drugged by McMaster, who calmly tells him when he wakes:

'I thought you would not mind – as you could not greet them yourself I gave them a little souvenir, your watch. They wanted something to take home to your wife who is offering a great reward for news of you. They were very pleased with it. And they took some photographs of the little cross I put up to commemorate your coming. They were very pleased with that too. They were very easily pleased. But I do not suppose they will visit us again, our life here is so retired . . . no pleasures except reading . . . I do not suppose we shall ever have visitors again . . . well, well, I will get you some medicine to make you feel better. Your head aches, does it not . . . We will not have any Dickens today . . . but tomorrow, and the day after that, and the day after that. Let us read *Little Dorrit* again. There are passages in that book I can never hear without the temptation to weep.'

Unlike Henty, after two weeks in Boa Vista Evelyn did eventually manage to escape, albeit by horse as the promised trade boats had failed to show up, and back towards Georgetown having given up on the idea of Manaós. On the second day, after going on ahead of his guide, he contrived to get lost and was extremely fortunate to stumble upon a hut belonging to an English-speaking Indian just when he and his horse could go no further, a stroke of luck the odds of which Evelyn estimated at 54 million to one. The Indian also happened to be heading to Bon Success, so within a couple of days Evelyn was safely back with Father Mather at St Ignatius, from where he wrote to Baby on Ash Wednesday telling her that he had been 'saved by the miraculous intervention of St Christopher' and bade her look forward to his return 'on account of my bearing and beauty and wit and nobility of character'.[32]

He did not reach Georgetown for a further six weeks, however, having rashly chosen a 'very unpansy'[33] route over the Pakaraima Mountains to the upper waters of the Potaro and so down to the Essequibo. 'One has to walk all the time as there is no trail for lamas,' he wrote to Baby, 'and one has a party of Indians in front with choppers clearing the path so it is very slow going.'[34] It was an even grimmer journey than he had envisaged, beset by heavy rain, kaboura flies and jiggers that regularly had to be dug out of the soles of his feet. When he eventually made it back he was relieved to find two 'delightful' letters from Baby and he replied that he had got 'a small dead alligator for Wincey [her dog]'.[35] He reached London a month later and promptly took himself off to a hotel in Bath 'to be in good architecture for a little after all those huts and forests', he explained to Baby,[36] and to attend to his backlog of mail.

Evelyn was mildly annoyed to see that an article he had written describing the Rupununi cattle trail had been rechristened by the *Daily Mail*

'My Escape from Mayfair' ('It will be about two years before I dare look anyone in the face again,' he told Baby). Rather more vexing, though, was the discovery that while he was away he had been accused of blasphemy and obscenity in a review of *Black Mischief* by Ernest Oldmeadow, the moralistic editor of Britain's oldest Catholic journal. '*The Tablet* says I am no Catholic,' Evelyn wrote to Baby, 'and yet I carried a torch for two miles in front of the B [Blessed] Sacrament in Trinidad [at Easter on his way home] and I was the only white man.'[37] Gratifyingly, twelve prominent Catholics had sprung to Evelyn's defence and in his absence written to *The Tablet* expressing their 'regard for Mr Waugh' and protesting at the journal's 'bad faith'. Evelyn himself now wrote a scathing 4,000-word 'open letter' to the journal's proprietor, Cardinal Bourne, the Catholic Primate of Great Britain, which Baby sensibly persuaded him not to publish ('Did I tell you I took your advice and rather deferred to your wishes, about the Cardinal's pamphlet?')[38] but which he nonetheless distributed among friends.

From Bath Evelyn went to Madresfield, where he got it into his head one 'bad night' that Baby was about to announce her engagement to Sir Michael Duff, a handsome, bisexual landowner from north Wales, and wrote to her withholding his congratulations 'until I am convinced that he is the solution for our particular problem'.[39] He realised the next morning this was not the case but sent her the letter anyway hoping it would amuse her. The four months away seemed only to have intensified his devotion and he was not shy of saying so. 'I think of you all the time,' he wrote in July. 'I believe you are the first woman I have ever been in love with . . . I love you so much.'[40] When he borrowed the Coopers' house by the sea at Bognor to make a start on *Ninety-Two Days* (dashed off at an astonishing rate within a month), he told Diana: 'Trouble is I think of the dutch girl all day – not sweet voluptuous dreams, no sir, just fretful and it sykeses the work.'[41] The same day he told Baby that he had wasted three sheets of notepaper from not knowing how to begin a letter to her – 'I wrote Sweet Tess and that looked silly and Dear Heart which was sillier still, and Lovely Teresa, which was better . . .'

Two days later, while staying with the Montagus at Breccles Hall in Norfolk, he wrote again: 'I don't think of much except you – your beauty, so fragile and intangible, a thing of fresh water and early morning and the silence of dawn and mist just alloyed with gold and deep, saturated restful greens, like sunrise on that river I travelled down last winter – and your intricate character, all mystery and frustration, a labyrinth with something infinitely secret and infinitely precious at its centre ... I couldn't understand anyone less and want anyone more ... Darling Tess your beauty is all around me like a veil so that every moment apart from you seems obscure and half real.'[42]

However fond Baby was of Evelyn, her inability fully to reciprocate his feelings continued to cause friction. 'It is hard to believe that you can't see me without wanting to have an affair with me,' she wrote to him, 'but if that is so I do _implore_ you not to feel bitter about it and not to behave as if we didn't perfectly understand each other and weren't very fond of each other _indeed_ quite apart from anything else. Please do try and understand what I mean and not be so unkind – You may have so many friends that you can afford to quarrel with me but there can't be many who are as fond of you as I am. So do please, Evelyn, be generous enough not to feel bitterly about me – If only you would be less obstinate about having evil intentions we could perfectly well go on seeing each other like we used to.'[43]

'I am afraid it must be my fault that you are cross with me,' she went on, 'perhaps you feel I made too much use of you during those weeks when I was sad – Forgive me if I did – it was only because I felt you were sympathetic and trusted you completely – _not_ only because you were a Catholic because after all there are a good many others who might have been able to produce priests and advice for me!'[44]

In this instance Baby's unhappiness seems to have stemmed from some kind of religious crisis and Evelyn told her how he had recently been asked by Lady Juliet Duff if it was true that she was going into a convent: 'No, I said, nothing is less likely except her marriage to someone she doesn't love.'[45] He had by then moved on to stay at Madresfield, where he hoped 'to do the work that got upset when I fell in love'.[46] The only other people were Maimie, Coote and Hughie, the latter 'deep in disgrace', so Evelyn told Baby, 'having been tipsy all the weekend and sykesed up the servants and attempted to murder C. Brocklehurst [a Sussex landowner and another of Baby's admirers – years later he left her money in his will]'. Evelyn was sleeping in 'oriental squalor' in Lady Sibell's old room, 'full of bad taste objects', and as usual had nursery as his study. 'My love to you all the time, everywhere,' he wrote to Baby.[47]

With Baby herself about to leave for a holiday in Italy with her mother and sister Zita, Evelyn had allowed her to persuade him to go on what he imagined would be a 'nightmare' Hellenic cruise with a group of fellow Catholics organised by Father Martin D'Arcy. 'You will think me insane when I tell you,' he wrote to Nancy Mitford, 'and you will be jolly well right.'[48] But Baby's imminent departure prompted yet another lovelorn outburst, possibly exacerbated by her confusing ambivalence:

Darling Evelyn,

Don't be cross with me and keep ringing off all the time – you <u>know</u> how fond I am of you and that you were the first person I wanted to see when I was miserable – so please don't ever doubt that, will you? But what do you expect me to do when you say that you might fall in love with me and that your intentions are evil! You see I enjoy that situation too much not to encourage it as much as I can in a subconscious way – and as I mean to try as hard as I possibly can not to behave badly, it wouldn't be very consistent of me to go on seeing you all the time, would it! And quite apart from that I have got such a <u>revulsion</u> suddenly from the ungenerousness of encouraging people as much as I can and then being prim in taxis – I know you will understand this although I explain it very badly – For once in my life I am <u>not</u> just being tiresome and enjoying creating a situation – at least I don't think I am! I am <u>really</u> very fond of you and should like to go on being your friend for the rest of our lives – and I should like to do some enormous thing for you so that you would know that I really mean all this – And if you are ever miserable and want anybody to be sympathetic I only hope that I shall be able to be as sweet to you as you have been to me – Thank you a <u>million</u> times for it, darling Evelyn – you have been an angel – and please do forgive me and not laugh at me for being priggish but I know you will understand me because you always do – If you weren't married you see it would be different because I might or I might not want to marry you but I wouldn't be sure – As things are, I <u>can't</u> be so unfair as to go on when I am quite determined about what I mean to do – Bless you – I might be Helen of Troy from the conceited things I find myself saying![49]

In the weeks leading up to his trip, while staying at Bognor, Evelyn had taken up skipping so as 'to make me prettier for the papist cruisers', he told Baby.[50] The cruisers were to have included 'old Hazel' [Lavery], but she missed the boat, which was a relief to Evelyn, who had been doing his best to avoid her since getting back from Guiana.

In the meantime, Evelyn spared Baby few of his yearnings: 'I love you and that's all there is to it and I know you a little and so realize that you find it hard to do both the hard and the good things that come easily to less remarkable people. You have almost every lovely quality – tolerance, temperance, patience, family affection, discretion, reticence, purity – all unattainable to me. But you're also lazy, cold and undecided. I knew all that long before I fell really in love with you.'[51]

Besides wanting to occupy himself while Baby was in Italy, another of Evelyn's motives for going on the cruise was to try and coax his old friend Alfred Duggan away from the bottle and back towards his lapsed Catholic faith, a mission which Evelyn was to pursue doggedly for many years to come and with eventual success, although on that particular trip Alfred was conspicuously drunk for much of the time and, as Evelyn told Diana, 'broke up badly during last days of voyage on account of switching from beer to Jugo-Slavian brandy'.[52]

Evelyn's more immediate achievement aboard SS *Kraljica Marija* was to make friends with two families of great importance to him in the future, the Asquiths and the Herberts. Of the latter, he made a sufficiently favourable impression on twenty-one-year-old Gabriel Herbert, a first cousin of his first wife, to be invited to go and stay at her family's house at Portofino after the cruise, and in the intervening week he persuaded Katharine Asquith and her son to join him for a few days sightseeing in Ravenna and Bologna.

Katharine, then aged forty-eight, was the widow of H. H. Asquith's brilliant son Raymond, who had been killed on the Somme in 1916. The next year her brother Edward Horner had also been killed in action and she inherited what was left of her family's Mells estate in Somerset and its beautiful sixteenth-century manor house, built for one of her Horner ancestors after the dissolution of Glastonbury Abbey.

A convert to Catholicism during widowhood and in some respects rather pious and high-minded, she nevertheless found Evelyn 'exceedingly amusing and a great collector of the ship's gossip',[53] as did her seventeen-year-old son Julian, 'Trim', who had succeeded his grandfather as the 2nd Earl of Oxford and Asquith in 1928 and whom Evelyn found 'studious, holy and respectful';[54] and her 'very doe-like and sweet' twenty-five-year-old daughter, Lady Helen, a teacher.[55]

The cruise was far more enjoyable than Evelyn had feared and he admitted to Baby he was 'glad you sent me'. Besides his various old and new friends, the ship was 'full of people of high rank,' he told the Lygon sisters, 'including two princesses of ROYAL BLOOD'. That there was 'not much rogering' appeared not to bother him unduly, nor that the food was 'appalling'. In fact the only obvious impediment to his enjoyment was the news that Baby had cut short her Italian trip to return to London. 'If I had realised you would be back so soon I wouldn't now be in the sea of Marmora,' he wrote to her on 1 September. 'If you had been a more enterprising girl you should have joined this cruise at Athens.'[56]

The ship eventually returned to Venice on 12 September, and after the few days sightseeing with the Asquiths, Evelyn made his way to Portofino, and to 'Altachiara', which the Herberts had named in translation of Highclere, although, like Guy Crouchback's 'Castello Crauccibac' in *Sword of Honour*, the locals always referred to it as the Villa Carnarvon. The house party there was presided over by Gabriel's mother Mary Herbert, a 'very decent hostess', according to Evelyn, and included Mary's Catholic friend Hilaire Belloc, various young friends of her children and the four Herbert siblings. The second-youngest of these, Laura, then aged seventeen, would eventually become Evelyn's second wife, although there is no evidence of the merest frisson on this first encounter; indeed he seems barely to have noticed her at all, beyond describing her in a letter to the Asquiths as 'a white mouse'.

* * *

Evelyn was of course still fixated by Baby Jungman, and in any case as a divorcee there seemed no prospect of his marrying anyone at all within the rules of the Catholic Church. Another of his friends on the recent cruise, Christopher Hollis, had noticed how Evelyn had gone to great trouble each day to obtain an English newspaper even though he had never seemed much interested in current affairs. 'Oh,' replied Evelyn when Hollis asked him why he did this, 'just to see if there is any good news – such as, for instance, the death of Mrs Heygate.'[57] For a time after his conversion, Evelyn had indeed taken it for granted that Shevelyn would have to die before the

Church would allow him to remarry, however by this time he had begun exploring with Catholic friends the possibility of applying to the Church to have his marriage annulled. It was presumably to talk about this that Evelyn had lunched with Shevelyn in July – an event referred to in passing in one of his letters to Baby. ('I wrote to my wife and she said lunch with me next week. I have grown my hair long and it has twelve white ones she said.'[58]) By this time Shevelyn's marriage to John Heygate was becoming unstuck and she was keen to do what she could to make amends so far as Evelyn was concerned. 'I felt that the whole thing was my fault,' she wrote later, 'and to pretend innocence was a lie . . . I was naturally anxious that he should get his annulment.'[59]

In October, Evelyn wrote to Coote Lygon: 'I shall be in London on Wed to take my poor wife to be wracked by the Inquisition.'[60] Beforehand the two Evelyns had lunch together again, during which Evelyn was 'pleasant,' Shevelyn recalled, 'and told me exactly what to say, which priest to be aware of and who was on his side. He was anxious to marry again and was afraid the girl would not wait.'[61]

The hearing itself took place in a large, gloomy room adjoining Westminster Cathedral, with 'a bevy of priests at a seemingly never ending table' as Shevelyn recalled, and four additional witnesses: Alec Waugh, Pansy Lamb, Shevelyn's sister Alathea and her husband Geoffrey Fry. Evelyn requested an annulment on the grounds of 'the lack of real consent', contending that, first, he and his wife had entered the marriage on the understanding that it could be dissolved at the wish of either party and, second, that children had been excluded for an indefinite period.

The second argument was eventually rejected over its failure to meet the required standard of proof, but the first argument prevailed after both Evelyns described themselves as nominal Anglicans (at best) at the time of their marriage, and testified that their church wedding had been a 'conventional formality' and that the words of the ceremony had meant nothing.[62] In support of Evelyn's case, Pansy Lamb went so far as to recall that 'They came to an agreement in my presence that, if the marriage was not happy, they would not be bound by it, and Miss Evelyn said to me that she had no intention of remaining married if the marriage did not turn out well. The arrangement was not a written contract but a mutual agreement, each accepting divorce as a definitive solution to possible misfortune.'[63] Even though the Westminster judges expressed doubts at the time about this evidence on the basis that it seemed to say 'more than the parties said themselves', the Rota eventually dismissed their reservations and granted a declaration of nullity: 'It is established beyond doubt on the evidence that the parties excluded the indissolubility of the bond of marriage by a specific act of will.'[64]

Almost three years were to pass before this judgment was delivered, however, due to what the Rota called 'reprehensible delays' in Cardinal Bourne's office at Westminster, where the papers concerning Evelyn's case lay forgotten until he eventually asked about them again in 1935. But at the time Evelyn was confident that his marriage would soon be annulled and so he felt free at last to propose to Baby Jungman. 'Just heard yesterday that my divorce comes on today,' he wrote to Maimie Lygon, 'so was elated and popped question to Dutch girl and got raspberry. So that is that, eh. Stiff upper lip and dropped cock. Now I must go. How sad, how sad.'[65]

15

I Can't Advise You in My Favour

After such a long and anxious build-up it was something of a relief for Evelyn finally to have got his proposal off his chest – even though the response was not the one he had wanted. Shortly afterwards the archbishop's office told him that while they were confident he would get his annulment, it was unlikely to come through for at least eighteen months. 'It is funny how things turn out,' he wrote to Baby when he heard this. 'Imagine my impatience and despair if I had been honourable and decided to wait till I was free before popping the question. Now having popped it and got my answer it is all more or less O.K.'[1]

Whether or not he was putting a brave face on it, in other respects Baby's rejection marked the low point of a difficult and desolate autumn, much of which he had spent by the sea at Diana Cooper's house in Sussex working on *Ninety-Two Days*, which he finished in the second week of November. 'It is a very sad life I lead,' he wrote to Coote Lygon, 'very lonely, very uncomfortable, in a filthy cottage in the ugliest place in England with only mice for company like a prisoner in the tower. Still I write my boring book, hand over fist and that is something.'[2]

Though he was buoyed by writing as fast as ever, rattling off up to 4,000 words a day, his birthday had been a forlorn and introspective affair. 'I was thirty on Saturday & feel sixty,' he wrote to Maimie Lygon. 'I celebrated the day by walking into Bognor and going to the Cinema in the best 1/6 seats. I saw a love film about two people who were in love; they were very loving and made me cry.'[3] Reaching the milestone had hit him hard, 'not the time wasted but the 45 years or so to come', he told Baby. 'You are between 20 and 30 and can always die young and that is all right, high promise unfulfilled, and so on. No one ever dies between 30 and 75.'[4]

However calmly he affected to take Baby's refusal to marry him, it was not long before Evelyn began beseeching her again. 'Of course what I asked for last night was out of all reason,' he acknowledged in early December. 'It is just that there are periods when one has to hope for a miracle because there seems no possibility of things going right by natural causes.'[5] Baby told him that she could no longer accept kisses or presents from him and sent back the chain he had bought her as a Christmas present, but as so often the messages soon became mixed again and when Evelyn went to Madresfield for Christmas, she sent him a sponge, which seemed to set him off again: 'I have clung to the last sponge you gave me through many changes of bathroom; I threw its shreds away today and will stick to the new one for months to come.'[6]

* * *

At such times the easiest way for Evelyn to cope was to go abroad and on 29 December he wrote to Baby from the SS *Raisai I Huid* bound for Morocco. 'You will say it was sly to go away without saying anything . . . But please believe it isn't only selfish – running away from pain (though it has been more painful than you know, all the last months, realizing every day that I was becoming less attractive and less important to you) – but also I can't be any good to you without your love and it's the worst possible thing for you to have to cope with the situation that had come about between us.'[7]

After disembarking at Tangier he took the overnight train to Fez, 'a city of astonishing beauty,' he wrote to Katharine Asquith, 'with running streams & fountains everywhere and enormous covered gateways in very narrow streets – no wheeled traffic, miles of bazaar, elaborate medieval fortifications, hills all round dotted with forts, olive trees, sand cliffs & spring grass, waterfalls. Dense crowds of moors and a few French soldiers – mostly Senegalese or Foreign Legion – practically no touting for tourists.'[8]

The more worldly Diana Cooper (who had seen him off) and the Lygon girls were treated to his tales from the red-light district: 'It was very gay and there were little Arab girls of fifteen & sixteen for ten francs each & a cup of mint tea. So I bought one but I didn't enjoy her very much because she had skin like sandpaper and a huge stomach which didn't show until she took off her clothes & then it was too late.'[9] More to his liking was a girl called Fatima whom he got to know on subsequent visits and briefly thought about installing in his own lodgings. 'She is not at all Dutch in her ways,' he told Maimie. 'She is brown in colour and her face is tattooed all over with blue patterns v. pretty but does not play the piano beautifully, she has a gold tooth she is very proud of but as we can't talk each other's language there is not much to do in between rogering.'[10]

Evelyn's other priority in Morocco was to write the novel he had been thinking about during the previous year and made a tentative start on in December at Chagford. Explaining the genesis of what eventually became *A Handful of Dust*, he later recalled that after writing 'The Man Who Liked Dickens' in British Guiana, 'the idea keeps working in my mind. I wanted to discover how the prisoner got there, and eventually the thing grew into a study of other sorts of savages at home and the civilised man's helpless plight among them.'[11]

The civilised man in his new book was Tony Last, innocent squire of Hetton Abbey, the savages his unfaithful wife Brenda and her young lover John Beaver. Like all Evelyn's previous novels, it was firmly rooted in his own experience, drawing on the bitterness he still felt over Shevelyn's betrayal coupled with his more recent rejection by Baby Jungman; however he was now attempting something much more serious than his previous black comedies. 'I peg away at the novel which seems to me faultless of its kind,' he wrote to Katharine Asquith. 'Very difficult to write because for the first time I am trying to deal with normal people instead of eccentrics. Comic English character parts too easy when one gets to be thirty.'[12] In early February 1934 he told her: 'The novel drags on at 10,000 words a week. I have just killed a little boy at a lawn meet & made his mother commit adultery & his father get drunk so perhaps you won't like it after all.'[13] Every so often he sent instalments back to his agent in London to be typed up. Though still undecided how it would end, he told Peters that the dénouement might possibly be the same as that of 'The Man Who Liked Dickens'.

Eventually it was, and when the book was published later in the year Henry Yorke was among those who found the ending 'so fantastic that it throws the rest out of proportion. Aren't you mixing two things together? The first part of the book is convincing, a real picture of people one has met and may at any moment meet again. Then comes the perfectly feasible, very moving, & beautifully written death of that horrible little boy after which the family breaks up. Then the father goes abroad with that very well drawn horror Messinger. That too is splendid & I've no complaints. But then to let Tony be detained by some madman introduces an entirely fresh note & we are in phantasy with a ph at once. I was terrified towards the end by thinking you would let him die of fever which to my mind would have been false but what you did do to him was far far worse. It seemed manufactured & not real.'[14]

Evelyn was unperturbed by his friend's assessment: 'Very many thanks for your letter of criticism,' he replied. 'You must remember that to me the savages come into the category of "people one has met and may at any moment meet again". I think they appear fake to you largely because you don't really believe they exist . . . I think I agree that the Todd episode is fantastic. It is a "conceit" in the Webster manner – wishing to bring Tony to a sad end I made it an elaborate & improbable one. I think too the sentimental episode with Therese in the ship is probably a mistake. But the Amazon stuff had to be there. The scheme was a Gothic man in the hands of savages – first Mrs Beaver etc. then the real ones finally the silver foxes at Hetton. All that quest for a city seems to me justifiable symbolism.'[15]

In his introduction to a 2003 edition of the novel, William Boyd suggested Evelyn was being disingenuous here, contending that what really happened was that he 'needed an ending and realized he had already written something that would do', and that 'rather than any huffing and puffing about Websterian conceits' the author's primary objective had been to bring Tony to a sad end in line with his belief in the cruel and frequently unfair workings of Fate. It is true that Tony's hellish destiny was in keeping with Evelyn's pessimistic world view and that he frequently reused what he had already written before – his letters abound with passages shamelessly lifted word for word from those to other correspondents. However the Websterian conceit had not been dreamt up on the spur of the moment in response to Yorke but had been in Evelyn's mind as early as February, when the book was still only half finished and he told Diana Cooper that it was 'rather like Webster in modern idiom'.[16]

* * *

Evelyn returned from Morocco in late February 1934, 'sweetened by solitude', he told Diana, and took himself straight off to Chagford to finish his novel, after which he planned to go and live in Oxford to write a life of Pope Gregory the Great. In the meantime, the American magazine *Harper's Bazaar* asked for an alternative ending to *A Handful of Dust* before they would agree to serialise it, given that 'The Man Who Liked Dickens' had appeared the previous year in *Cosmopolitan*. 'I'll get the happy ending done by Saturday,' he told Peters testily in early April, intending to rattle off 5,000 words describing Tony and Brenda's reconciliation. Evidently he procrastinated and several weeks later, when *Harper's* began to pester him about delivery, he exploded: 'God how I hate Americans ... They can't have the end tomorrow because it's not written but I'll do it this week if necessary.'[17]

By early July he was back in London and dropped in at the Lygons' townhouse off Belgrave Square where he found Hughie drinking gin in the library. Hughie announced that he was going to the Arctic island of Spitsbergen in two days' time with a young explorer named Alexander ('Sandy') Glen (later Sir Alexander Glen, chairman of the British Tourist Authority), whom Hugh had met recently though his sister Sibell. On the spur of the moment Evelyn decided to go with them.

After giving Glen £25 for his fare and buying some kit – skis, ice axes, balaclava helmets, windproof clothes, sleeping bag and mackintosh cover – he spent the evening before he left with Winnie, his favourite girl from Mrs Meyrick's 43 Club, who 'put up a good show of being sorry for my departure',[18] he recorded. The next morning he went to Farm Street Church 'to confess Winnie' and bought a birthday cake for Baby Jungman.

Having studiously refrained from contacting Baby for the past six months, now he was off on his travels again he felt emboldened to send 'My Darling Tess' his love for her birthday: 'You are nearly always in my thoughts wherever I am,' he wrote. 'Have a happy year and if ever you aren't happy and you think I could help you are to ask for me.'[19] By the time her birthday arrived they had reached Bergen and Evelyn noted in his diary that Baby 'ought now to be receiving a series of parcels from me with no name attached. It is more fun for her that way.'[20] A few days later, after threading their way northwards towards Tromsø, he wrote to Diana: 'I don't like Norwegians at all. The sun never sets, the bar never opens, and the whole country smells of kippers.'[21]

In the early evening of 17 July they finally caught sight of the south cape of Spitsbergen: 'Black mountains with glaciers flowing down to the sea between them – occasionally a magnificent burst of light on a narrow silver strip between iron grey sky and iron grey sea, the glaciers brilliantly white, the clouds cutting off the peaks of the mountains.'[22] From Advent Bay they took a whaling boat up the west coast to some remote mining huts, where Glen committed the cardinal sin of giving the whaler crew their bottle of rum as he said goodbye, causing 'very little pleasure to them and great concern to Hughie and me', according to Evelyn.

They spent the next two days on this desolate shore lashing the sledge, waxing their skis and repacking their provisions before rowing their small boat across the bay to another derelict hut: 'Seals bobbed in the water around us,' wrote Evelyn; 'there were innumerable small icebergs, some white and fluffy, others deep green and blue like weathered copper, some opaque, some clear as glass, in preposterous shapes, with fragile, haphazard wings and feathers of ice, pierced by holes. The whole bay was filled by their music, sometimes a shrill cricket-cry, sometimes a sharp, almost regular ticking, sometimes the low hum of a hive of bees, sometimes a sharp splintering, sometimes a resonant boom . . .'[23]

The plan was to climb a glacier and sledge across inland ice to some unexplored territory in the north-east of the island, but first they had to lug all their gear for three miles up a muddy mosquito-infested valley, requiring two trips a day with loads of up to 40lbs, 'beastly work' by Evelyn's account. They had hoped the worst would be over by the time they reached the ice, however an exceptional thaw had rendered the ice rough and hummocky and the snow so soggy that they could only manage five miles a day in ten hours of extreme labour. The glacier itself then proved too badly crevassed to negotiate, so they turned west towards the shore, where Glen promised they would find a trappers' cabin and a boat left by his last expedition.

Glen's invincible and to Evelyn's mind foolhardy optimism had long since begun to grate, besides which Evelyn did not especially relish taking orders from a twenty-two-year-old undergraduate. In his diary he referred to Glen sarcastically as 'the leader' and sprinkled the only account he published of their expedition (subtitled 'Fiasco in the Arctic') with a series of digs: 'G tried to swim, but quickly scrambled out, blue and shuddering, saying that it had warmed him . . . G had said that on the coast we could "live on the country". He and Hugh went out with their guns but came back empty-handed . . . G assured us that we should have a craving for fat as soon as we were on the ice. We did not find it so.'[24] Evelyn also chided him for being too eager to shoot seals just in case they might need to eat them, lecturing him on the sanctity of life for animals as well as humans.

It came as no great surprise to Evelyn that when they eventually reached the cabin the boat was not there. After sleeping for six or seven hours, Glen and Hugh set off to retrieve their sledge which exhaustion had obliged them to abandon en route, leaving Evelyn to sort out the cabin. When he had done that he lay down on the furs covering the bunk and sank into a deep sleep – from which he was urgently roused by Glen. One of the small streams that they had all crossed with ease a few hours earlier had since become a raging torrent and while Hugh, who was tall and strong, had managed to cross it and go on to fetch the sledge, Glen could not and thought Hugh would be extremely hard pushed to get back across without help. As Evelyn and Glen hurried back there, they heard the roar of the water half an hour before they reached it. 'When finally we stood on the bank the sound was so great that we could barely make ourselves heard, shouting in each other's ears,' Evelyn recalled. 'The flow was terrific, of no great depth as yet, and still divided by shingle banks into four or five streams, running at a dizzy speed, full of boulders and blocks of ice, whirling down in it.'[25]

Glen and Evelyn roped themselves together at the waist and began wading across water so cold that 'we did not feel the ice-blocks that pounded against us' and flowing so fast that it was impossible to stand without the support of the cord. When they eventually got to within reach of Hugh on the far bank they threw him the rope on a ski stick and began dragging him back across. But just as Glen reached shore the cord broke and Hugh and Evelyn were swept away and dashed against numerous rocks and ice blocks. It seemed an age before they eventually scrambled to safety and Evelyn had long since assumed they would not make it. To regain base camp avoiding the river they now had to make a three-day trek up into the mountains without map, tent, ice axes or rope. 'If I hadn't joined the Church of Rome,' Evelyn told Glen in the midst of this, as they sheltered from a storm beneath a rock, 'I could never have survived your appalling incompetence.'[26] When eventually they returned to England in late August he was scathing about the whole venture, describing it to Tom Driberg as 'hell – a fiasco very narrowly retrieved from disaster'.[27]

* * *

Ninety-Two Days was published in the spring to far better reviews than Evelyn had expected – *The New York Times Book Review* hailing it as a departure from 'the distortion of truth and the tawdry self-exploitation of the travel books of the recent degenerate era'[28] – yet when *A Handful of Dust* appeared on his return from the Arctic few critics considered it anything approaching the masterpiece it is now held to be, although Peter Quennell in the *New Statesman* thought it 'certainly the most mature and the best written novel Mr Waugh has yet produced'.[29] As far as Evelyn was concerned it was a success, however, not least since it was the Book Society's Book of the Month and was into its fifth impression by the end of the fourth week. 'Wherever I go,' he wrote to Maimie Lygon, 'the people shout Long Live Bo & throw garlands of flowers in my path.'

He was by then back staying with his parents, who had recently sold Underhill and moved to a flat on Hampstead Lane in Highgate. 'At present it is all dignity & peace,' he reported, 'but I expect we shall soon have a quarrel & black each other's eyes & tear our hair & flog each other with hunting crops like the lovely Lygon sisters. I am going to spend a very studious autumn writing the life of a dead beast. I think I shall stay here so that I shall not be tempted to the demon at the Savile and to go out with whores & make myself ill as I do if I am away from good parents.'[30]

The 'dead beast' was Edmund Campion, the sixteenth-century Jesuit priest and martyr, and the resulting biography not only raised Evelyn's stock in Catholic circles but also gave him a far deeper understanding of his adopted faith and 'a conception of the value of total surrender', as Christopher Hollis put it. When he had had enough of living under his parents' roof he went down to Chagford, where he interspersed his writing with days hunting and visits to friends such as the Asquiths at Mells. He also wrote two short stories, 'Mr Loveday's Little Outing'* and

---

* Originally entitled 'Mr Cruttwell's Little Outing', which would not have been wholly inappropriate as Cruttwell was to end his life insane.

'On Guard' – described to Coote Lygon as 'a funny short story about a looney bin and a very dull one about a dog who bit a lady's nose'.[31]

After Christmas Evelyn was asked by Gabriel Herbert to go and stay at Pixton Park in Somerset. It was his third visit to the cheerful and chaotic Herbert family home whose Irish shabbiness – 'pyramids of books on every table – dogs' dinners on sofa etc'[32] – would later inspire his portrait of Boot Magna Hall in *Scoop*, some of which was written there. Set in rolling parkland on the edge of Exmoor and originally surrounded by an estate of some 5,000 acres, this handsome stuccoed house had been built by the 2nd Earl of Carnarvon in 1803–5 and given to Gabriel's father, Aubrey, younger son of the 4th Earl (and half-brother of Shevelyn's mother), on his marriage to Mary Vesey in 1910. When Evelyn arrived he found a large party of boisterous young people and 'God they did make me feel old and ill', he told Maimie. But amid all the exhausting bouts of hockey and hunting and charades he soon found himself falling in love with the youngest of the Herbert sisters, Laura, the silent 'white mouse' whom he had barely noticed before but now confided to Maimie that he had taken 'a <u>great</u> fancy' to.

'What is she like? Well fair, very pretty, plays peggotty beautifully . . . She has rather a long thin nose and skin as thin as Bromo as she is very thin and might be dying of consumption to look at her and she has her hair in a little bun at the back of her neck but it is not very tidy and she is only 18 years old, virgin, Catholic, quiet and astute. So it is difficult. I have not made much progress yet except to pinch her twice in a charade and lean against her thigh in pretending to help her at peggotty.'[33]

Ostensibly shy, reserved and rather frail, Laura was very different to her more garrulous, hunting-mad elder sisters, as she was to all the girls with whom Evelyn had previously fallen in love. Yet as he perhaps sensed, behind the quiet, unassuming façade lay a resolutely independent character with an original, ironic sense of humour and a surprisingly violent temper, which she occasionally suppressed by taking herself off to bed until she had cooled down.

Her self-reliance may have stemmed from her distant relationship with her domineering mother – like her sister-in-law Winifred Burgh-clere, Mary Herbert was more obviously devoted to her husband than to her children – and the loss of her remarkable father when she was only seven after he contracted blood poisoning while having some teeth extracted as a supposed cure for his failing eyesight. Following the death of Aubrey Herbert – later immortalised in his granddaughter Margaret FitzHerbert's fine biography *The Man Who Was Greenmantle* – Laura's mother had promptly converted to Catholicism, however Laura stoutly resisted following her lead until she was well into her teens and thus old enough to know her own mind.

By the time she caught Evelyn's eye she was training to be an actress at RADA, having earlier attended a small boarding school in Wimbledon followed by a year at a Catholic finishing school just outside Paris (the Convent of the Holy Child at Neuilly, where 'Kick' Kennedy was finished a few years later). Besides the age gap and the fact that there was no immediate guarantee of his marriage being annulled, the most obvious impediment to Evelyn's courtship was the resistance of Laura's mother, who was far from thrilled about the reappearance of this slightly un-gentlemanly – as she reportedly saw him – character who had caused so much trouble for her sister-in-law several years earlier. 'I thought we'd heard the last of that young man,' remarked Lady Victoria Herbert, maiden aunt of both Laura and Shevelyn.

Mary Herbert was likened by James Lees-Milne to 'a magnificent, imperious stag by Landseer, perhaps an eagle . . . masterful and very clever . . . full of opinions and Catholic prejudices'.[34] Her first meaningful encounter with Evelyn at Portofino in 1933 had not been especially auspicious and early on during his stay she had pelted him with hard Italian buns and driven him from the house after he was rude about Ireland, where she had grown up at Abbeyleix as the only child of Viscount and Viscountess de Vesci. In general, though, he had been on his best behaviour, polite almost to the point of smarminess and as a recent convert keen to ingratiate himself with her famous Catholic guest Hilaire Belloc, whom Evelyn had met briefly on several previous occasions, most recently with Diana Cooper at Bognor. When Evelyn had gone and Mary Herbert asked Belloc what he made of him, he replied rather disconcertingly: 'He has the devil in him.'[35*]

Following the stay at Pixton just after Christmas, Evelyn's courtship of

---

* Many years later, Diana Cooper wrote to her son that while Graham Greene was 'a good man possessed of a devil' Evelyn 'contrary to this is a bad man for whom an angel is struggling'. John Julius Norwich (ed.), *Darling Monster: The Letters of Lady Diana Cooper to her son John Julius Norwich, 1939–1952*, p. 436.

Laura ran far from smoothly. In early February 1935, having invited her to London, he greeted her with a hangover and 'could only eat 3 oysters and some soda water,' he told Maimie Lygon, 'and I was sick a good deal on the table so perhaps that romance is shattered'.[36] In early May, while pegging away at the Campion biography at a succession of country houses, he wrote to tell Laura that he had begun to despair of ever seeing her again.[37] The next month he told Katharine Asquith that 'estranged is the word re M Herbert. High estimate of her charm and character undiminished but not able to see her without embarrassment.'[38]

In late July he had a final go: 'Darling Laura,' he wrote to her from St James's Club in Piccadilly, 'I am sad and bored and need your company. If you have a spare evening between now and when you leave London, please come out with me. Any time will suit me as I have no engagements that I cannot gladly break. Ask your mother first and tell her I wanted you to ask. That is, supposing you want to come. Perhaps you don't. I don't know where I shall be in the autumn so it may be a long time before we meet. Please come. I will behave respectfully, I promise.'[39]

His uncertainty as to his whereabouts in the autumn referred to his imminent departure for Abyssinia to report on the looming invasion by Mussolini, and it seems to have been the prospect of this, combined with Laura's mother's rigid opposition to him and Laura's equally determined independence from her, that eventually persuaded Laura to see him again. Soon after receiving the letter she asked him to Pixton for the weekend and it was on that occasion that she fell in love with him. 'I'm writing to you rather before I meant to,' she wrote boldly after he had left, 'but I feel like it – You can't know how happy I was & how much I loved having you here this weekend – I don't think I've ever loved anything so much . . . all my love to you darling I do love you so very much more than I can say – I do hope Abyssinia's fun & not dangerous.'[40]

'Darling darling Laura,' wrote a greatly relieved Evelyn from the Adelphi Hotel in Liverpool, as he prepared to embark for Africa, 'please don't find that you are just as happy without me. I am not nearly as happy without you. Bless you my darling love child.'[41]

A consummate opportunist when it came to his journalism, Evelyn had asked his agent to capitalise on his previous experience of Abyssinia when news broke of Mussolini's coming invasion. However in the end it was a word in Lord Rothermere's ear from his friend Diana Cooper – just as in *Scoop* Mrs Stitch mentions the young novelist John Boot to Lord Copper – that led to his highly lucrative employment as a correspondent by the *Daily Mail*, which had lost its star reporter (Sir Percival Phillips, who like Evelyn had reported on the coronation of Haile Selassie in 1930) to *The Daily Telegraph* just as the crisis loomed.

Besides his knowledge of the country – an extremely rare commodity on Fleet Street at that time – Evelyn could be counted on as an unflinching advocate of Rothermere's pro-Italian stance, viewing Mussolini as the most effective barrier against Hitler and Abyssinia as a barbarous country at the mercy of a capricious and violent government unable to cope with its lawless elements. 'It is entertaining to find a country where the noblemen feast on raw beef,' Evelyn had written in the *Evening Standard* earlier that year, 'but less amusing when they enslave and castrate the villagers of neighbouring countries.' The Abyssinian empire, he argued, had been taken bloodily and was held 'so far as it is held at all' by force of arms. 'In the matter of abstract justice, the Italians have just as much right to govern; in the matter of practical politics, it is certain that their government would be for the benefit of the Ethiopian Empire and for the rest of Africa.'[42]

As with previous trips, besides the *Daily Mail* contract, Evelyn looked to get two books out of his adventures: a non-fiction volume about the war, *Waugh in Abyssinia*, for which he was paid what was then the huge advance of £950 by Longman's, where his friend Tom Burns commissioned it; and a novel, which eventually became *Scoop*, inspired by the scorn he felt for the rest of the press corps, among whom he found the conscientious Stuart Emeny of the *News Chronicle* particularly ridiculous: 'All events for him had only one significance and standard of measurement – whether or no they constituted a "story". He did not make friends; he "established contacts". Even his private opinions were those of his paper . . .'[43]

But while Evelyn was inclined to disparage the whole business of journalism and his own aptitude for it, he actually possessed many of the qualities of an excellent newspaper reporter. One of his fellow correspondents in Abyssinia, W. F. 'Bill' Deedes, recalled: 'His ear was well attuned to the idiocies of this world. He was curious, thorough in any inquiry he made, very quick on the uptake, persistent and observant, and never nervous of embarrassing anyone.'[44] Deedes, whose quarter-ton of luggage famously found its way into Evelyn's portrait of William Boot in

Scoop, also admired Evelyn's bravery, his ability to intimidate friend or foe and to bluff his way out of a tight corner, and the fact that he 'seemed to be endowed with many of the qualities that good officers are supposed to possess'.[45] And he noticed that 'unlike a lot of so-called snobs, he was adept at conversing with people of small importance, though often baffling them with his brand of wit. He paid close attention to what they said to him, which is why dialogue in his novels rings so true.'[46*]

Deedes may have recognised his journalistic talent, but Evelyn did not cover himself in glory as far as the *Daily Mail* was concerned. The paper's biggest gripe was that he managed to be so comprehensively scooped by *The Daily Telegraph* on the most sensational story of the entire war – concerning a master of foxhounds from Berkshire called Francis Rickett who, on behalf of the brazenly named African Exploitation and Development Corporation, managed to obtain the sole rights to oil, minerals and other natural resources over half of Abyssinia, thereby giving Britain and America, to which countries the corporation belonged, a direct commercial interest in the maintenance of Abyssinian sovereignty.

Evelyn had chanced to travel out with the mysterious Mr Rickett and at the time thought there was something fishy about him, disbelieving his explanation that he was on a mission to deliver Coptic funds to the Abyssinian Orthodox Church and suspicious of the various lengthy cables he received en route, which he would pocket nonchalantly, remarking, 'From my huntsman. He says the prospects for cubbin' are excellent.'[47] But instead of tailing Rickett to find out what he was really up to, Evelyn took the eccentrically roundabout route of sending a leisurely letter of enquiry to Penelope Betjeman (several weeks away by mail), asking her to find out whether her Berkshire neighbour was a spy or an arms dealer or what.

When *The Daily Telegraph* broke the Rickett story a few weeks later, Evelyn was four days away from Addis Ababa in Harar (where he thought Italy was most likely to invade) so he could not even get back in time to file follow-up pieces until the story was already dead. The whole episode irreparably damaged his relations with the *Daily Mail* and eventually, fed up with their bad-tempered telegrams, he resigned. 'Well I have chucked

---

* Auberon Waugh later attested to his father's unexpected affability with the band that came to play Christmas carols each year at their home after the war: 'The common touch was certainly not something he cultivated, but in a rather surprising way, when he needed it, he had it.' Auberon Waugh, *Will This Do?*, p. 49.

the *Mail*,' he wrote to Diana Cooper. 'It was no good they sent me offensive cables twice a day & I took umbrage & they wanted me to stay in Addis and I took despair.'[48] But with book contracts still to fulfil he could not afford to leave Abyssinia just yet, and when his replacement was held up in Djibouti, he stayed on working for them until they finally terminated his contract at the end of November. He was away for more than four months in all, during which time he sent frequent letters to the girl whose love he had been assured of on leaving. 'I wonder how you are,' he wrote to Laura shortly after his arrival in Addis. 'In fact I wonder about you most of the day ... The thing I think about most is your eyelashes making a noise like a bat on the pillow. How compromising that sounds – you know what I mean, but the Ethiopians won't who read all my correspondence & telegrams ... Darling child I feel very far away from you.'[49] In October he hoped to be home by Christmas: 'I am lonely and bored and have all the material for a jolly good novel about journalists which I want to do before it gets stale to me.'[50]

In the event he spent Christmas in Bethlehem, followed by an overnight jaunt by charabanc across the desert to Baghdad for a weekend, then visits to Damascus and finally Rome, where he was 'crossed examined by beasts [priests] re my wife', he wrote to Maimie Lygon, and came away impressed after an interview with Il Duce. He returned to London at the beginning of February 1936, arriving 'in a lion-skin,' so his father recorded, 'which much excited Tuppence [their dog]'.[51] Laura was even more eager to see him providing her mother would let her. 'Please ring me up as soon as you reach London,' she had written. 'I've kept all this week free on the chance of your getting back & of my being allowed to see you. Darling Evelyn I can't tell you how happy it makes me thinking that you are coming back so soon – Even if I can't see you, it makes the whole difference knowing that you are near & out of any danger ... I am so longing to see you or even to hear your voice.'[52]

Evelyn was soon hard at work on his non-fiction book, *Waugh in Abyssinia*, much of which he wrote as a guest of Perry Brownlow, a distant cousin of Diana Cooper via her natural father Harry Cust and a great friend and lord-in-waiting of King Edward VIII, as he had just become, who like Evelyn spent a fair amount of time at Belton House, Lord Brownlow's stately home in Lincolnshire. In the spring of 1936, while writing his Abyssinia book, Evelyn stayed at another Brownlow property in

Shropshire, where he inhabited a flat above the estate office. 'So now I live here looking after the great Ellesmere estates,' he wrote to Maimie Lygon, 'god it is a responsibility I have afforested & deforested & distrained & debentured & still it won't come right.'[53]

Two weeks later from there he wrote Laura what amounted to an exceptionally straightforward and realistic letter of proposal:

Tell you what you might do while you are alone at Pixton. You might think about me a bit & whether, if those wop priests ever come to a decent decision, you could bear the idea of marrying me. Of course you haven't got to decide, but think about it. I can't advise you in my favour because I think it would be beastly for you, but think how nice it would be for me. I am restless & moody & misanthropic & lazy & have no money except what I earn and if I got ill you would starve. In fact it's a lousy proposition. On the other hand I think I could do a Grant [Eddie Grant, married to Laura's sister Bridget] and reform & become quite strict about not getting drunk and I am pretty sure I shall be faithful. Also there is always a fair chance that there will be another bigger economic crash in which case if you had married a nobleman with a great house you might find yourself starving, while I am very clever and could probably earn a living of some sort somewhere. Also though you would be taking on an elderly buffoon, I am one without fixed habits. You wouldn't find yourself confined to any particular place or group. Also I have practically no living relatives except one brother whom I scarcely know. You would not find yourself involved in a large family & all their rows & you would not be patronized & interfered with by older sisters in law & aunts as often happens. All these are very small advantages compared with the awfulness of my character. I have always tried to be nice to you and you may have got it into your head that I am nice really, but that is all rot. It is only to you & for you. I am jealous & impatient – but there is no point in going into a whole list of my vices. You are a critical girl and I've no doubt that you know them all and a great many I don't know myself. But the point I wanted to make is that if you marry most people, you are marrying a great number of objects & other people as well, well if you marry me there is nothing else involved, and that is an advantage as well as a disadvantage. My only tie of any kind is my work. That means that for several months each year we shall have to separate or you would have to share some very lonely places with me. But apart from that we could do what we liked & go where we liked – and if you married a soldier or stockbroker or member of parliament or master of hounds you would be more tied. When I tell my friends that I am in love with a girl of 19 they look shocked and say 'wretched child' but I don't look on you as very young even in your beauty and I don't think there is any sense in the line that you cannot possibly commit yourself to a decision that affects your whole life for years yet. But anyway there is no point in your deciding or even answering. I may never get free of your cousin Evelyn. Above all things, darling, don't fret at all. But just turn the matter over in your dear head.[54]

16

....

Goodness She is a Decent Girl

Evelyn was never going to be the world's easiest husband, however no one could accuse him of not having been entirely upfront about how difficult he was likely to be. In any case Laura's reply to his proposal must have been reasonably favourable as he told Diana Cooper in June 1936 that he had been periodically leaving his desk in Ellesmere for trips to see her and 'loving her a lot and she being exquisitely unDutch. Goodness she is a decent girl.'[1]

Yet however keen they were on each other, they could still not get married before the Pope had annulled Evelyn's first marriage and, while Laura remained a minor, her mother had given her consent. The first obstacle was removed on 7 July, when Evelyn returned to his club at dawn after a pilgrimage to Lough Derg in Ireland to find a telegram from Cardinal Godfrey in Rome: 'Decision Favourable.' That morning he found Laura and her mother at Farm Street Church, knelt behind them and after the service told Laura the news in the porch. For the next week he saw her every day, doing crosswords together, attending Mass, going to the cinema, dining twice at the Café Royal and once in Nancy Mitford's bedroom. On 16 July he was interviewed by Laura's mother at her townhouse on Bruton Street, where she told him that he and Laura must wait until October to be engaged and Christmas before being married.

Mary Herbert's resistance had possibly been softened by the announcement in late April that Evelyn had won the Hawthornden Prize, at that time Britain's most prestigious literary award, for *Edmund Campion*, which had been published the previous autumn while he was in Abyssinia and which his fellow Catholic convert Graham Greene hailed in *The Spectator* as 'a model of what a short biography should be'.[2] After hearing about the award, Henry Yorke wrote to Evelyn: 'I would congratulate you on it if it were not for the fact that you are the outstanding writer of our generation & that recognition of this kind has been due to you for a long time. It may sound ungracious to put it in the way I have just done but I do feel hotly that there is not one book you have published which is not very far beyond the books they have given the prize for up till now. It takes time for outstanding work to get through their thick skulls.'[3] It was presumably this prize that persuaded the dozy publishers of *Who's Who* that Evelyn might at last merit a mention in its pages – he was to appear for the first time in its 1937 edition (listing his sole recreation as 'travelling'), a scarcely believable seventeen years after his brother Alec's first entry in the hallowed annual reference work.

Evelyn replied to Henry that it was particularly gratifying that the prize should go 'to a specifically Catholic book' – knowing full well that this could do no harm to his reputation at Pixton.[4] Neither can it have damaged his marriage prospects that a week before his interview with Mrs Herbert, Maurice Bowra, again in *The Spectator*, had praised his recently published collection of short stories *Mr Loveday's Little Outing*. 'Mr. Waugh, like Mr. Maugham, succeeds at every kind of writing he attempts,' wrote Bowra. 'He manages the short story with the confident touch of an accomplished master ... Is it too much to ask that he will abandon biography to lesser men and give us more novels and more short stories like these?'[5]

But Evelyn relied heavily on his non-fiction and journalism to stay solvent, and with his expenses sure to rise after his marriage he now reached the reluctant conclusion that he needed to return to Abyssinia to beef up his half-written book with a concluding account of how the Italian conquest had turned out. After going to Pixton to say goodbye to Laura, he travelled out to Africa via Rome 'full of gloomiest forebodings', he told Katharine Asquith. 'I am sick of Abyssinia & of my book about it. It was fun being pro-Italian when it was an unpopular and (I thought) losing cause. I have little sympathy with these exultant fascists now.'[6] He arrived to find the fledgling colony in an ostensible state of chaos. 'Truth appears to be Wops in jam,' he wrote in his diary.[7] However by the time he came to finishing his book he was inclined to see the Italian invasion as having brought about the 'spread of order and decency, education and medicine, in a disgraceful place'; it was akin to 'the great western drive of the American peoples, the dispossession of the Indian tribes and the establishment in a barren land of new pastures and cities'.[8]

Leaving Laura this time had proved far more affecting than he expected. 'How I wish you were here,' he wrote to her from Assisi. 'Sweet poppet it seems such a waste to see lovely things & not be with you. It is like being one-eyed & goggling out of focus. I miss you & need you all the time. Most of all when I'm happy.'[9] The next day he wrote again:

> I need you all the time – when I'm vexed and uncertain & tired – but more than ever on a night like this when everything is unearthly & lovely. You see, darling child, so often when people fall in love & want to be married, it is because they foresee a particular kind of life to which the other is necessary. But I don't feel that. Sometimes I think it would be lovely to lead the sort of life with you that I have led alone for the last ten years – no possessions, no home, sometimes extravagant & luxurious, sometimes lying low & working hard. At other times I picture a settled life with a large household, rather acrimonious & rather frugal, and sometimes a minute house, and few friends, and little work & leisure & love. But what I do know is that I can't picture any sort of life without you. I have left half of myself behind in England and I am only dragging about a bit of myself now. And I don't at all regret the haphazard, unhappy life I've led up till now because I don't think that without it I could love you so much. Goodnight my blessed child. I love you more than I can find words to tell you.[10]

He told Mary Lygon: 'I cry a great deal on account of not seeing LAURA. But Lady Horner says absence is like the wind – it extinguishes a little flame & fans a big one with greater heat.'[11] However with Laura's mother insisting on their delaying the announcement of their engagement, Evelyn evidently did not feel bound by absolute fidelity just yet, and on his way back through Rome he recorded that he had 'intended to bathe, change, fuck, and eat a luxurious dinner. Instead spent the evening driving to pay my debt to the English College [presumably to do with his annulment] in smuggled lire.'[12] If there had been any lingering uncertainty in Laura's mind, Evelyn's absence in Abyssinia seems to have removed it. 'I have definitely made up my mind that I want to marry you more than anything I want in the world,' she wrote to him while he was away. 'I hope you're still wanting to marry me. I think I love you more every day.'[13]

Evelyn arrived back in London on 12 September to the shattering news that Hugh Lygon had died while on a motoring tour of Bavaria, having mysteriously fallen over and hit his head on the curbside, conceivably after drinking or suffering from sunstroke after driving in an open car. 'It is the saddest news I ever heard,' Evelyn wrote to Mary Lygon. 'I shall miss him bitterly.' During what *The Times* euphemistically described as Hugh's 'varied and adventurous career',[14] an unhappy stint in the City had been followed by an abortive attempt at training racehorses and a brush with the bankruptcy courts, but while he never overcame his alcoholism he had at last seemed to be making a success of his most recent venture of running one of the farms at Madresfield. 'It is so particularly tragic that he should have died just when he was setting up house and seemed happier than he had been for many years,' wrote Evelyn.[15]

Hughie's death had come only a few weeks after that of his mother, and while Lord Beauchamp, who was still living in exile in Venice, had been prevented from attending his wife's funeral after being warned as he prepared to disembark at Dover that he would be arrested if he set foot ashore, he determined to go to Hughie's funeral at Madresfield on 24 August come what may. On this occasion, to the fury of the Duke of Westminster, the Home Secretary suspended the warrant for his arrest. The next year, after his warrant was finally withdrawn, Boom returned to spend the last year of his life at Madresfield, in much the same way as Lord Marchmain returns in *Brideshead Revisited*.

As the final chapter of *Brideshead* shows, all this made a deep and lasting impression on Evelyn's imagination, however for the time being he had the distraction of his forthcoming marriage to Laura, in contented contemplation of which he was even prepared to make peace with John Heygate, who had written to him shortly after he returned from Abyssinia: 'I have done you a great wrong. I am sorry. Will you forgive me?' Evelyn replied on a postcard: 'O.K. E.W.'*

He had still not told his parents, but two weeks after he got back they heard from Alec on the telephone that his annulment had been accepted

---

* Heygate had originally written to Evelyn shortly after Shevelyn ran off with him, but received no reply. In 1936 a bishop told him that before being allowed to take Communion he must try and obtain the forgiveness of the man he had sinned against, whereupon he wrote again. As Heygate later told Auberon Waugh, the bishop 'seemed rather surprised' when he showed him Evelyn's answer, 'but was satisfied'. (Sir John Heygate to Auberon Waugh, 11 November 1973; AWA.)

by the Pope and that he hoped to be married after Christmas. 'But he has not written to us!' protested Arthur in his diary.[16] Five days later Kate received a note from Evelyn announcing that he was to be married in February and the day after that he finally got round to writing to his father, obliquely apologising for his 'unfilial' delay in telling him of his engagement.[17] A week or so later he brought Laura to Highgate. 'Great preparations for Evelyn & Laura,' Arthur recorded. 'The evening was delightful. She behaved charmingly; he was at his best; and the dinner was good.'[18] The next day, Arthur and Kate 'had a pleasant talk over dinner about our happy evening with Evelyn & Laura. Was very glad to see her so happy. By last post a dear little note came to K from Laura, thanking us for being "so sweet" to her, which sent us to bed happier still.'[19]

Evelyn also wrote to Baby Jungman, telling her that he wanted her to be the first to know – though of course one or two others knew already:

> She [Laura] is very young indeed. Very thin and pale with big eyes and a long nose – more like a gazelle really than a girl; completely free of any literary, artistic or social ambition, silent as the grave, given to fainting at inopportune moments, timid, ignorant, affectionate, very gentle, doesn't sing, Narcissus complex, looks lovely on a horse but often falls off, student of acting, but doesn't take it too seriously. Catholic but doesn't take that too seriously either, owns pretty nasty dog called Lump, but he looks like dying soon. I love her very much and I think there is as good a chance of our marriage being a success as any I know.[20]

The letter to Baby was written from Mells, where he was writing the final chapter of *Waugh in Abyssinia*, which he finished on 2 October. By the middle of the month he had moved on to *Scoop*, noting in his diary that he had 'made a very good start with the first page of novel describing Diana's early morning'[21] – Diana Cooper serving as his model for Mrs Stitch, some of whose less amiable traits betrayed Evelyn's growing ambivalence towards her on account of her pointed unfriendliness towards Laura. Within two weeks he had completed the second chapter, however his speedy progress was soon halted by his perennial need to make money and in early November he went to see the editor of *Nash's Magazine*, where he 'accepted money for jam job, thirty guineas a month for less than 2,000 words on anything I like'.[22]

Work aside, much of that autumn was spent looking for somewhere for him and Laura to live. The area around Mells seemed as good a place to start as any, not only because he was there at the time but also because it was very close to his aunts' home at Midsomer Norton and a convenient stop-off between London and Laura's family home at Pixton. Both soon set their hearts on an exceptionally pretty Georgian manor house within the bailey of the ruined castle at Nunney, however the owner, a 'homicidal squireen' in Evelyn's estimation, proved impossible to pin down. A few days before Christmas, having by then extended their search north into Gloucestershire, Evelyn recorded in his diary: 'Saw two no-good houses then Piers Court, Stinchcombe. Absolutely first-rate, delighted.'[23] 'Laura and I have found a house of startling beauty between Bath and Stroud,' he told Diana Cooper, 'so that is where we shall live.'[24]

Situated just above the village on the western escarpment of the Cotswolds, some twenty-two miles north-east of Bristol, Piers Court commanded spectacular views from its garden across the Berkeley Vale (a panorama since spoilt somewhat by the M5 motorway) to the Severn estuary and Forest of Dean beyond. But behind its handsome Georgian stuccoed façade the house itself was in considerable disrepair, without water, gas or electricity, and after spending Christmas at Pixton – hunting, shooting (or in Evelyn's case beating), and enduring what he wryly recorded as the Herberts' 'family fun' – they returned there in the new year to assess what needed to be done. With a view to having a carving placed on the blank pediment over the porch, around this time Evelyn also wrote to Alec to enquire about the validity of the Waugh coat of arms. On 22 January 1937 his offer of £3,550 for Piers Court and its surrounding forty acres was accepted – a week after he had spent the evening with his parents in Highgate and told them that Laura's grandmother, Lady de Vesci, was giving them £4,000 as a wedding present with which to buy the house.

Unable to compete with this, Arthur modestly asked them to choose some silver from what he had left of his grandfather's, wrapped up in flannel under his bed, and said he would give them £25 to buy 'something definite & lasting – to remind you of me'. 'I think that's decent,' Evelyn wrote to Laura, 'considering his reduced circumstances & the fact that he forked out handsomely for my mock marriage some years back.'[25]

Evelyn's grateful and sympathetic response made a change from his often curt attitude towards his father, with whom he had tended to be by turns sullen and censorious of what he called his 'affected conversation'.[26] To strain relations further, on one of his rare recent visits to his parents he had contrived to set Arthur's library alight, inadvertently destroying, as he later admitted, 'hundreds of inscribed copies from almost every English writer of eminence' – Arthur having had by Evelyn's reckoning 'more books dedicated to him than any living man'.[27] In the past few months, however, Evelyn had shown a good deal more tolerance and affection towards him, a welcome development that Arthur attributed to Laura's influence. 'Certainly we have had much more kindness from him,' he noted in his diary on New Year's Eve.[28] Two months later, after lunch at the Savoy Grill prior to Evelyn joining the board of Chapman & Hall, Arthur recorded pathetically: 'Evelyn very gracious & attentive to me.'[29]

But beyond the initial favourable impressions of his 'charming' prospective daughter-in-law, Arthur could never really fathom Laura. He was plainly extremely well disposed towards Alec's wife Joan, not so much because she was very rich – having inherited a fortune that Alec put at £300,000[30] (i.e. more than eighty times what Evelyn paid for Piers Court) from her Australian father – but mainly because she seemed so appreciative of everything about him that Evelyn found so annoying. However Arthur never felt anything like the same affinity with Laura. A few years later he wrote to Joan: 'Certainly my two daughters-in-law write very differently, and have very different temperaments. I shall never be able to make anything of Laura. We live in other worlds and talk another language. But I miss nothing. I find everything I want in Joan, the daughter of my heart.'[31]

Whether or not Evelyn picked up on Arthur's favouritism, he was rather less misty-eyed about his sister-in-law and brazenly mercenary when it came to her offer of some linen for their wedding present after she had already promised to pay for their honeymoon. 'I think now you should write to her,' he suggested to Laura from his writing den on Dartmoor where he was polishing off a lucrative film treatment* for Alexander Korda: 'say Evelyn has told you of her kind offer etc. and make out a big

---

* Evelyn had gone to Korda's studio to be told the plot of 'a vulgar film about cabaret girls'; the working title was 'Lovelies from America'. He was paid £750 for the script but the film was never made. *EWD*, p. 413n.

list of what we need – two double beds, three single (at least) & towels for five guests. You might hint at table cloths, table napkins etc. Sorry to put all this on you, but I really am very busy trying to get the film done & as it is correspondence takes ½ my morning.'[32]

The result evidently failed to come up to scratch: 'Joan Waugh is mean as hell,' remarked Evelyn sometime later. 'Well I suppose I must pay for having neglected her these last 2 years.'[33] Hers was not the only offering deemed below par. 'Presents have come in, mostly of poor quality,' Evelyn recorded in his diary in early February, 'except from the Asquiths who have given us superb candelabra, sconces, and table.'[34] The Coopers' glass chandelier would have been equally appreciated were it not for the fact that when it arrived, three months after the wedding, the Waughs' new butler gloomily announced 'a box full of broken glass outside for you'. As it turned out only a few bits were broken, and as Evelyn told Diana: 'If we can get it mended [which they soon did] it will be a superb ornament, in fact the whole of our hall and staircase has been planned and painted round it.'[35]

The wedding took place at eleven o'clock on a showery Saturday morning, 17 April, at the seventeenth-century Catholic Church of the Assumption (originally the chapel to the old Portuguese Embassy) on Warwick Street in Soho, preceded by a cocktail party for all the guests the evening before at 14 Gloucester Gate on the edge of Regent's Park, where the reception was also held. Among the three officiating priests, Father D'Arcy gave the address, although Evelyn thought him 'sensationally ignorant of simplest professional duties'. Laura's brother Auberon gave her away, having spent the journey to the church begging her to change her mind.[36]* The church was full of family and friends, including, as Tom Driberg reported in the *Express*, 'many fair women: Lygons, Jungmans [Baby and Zita], Lady Diana Cooper (straight from Windsor Castle), the Hon Mrs Peter Rodd (novelist Nancy Mitford: she wore a hat made of

---

* Auberon Herbert's disapproval of Evelyn was described by Alexander Waugh as 'the aristocrat's natural dislike of the *arriviste* or, as my father preferred, the "traditional jealousy between privilege and actual achievement". Auberon was no fool. He spoke six languages fluently, had a natural and unusual wit and was adored by figures as random and far apart as Sir Isaiah Berlin and Karol, his Polish butler, but to Evelyn, who deplored his manner of speech, the habitual twisting of his wrists by his face as he spoke, and the suffocating odour of his scent that wafted oppressively about his person, Auberon was no more than a spoiled idler.' *Fathers and Sons*, p. 272.

red and dark blue ostrich feathers, held together by bits of ribbon, which wasn't nearly as gauche as it sounds)'.

Among the more notable absentees was Evelyn's best man from his first marriage, Harold Acton, who had settled in Peking in 1932 to teach at the university and translate Chinese poetry after becoming fed up with his falling literary reputation in Britain. The reception was 'all over' by a little after one and Arthur Waugh recorded with apparent satisfaction that he was 'home by 1.40 to a slice of brawn and cheese'.[37]

Evelyn, meanwhile, repaired to his club bedroom to be toasted by his best man, Henry Yorke, along with Francis Howard, Douglas Woodruff, John Sutro, Perry Brownlow, Billy Clonmore and Hubert Duggan, after which he and Laura drove to Englefield Green to say goodbye to eighty-five-year-old Lady de Vesci, who had not made it to the wedding but may well have paid for it. They then flew from Croydon to Paris, where they caught the overnight express to Rome, arriving at Portofino the next afternoon by horse-drawn cab. 'Lovely day,' wrote Evelyn in his diary that evening, 'lovely house, lovely wife, great happiness.'[38]

Three weeks later Evelyn wrote to Katharine Asquith: 'Well it is o.k. being spliced. Very decent indeed . . . so far the marriage is an unqual-ified success.'[39] After ten days in Portofino he had taken Laura to Rome to be blessed by the Pope, who proved disappointingly inattentive, then Florence, then back to Portofino, where he resumed work on *Scoop*, which he admitted to his agent needed to be 'entirely rewritten' but promised would be ready in time for publication before Christmas.[40] Returning to England at the end of May, they borrowed a house in Chelsea from Laura's sister before moving finally into Piers Court in July where, as Evelyn told Diana Cooper, 'we are well and very happy indeed and the beauty of the house waxes daily'. They both became happier still when Laura discovered she was pregnant.

Work on the house, which they tended to refer to as Stinchcombe, or more often 'Stinkers', continued well into the next year, with Evelyn taking a keen interest in almost every detail. Besides designing his library and various other bits of joinery around the house, he filled the house with fine furniture and pictures, among them Rossetti's charcoal nude *Spirit of the Rainbow* ('My word it is ugly,' he told Diana) and Holman Hunt's painting *Oriana*, and a good collection of Victorian genre paint-ings, including works by George Smith and George Elgar Hicks.

He set about re-landscaping the garden, doing much of the physical work himself. Much is often made of Evelyn's supposed eager adoption of squirearchical ways, strolling about in his loud tweeds and chomping on a cigar. Yet he far preferred pulling brambles, planting trees and pegging out new lawns in the garden to hobnobbing with the local county set.

Several good friends lived within a fifty-mile radius – the Betjemans at Uffington in Berkshire, the Lygons at Madresfield, the Asquiths at Mells – although as neither Evelyn nor Laura had yet passed their driving tests, visiting them meant hiring a man to sit beside them in their car. Others from further afield were persuaded to come and stay, among them Pansy Lamb and Patrick Balfour, who reported to his mother: 'Lovely house: quite big, almost a "place". Evelyn v. happy & exaggeratedly domestic: they hardly see anybody. All right in the meantime, but I should think she would begin to want something more sooner or later. She is v. young & very much under Evelyn's thumb, & the question is how long she'll be content to stay under it. Wives must have *some* life of their own.'[41] But there would never be any evidence of the restlessness that he predicted.

When Diana Cooper came to stay after the birth of their first child she was assured beforehand that she would 'not notice baby or dog they are kept away'. Graham Greene, whom Evelyn had known for years but only recently befriended as a contributor of weekly book reviews to his short-lived literary magazine *Night and Day*, also came to stay with his wife Vivien: 'Yes, I normally wear a dinner jacket in the evenings,' Evelyn wrote to Mrs Greene, 'Laura a dressing gown. Do whatever is most convenient. I have asked a particular fan of Graham's & am sure he will dress for the meeting.'[42]

Local grandees held rather less appeal however. 'Count d'Oyley rang up to ask us to weekend at Berkeley,' runs a typical entry in Evelyn's diary. 'Refused, controlling temptation to explain that I do not go visiting the immediate neighbours.'[43] 'Started work again on novel,' he noted wearily on another occasion, a few months after they had moved in. 'Another lady with double-barrelled name called.'[44]

Across the fields at Stinchcombe Hill lived yet another double-barrelled name and unlikely soulmate for Evelyn, the keen yachtsman and shot Major Sir Francis Fetherston-Godley, then chairman of the British Legion and later retrospectively notorious for having consorted with the leaders of Nazi Germany on a visit there in 1935.* 'Dined with Lady Featherstone [sic] Godley,' recorded Evelyn after an evening chez the mustachioed major and his wife. 'Bad dinner, bad wine, middle-aged military men boasting about their ancestry.'[45] His opinion of the Catholic Misses Leigh at Nympsfield was initially more favourable – 'acute and decided and amusing' – although when they came with the local vicar to tea Evelyn noted: 'Sticky party'.[46]

By and large he got quite enough social life on trips to London, where he went from time to time to shop for books, artwork, architectural salvage and even basic ironmongery, as well as to discharge his new responsibilities as a director of Chapman & Hall. 'The month's figures showed a perceptible improvement,' he recorded after a board meeting that November, 'all directors accordingly highly sceptical.'[47] Their doubts were shared by Arthur, who wrote in similar vein early the next year: 'Heard that profits for 1937 exceeded 1936. Amazing but gratifying.'[48]

*　*　*

On 9 March 1938 Laura gave birth to their first child, a girl. 'The daughter large & blond,' Evelyn told his agent. 'No one has had the insolence to suggest it is like me.'[49] To Thomas Balston he wrote: 'I foresee that she will be a problem – too noisy for a nun, too plain for a wife. Well standards of beauty may change in the next 18 years.'[50] And to Baby Jungman: 'Dearest Tess, We have got a daughter – very large and ugly – and are going to christen it early next week. Would you be a godmother? Please do.'[51]

The little girl was christened Maria Teresa on 16 March at the church where Evelyn and Laura had married eleven months earlier, with Francis Howard and Katharine Asquith's son Julian (Trim) Oxford standing as the other godparents. Afterwards Evelyn wrote to Baby: 'It was sweet of you to be godmother and to come to the christening. I do hope that we shall see more of one another again one day.'[52]

Scoop was finally published in May, having taken Evelyn far longer to write than any of his previous novels. Described by Christopher Hitchens in 2000 as 'Waugh at the mid-season point of his perfect pitch; youthful

---

* A possible prototype for Colonel Hodge, owner of Much Malcock Manor, in Evelyn's short story 'An Englishman's Home' (1938).

and limber and light as a feather',[53] at the time it received favourable if not ecstatic reviews. 'Superb entertainment', said *The Tablet*;[54] 'exceedingly amusing', thought the *New Statesman*.[55] 'His job is to provide laughter,' declared *The Daily Telegraph*'s critic, 'and how well he does it.'[56] Perhaps the most perceptive review came from Evelyn's former pupil at Arnold House, Derek Verschoyle, who admitted that he found Europe 'a more effective background to his [Waugh's] characters than the other continents', but wrote that almost all his contemporaries could take lessons from him in technique. 'His books are so easy to read that it is possible to overlook how intricately they are organised. They are exactly of the length and of the form which their subject requires; there is never a word wasted or an emphasis misplaced.'[57]

It was in the afterglow of this latest success that Evelyn's parents paid their first visit to Piers Court, which Arthur pronounced himself 'delighted' with,[58] evidently relishing the luxury of having the butler unpack his suitcase and bring him his morning tea. There may have been vague feelings of bemusement and perhaps even envy that both his sons had ended up in such relatively large country houses, Alec and Joan having recently bought Edrington, a Queen Anne rectory on the Hampshire–Berkshire border which Evelyn had then sent them Sibyl Colefax to decorate. In both cases the money to buy the house had come from the wife's side of the family, however the difference was that Alec always felt that Edrington was Joan's and that his writing did not support it and had thus chosen a tiny room in the attic as his study. In Evelyn's case his pen paid for all the family's expenses and accordingly he felt no compunction about choosing the best room on the ground floor for his library, installing bookshelves in a series of handsome bays and a fine writing desk – all of which would be dismantled and transported in their entirety after his death to the University of Austin in Texas. The room was already filling up with a collection of books that Arthur admired on his visit and in years to come served as an essential place of refuge for Evelyn from the distractions and annoyances of family life. A few years later Kate Waugh asked two of his young children whether they had ever been inside it. 'Oh no,' they said, 'but we have peeped through the window.'[59]

Evelyn managed to be friendly for most of his parents' four-day visit, meeting them at Stroud station when they arrived, showing them around the garden and taking them on various expeditions to see the surrounding sights. On the final evening, though, Arthur perhaps sensed that he was once again beginning to get on his son's nerves: 'Evelyn and Laura both very tired,' he recorded in his diary. 'Too much entertaining! After dinner K & Laura played chess. Evelyn read & I kept quiet.'[60]

Scoop was more successful commercially than any of Evelyn's previous novels, yet with a family to feed he remained as receptive as ever to new opportunities for making money and very shortly after its publication accepted a lucrative commission from the oil magnate Viscount Cowdray's son Clive Pearson – 'a very rich chap,' so Evelyn described him to Peters, who 'wants me to write a book about Mexico'.[61] The Mexican President Cárdenas had recently expropriated several oilfields belonging to the Pearson family, along with those of various other foreign companies; and in return for an expenses-paid trip for himself and Laura and a cheque for £989, extracted by Peters before they set off, Evelyn agreed to write a book exposing the rank injustice of all this and countering the impression propagated by Britain's left-wing press that General Cárdenas was a progressive reformer. An additional draw for Evelyn was the opportunity to denounce the regime's persecution of the Catholic Church.

Evelyn and Laura left on 30 July and travelled out via New York and Havana, arriving in Mexico City in mid-August and putting up at the Ritz: 'Uncle Clive's beneficence followed every state and we have had the smoothest possible journey,' Evelyn wrote to his mother-in-law. 'Mexico is a puzzling place & I cannot say we feel at all at home here yet. It is like sitting in a cinema, seeing the travel film of a country one has no intention of visiting. Thousands of American tourists, a handful of disgruntled English businessmen, homicidal traffic, noise, dust – all very far from Stinkers.'[62]

The Mexican trip lasted almost three months and the resulting book, whose provocative title *Robbery Under Law* further fulfilled Evelyn's obligations towards 'rich Pearson', was not finished until April 1939, when Evelyn described it to Diana Cooper as 'like an interminable *Times* leader of 1880', a reasonable appraisal of the uncharacteristically stodgy chapters dealing with oil and the Catholic Church. But although Harold Nicolson, generally a great admirer of Evelyn's writing, called it a 'dull' book in *The Daily Telegraph*, others were surprisingly enthusiastic, not least *The Guardian*, which praised Evelyn for recounting his experiences 'with great agreeableness'.[63] In America, which unlike Britain still maintained

The Evelyns photographed by Alastair Graham in the garden at Barford, shortly after their engagement in May 1928.

Their 'spick and span bandbox of a house' at 17a Canonbury Square, and (*below right*) the portrait painted by Henry Lamb for Bryan Guinness – hence the glass of stout – earlier the same year, 1928, shortly after Evelyn had finished *Decline and Fall*.

AS A CHILD IN THE YEAR 1860 : THE HON. MRS. EVELYN WAUGH.

Shevelyn photographed by *Sketch* at the Guinnesses' 1860 party in the same costume as she was seen by *The Tatler* at a later party, lounging on deck in 'a very amiable position' with John Heygate.

The Evelyns at a 'Tropical' fancy-dress party during their failed reconciliation-fortnight.

After the collapse of his marriage, Evelyn sought refuge with Bryan and Diana Guinness, seen here on honeymoon in 1929.

House party at Pakenham Hall, 1930: Alastair Graham, Evelyn, Elizabeth Harman (later Longford), and, just out of shot with a tennis racket, John Betjeman.

Below: Evelyn in observation mode at Pool Place, with Rupert Mitford (Nancy's uncle), Nancy Mitford and Pansy Lamb, 1930.

Below right: Evelyn in Kenya in 1931.

Alec and Evelyn at Villefranche, South of France, 1931.

Teresa 'Baby' Jungman, whom Evelyn fell deeply in love with in 1930, and (left) below, posing with her sister Zita as the Gemini sign of the zodiac.

Another who eluded his advances was Eileen Agar (*above*), but more receptive girlfriends included (*clockwise from above right*) Joyce Fagan, Audrey Lucas, Hazel Lavery and Pixie Marix.

AUDREY SCOTT

Evelyn with Sybil Colefax, Phyllis de Janzé and Oliver Messel in 1931.

Alec Waugh and Joan Chirnside after their engagement in 1932.

Left: Evelyn, Hamish St Clair Erskine, Coote Lygon and Hubert Duggan at Madresfield, early 1930s.

Below: Evelyn between Maimie and Coote (in specs) Lygon.

Left: Evelyn at Captain Hance's riding academy, labelled by himself.

Madresfield as it looks today.

Evelyn is congratulated by his father after winning the Hawthornden Prize in 1936.

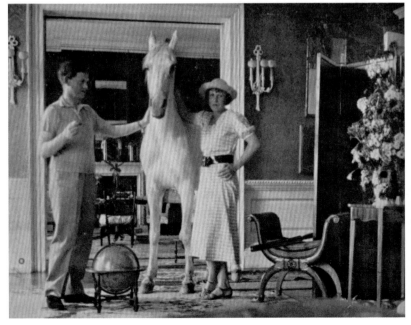

Evelyn with Penelope Betjeman and her horse in the drawing-room at Faringdon House.

an embassy in Mexico and where it thus bore the more diplomatic title *Mexico: An Object Lesson*, the book found even more favour with *The New York Times*: 'Soberly conceived and wittily executed in the best traditions of the familiar essay, it is one of those astringent volumes which appear every now and then as an antidote to complacency, sweetness and light. The evident sincerity of the author, the high quality of his literary talent and the calm logic with which he pursues his theme entitle him to a hearing in this country.'[64]

Although Evelyn was a hired gun, the thrust of what he had contracted to write was very much in line with his conservative political outlook, so there was an integrity to his account which reviewers responded to, besides which it may not have escaped their notice that his friend Graham Greene, whose political views were a long way to the left of Evelyn's, had reached many of the same conclusions in his own more famous travel book on Mexico, *The Lawless Roads* (inspiration for *The Power and the Glory*), which came out shortly before *Robbery Under Law*.

In any event, by the time Evelyn's book appeared in June 1939 the British public cared very little about what was going on in Mexico due to ominous developments much closer to home, Hitler having invaded Czechoslovakia in March and more recently told his military commanders to get ready for war against Poland in order to expand Germany's *Lebensraum* in the east and secure its food supplies via the Baltic port of Danzig. Evelyn himself had been mentally hunkering down since the beginning of the year: 'We are here immovable until the outbreak of war,'[65] he wrote to Baby Jungman from Piers Court on New Year's Day 1939. He saw the looming conflict as a crusade against the forces of totalitarianism in whichever form and on 22 August, shortly after his parents' second stay at Stinchcombe, he recorded: 'Russia and Germany have agreed to neutrality pact so there seems no reason why war should be delayed.'

Since finishing *Robbery Under Law* he had been working hard on a new novel (eventually published unfinished as *Work Suspended*), but had lately found himself restless and unable to concentrate and had instead been throwing his energy into the garden. On 24 August he recorded: 'Working in the afternoon in the garden, clearing the alley, I thought: what is the good of this? In a few months I shall be growing Swedes and potatoes here and on the tennis court; or perhaps I shall be away and then another two or three years of weeds will feed here until the place looks as it did when we came here two years ago.'

With Laura expecting their second child that November he was as happy and settled as he had ever been, yet at the same time he was uneasily aware that their idyll was likely to be brief. Not unnaturally, he did his best to shut the international crisis out and prided himself on being 'the only English family to eschew the radio'.[66] When Diana Cooper came to stay with her devoted friend and admirer Conrad Russell, she wrote afterwards to say how impressed she was by the 'excellencies' of his 'terribly covetable' house and how delighted she was to see him 'so happy and so serene'. Yet she failed to understand why the international crisis – 'a subject which by its nature must be constantly present in all our minds' – had to be so taboo. Evelyn had forbidden her even from getting her radio from the car to listen to a speech by the Foreign Secretary, Lord Halifax, and when at the end of dinner she attempted to bring the subject up she was met with a 'very nasty snub' from Evelyn. 'I saw both butlers blanch at your tone,' she told him. 'Why is it Bo?'[67]

On Monday, 26 August, with Germany poised to attack Poland, the local schoolmistress called to tell Evelyn that Piers Court had been designated as a billet. 'My heart sank,' he recorded. 'But it is not for children but for five adults who are coming to arrange for children's arrival and go in a week's time.' Having made arrangements, however, 'removing all valuable objects from the rooms I am giving them', they learned that there were fewer evacuees than anticipated and they would be spared after all, so instead they took a bed and some clothes to a destitute family the vicar was sheltering in his stable loft.

After breakfast on Sunday, 3 September, Evelyn gave in to temptation and listened to the Prime Minister, Neville Chamberlain, broadcast on the radio that war had begun. 'He did it very well', he told his diary. Two days later he placed an advertisement in the personal columns on the front page of *The Times*: 'MR. EVELYN WAUGH wishes to LET PIERS COURT, near DURSLEY, GLOS. FURNISHED for duration of war. Old house recently modernized: 4 reception, 10 bed, 4 bath, & co.: 4 acres or more. Low rent to civilized tenant.'[68]

17

....

A War to End Waugh

'How sad it all is!' wrote Evelyn's mother when she saw they were letting Piers Court. 'May the duration of the war be short & your return to your lovely home be soon.'[1] But Evelyn was pessimistic about how long it might last and although he had given the impression of ignoring its approach, privately he had been thinking about little else. The obvious thing for him to do was to apply to the Ministry of Information, where friends such as Graham Greene and Tom Burns were soon busy peddling propaganda. However as an artist and adventurer he felt drawn towards something substantially more active and exciting. 'My inclinations are all to join the army as a private,' he confided to his journal. 'Laura is better placed than most wives, and if I could let the house for the duration very well-placed financially. I have to consider thirty years of novel-writing ahead of me. Nothing would be more likely than work in a Government office to finish me as a writer; nothing more likely to stimulate me than a complete change of habit. There is a symbolic difference between fighting as a soldier and serving as a civilian, even if the civilian is more valuable.'[2]

With no takers yet for his patriotic services or his house, life at Piers Court continued much as usual for the time being, with Evelyn devoting his time to planting box hedges, building a wall and erecting a Gothic balustrade with the help of the gardener Prewitt. But at the end of September some Dominican nuns took the house for £600 a year for use as a girls' school and Evelyn and Laura decamped to Pixton, where they found a household of fifty-four, including twenty-six evacuated children. 'We ate in the hall,' Evelyn recorded that evening, 'making a fine target for the children's spittle from the top landing.'[3]

'I can't think of a worse torture,' Henry Yorke wrote to commiserate, 'than being stuck with your in-laws & the frightful children.'⁴ Evelyn grabbed every opportunity to escape to London and in late October he had an interview there with Ian Fleming – then only a slight acquaintance – for a job in naval intelligence. The next day he was delighted to be accepted by the Welsh Guards, only to be told a few days later that they were full up after all. By now beginning to despair, Evelyn suspected 'there must be someone at the War Office occupied in blocking my chances',⁵ which was conceivable given his words of admiration for Mussolini in *Waugh in Abyssinia* and for Franco in *Robbery Under Law*, although subsequent whispers that his interviewers had thought his suede shoes 'unsuitable'⁶ suggests it was more likely pure snobbery on their part.

On his return to Pixton he recorded that 'a fresh wave of lice has effected an entry'.⁷ And the next day: 'Work out of the question as the evacuated children are now admitted to the garden at the back of the house under my windows. Impetigo, thrush, and various ailments are rampant.' The only thing for it was to take himself off to his writing refuge at Chagford. 'It was sweet of you to let me go without protest,' he wrote to Laura from the Easton Court Hotel. 'It was the only sensible course. I shall be able to work here. I hope to get the novel really under way before the birth.'⁸ A couple of days later he reported: 'I work all morning. Then walk. Then a little work. Then a bath, a cocktail, dinner, and the crossword and early bed & long sleep. Except for one thing [Laura not being there too] an idyllic existence – but that one thing makes the crucial difference.'⁹

Within four days he had added 4,000 words to the 15,000 he had completed before war broke out. Laura came to meet him in Exeter on his birthday and again the following weekend, but otherwise he toiled on alone with the novel, by now sufficiently absorbed to have temporarily ceased worrying about not being on active service.¹⁰ On 16 November he moved to a boarding house near Pixton to await the birth of their baby and the next day drove over after Laura went into labour. Afterwards he told Maimie Lygon: 'Laura has had a son. Will you be its god-mother? It is to be called Auberon Alexander. It is quite big and handsome & Laura is very pleased with it.'¹¹ Maimie had herself recently married the Russian émigré wine merchant Prince Vsevolod Ivanovich Romanov, nephew of the last Tsar, and was thus now Princess Romanovsky Pavlovski, which Evelyn promised her Auberon would be made to say as soon as he learned to speak. Laura seems to have minded far more than Evelyn about having a boy. 'I am fretting about your anti-daughter feeling,' Evelyn had written to her beforehand. 'Daughters are a great comfort to their parents compared that is with sons.'[12]

Four days after Auberon's birth, Evelyn went up to London to see the Royal Marines, his application having been 'strongly supported'[13] by Winston Churchill at the instigation of Brendan Bracken, whom Evelyn had known vaguely since the early 1930s.* Staying at Highgate, Evelyn found his parents 'markedly unsympathetic to my project of joining the war'.[14] His interview the next day was preceded by a medical examination in a flat in St James's: 'I went first to have my eyes tested and did deplorably,' he recorded. 'When asked to read at a distance with one eye I could not distinguish lines, let alone letters. I managed to cheat a little by peering over the top. Then I went into the next room where the doctor said, "Let's see your birthday suit. Ah, middle-aged spread. Do you wear dentures?" He tapped me with a hammer in various organs. Then I was free to dress.' At the interview itself at the Admiralty, a friendly colonel told him: 'The doctors do not think much of your eyesight', but after asking him to read a large advertisement across the street he accepted him nonetheless, adding breezily: 'Anyway most of your work will be in the dark.'[15]

Evelyn's day got even better that afternoon when the editor of the American *Life* magazine commissioned two articles 'at the startling price of a thousand dollars', which went a long way towards settling his immediate debts. Cue champagne at his club, a magnum at dinner with Patrick Balfour, then three more bottles and one of rum with Kathleen Meyrick at a nightclub. 'I was sick at about five.'[16]

Required to report for duty with the Marines on 7 December, he spent the intervening week recovering from this bender at Pixton with Laura, who was now suffering from pleurisy. Travelling down to Chatham, his fellow officers struck him as 'the kind of nondescript body one might have conscripted out of the first omnibus one saw in the Strand'. But he perked up on arrival, when they were greeted with pink gins and he was given a large bedroom to himself with a fire continually blazing in it. 'The food is

---

* After their first encounter, in 1931, staying with the Brownlows at Belton, Evelyn whimsically told Maimie Lygon that 'there was a pretty auburn-haired girl called Brendan Bracken dressed up as a man' and that he could not resist sleeping with her (Christopher Sykes, *Evelyn Waugh*, pp. 113–14). However much Evelyn subsequently owed to Bracken as a fixer, he always thought him a preposterous fraud and, later feeling let down, used him as the basis for the obnoxious Rex Mottram in *Brideshead Revisited*.

absolutely excellent,' he told Laura. 'On the first evening there was a cold supper on account of a play which was being given us in our own theatre. I was led to the supper table with profuse apologies and found lobster, fresh salmon, cold birds, hams, brawn exactly like the cold table at the St. James's. Afterwards several rounds of excellent vintage port.'[17]

The next week they began a six-week intensive infantry course consisting of map-making, sanitation, small-arms, military law, endless arms drill and the dreaded PT.[18] Evelyn was the first to admit that even with his newly grown moustache, 'as smart a little moustache as Errol Flynn,' as Diana Cooper described it,[19] he did not look very impressive in his uniform: Mary Pakenham said he was the only person she knew who was made less distinguished-looking by wearing it. But he nonetheless thought himself quite good at ordinary military drill, an assessment with which his colour sergeant did not always agree: 'Lieutenant Wuff, press on that rifle butt and keep your precious eyes to the front. To the front I said! You're not 'ere to collect daisies!'[20]

On the whole, though, the life suited him very well. 'Marine barracks are like a senior common room without the bore of dons talk,' he told Helen Asquith, '– good Georgian architecture, old silver & mahogany, vintage port – all the concomitants of university murder stories with enough physical exercise to give one an appetite; no responsibilities, no intellectual exercise except in attempting to convince the Protestant chaplain of the authenticity of Our Lord's miracles.'[21]

After all this, Christmas at Pixton with its notoriously bad cooking came as a rude shock, especially since the house was now full of 'slum children' and 'silent professional spinsters, ironically called "helpers"'. With Laura still convalescing in bed, he chose to eat most of his meals on a tray in her room. Returning to Chatham just after New Year, he spent the next weekend with Tom Burns in London and was touched to be reconciled with Baby Jungman over cocktails. 'The Dutch Girl has got a new youth out of the war,' he told Laura, '(and the death of her King Charles spaniel). She dances with Canadian soldiers at night clubs three nights a week and sits up in an A.R.P. post the other four.'[22] That summer she would be swept off her feet by one of her dance partners, a walrus-mustachioed Scot called Graham Cuthbertson who was serving in a Canadian regiment. Frank Pakenham later recalled: 'He obviously had plenty of sexuality. Perhaps it needed someone like that to overcome Baby's chasteness, which possibly he did not even notice.'²³ Most of Baby's former suitors seemed to think he was a bounder, however Evelyn chivalrously told her that her marriage was 'the first good news since the Graf Spee' and that her husband 'must be a prodigy to have triumphed where so many have fallen'. 'Do let us all four meet. Laura joins with me in sending her true love. I pray you may be as happy in marriage as I have been these last three years.'²⁴ The marriage soon produced two children, yet despite Evelyn's prayers it was not long before the couple drifted apart.

* * *

In mid-January the Marines moved to a grim disused holiday camp at Kingsdown near Deal, which was so cold and uncomfortable that Evelyn sought refuge whenever he could at 'a club for old buffers' – the Deal & Walmer Union. Their affable new colonel, Godfrey Wildman-Lushington, expected them to be under canvas by April, which Evelyn did not much like the sound of. The colonel also spoke of 'extreme athletic fitness as essential for active service,' Evelyn told Laura, 'so I think you can rest easy in your mind that I shall be left behind with the luggage when the more sensational adventures are attempted'.²⁵ Yet despite being a conspicuous bon viveur who evidently hated PT and was growing stouter by the day due to overindulgence in the officers' mess, Evelyn managed the gruelling thirty-mile marches with all his kit remarkably well; one regular officer later noted that he had 'a very good pair of lungs on him' and was 'surprisingly fit'.²⁶

The brigade commander, Albert St Clair-Morford, was a striking character and the obvious prototype for the lovably bloodthirsty Brigadier Ritchie-Hook in *Sword of Honour*: '[He] looks like something escaped from Sing-Sing,' Evelyn recorded after the brigadier's first lecture, 'and talks like a boy in the Fourth Form at school – teeth like a stoat, ears like a faun, eyes alight like a child playing pirates, "We then have to biff them, gentlemen." He scares half and fascinates half.'²⁷

The next month, Evelyn visited St Clair-Morford at his home, 'a depraved villa of stockbroker's Tudor,' as Evelyn perceived it. 'I said in a jaggering way, "Did you build this house, sir?" and he said "Build it! It's 400 years old!" The Brigadier's madam is kept very much in her place and ordered about with great shouts. "Woman, go up to my cabin and get my boots." More peculiar, she is subject to booby-traps. He told us with great relish how the night before she had had to get up several times in the night to look after a daughter who was ill and how, each time she returned, he had fixed up some new horror to injure her – a string across the door, a jug of water on top of it etc. However she seemed to thrive on this treatment & was very healthy & bright with countless children.'[28]

Evelyn was as infected by the brigadier's bellicosity as he was entertained by his eccentricity and told John Betjeman, who had been turned down by the RAF on medical grounds:[29] 'Don't on your life get into a pansy mobile base defense unit. Infantry brigade is the thing ... The only way to bring this business to a happy conclusion is to kill great numbers of Germans. If we go on thinking only of defence there will be nothing worth defending. Why do you prefer defence? I can't understand it.'[30]

Evelyn had seen a lot more of Laura since Christmas, lodging with her for a time away from barracks in a local hotel and spending weekends together in London. In April, just as she had begun to feel well again for the first time since the birth of Auberon, she was somewhat less than elated to find she was pregnant yet again. 'It is sad news for you that you are having another baby and I am sad at your sorrow,' Evelyn wrote to her. 'For myself, surrounded with the spectacle of a world organized to kill, I cannot help feeling some consolation in the knowledge that new life is being given. Your suffering will be to give life, ours, if we have to suffer, to take it. A child that is a danger & distress now may be your greatest happiness in the future. If I do not live through this war, you will have your children's love & their need of you.'[31]

The consensus among the vast majority of chroniclers of Evelyn's military career is that he was 'not good with men' and was disliked by his troops because of his sarcasm and impatience and tendency to talk over their heads – he was once memorably overheard gently advising a group of nineteen-year-olds that 'Whistling and catcalls is a form of courtship that rarely leads to union.'[32] There was almost certainly some truth in reports of his unpopularity, although the evidence for it seems to consist almost entirely of the testimony of his fellow officers rather than the recollections of the troops themselves, several of whom gave evidence to the contrary. There are also several other indications that for much of the time Evelyn got along perfectly well with his men, who enjoyed his boldly nonconformist approach to soldiering even if his irritability sometimes got the better of him. He defended his men in several courts-martial and in defiance of the colonel's orders gave one young marine a night's leave so that he and his 'young lady' could compete in a dancing competition. As Evelyn told Laura, the man returned 'with a silver cup as high as himself, champion of the South of England'.[33] At the beginning of April he told Laura that he was the only temporary officer in his battalion to have been given command of a fighting company. 'But I am sad to leave my platoon whom I was greatly attached to.'[34]

The next month brought promotion to captain and a predominantly favourable report from Colonel Wildman-Lushington and Brigadier St Clair-Morford: 'A natural commander and experienced man. He works hard and gets good work out of his subordinates but must curb a tendency to lean on his 2nd in Command. Possesses any amount of moral courage and has self-confidence when on subjects he knows. A little impatient. I believe that with more military experience he will make a first class Company Commander.'[35]

In August, however, Evelyn was abruptly relieved of his command after he was overheard loudly berating his quartermaster sergeant in front of the men for the lack of drinking water on their train to Birkenhead, en route for Scapa Flow and then – after a two-week voyage – West Africa. Shortly prior to this he had gone to see Brendan Bracken about transferring to the commandos being formed by Sir Roger Keyes as director of Combined Operations, but he now worried that it would look like he was leaving under a cloud, and just as his battalion was about to see action for the first time. Rather than take up the offer of immediate transfer, he therefore accepted an appointment as battalion intelligence officer, an information-gathering role that was perhaps better suited to his particular talents than that of company commander. The action that he had been hankering for, however, proved elusive. Their part in an attempt to install General de Gaulle and the Free French in Dakar was eventually aborted due to a combination of what nowadays might be termed adverse weather conditions and the general not receiving as cordial a welcome as hoped. Afterwards Evelyn wrote to Laura that in the hours leading up to what had promised to be a very hazardous operation, 'my thoughts were with you, & with you only, all the time' but that ultimately 'bloodshed has been avoided at the cost of honour'.[36]

A few days later he wrote to her: 'I realised [then] how much you have changed me, because I could no longer look at death with indifference. I wanted to live & I was pleased when we ran away.' But whenever he did see action in future Evelyn showed himself to be almost entirely impervious to danger and his subsequent enforced retreats, far from bringing any sense of relief, seemed to cause only profound feelings of shame and disillusionment.

* * *

It was on his way back in Gibraltar that Evelyn received a letter from Lieutenant-Colonel Robert Laycock to say he had a post for him in his commando, which Evelyn rather tactlessly described to his worried parents as 'a more melodramatic force than the Marines'.[37] A vague acquaintance since the early 1930s through the Lygons, Bob Laycock was the officer Evelyn would come to admire above all others he served with. Then aged thirty-three, four years younger than Evelyn, brave, charming and supremely well connected, he was the son of the raffish Nottinghamshire landowner Brigadier-General Sir Joseph 'Joe' Laycock, KCMG, DSO, who was said to have fathered two children with Edward VII's mistress Daisy Warwick before luring Bob's famously beautiful mother away from her previous husband, the Marquess of Downshire.[38] Bob Laycock was himself married to a daughter of Freda Dudley Ward, chief mistress to the Prince of Wales before Wallis Simpson. After Eton and Sandhurst he had joined the elite Royal Horse Guards in 1927 and combined a glittering cavalry career with such adventures as sailing halfway round the world before the mast in a Finnish windjammer.[39] On the outbreak of war his scientific expertise had taken him to Cairo as an anti-gas staff officer, a dull and dead-end job from which he managed to escape with the help of David Niven, the film star.

Niven was soon to marry Laycock's niece and had no hesitation in recommending his future uncle to his boss at the War Office, Dudley Clarke, who was founding the commandos to carry out offensive raiding operations behind enemy lines in occupied France, inspired by the Boer horsemen who had harried the British in his native South Africa. Laycock's sailing background meant he was ideally suited to seaborne raids and landing operations and by Niven's account, Clarke 'immediately decided that this was just the man he wanted'.[40] Laycock thus set about raising 8 Commando. An officer of great initiative, imagination and daring, within three years he would be the youngest major-general in the army.

'The business of forming a unit of volunteers, officered by my own friends, seemed, and still does seem to me, the pleasantest way of going to war,' Laycock recalled.[41] Many of his officers were recruited at the bar of his club, White's, of which Evelyn was not yet a member but soon would be. Although Laycock's officers were chosen from those who, like Evelyn, had volunteered for hazardous service, he was looking for those whom he felt he could trust. A great fan of Evelyn's novels, Laycock later remembered agreeing to Bracken's suggestion that he take Evelyn on the grounds that he was 'often even funnier in fact than in fiction' and 'could not fail to be an asset in the dreary business of war'.[42]

* * *

Before joining his new unit in Ayrshire, Evelyn spent his leave at Pixton and visited Piers Court, which he found 'over-flowing with refugees' and the garden 'rapidly relapsing into jungle'. He also went to London at the height of the Blitz, staying with his parents at Highgate, where he also saw Alec who had been evacuated from Boulogne after the fall of France and was now taking the opportunity of his family's absence in Australia to pursue a love affair with a tall, bosomy, much younger woman, whom Evelyn had first met at their writing retreat in Devon and christened 'the Chagford giantess'.

In mid-November Evelyn travelled north to Largs on the Ayrshire coast where 8 Commando was stationed, with the town's Marine Hotel serving as their officers' mess. There he found various friends and acquaintances, including the former Reuters correspondent Robin Campbell, whose father had been ambassador to Paris until France fell.[43] There was also Harry Stavordale, whom he knew from Oxford, whose spectacular family home, the Jacobean Holland House in London's Holland Park, had just been destroyed in the Blitz; and Randolph Churchill, the prime minister's spoilt and rumbustious son with whom Evelyn had had a love-hate relationship since they had both been made godparents to Diana Guinness's son Jonathan. These plus a few others led by Earl Fitzwilliam's ill-fated heir Peter Milton* – 'very agreeable but a bit much for me', Evelyn told Laura – made up 8 Commando's 'smart set', a group of rich playboys whom Evelyn could not afford to join yet looked upon with indulgent amusement. 'The smart set drink a very great deal,' he told Laura, 'play cards for high figures, dine nightly in Glasgow, and telephone to their trainers endlessly.' Having reverted to the pay of a lieutenant, Evelyn was meanwhile obliged to live in 'dignified poverty'.[44]

Evelyn relished the smart set's unconventionality and thought their 'gaiety and independence' would prove an asset in action.[45] To begin with he served as liaison officer with Campbell and Stavordale. 'I have done nothing so far except take a cuckoo clock to pieces & play a lot of ludo,' he told Laura. 'All the officers have very long hair & lap dogs & cigars & they wear whatever uniform they like.'[46] A week later he reported that life in 8 Commando was growing 'more like a house party daily & I think a minor operation might be salutary to check the lotus eating . . . Today there was a grand inspection & I walked behind with the staff detecting, with my trained, Marine eye many imperfections which escaped the foot guards.'[47]

At the end of November Evelyn was to have undergone training in field-craft at Inverailort Castle in the Highlands, accompanied by Randolph Churchill, who had been expelled from the previous course by Lord Lovat for heckling one of his NCO instructors, several of whom were ghillies or stalkers on his estate at Beaufort.[48] (Another instructor was Shimi Lovat's cousin, David Stirling, later to found the SAS.) In the event Evelyn did not go because on the evening of Saturday, 30 November Mary Herbert telephoned from Pixton to say that Laura had gone into labour early with the baby she had been expecting since that spring.

Evelyn caught the sleeper the next day, arriving at Tiverton station at 10.30 on the Monday morning. 'Laura's baby was born prematurely on Sunday and lived for only twenty-four hours,' he wrote to his mother later that day. 'She was baptised, Mary, before she died & will be buried in Brushford churchyard tomorrow.' The letter then bizarrely went on: 'It was an easy birth and Laura is in excellent health . . . I have got three days' leave & return to my commando on Friday. Life is more easygoing there

---

* Heir to an estimated £45 million, including England's largest country house, Wentworth Woodhouse, Viscount Milton was later romantically linked to the widowed Marchioness of Hartington, the former 'Kick' Kennedy, sister of the future President J. F. Kennedy. In 1948 they were both killed when the plane in which they were travelling crashed in France.

than in the Marines; many old friends and acquaintances are with me, and I find the life highly enjoyable . . .'[49]

Arthur, who had always longed for a daughter, was shocked by Evelyn's apparent lack of concern at losing one of his own and additionally hurt by the fact that the news had not reached him until after the funeral. 'There seems something quite pathetic in this little star of life,' Arthur wrote to Alec's wife Joan in Australia, 'which just flickered and went out. She wasn't wanted and she did not stay. Evelyn announced her coming as "to the regret of all and the consternation of some". Well, she didn't trouble them for long, and she is spared a great deal.'[50]

Evelyn's grandson later attributed his strangely dispassionate reaction to an instinctive compulsion to 'prove his immunity to Arthur's worst fault – sentimentality', as a result of which Evelyn 'struck attitudes of immoderate detachment, exaggerated often to the point of absurdity. The more emotional Arthur became, the more Evelyn vaunted his *sangfroid*.'[51] This seems perfectly plausible, although Evelyn's account of the loss of his daughter in his diary was also curiously unemotional, apart from the sorrowful admission: 'Poor little girl, she was not wanted.'[52]*

By 7 December, Evelyn was back with the commandos in Scotland and soon off to the Isle of Arran to train for an assault on the Italian island of Pantelleria. He had been 'very sad leaving you alone', he told Laura, but doubted he would be able to make it back to Pixton for Christmas: 'You well know how glad I am to avoid that.'[53] He was glad too that Penguin had agreed to publish his unfinished novel under the title *Work Suspended*. There was, he told Laura, 'too much good material there to let it disappear',[54] and he thought it the best thing he had written as far as it went. With its first-person narrative and descriptive, nostalgic prose, *Work Suspended* is the stylistic precursor of *Brideshead Revisited* and may conceivably have become the better novel had the war not intervened.[55]

In the event, Christmas Day was spent aboard the troopship *Glenroy*, whose captain enlivened dinner by setting the tablecloth on fire and then being sick where he sat. Evelyn spent most of the day asleep. Not

---

* Although she lived for barely twenty-four hours, Mary had the distinction of being the only one of Laura's children who was breastfed, the doctor having said that that was her only hope. Perhaps because of the trauma of losing her, Laura later remembered that her daughter had lived for a week, but Evelyn's diary appears to refute that.

long afterwards the planned Pantelleria raid was cancelled, much to the exasperation of Keyes, who knew that his commandos had been brought to a peak of readiness for action and that it would become far more diffi-cult to keep them motivated if they were continually stood down. It was against this background in late January that Evelyn's unit was suddenly told to pack their bags for North Africa as part of 'Force Z' (later renamed Layforce) under the overall command of Bob Laycock.

Keyes, whose son Geoffrey was serving with 11 Commando, saw them off himself and afterwards wrote to Churchill that they were 'the envy of all those who were left behind. I gave your love to Randolph, who is delighted to be one of the lucky ones. So many of our mutual friends have sons in that splendid party. It is the flower of my striking force.'[56]

Evelyn had been appointed acting brigade major and on the long voyage out round the Cape of Good Hope shared a small cabin with the prime minister's son and Harry Stavordale, 'both of whom have brought luggage enough for a film star's honeymoon,' he told Laura. While Churchill grew a moustache, Evelyn attempted a beard. 'At present it looks peculiarly repulsive,' he admitted to Laura, 'a mass of isolated, coarse hairs of varie-gated colouring, but it gives me an interest as they say, like a pet or a pot flower.'[57] Two weeks later he wrote: 'As the voyage goes on the commando gets more & more like the Russian cavalry of Tolstoy's *War & Peace*. At the last settling day for gambling poor Randolph was £800 down. Poor Pamela will have to go to work.'[58] (This proved to be the last straw in the Churchills' already unhappy marriage; they eventually divorced in 1946.) Evelyn, meanwhile, made do with 'a little poorer game with the poor', he told Laura. 'All my gaming winnings are for you. There is another pound or two coming to you at next settling day.'[59]

Before leaving, Evelyn had written to his butler Ellwood asking him to be his batman but got no reply and a nineteen-year-old archaeologist called Ralph Tanner had volunteered instead – 'very high brow,' Evelyn described him to Laura, 'a pleasant young man'. Scarcely credible though it seemed to Evelyn's would-be detractors, Tanner found his new em-ployer equally pleasant. When, years later, an interviewer from *Punch* magazine suggested that Evelyn had been 'so unpopular that he had to be protected from other soldiers', Tanner replied: 'Absolute rubbish. He fitted in very well. He was everything you'd expect an officer to be.' 'A bit of a tyrant, you mean?' asked the doggedly sceptical interviewer. 'Not at all,' said Tanner. 'He didn't exploit you the teeniest, weeniest bit?' 'I'd say he behaved as a model employer to a servant'. 'Oh . . .'[60]

Evelyn's reputation for rudeness was 'totally alien to the Waugh I knew', Tanner added, recalling that he was ticked off only a couple of times when he served hot gravy with cold meat and when he got polish on the wrong side of his Sam Browne belt so that it came off on his uniform. In another unpublished interview, Tanner also recalled having had 'some absurd idea that if you went into the tropics, you had to have flannel spine pads, and I remember saying to him, "Do you wish me to make spine pads for you?" He looked a little bemused, but said, "No, I don't think that will be necessary." He wasn't at all sarcastic.'[61]

So considerate was Evelyn that Tanner recalled 'waiting up for him with some hot water, just to return the courtesy'. The only gossip Tanner heard about him among the troops, meanwhile, was that he was 'a bit fond of the honourables'[62] and that he had insisted on sharing a cabin with Randolph Churchill and Lord Stavordale. The implication is of course that Evelyn was a snob, which was perhaps not an entirely outrageous assessment, yet in fairness to him both of these were old friends of his and in any case he would have been hard pushed to find cabin mates among the officers of 8 Commando who did not, broadly speaking, fit the 'honourables' description.

* * *

Layforce eventually entered the Suez Canal in early March with promises that they would soon have a 'bellyful of fighting'.[63] But just as they began serious training for yet another abortive mission – an attack on the island of Rhodes – the Germans reoccupied Cyrenaica and General Wavell felt he could no longer spare the air cover and destroyer escorts that would allow them to strike in the Dodecanese or anywhere else.

Layforce was ordered to Alexandria, but while their commanding officer strove to get his men into action, his commandos were repeatedly called back from operations on which they had been sent out. One wag suggested they be renamed 'Belayforce' and some mock-Churchillian graffiti appeared on the troop deck: 'Never before in the history of human endeavour have so few been so buggered about by so many.'[64]

On 19 April they at last went into action with a night raid on the

Libyan coastal town of Bardia, which reports suggested was held by 2,000 of Rommel's *Afrika Korps*. The aim was to disrupt the enemy's lines of supply and communication and cause Rommel to 'look over his shoulder' and divert his troops away from the front line. But as they crept ashore it soon became apparent that the town was deserted apart from a solitary motorcycle patrol, which evaded their clumsy attempts to shoot it down and was thus fortunately able to relay news of the raid, with the result that a German brigade was diverted from the front line at a crucial time. In almost all other respects the operation was a shambles: one boat failed to get into the water; another ran aground and had to be destroyed; an officer was shot and killed by his own men; another man was injured by his own grenade; a party of sixty commandos returned down the wrong wadi and was left ashore and later captured. Evelyn later obligingly portrayed the raid as a success in a propaganda piece he had lucratively been contracted to write for *Life* magazine – 'it seems that you are being asked for a piece of fiction rather than an article,'[65] his agent told him – however he knew perfectly well that it had been botched. In his diary Evelyn recalled that some of the officers complained to him that their commanding officer, Lieutenant-Colonel Felix Colvin, had behaved badly. However, Evelyn thought that 'no one had behaved well enough for them to be able to afford a post-mortem' so did not pass their criticism on to Laycock. 'Perhaps if I had we might have been saved some shame in Crete,' Evelyn reflected.[66]

Crete was to be the scene of Layforce's next action, their arrival on the island coming six days after the German airborne invasion of 20 May. Before leaving Alexandria Evelyn recalled hearing that 'the Maleme aerodrome garrison was hard-pressed' but that otherwise the situation was 'well in hand'.[67] This misinformation owed much to the reluctance of the Allied Commander-in-Chief on Crete, Major-General Bernard Freyberg VC, to admit to Wavell how quickly the airport had fallen and to warn him that the island could no longer be held.

In any event by the time Layforce reached Suda Bay on the island's north coast close to midnight on 26 May, the battle was already lost and they were greeted by scenes of apocalyptic chaos. The lighters which came to take them ashore were full of wounded and a bedraggled and hysterical naval officer burst through the captain's door with anguished cries of: 'My God, it's hell, we're pulling out!' The commandos all stared at him aghast and Evelyn was contemptuous of what he saw as the man's cowardice, desperate as he was to have a proper go at last at the Germans.[68] Laycock later recalled telling the wretched man to shut up.

With very limited time to land, they had to dump most of their kit before going ashore. Once on the quayside, Laycock and Evelyn, acting as his intelligence officer, then left their brigade major, Freddy Graham, to get the men into defensive positions while they went off in search of the commander of British troops on the island, Major-General E. C. Weston, whom they found asleep on the earth floor of a rustic hovel serving as his headquarters. There they were told the full extent of the retreat and that, far from raiding aerodromes and seaports as promised in Alexandria, they were to assist in the rearguard covering the withdrawal over the White Mountains to Sphakia, a small fishing harbour on the south coast. It was getting light by the time they reached 'Creforce' headquarters, where Laycock asked Freyberg whether they were to hold the defence 'to the last man and last round', to which the general replied: 'No, a rearguard. Withdraw when you are hard pressed.'[69]

Back with his commandos, Laycock drew up instructions for a timed rearguard action lasting two days and Evelyn set off with Tanner to deliver the orders to Lieutenant-Colonel Colvin, the officer he had shielded from criticism after Bardia. Driving through no man's land, Evelyn appeared oblivious to the Stukas circling overhead and later dismissed their sorties as 'like German opera – too long and too loud'.[70] When the truck could go no further, he left his companions and proceeded on foot, walking for half an hour through scrub and rock before eventually coming across a commando officer who took him to a farm building and pointed under a table. There was Colvin, as Evelyn recorded, 'sitting hunched up like a disconsolate ape'.[71] Evelyn saluted the shell-shocked colonel (who was to serve as the model for Major 'Fido' Hound in *Sword of Honour*), gave him his orders and eventually took him back to headquarters, where, by Evelyn's pitiless account, every time a plane went over the wretched man 'lay rigid with his face in the gorse for about four hours'. At sunset Colvin went back to his battalion, only to return a few hours later 'with a confused account of having been ambushed on a motor cycle,' Evelyn wrote. 'His battalion was fiercely engaged he said (this was balls), and without explaining why he was not with them he gave us the order to withdraw. It all seemed fishy . . .'[72] They nevertheless obeyed and marched all through the night, with Colvin telling them 'We must get as far as we can before light'. The moment daylight came the colonel 'popped into a drain under the road and sat there', recorded Evelyn. After an hour's sleep, Evelyn decided to assess the situation for himself and walked back across the hills through various villages they had passed in the night to within half a mile of where the enemy was being held, where he eventually found Bob Laycock. They drove back to Colonel Colvin, still in his drain; 'Bob as politely as possible relieved him of his command'[73] – this was later repeated with some 'good round swearing'[74] after the colonel was found to have ordered his men to retreat from their position covering the redeployment of another Layforce battalion.

That night Evelyn and Laycock took the truck and fell back as far as Imbros, on the southern side of the White Mountains, from where the road descended 2,000 feet down a deep ravine to Sphakia. After resting up in a vineyard, at noon they continued on down a series of sharp hair-pins past caves full of ragged stragglers in vain search of an embarkation officer. That evening they eventually found the cave now serving as General Freyberg's headquarters, where they were given half a cupful of sherry and a spoonful of beans and told: 'You were the last to come so you will be the last to go.'[75]

Their return journey in the dark proved far more difficult and 'after an hour or two's scrambling and a bad fall for Bob' they spent the rest of the night at a little shrine on the hilltop, from where they could hear the shouts of Royal Navy sailors embarking troops on the coast below. Layforce spent the next day and a half protecting the Sphakia gorge before Evelyn and Laycock returned to the Creforce cave in the afternoon for further orders ahead of what was to be the last night of the evacuation. At around three o'clock that night, they and just over 200 members of Layforce were evacuated on the last ship to leave the island.

* * *

Over the past twenty-five years, Bob Laycock has been widely accused of lying and acting in direct contravention of orders and jumping the queue for evacuation from Crete, while Evelyn has been charged with falsify-ing the Layforce diary to cover up for him. These allegations were first made by Antony Beevor in his highly acclaimed and prize-winning book *Crete: The Battle and the Resistance* (1991), and with added vigour in an article he wrote for *The Spectator* – punningly entitled 'The First Casualty of Waugh' – shortly before the book's publication. His thesis has been almost universally adopted since. Leaving aside for a moment the direct evidence for the alleged wrongdoing – which is less compelling than one might imagine – one can see why the theory has caught on, stemming as it does from the strong sense of disillusion that permeates Evelyn's fictionalised account of the retreat from Crete in *Officers and Gentlemen*, the second novel in his *Sword of Honour* trilogy, and in particular his depiction of the discreditable flight of Ivor Claire, whose Hookforce diary is later burnt by Guy Crouchback to remove the only evidence of his questionable conduct. *Officers and Gentlemen* was published in 1955 and dedicated 'To Major General Sir Robert Laycock KCMG CB DSO. That every man in arms should wish to be.'

When Evelyn sent his mischievous friend Ann Fleming a copy, she telegraphed back: 'Presume Ivor Claire based Laycock dedication ironical Ann.' Evelyn's response was: 'Your telegram horrifies me. Of course there is no possible connexion between Bob and Claire. If you suggest such a thing anywhere it will be the end of our beautiful friendship . . . For Christ's sake lay off the idea of Bob = Claire . . . Just shut up about Laycock, Fuck You, E Waugh.'[76]

The violence of Evelyn's reaction indicated to many people that he had been rumbled, and as Beevor reasonably remarked, his subsequent diary entry hardly dispelled the suspicion: 'I replied that if she breathes a suspicion of this cruel fact it will be the end of our friendship.'[77] However since then a substantial body of contrary evidence has been excavated from scattered military archives by the Waugh scholar Professor Donat Gallagher and now several other key documents – including a previously unseen memoir by Bob Laycock – have come to light that go a long way towards refuting the accusations against Evelyn and his military mentor. So it is worth re-examining what happened after Evelyn and Laycock reached the Creforce cave on the afternoon of 31 May.

* * *

When they got there they found General Weston in charge, Freyberg having left the island by flying boat the previous evening. As Laycock recalled in his memoir, Weston seemed to be in extremely low spirits and warned them that both ammunition and food were in very short supply. Laycock reassured the general that his commandos had been trained to forage and that, having picked up countless rounds abandoned during the retreat, they also had more ammunition than they could possibly shoot off. They left the cave with orders which Evelyn later recorded in the Layforce war diary: 'Final orders from CREFORCE for evacuation (a) LAYFORCE positions not to be held to the last man and last round but only as long as was necessary to cover withdrawal of other fighting forces. (b) No withdrawal before order from H.Q. (c) LAYFORCE to embark after other fighting forces but before stragglers.'[78]

That evening Laycock was again summoned to Weston's cave and 'found him looking more utterly dejected than I can describe'. Weston was due to leave in a few hours by aeroplane and, as Laycock recalled:

> He looked at me without appearing to see me for a moment or two and then said very slowly and very quietly: 'I am now going to say something which, even in my most ghastly nightmare, I never dreamed that I could say to a British officer on the field of battle. Take down this order.' I turned to Freddy [Graham] who produced a notebook and pencil. Again in a voice so subdued that we could hardly hear him General Weston started to dictate. 'From GOC Crete to Remnants Creforce. You will provide yourself with a white flag. Tomorrow morning at first light you will seek out the Commander of the German forces and surrender to him.'
>
> When he had finished, Freddy handed the message to me. I gazed at it for some time before asking Weston whether he would consider it very insubordinate if I flatly refused to obey it.

Laycock pointed out that his commandos had plenty of fight left in them and suggested to Weston that either he could stay and organise guerrilla warfare in the hills, which some of his commandos eventually undertook on their own initiative, or he could evacuate as many of his brigade staff and men as could get down to the beach in time. After some thought Weston told Laycock that the second alternative seemed more likely to pay dividends for the future war effort. The general also took account of the fact that the Germans appeared to be 'making no attempt to give us the coup de grace', as Laycock wrote, and therefore as far as he was concerned 'the responsibility of Layforce to provide a rearguard to a force which was due to surrender in a few hours time had lapsed'.[79] By his own account, Laycock was thus authorised to delegate the responsibility for surrendering, a task which he initially assigned to Lieutenant-Colonel Colvin but which was eventually undertaken by a more senior New Zealander.

Beevor later accused Laycock of lying about his authorisation to evacuate, apparently overlooking the fact that General Weston recorded in his dispatches that he had sent for Colvin to make the surrender, thus effectively corroborating Laycock's testimony that he had been given permission to go. Freddy Graham recalled the circumstances of the crucial last meeting with Weston rather differently, but the conclusion was essentially the same – that Laycock was at liberty to evacuate his brigade headquarters along with as many of his men as he could muster. It is unclear whether Evelyn was at the same meeting, however in his private diary he later recalled that Weston 'had at first charged Bob with the task but later realised that it was foolish to sacrifice a first-class man for this and chose instead Colvin . . . Weston said that we were to cover the withdrawal and that a message would be sent us by the embarkation officer on Sphakia beach when we could retire.'[80]

In the event no message arrived and sometime after midnight Laycock grew concerned that time was running out for his commandos to make it from their various rearguard positions to the beach in time. He thus took Evelyn and Graham and hurried to Sphakia to try and find the beach officer, but the officer had already left by flying boat along with Weston and the rest of the Creforce staff at 11.50 p.m. Laycock now took matters into his own hands and sent Evelyn's batman, Tanner, as a runner with orders to his troops protecting the perimeter to withdraw.

By his own account, Evelyn meanwhile 'rescued a party of Greek boatmen whom the Australians wished to shoot as spies' and, deciding that there was nothing more they could do, he and Laycock and the rest of Layforce brigade HQ embarked in a small motor boat and boarded the destroyer *Kimberley*, which would be the last ship to leave at around three o'clock in the morning.

Evelyn later wrote in the Layforce diary: 'On finding that the entire staff of Creforce had embarked, in view of the fact that all fighting forces were now in position for embarkation and that there was no enemy contact, Col. Laycock on own authority, issued orders to Lt-Col. Young to lead troops to Sphakion by route avoiding the crowded main approach to town and to use his own personality to obtain priority laid down by Div. orders.'[81] In his *Spectator* piece Beevor wrote: 'It would be hard to compress more distortions of the truth into a single sentence.'[82] Yet everything that Evelyn recorded seems to have been perfectly correct. There was no enemy contact because the Germans chose to fight during the day and rest at night and so fighting had stopped at 8.45 p.m. Beevor contends that Evelyn's most serious fabrication was the assertion that 'all fighting forces were in position for embarkation', given that by Beevor's reckoning neither the Australian 2/7th Battalion nor the Marines, both of which had priority over Layforce, had then reached the beach. However both these units arrived at the entrance to the small beach before Laycock issued his orders to withdraw, only to find their way blocked by a combination of violent rabble and overzealous Movement Control officers. The time can be fixed because one of them recalled hearing General Weston's Sunderland take off soon after they got there.[83] Most of Layforce's troops found their way similarly blocked in the narrow sunken path to the beach. The few commandos who did manage to get away had hurried from the far western perimeter and made it onto the beach via a far less crowded side lane. The first 120 of them clambered aboard the last landing craft to leave, at 2.30 a.m.[84]

The fact that around 550-higher priority Australians and Marines failed to get away despite having reached the shore at around the same time owed far more to the complete breakdown in organisation than any supposed queue-barging by Layforce's commandos. The total taken off that night was 1,000 fewer than the planned 5,000 and numerous testimonies tell how the last landing craft were loaded with any soldiers to hand, including a great many who were not designated fighting troops. By all these accounts it seems most likely that, had the commandos not boarded when they did, their places would have been taken by lower-priority troops. Had there been better organisation many more fighting troops would have got off, including the Australians and the Marines, but that was hardly Bob Laycock or Evelyn Waugh's fault.

Freddy Graham later told Michael Davie that Evelyn had never so much as hinted that he thought Laycock should have stayed behind on Crete 'perhaps because he [Evelyn] had a personal horror of being captured!'.[85] Evelyn's strong aversion to the idea of being taken prisoner was also attested to by Laycock, who recalled Evelyn telling him that he was 'determined not to suffer the ignominy of capture' and wanted to ask a padre whether it would be considered suicide if he drowned in an attempt to swim back to Egypt.[86] Their evacuation removed the necessity for this drastic action, however Evelyn was evidently not entirely happy as they embarked on the last ship to leave the island, as Laycock recalled: 'By the look on his face at the time I gathered that Evelyn believed this to be a dishonourable thing to do though it made sense to me for, at least, we lived to fight another day.'[87]

But given time for reflection, the moral rightness of their departure became less clear to Bob Laycock too:

> Was I right in using arguments which influenced Weston to countermand his original orders? Should I, personally, have embarked that night knowing that nearly three-quarters of my command was still ashore? Probably not. There is much to be said in support of the principle that the Captain is the last to leave the sinking ship. At the time, however, my motive seemed reasonable enough and I am confident that my Brigade Staff, with the possible exception of Evelyn, heartily agreed with my contention that we would be more use to our country by returning with the remnants of Nos. 7, 50 and 52 Commandos to rejoin Nos. 8 and 11 in Egypt than by spending the rest of the war in a prisoner of war camp. Once the order to surrender was given I maintained that every able-bodied man who succeeded in getting back to Egypt had done the right thing. 'Qui s'excuse s'accuse.' I have never been happy about leaving Young and his gallant men behind.[88]

Evelyn's violent response to Ann Fleming and the apparently incriminating reference in his diary to 'this cruel fact' was possibly his way of acknowledging that the discreditable flight of Ivor Claire did in some way embody his remembered sense of moral unease and uncertainty during their evacuation from Crete. At the same time he still hero-worshipped Bob Laycock as the commander par excellence, besides being a steadfast friend and supporter. Evelyn was doubtless therefore genuinely appalled that a notorious gossip such as Ann Fleming might start putting it about that Laycock's evacuation from Crete was equivalent to that of Claire, who had deserted his men and contrived to get himself evacuated contrary to orders to fight until the last man and then surrender.

In *Officers and Gentlemen*, the character most like Laycock is Tommy

Blackhouse, who falls down a companionway on the way out to Crete and is thus saved him any responsibility for the ensuing debacle. Ivor Claire, meanwhile, contained elements of several members of 8 Commando's 'White's Club gang', none of whom were with them on Crete. According to Laycock, Claire's numerous apparent models included Eddie Fitzclarence, Bones Sudeley, Peter Beatty, Randolph Churchill, Philip Dunne and Peter Milton.[89]

If Evelyn later felt ashamed over what he called 'my bunk from Crete', there was doubtless also an element of guilt about the fact that so many – including most of Layforce's commandos – had been left behind to surrender. Others who got away felt much the same way. There was also a feeling that he had taken part in a military disgrace, and a deep sense of disillusionment at the way the Allies as a whole had capitulated so tamely when the island could and should have been held. As Beevor himself neatly summarised it: 'The loss of Crete was the most unnecessary defeat in that initial period of Allied humiliation at the hands of Hitler's Wehrmacht.'[90]

Christopher Sykes remembers Evelyn telling him shortly afterwards that he 'had never seen anything so degrading as the cowardice that infected the spirit of the army; said that Crete had been surrendered without need; that officers and men had been hypnotised into surrender by dive bombing'. Tanner, too, told Beevor that 'it struck me that everyone was being cowardly, no-one was moving as a military unit, everybody was out for himself'.

Antony Beevor is an outstanding and very readable military historian, however his case against Bob Laycock and Evelyn Waugh is highly dependent on supposition, much of which is refuted by evidence that has come to light since he wrote his book. In any event, for whatever reason, it appears from the transcript of his interview with Evelyn's batman Ralph Tanner that he had already made up his mind about the queue-jumping before he spoke to the witness who, one would think, was reasonably well placed to tell him what happened. 'There's no question that Laycock was a very brave man,' Beevor said to Tanner during the conversation, 'but there's no doubt about it, he tried to get out before they were supposed to, and tried to get as many of Layforce off as he could, but they were very much jumping the queue, in front of the Australians and the Marines.'[91]

It is perhaps telling that in her own fine biography, Selina Hastings mistook this quote as having come from Tanner and cited it in support of

Laycock and Evelyn's supposed misdeeds. The shorthand typist had begun transcribing the theory advanced by Beevor during his conversation with Tanner with a capital 'T', short for 'The' ('The controversial area is . . .') as opposed to 'Tanner' as Selina Hastings presumably thought. The slip is understandable given that Tanner said nothing in the whole interview to imply that Laycock and Waugh had acted in any way improperly or irresponsibly. In answer to the suggestion that Evelyn falsified the Layforce diary, Tanner said: 'As far as I knew, all Evelyn Waugh's comments in his diary were accurate.'[92]

Neither was there any accusation of wrongdoing from the Layforce officers who were left behind, Colonel Young saying he was 'strongly of the opinion' that Laycock going was 'justified' and 'required'. The official British 'Narrator' of the campaign, Colonel E. E. Rich, recorded that 'Layforce was ordered late in the evening to embark' and regretted the failure of them all to 'reach the boats'.[93] The Narrator's report is especially significant as it was submitted to all senior officers for their comments. The Inter-Service Committee report under Brigadier Guy Salisbury-Jones said much the same, amid some very blunt criticisms of senior officers. It is also hard to believe that Laycock would have gone on to the plum wartime jobs that he did had there been any suspicion regarding his actions on Crete hanging over him.

18

....

Head Unbloodied but Bowed

With so many of Layforce taken prisoner on Crete, the unit was soon disbanded and at his own request Evelyn rejoined the Royal Marines. His route back to England avoiding U-boats again took him via Cape Town, then across the Atlantic to Trinidad, up the American coast and across to Iceland before finally reaching Liverpool in early September 1941. He put the two-month trip to use writing *Put Out More Flags*, a riotous satire chronicling Basil Seal's non-military adventures during the Phoney War which seemed to capture the zeitgeist better than any of his books since *Vile Bodies* in 1930, albeit while suffering from similar defects of disjointedness. Although Evelyn dismissed it in a letter to his father as 'a minor work dashed off to occupy a tedious voyage', it promptly sold 18,000 copies early the next year, despite wartime paper restrictions.

Less than a month after Evelyn got back to London, his brother Alec left for Syria on a two-year posting as publicity agent to General Spears which, as Evelyn told Laura, 'is sad for my parents & for me as it means I now have them on my conscience'.[1] At the age of seventy-five and in frail health, Arthur Waugh felt particularly forlorn at the prospective departure of his favourite son, fearing that he might never see him again. In this rare instance he was relieved when Evelyn rang to invite himself to lunch on the day Alec left, recording in his diary that 'as it turned out it was a very good move, as he was amiable and cheerful and helped to stave off the anxiety of Alec's departure. He and Evelyn left us at 4 p.m. It was a ghastly wrench to say goodbye, especially as he was so kind and gentle. But his taxi vanished through the drive and we were left sorrowing.'[2]

Alec caught a sleeper to Glasgow that evening after a small leaving party in his flat, with champagne and sandwiches made by his mother. Evelyn initially declined his brother's invitation as he had just been given clearance from Brendan Bracken to do his piece about the Bardia commando raid for *Life* magazine and wanted to get it done before he rejoined the Marines. He was still struggling with it late the next evening and wrote to Laura that 'everything I try to write comes out in clichés'.[3] The finished article certainly has its *Boy's Own* moments, although a greater difficulty for Evelyn was that Peters had syndicated it to the London *Evening Standard* without telling him and a melodramatic report by Beverley Nichols subsequently appeared in the *Sunday Chronicle* describing Evelyn as a 'hard-bitten, sun-scorched Commando, with the dust of the desert in his eyes, and a rifle in his hand . . . The ex-dilettante, writing exquisite froth between cocktails, has proved one of the toughest of the lot . . . Few of us in the old days could have imagined Evelyn crawling up the escarpment at Bardia in the dead of night . . .'[4]

Nichols's portrayal was perhaps slightly tongue-in-cheek, but one can well imagine it infuriating certain other commandos who regarded themselves as rather tougher than Captain Waugh. It also earned Evelyn a stern reprimand for not having sought the approval of the Marine Office after Brendan Bracken, as Evelyn saw it, 'backed out of his responsibility' – thereby sowing the seeds for his unflattering portrayal as Rex Mottram in *Brideshead Revisited*, 'half a man posing as a whole one'.

On his last day in London before resuming military life, Evelyn saw Baby Jungman, as he still referred to her despite her marriage, now 'with a vast baby solely in her charge', he told Laura. 'She has changed a great deal with contact with rough Canadians and loss of virginity and is now frank in thought, coarse in speech & likes a stiff whisky. Very surprising.'[5] He returned to duty at Hayling Island on the Hampshire coast 'with the most profound misgiving'.[6] Unable to recapture the adventurous enthusiasm with which he joined up at Chatham, he told Laura that life at his new base was 'squalid, idle & lonely', albeit philosophically adding that it was 'suitable payment for fun with the commando & for my safe & happy return from Egypt'.[7] In November they moved north to Hawick, 'a grim, picturesque little town', as Evelyn described it, made grimmer by the intense cold and wind and rain, and the dreaded wireless playing ceaselessly in the mess. 'Weary, wet, lonely, bored,' he concluded a letter to Peters. 'There is no one here with any sense of humour,' he complained to Laura, 'but they never stop laughing.'[8] His boredom was relieved only by the books that *The Spectator* and *The Tablet* sent him to review, and in early January 1942 by a company commander's course which chanced to take place at Bonaly Tower, on the outskirts of Edinburgh, where Evelyn recognised the Cockburn coat of arms on the staircase and discovered that it had been built (by the architect William Henry Playfair in 1836) for his great-great-grandfather, Lord Cockburn.

At his suggestion, Laura joined him for part of the time ('it is absolutely glorious that you can come', he told her)[9] and they stayed at the Caledonian Hotel on Princes Street before transferring to humbler and more economic quarters, with Evelyn taking a taxi each day out to Bonaly. He thought the teaching staff 'admirable', apart from the intrusively perceptive psychoanalysts: 'I was interviewed by a neurotic creature dressed as a major, who tried to impute unhappiness and frustration to me at all stages of adolescence.'[10]

In February he returned to Hawick with his thoughts about the war growing gloomier by the day, the alliance with the Soviet Union having removed its 'heroic and chivalrous disguise', as he saw it, and rendered it instead 'a sweaty tug-of-war between teams of indistinguishable louts'. 'Do you understand now,' he wrote to Diana Cooper, alluding to his brusqueness when she came to stay at Piers Court in 1939, 'why I would have no wireless or talk of Central Europe at Stinchcombe? . . . Are there corners where old friends can still talk as though they were free? If there are, they must say in those corners that there is nothing left – not a bottle of wine nor a gallant death nor anything well made that is a pleasure to handle – and never will be again.' It was in this foul mood that on 2 April he made his first appearance on a BBC radio discussion programme, *The Brains Trust*, during which he managed roundly to offend all the other panellists by refusing to have lunch with them beforehand, making fun of them during the broadcast and finally suggesting that they all give their fees to the War Fund.

Desperate to get back to soldiering among friends, he wrote to Bob Laycock: 'I wish I were back with you. I suppose that there is no opening?' Laycock had recently returned from Egypt to command the Special Service Brigade, having earlier gone missing after the abortive raid on Rommel's headquarters in Libya, when Geoffrey Keyes was killed and posthumously awarded the VC and Evelyn's friend Robin Campbell severely wounded in his leg, which he eventually lost in a prisoner-of-war camp. 'It looks unlikely that [Laycock] has survived,' Evelyn noted at the time; 'but in White's everyone says he is too "fly" to be caught.' Sure enough, Laycock had miraculously presented himself to some British troops on Christmas Day after six weeks living off berries behind enemy lines, attributing his survival to his knowledge of the habits of foxes, in gratitude for which he never went hunting again. Though he knew perfectly well how difficult Evelyn could be, Laycock remained fond of him and in addition had been much impressed by his courage and coolness under fire on Crete. He agreed to have him back as an intelligence officer. '"The Blues" [Royal Horse Guards] have accepted me,' Evelyn wrote to Laura, 'so I can now grow my hair long and wear a watch chain across my chest, and you can have a suit made of their check tweed.'[11] After joining his new unit at Ardrossan on the Ayrshire coast, Evelyn wrote to Coote Lygon from 'a nice black market hotel where I have grape fruit and large dishes of eggs daily'. 'Chucker Laycock has proved most unchucking,' he purred, 'and I am back with him & Philip Dunne and other old chums.'[12]

Two weeks later, still feeling chipper, he wrote a much-quoted letter to Laura which showed how much he delighted in things going wrong, to say nothing of his flair for embellishment and preference for the most picturesque form of whatever story he happened to be telling:

So No.3 Cmdo were very anxious to be chums with Lord Glasgow [whose Kelburn estate lay just north of the commandos' base at Ardrossan] so they offered to blow up an old tree stump for him and he was very grateful and he said don't spoil the plantation of young trees near it because that is the apple of my eye and they said no of course not we can blow a tree down so that it falls on a sixpence and Lord Glasgow said goodness you are clever and he asked them all to luncheon for the great explosion. So Col. Durnford-Slater D.S.O. said to his subaltern, have you put enough explosive in the tree. Yes, sir, 75 lbs. Is that enough? Yes sir I worked it out by mathematics it is exactly right. Well better put a bit more. Very good sir.

And when Col. D. Slater D.S.O. had had his port he sent for the subaltern and said subaltern better put a bit more explosive in that tree. I don't want to disappoint Lord Glasgow. Very good sir.

Then they all went out to see the explosion and Col. D.S. D.S.O. said you will see that tree fall flat at just that angle where it will hurt no young trees and Lord Glasgow said goodness you are clever.

So soon they lit the fuse and waited for the explosion and presently the tree, instead of falling quietly sideways, rose 50 feet into the air taking with it ½ acre of soil and the whole of the young plantation.

And the subaltern said Sir I made a mistake, it should have been 7½ lbs not 75.

Lord Glasgow was so upset he walked in dead silence back to his castle and when they came to the turn of the drive in sight of his castle what should they find but that every piece of glass in the building was broken.

So Lord Glasgow gave a little cry & ran to hide his emotion in the lavatory and there when he pulled the plug the entire ceiling, loosed by the explosion, fell on his head.

This is quite true.[13]

Laura was at this time expecting another child and in advance of the birth Evelyn suggested: 'James if a boy; if a girl it is kinder to drown her than to bring her up like her poor sister.' If this was not meant to be taken too literally, Evelyn was genuinely concerned that Teresa had not been getting enough attention at Pixton. Staying there that Easter, he had found Bron 'sanguine and self-confident' and Teresa 'contrary to accounts, a civil, intelligent and self-possessed little girl', however also 'inarticulate and pasty faced'. He thought a 'long visit' to his mother in Highgate might 'undo some of the mischief of Pixton neglect', so after Easter they went up to London, Laura taking the children to Highgate while Evelyn treated himself to a night on the tiles with Frank Pakenham and Maimie Lygon, eventually crawling into bed at the St James's Club. Two weeks later, by which time he was back with his unit, he received a letter from his father: 'I am enjoying Teresa's visit very much. And find her a gentle affectionate & lovable little creature . . . Mother has given up her time to her entirely – having ceased to play bridge or attend at the Red Cross depot.'[14]

Laura's baby girl was born on 11 June 1942 at Pixton and christened Margaret Evelyn two weeks later. Evelyn got there shortly after the birth but was recalled before the christening to a photographic interpretation course in Derbyshire, where he soon made a point of reciprocating Bob Laycock's loyalty to him by reporting some 'insolent' remarks he had heard in a lecture about the Rommel raid, which Laycock admitted 'made my blood boil'.[15] 'I think this wicked colonel [the lecturer] will be severely beaten,' Evelyn smugly told Laura.

However in August he undid his good work somewhat by arriving at dinner with the Laycocks considerably the worse for wear after 'a hard day's drinking'. 'From that evening I began to trace a decline in my position in Bob's esteem,' he recorded. 'The next ten days I wandered aimlessly in the triangle Ritz, St James's, Claridge's, spending most of the time with Randolph or Phil [Dunne].' That autumn Evelyn's diary chronicled regular binges culminating in assorted minor disasters. After a 'beautiful day of overeating and overdrinking' at the home of Harry Stavordale at Evershot, near to the Sherborne camp where they were stationed after Ardrossan, he recorded: 'Called at 6.30 [a.m.]. Still very confused with drink and smelling of "orange gin". Drove as far as Camberley in a stupor where we had a collision which destroyed the car.'[16] 'You see,' he wrote to Laura, 'I do get into mischief when I am Whiskerless do I not.'[17] (Whiskers was Evelyn's pet-name for Laura.)

That Christmas he described a party of 'great drunkenness' at Longleat with another old friend, Daphne Weymouth, the morning after which he called on Olivia Plunket Greene, to whom he had remained characteristically steadfast as she had descended into alcoholism. She was by then living in a cottage on the Longleat estate and Evelyn 'found her with no trousers on completely drunk and Gwen blacking the grate. Then I came back to Sherborne and off we went again, to a great dinner party given by Bill Stirling & Peter Milton. Last night I suffered from the delusion that black rooks were flying round and round my bed room.'[18]

* * *

On 28 October, his thirty-ninth birthday, Evelyn had recorded: 'A good year. I have begotten a fine daughter, published a successful book, drunk 300 bottles of wine and smoked 300 or more Havana cigars. I have got back to soldiering among friends. This time last year I was on my way to Hawick to join 5 R.M. I got steadily worse as a soldier with the passage of time, but more patient and humble – as far as soldering is concerned. I have about £900 in hand and no grave debts except to the Government; health excellent except when impaired by wine; a wife I love, agreeable work in surroundings of great beauty. Well that is as much as one can hope for.'[19]

However he still yearned for more military action, the dearth of which was highlighted by Laycock's acceptance of 'sporting invitations far ahead', as Evelyn ruefully noted in his diary, not to mention the various successful raids recently carried out by other commandos, most notably by No. 4 Commando at Dieppe in August 1942, where Shimi Lovat's capture of the Varengeville battery had earned him a DSO to add to the MC he had been awarded after an earlier raid at Boulogne. Lovat was one of the most dashing commandos of them all, a fearless Highland chieftain famously described by Winston Churchill as 'the handsomest man to cut a throat', however Evelyn thought him a show-off and privately pronounced him 'a *Palais de Danse* hero'.[20] Years later in the *Sword of Honour* trilogy he mercilessly caricatured him as the former hairdresser Trimmer/McTavish.

Evelyn was at first impressed by Lovat's qualities as a soldier. After watching the film of Dieppe at the Combined Operations Club and hearing a fairly full account of the operation, he could only conclude that 'Shimi Lovat did brilliantly, the only wholly successful part of the raid'.[21] But in due course his admiration for him was overtaken by feelings of irritation: 'I have had a very great victory in a very minor battle [a dispute about maps] with Shimi,' he told Laura in October, 'and hate him instead of Wakefield.'[22] Sometime later he reported: 'Shimi has tried to make me lecture to his commando so I have countered by offering a series of lectures on imperial geography to be followed by a written examination for all ranks or, alternatively, a popular talk in praise of David Stirling. That will annoy.'[23] And the next year: 'Shimi's conceit is boundless. I thought perhaps that now he had done something he might pipe down a bit. Instead he is planning to become the Voice of the Army in the House of Lords.'[24] The dislike was evidently mutual, and years later Lovat devoted three pages of his autobiography to vilifying Evelyn as a slovenly soldier and brazen social climber, 'a greedy little man – a eunuch in appearance – who seemed desperately anxious to "get in" with the right people'.[25]

The simmering tension between the swaggering aristocrat and impertinent parvenu came to a head in the summer of 1943 after Bob Laycock departed for North Africa as part of Operation Husky – the Allied invasion of Sicily – leaving orders that Evelyn continue in his recent post as liaison officer at Combined Operations Headquarters in London before joining him when transport became available.

Though annoyed not to be included in the initial party, Evelyn was distracted for the time being by the death of his father in the early morning of the same day that Bob Laycock left. Evelyn was with Laura in London at the time and spent the next few days staying at his parents' Highgate flat going through his father's papers – 'he kept up a large correspondence with very dull people,' Evelyn noted – and having bookplates engraved so that he and Alec could keep his books together in their respective libraries. He displayed little emotion either in his diary or in his replies to letters of condolence, his main concern being for his mother, whose nerves had already been shattered by the Blitz. 'It is a disagreeable world for the old and I think he was glad to leave it,' Evelyn wrote to Tom Driberg, who had recently been elected an independent MP. 'His only regret would be leaving my mother. I am in a backwater of the war at the moment but hope for adventure soon.'[26]

Evelyn wanted very much to go to North Africa in early August and wrote to Alec suggesting that if he could get home from Syria, 'it would be a good thing as our mother is desoeuvree and lonely . . . the best thing would be for you to live with her . . . I hope you will be able to get back to see to things after I have left.'[27] However Shimi Lovat suggested that a course at the fearsome commando training depot at Achnacarry in Scotland might not go amiss after so long at a desk job. This was a very unattractive proposal for Evelyn as it threatened to delay his departure to the point at which he could no longer be of any use to Laycock in Sicily. It would also have entailed his coming under the jurisdiction of the training depot's commandant Colonel Vaughan, an ex-drill-sergeant and renowned stickler with whom he had recently clashed, accusing him of making a homosexual pass after the colonel reprimanded him for acknowledging him disrespectfully with a casual wave of his riding crop.

Evelyn responded that Laycock had explicitly stated that he should remain in his post until embarkation and that he had 'good personal reasons [following his father's death] for wishing to remain in London as long as possible'.[28] Lovat wrote back that Laycock's orders had been 'automatically cancelled' (by his superior, General Charles Haydon) and that Evelyn was to report to the depot on 1 August. 'You will not proceed overseas unless passed fit by Achnacarry. I hope I have made myself clear.'[29]

Interpreting this as a deliberate act of provocation on Lovat's part motivated by personal malice – a fellow officer at Brigade HQ later described it as 'a childish and obvious bit of intimidation'[30] – Evelyn requested an interview with General Haydon to discover why an exception was being made in his case, pointing out that if doubt existed about the fitness of an officer for foreign service, the usual procedure was to refer him to the medical authorities; Evelyn had incidentally been pronounced fit by a Harley Street consultant after referring himself. But Haydon proved even less amenable and insisted that he not only do the depot course but also an intelligence course. He concluded their interview by saying that Evelyn had brought nothing but discredit to the Brigade since he joined and advised him that for the Brigade's good he should leave as soon as possible. Calculating that by the time he had done the two courses it would be too late anyway for him to go to Sicily, Evelyn complied, explaining afterwards to Bob Laycock: 'A cad [Lovat] and a lunatic [Haydon] make a formidable couple when they are hunting together.'

For his part Haydon later wrote to Laycock to explain that 'Evelyn Waugh has caused trouble and is going', adding: 'I know very well that this will disappoint and probably annoy you, because I am aware that you have a high opinion of Waugh's personal courage in the field. This is not in question . . .' Laycock certainly was annoyed and when he heard from another officer how Evelyn had been 'bullied by Lovat and Haydon', he remarked to his wife, 'How feeble of them – I am angry'.[31] His reaction appears to refute the suggestion made by both Christopher Sykes and Shimi Lovat that he had never intended for Evelyn to join him in Sicily.

Evelyn's tendency to rub certain people up the wrong way had clearly contributed to his own downfall – even Laycock had earlier warned him that he was 'so unpopular as to be unemployable'. Given that Evelyn recorded Laycock's comment without protest in his diary, he was evidently alive to his own shortcomings when it came to getting on with people whom he disliked. Less forgivable as far as some of his fellow officers were concerned was his occasional tendency to tease, or as some saw it 'bully',[32] his own men, although on the other hand several he commanded later recalled how much they liked him. But while Laycock was well aware of Evelyn's faults, the idea that he had somehow secretly connived in his sacking – even if Evelyn initially believed this to have been the case – is not only contradicted by the surviving correspondence but also seems unlikely given the past tensions between Bob Laycock and Shimi Lovat.

'My dear Shimi,' Laycock had written to him the previous year. 'When will you learn some tact? I know that it is uphill work dealing with officers who, to put it snobbishly, do not come from the same social status as those with whom you used to deal with in peacetime ... yet nevertheless you *must* learn to bear with them.'[33] And on another occasion, after receiving a complaint about 'one of your temperamental prima donnas in the shape of Lovat',[34] Laycock rebuked him for 'pointless bad manners when dealing with junior staff officers' and 'not giving a damn for anyone and telling all and sundry where to get off'.[35]

The account Shimi Lovat wrote in his autobiography* of Evelyn's 'sacking' from the Special Service Brigade was published well after the other main protagonists had died and went unquestioned by Evelyn's subsequent biographers, even though the author was hardly an impartial witness. The claim that Evelyn had spent his compassionate leave mostly at White's was perfectly consistent with his normal habits yet seems unlikely in this particular instance given all he had had to do sorting through his father's papers and dealing with the funeral and so forth. 'It has been marvelous to have had Evelyn in London,' his mother wrote to Alec on 3 July, four days after the funeral, 'he has seen to everything in a kindly and efficient manner ... I don't know what I should have done without him.'[36]

Several of Lovat's other assertions are equally questionable – for instance his claim that Evelyn 'stormed in unannounced to General Haydon's office' when he plainly wrote to request an interview; and the notion that he was 'sacked on the spot for insubordination', when even by Haydon's account Evelyn was advised to resign. These may seem rather pedantic points, yet when taken together and then exaggerated by subsequent chroniclers they have further distorted the truth about Evelyn Waugh's war. Whilst more than capable of putting people's backs up and far from the ideal company commander, there were other ways in which Evelyn could be very useful to the military. He had an extremely good brain, of great value when it came to planning operations, at headquarters and in the field; he excelled at knocking the long-winded written drafts into concise and readable shape; and above all he was extraordinarily brave and cool under fire. Laycock was himself a well-read and witty man and undoubtedly found Evelyn very entertaining. However it is hard to believe that he would have wanted him on his staff had he not also been impressed by some of his qualities as a soldier.

At first Evelyn felt extremely aggrieved at his treatment and wrote a

---

* *March Past*, (Weidenfeld & Nicolson, 1978).

long letter to Laycock setting out 'the facts relevant to my leaving the Brigade so that when you have the leisure to look at them, you will know that it is not I who has let you down'.[37] He wrote an equally long letter to the head of Combined Operations, Lord Louis Mountbatten, however by the time he eventually saw him, in early August, he had grown bored of the whole saga and they met on 'terms so cordial as to be almost affectionate'.[38] At the end of that month, back with the Royal Horse Guards at Windsor, he reflected:

> I dislike the Army. I want to get to work again. I do not want any more experiences in life. I have quite enough bottled and carefully laid in the cellar, some still ripening, most ready for drinking, a little beginning to lose its body. I wrote to Frank [Pakenham] very early in the war to say that its chief use would be to cure artists of the illusion that they were men of action. It has worked its cure with me. I have succeeded, too, in dissociating myself very largely with the rest of the world. I am not impatient of its manifest follies and don't want to influence opinions or events or expose humbug or anything of that kind. I don't want to be of service to anyone or anything. I simply want to do my work as an artist.[39]

The opportunity to return to writing would come sooner than he thought, although for the time being he persisted in trying to get back into action as a soldier and began badgering Shimi Lovat's cousin Bill Stirling about a place in 2 SAS, which he had formed after the capture of his brother David in North Africa. 'I dread the prospect of organization and training and a hundred new acquaintances,' Evelyn wrote in his diary. 'But after my treatment by Haydon I must "make good" as a soldier. Nothing can upset him more than to find me promoted as a result of his intemperance.' Evelyn had stayed with Stirling at Keir, his palatial home in Perthshire, the previous year while his brother David was still missing after the Benghazi raid and they had since furthered their acquaintance at the bar of White's. For the time being Stirling put Evelyn to work drafting a cogent case to be presented to the War Office for the regiment's expansion. 'He is a great change as a master from Bob,' Evelyn wrote to Laura, '– vague, mystical, imaginative, impatient, chivalrous, moral, slow witted, unconventional, unsmart, aristocratic, – in every quality dramatically opposed to Bob and in many ways preferable.' With his posting eventually fixed, Evelyn was all set to go out with Christopher Sykes and join the rest of the SAS in North Africa in mid-November, however the Allied campaign in the southern Mediterranean went far better than expected and they were eventually deemed surplus to requirements. Instead they were sent on a parachuting course at Tatton Park in Cheshire, from where Evelyn wrote to Laura: 'Parachuting is without exception the most exhilarating thing I have ever done. All the tedium of the last months has been worthwhile for the few seconds of first leaving the aeroplane. I felt absolutely no reluctance to jump – less than in taking a cold bath.'[40] In his diary he recalled stepping from the noisy aeroplane 'into perfect silence and solitude and apparent immobility in bright sunshine above the treetops'. Years later, when the whole experience had fully ripened in his memory, he described the rapture felt by his fictional alter ego Guy Crouchback on his first parachute jump,

> ... something as near as his earthbound soul could reach to a foretaste of paradise, *locum refrigerii, lucis et pacis*. The aeroplane seemed far distant as will, at the moment of death, the spinning earth. As though he had cast the constraining bonds of flesh and muscle and nerve, he found himself floating free; the harness that had so irked him in the narrow, dusky, re-sounding carriage now imperceptibly supported him. He was a free spirit in an element as fresh as on the day of its creation.[41]

But Evelyn's foretaste of paradise was as short-lived as Crouchback's and on his second jump he landed badly and cracked the fibula in his left leg, an injury that would eventually grant him the time he needed to write *Brideshead Revisited*, the climax of which had been forming in his mind ever since his efforts that October to save the soul of his dying lapsed Catholic friend Hubert Duggan.

A stepson of Lord Curzon, Duggan had been Conservative MP for Acton for more than a decade and Evelyn had known him vaguely since being at Oxford with his elder brother Alfred, although he and Hubert had only really become friends in the early 1930s at Madresfield after both had been deserted by their wives in strikingly similar circumstances and Hubert began an affair with Maimie Lygon. They had grown closer still during the war, when Hubert was the only one of Evelyn's friends he made a godparent to his daughter Margaret. By this time Hubert was living 'in sin' with Diana Cooper's long-standing friend Phyllis de Janzé, a renowned beauty and fellow divorcee ten years his senior (and the ex sister-in-law of Alice de Janzé who had shot Evelyn's friend Raymond de Trafford), but Phyllis died in April 1943 and shortly afterwards Hubert fell gravely ill with tuberculosis.

'The news of Hubert is very bad indeed,' Evelyn wrote to Laura that September. 'He is allowed to see no one ... He never sleeps and drugs put him into a delirium but not to sleep. He is in the blackest melancholy and haunted by delusions. There is nothing which can be done for him medically. Supernatural aid needed.' For three weeks Evelyn visited his stricken friend almost daily at his house on Chapel Street in Belgravia, until eventually one day Hubert began to talk about religion 'and of re-turning to the Church', as Evelyn put it, however Hubert worried that it would be a betrayal of Phyllis to profess repentance of his life with her. The next day Evelyn consulted a Catholic chaplain and was given a medal. 'Just hide it somewhere in the room,' said the priest. 'I have known most wonderful cases of Grace being brought about in that way.'

When Evelyn got to Chapel Street later that morning, Lady Curzon told him that Hubert was not expected to live through the day, so Evelyn went immediately to Farm Street to fetch Father Devas. Like Lord Marchmain's mistress Cara in *Brideshead*, Hubert's sister did not want the priest there, but Evelyn brought him in nonetheless and after he had given Hubert absolution Hubert said, 'Thank you father!' which was taken as his assent. Evelyn returned to the house that afternoon to find the sister still hostile, yet Father Devas gently explaining his intention to anoint Hubert. 'Look all I shall do is just to put oil on his forehead and say a prayer. Look the oil is in this little box. It is nothing to be frightened of.'

'And so,' Evelyn recorded, 'by knowing what he wanted and sticking to that, when I was all for arguing it out from first principles, he got what he wanted and Hubert crossed himself and later called me up and said, "When I became a Catholic it was not from fear", so he knows what happened and accepted it. So we spent the day watching for a spark of gratitude for the love of God and saw the spark.'[42]

Believing that he had been granted God's pardon, Hubert briefly rallied but died twelve days later. Evelyn attended a Requiem Mass for him at Farm Street on 3 November and in late January 1944 he asked for time off from the Army in order to write his book. The letter was addressed to the commanding officer of his regiment, the current Duchess of York's grandfather Colonel A. H. Ferguson, from whom Evelyn requested three months' leave on the basis that 'entertainment is now regarded as a legitimate contribution to the war effort'. He went on: 'It is a peculiarity of the literary profession that, once an idea becomes fully formed in the author's mind, it cannot be left unexploited without deterioration. If, in fact, the book is not written now it will never be written.'[43]

Ferguson at first refused, taking the view that his time would be better spent training the Home Guard at Windsor; however after enlisting the support of Brendan Bracken at the Ministry of Information, Evelyn eventually got his leave. Laura not unreasonably saw this as an opportunity to see more of her husband and suggested they take a cottage at Pixton, but Evelyn was always the most ruthlessly self-protective of artists and that idea was quickly scotched. 'The reason is that I long for your company at all times except one,' Evelyn explained. 'When I am working I must be alone. I shall never be able to maintain the fervent preoccupation which is absolutely necessary to composition, if you were at close quarters with me . . . I shall see if they can take me at Chagford.'[44]

Thus on the last day of January he checked into the Easton Court Hotel determined to begin writing by ten the next morning. 'I still have a cold,' he noted in his diary that evening, 'and am low in spirits but I feel full of literary power which only this evening gives place to qualms of impotence.' He remained ensconced there for the next four weeks, intensely engaged in what he already believed was going to be his most significant and self-revealing book, at once a highly romanticised representation of aspects of his own life and, as he later wrote for the dust-jacket, 'an attempt to trace the workings of the divine purpose in a pagan world, in the lives of an English Catholic family'.

19

A Book to Bring Tears

On 2 February 1944 Evelyn wrote to Laura from Chagford: 'So the nut started rather stiff & I had to write the first thousand words of magnum opus three times before they came right but now things are going better and I have done 2,387 words in 1½ days. It shall be 3,000 this evening & soon I hope to get 2000 a day. It is v. high quality about Col. Cutler* and how much I hate the army.'[1]

By the end of the first week he was up to 10,000 words and wrote to his agent that if left undisturbed by the military he hoped to finish the book by the middle of May. He suggested that Chapman & Hall might like to reserve some paper in order to publish it for Christmas but was concerned that their production standards might not do his great work justice. 'I should like this book to be in decent form,' he told Peters, 'because it is very good.'[2] From time to time he got bogged down rewriting. 'Every day I seem to go over what I did the day before and make it shorter. I am getting spinsterish about style.'[3] But at other times progress was far more satisfactory and on one day he sat down after dinner and rattled off 3,000 words in three hours. By the end of the fourth week he had completed 33,000 words and had reached the end of the third chapter, when Charles watches Julia drive away from Brideshead Castle and Sebastian tells him 'We'll have a heavenly time alone.'

But before he could start on the next chapter he was summoned to London to become ADC to Major-General Ivor Thomas, to whom he promptly behaved so obnoxiously that the general refused to have him.

---

* Colonel S. G. Cutler had been his commanding officer in the Royal Marines in 1942, a 'pompous booby' in Evelyn's estimation and one of his chief military bugbears alongside Tom Churchill, Shimi Lovat and Roger Wakefield.

'The primary lack of sympathy seemed to come from my being slightly drunk in his mess on the first evening,' Evelyn nonchalantly recorded. 'I told him I could not change the habits of a lifetime for a whim of his.'[4] To Laura he wrote: 'The worst I did was to pour claret in his lap.'[5] But no sooner had he escaped from one general than another one was conjured for him. Evelyn knew the next one vaguely of old, a substantially more easy-going Old Etonian called Miles Graham whom he deemed 'a slightly superior type': 'So the new general is very much less assuming than Tomas [*sic*],' he told Laura, '& fully appreciates, or appears to appreciate, the importance of a gentleman leading his own life.' Graham immediately gave him six weeks' leave but twenty-four hours later cancelled their arrangement altogether, perhaps having reflected on what he was letting himself in for.

Returning to Chagford after his ten-day break, Evelyn took a while to get back into his stride, but eleven days later he sent off another 13,000 words to be typed up, and six days after that a further 7,800. 'I am writing a very beautiful book,' he told Coote Lygon, 'to bring tears, about very rich, beautiful, high born people who live in palaces and have no troubles except what they make themselves and those are mainly the demons sex and drink which after all are easy to bear as troubles go nowadays.'[6] He was greatly relieved to be back doing what he loved best and also away from London where, as he admitted to Coote, 'it is not unfair to say I never draw a sober breath. I was beginning to lose my memory which for a man who lives entirely in the past, is to lose life itself.'[7] The hotel's other guests were mostly elderly women who did not disturb him apart from when it was sunny and they emerged 'like lizards' and annoyed him by sitting right outside his window.[8] Despite this and a few brief intrusions by trysting couples, by 29 March he had written a total of 62,000 and was up to the end of Book Two.

* * *

It was at this point that Laura came for her last brief visit to Chagford before the birth of her fifth child, Harriet, who was born in May. Neither Evelyn nor Laura ever appeared greatly to relish having children and Evelyn had greeted the news of Laura's latest pregnancy with his customary commiseration. 'I do hope that your nursery life is not proving unendurable,' he wrote to her. 'I think I have not said enough about how deeply I admire your patience & resignation in this and in the threat to your future happiness in the birth of another child. If I have seemed to make light of it, that is my rough manner; my heart is all yours & sorrowing for you.'[9] Their son Bron later recalled his mother as having scarcely featured in his early life at Pixton and being unaware that motherhood involved 'any particular emotional proximity'. His father, he remembered, 'featured not at all'.[10]

Bron had vague memories of him occasionally turning up in uniform, but most of the time Evelyn evinced a breathtaking determination to stay away. 'I shall not visit my children during Christmas leave,' he had written to Laura in December 1941, 'they should be able to retain the impression formed of me for another three months. I can't afford to waste any time on them which could be spent on my own pleasures. I have sent them some kippers as compensation.'[11] And the next year: 'I am very glad not to be with my children for Christmas. There is an hotel at Shaftesbury with a very splendid sideboard. I think we might take a week end there soon when you are fuckable.'[12]

But as much as Evelyn recoiled – or at least affected to recoil – from spending time with his children, he constantly craved the company of his wife. 'If by any chance my children should die,' he wrote to Laura at the time of her latest pregnancy, 'do come to London. I miss you every hour.'[13] Though he sometimes chided her for her careless appearance – 'Try and get your teeth white before we meet,'[14] he wrote before a brief rendezvous that spring – or bombarded her with bossy instructions about their house or children or how to liven up her correspondence, his letters to her were more often tender as well as funny, abounding in heartfelt expressions of his love for and need of her, and the various ways he missed her – 'bitterly', 'unspeakably', 'unbearably', 'unendurably' and so on. After the evacuation from Crete in June 1941 he had written to her: 'What a lot we shall have to say to each other when we meet. I feel that all our future life will be spent in telling how we have spent this year apart. In danger I have one fear, that it means further separation from you.'[15]

* * *

Just before Easter, Evelyn was again summoned to London for a proposed assignment to conduct journalists around the Second Front, which was due to open that summer. 'It is not quite as disastrous as it might be,' he reflected, 'for I have come to a suitable halting stage in the book and a week or two away from it may do no harm.'[16] But, as so often, the job never materialised and instead he passed an idle two weeks at White's catching up with old friends and drinking 'a great deal of good wine which is getting scarce daily but still procurable by those who take the trouble'.[17] He then went down to Pixton, where he completed the revision of the first two sections of *Brideshead*. Lady de Vesci's ancient stepmother Grace, Lady Wemyss, was also staying and as Evelyn recorded, 'Auberon surprised her in her bath and is thus one of very few men who can claim to have seen his great great grandmother in the raw.'[18] Returning to London he gave dinner to his old friends John Sutro and Harold Acton, the latter of whom had been working for RAF intelligence in India. Feasting on gulls' eggs, consommé, partridge, haddock on toast and nearly a bottle a head of Perrier-Jouët 28, Evelyn was riveted by what he called Harold's 'descriptions of service life as seen by a bugger . . . He combines his pleasures with keen patriotism.'[19]

With nothing yet fixed for him to do, Evelyn returned for a week to Chagford, where he 'painfully picked up the threads of a very difficult chapter of love-making on a liner'.[20] He managed to despatch the first chapter of Book Three (12,000 words) a week later yet was unsure as to the success of this section. 'I feel very much the futility of describing sexual emotions without describing the sexual act,' he recorded in his diary; 'I should like to give as much detail as I have of the meals, to the two coitions – with his [Charles's] wife and Julia. It would be no more or less obscene than to leave them to the reader's imagination, which in this case cannot be as acute as mine. There is a gap in which the reader will insert his own sexual habits instead of those of my characters.'[21]

Back in London he again enlisted the help of Bob Laycock to rescue him from the spectacularly unsuitable jobs that the War Office kept proposing (the current choice was between adjutant to a transit camp in India and assistant registrar in a hospital) and to persuade Bill Stirling to take him back at 2 SAS with as much leave as he needed to finish his book. Deeply appreciative of Stirling's help, Evelyn promptly asked him to be one of Harriet's godparents, along with Basil Bennett, owner of the

Hyde Park Hotel where he now tended to stay when in London; Mary Herbert's secretary Miss Haig, 'an inexplicable whim of Laura's' as Evelyn put it; and Laura's other choice, Gretel Coudenhove-Kalergi, an elderly Austrian countess who had been staying with her maid at Pixton when war broke out and decided to remain there for the duration, and then for a few more years after it had finished, all the time 'occupying two of the best bedrooms on the first floor', so Evelyn's son Bron later recorded with a degree of retrospective bewilderment, and 'joining a large population of retired nannies, housekeepers and maids who occupied different parts of the house, living their own lives and jealously protecting their own territory'.[22]

Harriet's fifth godparent was Nancy Mitford, to whom Evelyn looked 'not so much for spiritual instruction,' he assured her, 'as for knowledge of the world, savoir faire, joie de vivre and things of that kind'.[23] Evelyn had known Nancy since his marriage to Evelyn Gardner and later throughout his brief but deep friendship with Nancy's sister Diana Guinness, during which time Evelyn mentored Nancy in her early endeavours as a novelist. In the early 1930s they often saw each other with literary friends such as the Sitwells, Cyril Connolly, Robert Byron and John Betjeman and at house parties with the Weymouths, Pakenhams and Churchills. After Nancy married Peter Rodd, whom Evelyn disliked for his curious combination of pedantry and fecklessness, there was a distinct lull in their friendship, however by 1939 that marriage was all but over and Evelyn soon became a regular patron of Heywood Hill's bookshop in Mayfair where Nancy worked for much of the war and which he regarded as 'the one centre of old world gossip left'.[24] From then on theirs developed into one of the most famous literary friendships.

By the middle of May Evelyn was back into his stride and well on his way to finishing *Brideshead*, which he eventually brought to its climax on D-Day, 6 June: 'This morning at breakfast the waiter told me the Second Front had opened. I sat down early to work and wrote a fine passage of Lord Marchmain's death agonies ... I sent for the priest to give Lord Marchmain the last sacraments. I worked through till 4 o'clock and finished the last chapter – the last dialogue poor – took it to the post, walked home by the upper road. There only remains now the epilogue which is easy meat. My only fear is lest the invasion upsets my typist at St. Leonard's, or the posts to him with my manuscript.'[25] Laura came to stay with him for a week while he corrected the typescript, and on 20 June he reported to Peters: 'I have delivered complete ms. "Brideshead Revisited" to Chapman & Hall. Duplicate for yanks is coming to you as soon as a friend in Oxford [Martin D'Arcy] has vetted it for theological howlers.'[26]

With his book finished, Evelyn was now obliged to join up with 2 SAS for training at one of Bill Stirling's shooting lodges in Perthshire, but before leaving he spent a few nights in London where he found himself strangely (for him at least) rattled by the V-1 flying bomb raids prompted by the recent Allied landings in Normandy. 'I heard one flying near and low and for the first and I hope the last time in my life was frightened,' he recorded. 'Thinking this disagreeable experience over I think it was due to weakening my nerves with drink (I was drinking heavily all those days in London) and have therefore resolved today never to be drunk again.'[27] From Scotland he wrote to Laura: 'I have given up drunkenness for life. Are you pleased or sad? It is a cutting of one of the few remaining strands that held me to human society.'[28]

The new commanding officer of 2 SAS, Brian Franks, evidently had qualms about having Evelyn under his command, however by a stroke of luck news promptly arrived that Randolph Churchill wanted Evelyn to join him in Yugoslavia as part of Fitzroy Maclean's military mission to Tito's Partisans. Maclean had no hesitation in endorsing Randolph's idea, having heard reports of Evelyn's bravery in Crete and believing that his early travels further testified to his enterprise and resilience. Besides, he later admitted, 'here, at last, was someone well qualified to contain Randolph, someone whom, with minor adjustments, he might even regard as his social and intellectual equal'.[29] Maclean was keen to send a new mission to Croatia where Tito's guerrillas were especially hard pressed in their resistance against the occupying Germans, and duly gave instructions for Churchill and Waugh to be infiltrated 'soonest'. Randolph told Evelyn that as his second-in-command he was counting on him 'to heal the Great Schism between the Catholic and Orthodox churches', which was proving a hindrance to his war policy.[30] Evelyn 'accepted eagerly', and after saying goodbye to his family at Pixton and his mother in London, on 4 July he set off on a roundabout journey via Gibraltar and Algiers, where he joined a house party at the British Embassy with the 'wonderfully unambassadorial' Coopers. The other guests included Evelyn's old friend Bloggs Baldwin, Victor Rothschild, Virginia Cowles and the journalist

Martha Gellhorn, a great friend of Diana Cooper's who was by then estranged from her husband Ernest Hemingway and according to Evelyn went about 'stark naked most of the day & very repulsive'.[31]

Evelyn read Gellhorn's novel *Liana* on a chaise-longue but pointedly said nothing about it when he had finished; she later called him 'a small and very ugly turd'.[32] His hostess also commented on how glum he was being. It is possible that he had got wind of the fact that Diana and Bloggs had recently begun a 'lighthearted' affair – a rare occurrence in Diana's life – and was slightly jealous. In any event he responded that he had never been happier, having just written a novel he considered to be a masterpiece, in addition to having a wife he adored, four fine children, splendid health and 'an active life calling him to Yugoslavia with his beloved Randolph ... I said I wished he could reflect his happiness a little more, Diana recalled. 'He said that other people had said the same.'[33]

From Algiers it was on via Catania, Naples and Bari to the island of Vis off Croatia's coast where Evelyn soon had his first and only encounter with Marshal Tito, whom he instinctively disapproved of for his Communism and anti-Catholic stance. Evelyn had also already decided that the marshal was a woman, his favourite of several rumours that had circulated before the mysterious resistance leader's identity became more widely known. Maclean later recalled introducing the two of them a few days later as Tito emerged from the sea in some very brief swimming trunks. 'Will you please ask Captain Waugh why he thinks I am a woman,' said the marshal. Evelyn did not record this slightly awkward encounter in his diary – which he continued to keep in serene disregard of standing instructions – however he later maintained that Tito's 'bathing dress' left him in no doubt about 'her' sex.

Their next destination was the Partisans' Croat headquarters in the rundown little spa of Topusko, amid a patch of liberated hills and woodland on the mainland, to which they flew under cover of night. But as their Dakota transport came in to land Evelyn was conscious in the darkness of it first descending and then shooting upwards, 'and the next thing I knew was that I was walking in a cornfield by the light of the burning aeroplane talking to a strange British officer about the progress of the war in a detached fashion and that he was saying "You'd better sit down for a bit skipper". I had no recollection of the crash nor, at the time, any knowledge of where I was or why, but a confused idea that we had made a forced landing during some retreat.'[34]

Soon after Evelyn came round he saw Randolph in tears as his servant had been among ten of those on board who had been killed instantly. As Randolph later wrote to Laura, it was 'really providential'[35] that he and Evelyn had survived, given that the plane's engines had stalled at about 400 feet and it burst into flames immediately upon hitting the ground. Both of them had been badly burnt, Evelyn on his head and both hands and legs.

Bandaged like mummies, they were eventually transferred to hospital in Bari and soon visited by Hermione Ranfurly, who was amused by their periodic shouting matches and 'arguments about nothing in particular'.[36] Coote Lygon also came from her nearby WAAF base and recalled Randolph 'creating a fine fuss' about his knee and Evelyn telling her about his recently completed novel, *Brideshead Revisited*, the proofs of which he was eagerly awaiting from his publishers: 'It's all about a family whose father lives abroad, as it might be Boom [Coote's father Lord Beauchamp] – but it's not Boom – and a younger son: people will say he's like Hughie, but you'll see he's not really Hughie – and there's a house as it might be Mad, but it isn't really Mad.'[37]

During Evelyn's subsequent convalescence in Rome he was operated on for a painful abscess on the back of his neck and suffered also from homesickness: 'I feel I have been away many months,' he wrote to Laura, 'tho it is less than two, and long to be with you again.'[38] He saw Diana Cooper and Bloggs Baldwin again and otherwise spent his time visiting churches and art galleries and reading. By mid-September he and Randolph had sufficiently recovered to return to Topusko, where they established their mission in a small farm on the edge of the town, looked after by a hardworked cook-cum-housekeeper called Zora and a bibulous handyman known as Stari, who had lived for some years in America and replied to their every request with a cheery and unreliable 'Sure, Boss, I'll fix it!'[39] The work of the farm, meanwhile, appeared to Evelyn to be 'mainly in the hands of a little girl of five or so'.[40]

Evelyn made sure to get a bedroom to himself, 'away from Randolph,' he told Laura, 'whose rhetoric in his cups I find a little wearisome'. The spa town's medical baths had lost their windows to the war but were otherwise undamaged, and as Evelyn reported, 'we go there daily & sit in radio-active hot water which I find very enervating. The town has been laid out entirely for leisure, with neglected gardens and woodland promenades reminiscent of Matlock. It suits our leisured life well. We do very little & see little company except a partisan liaison officer, the secretary general of the communist party, the leader of the Peasant party & such people. We also arrange for the evacuation of distressed Jews.'[41]

Evelyn was in 'admirable' health, he reported in a subsequent letter home, and 'my nut very clear – so clear that I hunger to rewrite Mag. Op'. The only available alcohol was a local spirit called *rakia* which to Evelyn stank of somewhere between sewage and glue, so he had little difficulty in sticking to the non-drinking pledge he had made in London. He was thus sleeping unusually well by his standards – 10.30 until 6.30 – however at other times the uninterrupted boisterousness of Randolph was proving a considerable strain. 'The good time of day for me,' he told Laura, 'is the first two hours of daylight before Randolph is awake.'

In mid-October they were joined by Freddy Birkenhead, F. E. Smith's son and Winston Churchill's godson, whom Randolph had fagged for at Eton. Evelyn, too, knew him fairly well and described him to his mother as 'an old friend who is always amusing in a surly & sour way'. But 'more than the pleasure of his company I value him as taking Randolph off my hands a bit'.[42]

Birkenhead was accompanied by Major Stephen Clissold, a 'gentle schoolmaster', as Evelyn described him, besides being a fluent Serbo-Croat speaker and expert on the Partisans. Clissold later remembered the sensation on arrival of finding himself 'in the midst of an old boys' reunion, an unexpected house-party in which I felt something of an intruder', although Evelyn proved an unexpectedly 'affable companion, who did what he could to put me at my ease'.[43]

The tension between Evelyn and Randolph was immediately apparent, though. 'There he is!' roared Randolph as Evelyn returned from meeting the newcomers at the airfield. 'There's the little fellow in his camel-hair dressing-gown!' Evelyn gave Randolph a stare 'cold and hostile as the Arctic Ocean', recalled Birkenhead, 'and remarked with poisonous restraint: "You've got drunk very quickly tonight. Don't send any more signals."'[44]

A week or so later they were all awoken early one morning by cries of 'Avion! Avion!' and the menacing drone of German planes overhead.

Though generally as insanely fearless as Evelyn, Randolph on this occasion became hysterical, convinced that they were being deliberately targeted because of his father. As the others all scrambled for cover in a ditch, Evelyn calmly strolled from the farmhouse wearing a white duffel coat that seemed designed to attract fire. 'You bloody little swine, take off that coat!' yelled Randolph. 'TAKE OFF THAT FUCKING COAT! It's an order! It's a military order!'

Evelyn made a point of keeping the coat on and deliberately took his time lowering himself into the trench, pausing as he did so to remark to Randolph: 'I'll tell you what I think of your repulsive manners when the bombardment is over.' Birkenhead later recalled that Evelyn's behaviour 'endangered all of us'[45] as the mission was sprayed with machine-gun fire and bombs dropped near enough to blow its windows out. However Clissold remembered the raid more nonchalantly as a 'rather ineffectual enemy visitation' during which 'no bomb fell near us'.[46]

In any event Randolph soon became anxious to clear the air and apologised to Evelyn for his sharpness. In an echo of his scorn for the wretched Colonel Colvin on Crete, Evelyn replied: 'My dear Randolph, it wasn't your manners I was complaining of: it was your cowardice.'[47] When Randolph pleaded for kinder treatment Evelyn remained unmoved, explaining to his diary that

> in these matters he is simply a flabby bully who rejoices in blustering and shouting down anyone weaker than himself and starts squealing as soon as he meets anyone as strong. In words he can understand, he can dish it out, but he can't take it . . . The facts are that he is a bore – with no intellectual invention or agility. He has a childlike retentive memory and repetition takes the place of thought. He has set himself very low aims and has not the self-control to pursue them steadfastly. He has no independence of character and his engaging affection comes from this. He is not a good companion for a long period, but the conclusion is always the same – that no one else would have chosen me, nor would anyone else have accepted him. We are both at the end of our tether as far as war work is concerned and must make what we can of it.[48]

In a bid to stem the flow of Randolph's incessant chatter, Evelyn and Freddy bet him £20 that he could not read the Bible in a fortnight.

Randolph proceeded to spend the next two weeks noisily reading quotations aloud or, as Evelyn told Nancy Mitford, 'slapping his side & chortling "God, isn't God a shit!"'[49] In the long run, Evelyn and Randolph's friendship would prove remarkably resilient, however at its lowest point at Topusko Evelyn wrote to Laura: 'I have got to stage of disliking Randolph which is really more convenient than thinking I liked him & constantly trying to reconcile myself to his enormities. Now I can regard him as one of the evils of war like Col. Cutler or Tom Churchill or Roger Wakefield and so live with him more harmoniously.'[50]

Evelyn's relations with Birkenhead were ostensibly more harmonious, Birkenhead later recalling Evelyn as 'friendly and charming' towards him and pathetically grateful for the 100 cigars he had brought with him, along with various replacements for items he had lost in the air crash – two pairs of shoes, a pot of shaving cream, a pair of hairbrushes, razor blades, plus a letter from Laura. However Birkenhead shared Randolph's weakness for the bottle and in the uneasy aftermath of the raid he too began to get on the temporarily abstinent Evelyn's nerves.

'At luncheon Randolph and Freddy became jocular,' Evelyn recorded a couple of days afterwards.

> They do not make new jests or even repeat their own. Of conversation as I love it – a fantasy growing in the telling, apt repartee, argument based on accepted postulates, spontaneous reminiscence and quotation – they know nothing. All their noise and laughter is in the retelling of memorable sayings of their respective fathers or other public figures; even with this vast repertoire they repeat themselves every day or two – sometimes within an hour. They also recite with great zest the more hackneyed passages of Macaulay, the poems of John Betjeman, Belloc, and other classics. I remarked how boring it was to be obliged to tell Randolph everything twice – once when he was drunk, once when he was sober.

A couple of weeks later he told Laura: 'Drunkenness is a very sad thing for the sober. Freddy is fuddled most evenings and, I suppose, just as he was in White's when I thought him the wittiest of Worm friends – now I find him repetitive & trite.'[51]

In the essay he wrote about their time together in Yugoslavia for the collection *Evelyn Waugh and His World* (1973), Birkenhead described

Evelyn in generally affectionate terms. However, possibly prompted by the various unflattering references to himself in Evelyn's published letters and diaries, he later told Hugh Trevor-Roper (himself not a great fan of Evelyn's either) that he had actually thought him 'an odious, indeed a psychopathic character', ruefully adding: 'I should have dealt far more hardly with him had his widow not still then been with us, & had I not wished to avoid, perhaps cravenly, the insane malice of his repulsive son.'[52] Birkenhead also thought that Evelyn's virulent hatred of Communism limited his usefulness as a liaison officer to the Partisans; however Clissold offered a different perspective, recalling Evelyn as 'punctilious in carrying out the duties assigned to him' and commenting that his diaries showed 'a good deal of prescience and insight' about the Partisans' lack of real interest in fighting the Germans as opposed to getting on with their own civil war.[53] Fitzroy Maclean, too, was at pains to stress that Evelyn 'did his job very efficiently' and that overall he had been 'very keen on being a good officer and succeeded in that'. But in any event Evelyn had now had quite enough of soldiering and was longing to go home. 'The war seems to me to have rolled itself in blubber like an Eskimo & settled down for the winter,' he wrote to Laura that November. 'I don't see much hope of getting back before the spring.'[54]

Evelyn's homesickness was exacerbated not just by his weariness of Randolph but also the knowledge that fifty privately printed advance copies of *Brideshead Revisited* had been sent out to his family and friends in England. Evelyn begged Nancy Mitford to tell him 'what everyone says behind my back' while more confidently telling his mother that he expected 'a great success' when the public edition eventually came out the next spring.[55]

While the war rolled on interminably in Yugoslavia the least Evelyn required was a respite from Randolph, a feeling that was evidently mutual, with Randolph cabling that he was 'Waugh-weary'. In early December they got their wish when Evelyn was posted to Dubrovnik to mediate between British troops and the Partisans, with permission also from Fitzroy Maclean to write a report on the subject closest to his heart, the local situation of the Roman Catholic Church.

Christmas in his new posting was spent entirely alone, 'which next to being with you,' he wrote to Laura, 'is what I like best'.[56] It was, he told her, 'a joy to be surrounded by first class architecture again', and though his quarters were in 'a slum' he had a jeep at his disposal, 'an excellent Dalmatian cook', two other servants, plenty of wine and an Alsatian dog.

In the new year reactions to *Brideshead* began to arrive, first of all from Nancy, who wrote reassuringly that she thought it 'a great English classic in my humble opinion' and that she was 'literally dazzled with admiration'. A subsequent postcard informed him that 'people are giving luncheon parties to discuss the book & the Windsors have given it to everyone for Xmas. Rather low-brow circles I fear but still!'[57]

Nancy shared Evelyn's gift for writing letters as if in a gossipy conversation. Hers were sharp, provocative and often very funny. It was a talent that would endear her to Evelyn for the rest of his life; however it also served to highlight the fact that Laura was a far from sparkling correspondent. 'Sweet whiskers,' Evelyn wrote to her,

do try to write me better letters. Your last, dated 19 December received today, so early expected, was a bitter disappointment. Do realize that a letter need not be a bald chronicle of events; I know you lead a dull life now, my heart bleeds for it, though I believe you could make it more interesting if you had the will. But that is no reason to make your letters as dull as your life. I simply am not interested in Bridget's children. Do grasp that. A letter should be a form of conversation; written as though you were talking to me. For instance you say my Christmas presents have arrived and Eddie is pleased. What do you think of the book? Your copy is still binding but you must have seen his. You know I have not seen one. Tell me what it is like. It is dedicated to you. Are you pleased to see it in this form? Are you curious to know what changes I have made in the final proofs. There are many changes in this copy from what you read before. Can you not see how it disappoints me that this book which I regard as my first important one, and have dedicated to you, should have no comment except that Eddie is pleased with it.[58]

After the unbroken solitude of his Christmas, he celebrated the Orthodox equivalent in early January at what was billed as a tea party, although as he told Nancy, 'One never knows what one will get in this country.' Without a word of greeting from their military hosts the guests were soon served with '(a) Green Chartreuse (b) tea and ham sandwiches (c) cakes and cherry brandy & cigarettes (d) two patriotic speeches. Then it seemed reasonable to think the party was over, but no, in came cold mutton & red wine. It is unsettling at my age.'[59] A few days later Evelyn took pity on an elderly sculptor he had met called Mr Paravacini who was short of food and money. Evelyn commissioned a portrait bust of himself in return for £50 and some rations while he was at work: 'I doubt his ever getting the stone or finishing it,' Evelyn wrote in his diary; 'if he does it will be the next best thing to having myself stuffed.'[60] 'It is very masterly,' he told Laura when the bust was under way, 'rather bad tempered in expression but most forceful like Beethoven rather. It will be a beautiful possession for you – indeed a series of possessions for all as I propose to have it cast in bronze and terra cotta & lead & iron & so forth and to travel with it as Gerry Wellesley used to travel with the bust of his great ancestor. You can imagine what an interest & excitement it has been to me.'[61]

Meanwhile, he felt increasingly worn down, surrounded by 'so many unhappy people who look to me for help which I can ill supply,' he told Laura. 'It seems to comfort them to come & tell me how miserable they are; it saddens me. But is it not odd? Would you have thought of me as having a kind nature? I am renowned for my great kindness here.* At our headquarters in Bari however I am looked on as very troublesome and offensive.'[62†]

Evelyn's latest outrage had been to refuse to be transferred to Trebinje on the grounds that he had not finished his investigations into the Dubrovnik clergy and the alleged killing of fifty-two Roman Catholic priests by Partisans. However a few days later he did obey a command to return to Bari, where he then obtained permission to visit Pope Pius XII in Rome to report on what he had discovered, although His Holiness appeared to grasp almost nothing of what he said. 'The sad thing about the Pope,' Evelyn wrote to Laura after his private audience, 'is that he loves talking English and has learned several elegant little speeches by heart parrot-wise & delivers them with practically no accent, but he

---

* After the war, one of those who served with Evelyn in Dubrovnik wrote to his MP from Yugoslavia to say how he was 'known and loved by a surprising number of civilians here, for his efforts on their behalf' (Signalman Leslie John Murphy to Lieutenant-Colonel Sir Thomas Moore, 20 September 1945, cited in Donat Gallagher, *In the Picture*, p. 265).

† Evelyn's immediate superior in Bari, Major John Clarke, later recalled having had his life made hell by Maclean's 'incredibly stupid' decision to send Evelyn to Dubrovnik 'to tickle up the RC clergy' and that he 'stirred up a hornet's nest' (Frank McLynn, *Fitzroy Maclean*, p. 245).

does not understand a word of the language.' When Evelyn had finished expounding on the desperate plight of the Dubrovnik clergy, the Pope 'made a little English speech, inopportunely the one he keeps for sailors telling them how much he enjoyed a naval review at Portsmouth in 1920 something'.[63] A week after his audience Evelyn left Rome with his report on the Church in Croatia half written and flew via Naples to London, arriving there on 15 March.

Evelyn's report on 'Church and State in Liberated Croatia' eventually ran to some 7,500 words. It was first presented to Fitzroy Maclean, who pronounced it to be 'reasonably fair'; however when Evelyn tried to circulate it further the Permanent Under-Secretary of the Foreign Office, Sir Orme Sargent, sternly forbade it, seeing it as blatant propaganda against the British government's policy of support for Marshal Tito. All that Evelyn managed in the end was to get a question asked in the House of Commons in May about what measures were being taken to protect the Croat Catholics, to which the Foreign Secretary, Anthony Eden, replied that such matters fell outside the British government's responsibilities and must remain those of the Yugoslav state.

Observers far more sympathetic to Tito and the Partisans accused Evelyn of bias in his report and of omitting evidence that Catholic priests had collaborated with the Ustaše terrorists who supported the Italians during the fascist occupation of Yugoslavia. Evelyn freely admitted that some Catholic priests had been guilty of horrific crimes, but insisted that such cases were rare. In any event, even allowing for the possibility of bias on his part, the persistent ill-treatment of priests in post-war Yugoslavia would show his diagnosis of Communist persecution of the Catholic Church to be broadly correct. Evelyn meanwhile remained a fierce critic of Tito, and when Eden invited him to Britain on a state visit in 1952 at the height of the Cold War, he wrote an article angrily denouncing 'Our Guest of Dishonour'.

20

....

The Occupation

The war had been frustrating and disillusioning for Evelyn, but the change of habit had at least stimulated him as an artist and he had written two fine novels, the latest of which was about to make him rich ('stinking rich', he assured Laura) and famous. *Brideshead Revisited* was published at the end of May 1945, three weeks after VE Day. Evelyn was quite sure at the time that it was his most important work, his 'magnum opus' as he had called it ever since he started writing it in February 1944. 'For the first time since 1928,' he told Nancy Mitford, 'I am eager about a book.'[1]

Not all his friends enjoyed it, Katharine Asquith being prominent among those who did not, however reactions to his privately bound advance copies were mostly very positive. Like Evelyn, Graham Greene would later revise his opinion, however at first he rated it even better than *Work Suspended*, his previous favourite. Another Catholic friend, Daphne Acton, was 'ecstatic in her praise', Martin D'Arcy reported, while Ronnie Knox was 'at first antagonistic' but later 'in tears over the deathbed scene, & by the last chapter an ardent convert'.[2] The future Catholic convert Penelope Betjeman wrote: 'I think it is as good as Madame Bovary.'[3]

Among non-Catholic friends the unsurprising consensus was that there was 'too much Catholic stuff'.[4] Yet even the irreligious and increasingly egalitarian Henry Yorke,* who confessed to finding *Brideshead*'s subject matter deeply distasteful, could only conclude that 'to my mind you carry

---

* Henry Yorke/Green's most recent novel, *Loving*, published two months before *Brideshead*, was also about the country house in decline yet so different in perspective that Evelyn privately described it as an 'obscene book about domestic servants' and lamented that his friend had become a 'fierce proletarian convert'. 31 March 1945; *EWD*, p. 624; EW to Patrick Kinross, 1 August 1945; AWA.

out what you set out to do better than any English writer now writing'.[5] Meanwhile Nancy reported that Raymond Mortimer had pronounced it a 'Great English classic' and Cyril Connolly had found it 'impossible to put down'.[6]

Connolly, though, was also among those who did not care for some of the 'purple passages', an opinion that Evelyn would later come to share. In his preface to the revised 1960 edition, he explained that *Brideshead* had been written during 'a bleak period of present privation and threatening disaster – the period of soya beans and Basic English – and in conse- quence the book is enthused with a kind of gluttony, for food and wine, for the splendours of the recent past, and for rhetorical and ornamental language which now, with a full stomach, I find distasteful'.[7]

After the book was published in May, the first letter of congratulation Evelyn received was a typically extravagant outpouring from Harold Acton, who claimed to have 'slid my paperknife through the still virginal pages like an itching bridegroom and was panting, trembling and ex- hausted by the time I had finished cutting them'.

After he had caught his breath and begun reading the book, Acton had been

swept alternatively by pleasure and pain: pleasure at your ever-increasing virtuosity and mastery of our fast-evaporating language, for there are subtler nuances of prose in this than perhaps any of your writings; pain, at the acrid memories of so many old friends you have conjured, with ac- companying passion which I am surprised to find still smouldering in my bosom after all those years. It is the only successful evocation of the period that I know. But like the period itself, it leaves a melancholy dirge-like after- taste. So far one has survived, but for how long and into what?[8]

Among the early newspaper reviews, the *Manchester Guardian* was predictably prejudiced against *Brideshead*'s subject matter while con- ceding 'the brilliance of his writing'.[9] The *Times Literary Supplement* questioned whether Evelyn had managed to trace the workings of divine purpose with any 'marked clarity' and thought 'the decorations of the tale' were devised to better advantage than the working out of his overall theme. Reservations were also expressed about what seemed to be the au- thor's excessive reverence for the aristocracy. The *New Statesman* found

Brideshead 'deeply moving in its theme and its design' and 'a fine and brilliant book', yet suggested that 'a burden of respect for the peerage and Eton, which those who belong to the former or have been to the latter, seem able to lightly discard, weighs heavily on him'.[10] Even more damning was Edmund Wilson's assessment in *The New Yorker* early the next year: 'Waugh's snobbery, hitherto held in check by his satirical point of view, has here emerged shameless and rampant . . . his cult of high nobility is allowed to become so rapturous and solemn that it finally gives the impression of being the only real religion in the book.'[11]

Wilson was America's pre-eminent critic at the time and had previously singled out Evelyn as 'the only first-class comic genius that has appeared in England since Bernard Shaw'.[12] Given his antipathy towards both Catholicism and conservatism, *Brideshead* was always going to be less to his liking than Evelyn's earlier books; however he may also have felt that he had a score to settle, having been teased mercilessly by Evelyn at Cyril Connolly's table about his failure to find a British publisher for his recent novel on the grounds of obscenity. The next day Evelyn recorded in his diary having 'chucked an appointment to show London to insignificant yank named Edmund Wilson'.[13]

Evelyn shrugged off Wilson's criticisms and in any case could argue that the various aristocratic characters in his book were never sanctified and mostly decidedly flawed. It was also a gratifying irony for him that 'the age of the common man' ushered in by the post-war anti-elitism also fuelled nostalgia for the disappearing aristocratic way of life that made *Brideshead* such a spectacular bestseller. The first edition sold out in the first week of publication in Britain, and in America the book quickly sold more than half a million copies.[14] When it was made America's Book of the Month in July Evelyn calculated that it was worth '£10,000 down and a probable £10,000 from ordinary sales and cinema rights',[15] and he began to look forward to an annual income of at least £25,000 over the next five years.

But the satisfaction he had always taken in making money was soon competing with the fear of losing it in tax, especially after the post-war general election victory of the Labour Party, whose government Evelyn was soon referring to as 'the Attlee terror'[16] or simply 'the Occupation'.[17]

The pleasure he took in things going wrong, particularly for self-important politicians, meant that at first he found much to enjoy in the shock result.* Having failed to persuade Laura to come up from the country for Ann Rothermere's election night party, he reported afterwards that 'although the champagne was exiguous & the vodka watery the spectacle of consternation as details of the massacre spread was a strong intoxicant'.[18] But as the establishment of what he called 'Welfaria' got under way, he began to reflect miserably on what he saw as the new regime's commitment to obliterate all class distinctions, getting rid of a structure which for Evelyn lay at the very heart of English culture and which 'influenced, and often determined, all social and personal relations' and had grown over the centuries 'so complex that no foreigner and few natives could completely comprehend it'.[19] He contended that during his lifetime England had changed from being one of the most beautiful countries in the world to being one of the ugliest, adding that: 'German bombs have made but a negligible addition to the sum of our own destructiveness. It is arguable that the entire process is traceable to the decay of aristocratic domination.'[20]

Among those who had been newly elected as MPs, Evelyn saw Christopher Hollis and Hugh Fraser (with whom he got along better than with his brother Shimi Lovat) as 'the hope of the Catholics';[21] Randolph Churchill, meanwhile, was among those of his friends who had failed to win seats. Unable to move back into Piers Court until September and unwilling to live even temporarily at Pixton, Evelyn arranged to go and stay with Randolph, with whom he was by then reconciled, at Ickleford in Hertfordshire. Evelyn found Randolph 'crestfallen but not crushed' by his election defeat,[22] although he had also recently separated from his wife Pamela and the only furniture in his rented old rectory were odd bits that she had left behind. 'The plan is to stay until White's reopens,' Evelyn noted in his diary, 'but I am not confident that we shall live harmoniously so long.'[23] Anywhere was preferable to living with his in-laws, however, and he remained there on and off throughout August, joined for the last two weeks by Bron, who was just short of his sixth birthday and a potential playmate for Randolph's slightly younger son Winston.

After a few days Evelyn told Laura that his son's visit had been 'an unqualified success', adding that he had so far 'behaved admirably and won

---

* Evelyn never voted himself, explaining: 'I do not aspire to advise my sovereign in her choice of servants.' *The Spectator*, 2 October 1959; *EAR*, p. 537.

golden opinions on every side'. However when he took him to London to stay with his grandmother and show him some sights, Evelyn reported:

> I have regretfully come to the conclusion that the boy Auberon is not yet a suitable companion for me. Yesterday was a day of supreme self-sacrifice. I fetched him from Highgate, took him up the dome of St. Pauls, gave him a packet of triangular stamps, took him to luncheon at the Hyde Park Hotel, took him on the roof of the hotel, took him to Harrods & let him buy vast quantities of toys (down to your account) took him to tea with Maimie who gave him a pound and a box of matches, took him back to Highgate, in a state (myself not the boy) of extreme exhaustion. My mother said 'Have you had a lovely day?' He replied 'A bit dull'. So that is the last time for some years I inconvenience myself for my children. You might rub that in to him.[24]

Evelyn and Laura finally moved back into Piers Court two weeks later after almost exactly six years away, leaving the children at Pixton while they put the house back in order. 'Arrived on a grey, fly-infested, heavy evening with a hangover and the excitement of homecoming contending,' Evelyn recorded. 'At first sight the garden was rank, the paths lost, the trees stunted or overgrown irregularly; inside everything damp but superficially tidy. Slept ill.' The next day he wrote: 'Nuns half out, ourselves half in. Laura saying how perfect everything looked, I detecting losses and damage everywhere.'[25]

Evelyn later admitted to having returned home with 'many sentimental tremors' only to find that 'my love for it was quite dead, as so many soldiers found about their wives but not me thank God'.[26] Yet within a week the tanks were full enough for a hot bath, his library was back in order and he had begun to resume his pre-war routine. 'It is delightful to be writing to you again on Piers Court paper,' he told his mother,

> at my own writing table face to face with Queen Victoria in bronze and George III in paint. We have had an arduous week moving in. The nuns left things superficially clean and in as good condition as one could expect after six years school-use, but all the furniture was misplaced, moths had ravaged carpets, paint has gone and innumerable small breakages come to light daily. The water supply had been diverted from the village and is only

slowly returning; our first two or three days we could not light the boilers and had to carry all water up in buckets from the well. The garden is in poor shape, many paths entirely lost, but the trees & hedges well grown & the quinces, in particular, bearing well. The stables have been repaired after their collapse.[27]

It took several months to reassemble their household staff and for much of that autumn they were reliant on Laura's somewhat erratic cooking and housework, 'vague but pertinacious' as Evelyn described it. 'Little Laura and I live alone here in circumstances of very grave austerity,' he told Maimie. 'We have 27 hens which lay sometimes 3, more often 2 eggs a day and keep L. L. constantly busy cramming them with rich foods. She and I live on dry bread & vintage port . . .'.[28] To Randolph he reported: 'Laura broods despondently over the kitchen range and periodically raises columns of black smoke, announces that our meat ration has been incinerated, and drives me to dinner at a neighbouring inn.'[29]

The return of the butler Ellwood in mid-November was evidently an uplifting event: 'silver, boots, and furniture shine,' purred Evelyn. Less so was the arrival of Teresa and Bron just before Christmas. 'By keeping the children in bed for long periods we managed to have a tolerable day,' Evelyn recorded. 'The children leave for Pixton on the 10th. Meanwhile I have my meals in the library.'[30] Shortly after New Year 1946 he wrote to Diana Cooper:

I have my two eldest children here, a boy and a girl; two girls languish at Pixton; a fifth leaps in the womb. I abhor their company because I can only regard children as defective adults, hate their physical ineptitude, find their jokes flat and monotonous. Both are considered great wits by their contemporaries. The elder girl has a precocious taste for theology which promises well for a career as Abbess; the boy is mindless and obsessed with social success. I will put him into the Blues [the Royal Horse Guards] later, meanwhile he goes to boarding school at the end of the month with the keenest expectation of delight.[31]

Six when he was packed off to prep school, Bron later recalled: 'Papa's best practical joke was played in my first term when I was still very nervous. He told me he proposed to change his name to Stinkbottom. When he had done so, the headmaster would summon the school together and say: "Boys, the person you have hitherto called Waugh will in future be called Stinkbottom." School assembly was held every morning, and every morning I felt a slight tightening of the chest as Mr Dix came forward to make his morning announcements.'³²

* * *

After the war Evelyn had begun working on a new novel about St Helena, the research for which entailed 'a very interesting correspondence with Mrs. Betjeman about horses & sex', he told Nancy Mitford. Evelyn had first met Penelope Chetwode in the early 1930s staying with the Pakenhams in Ireland when she was engaged to John Betjeman. Fresh from his lessons at Captain Hance's equitation academy, Evelyn was very keen to go riding with the gamine Penelope but she had taken the Pakenhams' only good horse and his mount, an unbroken and completely unmanageable bay cob, promptly carted him off at a gallop towards Lough Derravaragh. When Penelope followed she came across the horse grazing calmly by the lake and heard Evelyn calling her from the branch of a tree where he had eventually been deposited. It was the start of a great friendship, admiring of his bravery and literary genius on her part, flirtatious and at times boldly suggestive on his. 'Be a good girl about this,' he wrote from Abyssinia in 1935 when asking for information about the mysterious Mr Rickett, 'and I will reward you with a fine fuck when I get back.'³³

If this sounds like a joke or at least wishful thinking on Evelyn's part, he was later said to have complained to Osbert Lancaster in a moment of bitterness, 'She always laughs when I come'.³⁴ For her part Penelope recalled being alarmed when he made advances on her both before and after her marriage, maintaining that 'he never attracted me in the very least'.³⁵ Years later, shortly before Evelyn died, Auberon asked him whether he had ever been to bed with Lady Betjeman, to which he replied, 'Since you ask, yes.'³⁶

Whether or not this was a tease, Evelyn clearly found Penelope attractive and given that John Betjeman almost certainly knew this, Evelyn's letter to him in May 1945, explaining that he was modelling the Empress Helena's early life on the horse-mad Penelope's own 'hipporastic' experiences, bordered on the sadistic: 'She [Helena] is 16, sexy, full of horse fantasies. I want to get this right. Will you tell her [Penelope] to write to me fully about adolescent sex reveries connected with riding. I have no experience of such things, nor has Laura. I make her always the horse & the consummation when the rider subdues her. Is this correct? Please make her explain. And is riding enough or must she be driven? Are spurs important or only leather-work?'[37]

After hearing nothing, Evelyn eventually asked Penelope directly: 'I describe her as hunting in the morning after her wedding night feeling the saddle as comforting her wounded maidenhead. Is that O.K.? After that she has no interest in sex . . .'[38] Penelope had by then read an extract of Evelyn's work in progress in *The Tablet* and replied that she thought the descriptions of Helena hunting 'very good but whatever will Fr Darcy say?'. She further confided that 'my first experiments in horse sex were when I drove my donkey round the pine-woods at Aldershot in father's cavalry bit when I was 11', and that she had 'found it very difficult to separate sex & religion after I married & frequently used to drive a severely-bitted carriage horse in flights of fancy with an Anglo or Roman priest seated at my side. Couldn't the Empress take great pleasure in driving a Druid about in a chariot? . . . Pray consign this to your kitchen boiler when studied.'[39]

Aside from Evelyn's nosy questions about his wife, John Betjeman also had to put up with regular barrages about his own religious views. 'I have been painfully shocked by a brochure named "Five Sermons by Laymen",' Evelyn wrote to him just before Christmas 1946:

Last time I met you you told me you did not believe in the Resurrection. Now I find you expounding Protestant devotional practices from the pulpit. This WILL NOT DO . . . Your ecclesiastical position is entirely without reason. You cannot possibly be right. Marxist Atheists might be. Zealous protestants may be (i.e. it is possible to say that from the word go the Church was all wrong & had misunderstood everything Our Lord told them, & that it required a new Divine Dispensation in the sixteenth century to put people on the right track again. That is just possible.) What is inconceivable is that Christ was made flesh in order to found a Church, that He canalized his Grace in the sacraments, that He gave His promise to abide in the Church to the end of time, that He saw the Church as a human corporation, part of his Mystical Body, one with the Saints triumphant – and then to point to a handful of homosexual curates and say: 'That is the true Church.'[40]

On the point of going over to Rome herself, Penelope Betjeman was as keen as Evelyn was for her husband to convert to Catholicism, however she worried that Evelyn went too far, and in April 1947 she told him that John was 'in a dreadful state he thinks you are the devil and wakes up in the middle of the night and raves and says he will leave me at once if I go over'. Two months later she wrote: 'The ONLY thing is to leave him alone at present. He has dreadful persecution mania where Catholics are concerned . . .'[41] Evelyn replied: 'I am by nature a bully and a scold, and John's pertinacity in error brings out all that is worst in me. I am very sorry. I will lay off him in future.'[42] Two months later, Evelyn recorded in his diary: 'To Farnborough to make my peace with the Betjemans. Successful in this . . . Penelope seems resolved to enter the church in the autumn and John to desert her when she does so.'[43]

* * *

Another long-standing friend who was regularly put through the mill was Cyril Connolly. The commercial success of *Brideshead* meant that Evelyn could now afford to pick and choose what journalism he did, and in the autumn of 1945 when Douglas Woodruff at *The Tablet* asked if he might like to supply a 'trenchant' review of Connolly's *The Unquiet Grave*, Evelyn obliged with a piece which, as he cheerfully told Nancy Mitford, 'shook out a few feathers'[44] and might well have ended their friendship had Connolly not sensibly refrained from reacting.

Evelyn and Connolly had been on-off friends since Oxford. Evelyn greatly admired him as a critic – as well he might, given that Connolly was one of his most consistent champions – was fond of him as a drinking companion and realised they had much in common besides their shared literary, artistic and epicurean interests, both being easily bored, notoriously moody, unpredictable and at times spectacularly rude. Yet Connolly's all too evident wariness of Evelyn also made him the recurrent butt of his bullying, and he was relentlessly teased for his left-wing opinions and castigated for his laziness and lack of religion. 'Connolly has many injuries to revenge,' Evelyn admitted in 1951 when he heard that he was researching a profile of him for *Time* magazine. 'I can't blame him if he takes the opportunity.' But he warned him that when the piece appeared (it never did), 'I shall horse-whip you on the steps of White's'.[45]

Reviewing *Enemies of Promise* in 1938, Evelyn had described Connolly as the only man under forty who showed any signs of raising literary criticism to an art form, yet tore into the book as 'structurally jerry-built'.[46] *The Unquiet Grave* had already been widely acclaimed as a potential classic, however Evelyn, while acknowledging that the book contained sentences 'as beautiful as any passages of modern English prose that I know', suggested that Connolly had been 'duped and distracted by the chatter of psychoanalysts' and that he had given 'full rein to the tosh-horse whose hooves thunder through the penultimate passages'.[47] When Nancy had first sent Evelyn the book in Yugoslavia in 1944, he reported back that the passages about Christianity in particular were 'real twaddle' and concluded that 'Connolly has lived too much with communist young ladies. He <u>must</u> spend more time in White's.'[48]

White's remained the place that Evelyn chose to spend most of his time whenever he was in London, and in March 1946 a friend there, Mervyn Griffith-Jones, a former comrade in No. 8 Commando and now a prosecutor at Nuremberg, invited him to attend the trials as an observer. The ancient Bavarian city had been almost completely destroyed by Allied bombs in the final months of the war and Evelyn found 'a waste of corpse-scented rubble with a handful of middle-aged, middle-class Germans in Homburg hats picking their way through ruins. We drove to the Sports Palace which is intact but probably due for demolition – typical modern functional magnificence designed for mass parades, now full of German Jews in American uniforms photographing one another in the act of giving the Nazi salute from Hitler's rostrum.'[49]

He observed the next day's court proceedings as a VIP, sitting in the front row of the gallery and watching the various high-ranking Nazis as they came and went from the dock. Göring had 'much of Tito's matronly appeal', Evelyn told Randolph Churchill, while Ribbentrop looked 'like a seedy schoolmaster being ragged. He knows he doesn't know the lesson and he knows the boys know.'[50]

Always fascinated by the macabre, after the court rose for the day Evelyn 'went to see the room where a French Jew keeps lampshades of human skin, shrunken heads, soap said to be made of corpses and so forth'. After two days he had had enough of listening to legal arguments and flew on to stay with the Coopers in Paris, where Duff had recently become Ambassador. Evelyn initially surprised everyone with his mellow mood, but soon set about baiting the other guests, treating Julian Huxley as 'a crypto-Communist zoo-keeper with no interest in life beyond the diet of his panda' and describing Peter Quennell to Diana in terms 'so foetid and sinister,' she recalled, 'that it will colour most unfairly my sentiments for him'.[51] 'Poor Wu,' she wrote to Conrad Russell afterwards, '– he does everything he can to alienate himself from the affection he is yearning for.'[52] Also at the embassy was his brother-in-law Auberon Herbert, and when he left for Brussels Diana implored Evelyn to follow him downstairs and tell him that he liked him. 'He believed it,' Evelyn noted in his diary.[53]

In June that year Evelyn went to Spain with Douglas Woodruff to attend a centenary celebration of 'a Thomist philosopher whose name escapes me' (Francisco de Vitoria), the inspiration for his novella *Scott-King's Modern Europe*, arriving back on 2 July two days after Laura had given birth to their sixth (fifth surviving) child, James.

At the end of that year Duckworth published a compilation of Evelyn's travel writing, *When the Going Was Good*, with a preface promising that 'my own travelling days are over'. However there would soon be more expeditions, including to Scandinavia the next year to write two travel pieces for *The Daily Telegraph*, and several visits to the United States. The first of these took place in early 1947 after Metro-Goldwyn-Mayer offered an all-expenses-paid trip for himself and Laura to Hollywood to discuss a possible film treatment of *Brideshead Revisited*. The handsome terms that Peters negotiated on Evelyn's behalf were that he would be paid $2,000 (more than $20,000 in today's money) a week throughout their stay, which in the end lasted over two months, with the promise of an eventual $140,000 ($1.5 million) if a film deal was agreed, minus whatever MGM had already spent.

Peters was understandably nervous at the prospect of Evelyn's visit given his frequently declared hostility to 'the bloody yanks', who embodied so much of what he hated about the modern world. In February 1946 Evelyn had written to Maimie Lygon: 'My book has been a great success in the United States which is upsetting because I thought it in good taste before and now I know it can't be.'[54] Worse than the popular applause was the fan mail that came in its wake. 'I have momentarily become an object of curiosity to Americans,' he wrote in an article that spring for *Life* magazine, 'and I find that they believe that my friendship and confidence are included in the price of my book.' Some of the correspondence was not so friendly: 'An offensive letter from a female American Catholic,' Evelyn noted in his diary in March. 'I returned it to her husband with the note: "I shall be grateful if you will use whatever disciplinary means are customary in your country to refrain your wife from writing impertinent letters to men she does not know."'[55]

The *Life* piece gave Evelyn the opportunity of 'answering collectively all the inquiries I have received', but he also used it as a wider statement of his artistic aims and to respond to a few of the more pointed criticisms, including the charge of snobbery. 'Class-consciousness, particularly in England, has been so much inflamed nowadays that to mention a noble-man is like mentioning a prostitute sixty years ago. The new prudes say, "No doubt such people do exist but we would sooner not hear about them." I reserve the right to deal with the kind of people I know best.'[56]

Before Evelyn set off for America, Peters warned him from New York: 'I must tell you that you have the reputation here – both at M.G.M. and everywhere else – of being a difficult, tetchy, irritating and rude customer. I hope you will surprise and confound them all by behaving like an 18th century ambassador from the Court of St. James's. They are children; and they should receive the tolerance and understanding that you show to children. You would (I hope, will) be surprised by the result.'[57] Evelyn replied calmly that 'I mean to do business with the Californian savages if it is possible . . . I am sure Matson [Evelyn's New York agent] and his fellow countrymen are, as you say, just little boys at heart, but I believe little boys should be very frequently whipped and sent to bed supperless.'[58]

Evelyn and Laura sailed for New York on 25 January 1947 shortly after an unsuccessful operation for piles which put him in a foul mood on arrival, when he was soon inveighing against the 'tasteless' food at the Waldorf Astoria, wine ruined by 'bad cellarage' and electric shocks every time he touched something metal. He objected to the talkative taxi drivers ('It's an outrage to be charged for such boredom')[59], the chewing of gum and the habit of smoking between courses. As for New York's famous tall buildings, he wrote to Diana Cooper: 'They are nothing nothing nothing at their best. At their worst, that is to say when they attempt any kind of ornament they are actively wicked. Compare them with the kind of things you have at your doorstep – Horse Guards Parade, Banqueting House, St Martin-in-the-Fields, Westminster Abbey – or what I have within a five mile radius of Stinkers. Think of the infinity of aesthetic problems which a real architect has to solve every yard – and then of these great booby boxes. Interiors <u>all</u> vile.'[60]

At least Laura appeared to be enjoying herself and she managed to get through $2,000 'in a very few minutes' when let loose in an expensive dress shop. After four days they continued their journey aboard the sumptuous 20th-Century train to Chicago, then onwards to Pasadena, where they arrived on the morning of 6 February to be met by a car from MGM to take them to the Bel Air Hotel. Alec Waugh later described what he had heard of Evelyn's arrival in California: 'The sun was shining, tropical flowers were in bloom, all the young people were dressed in shorts and slacks and open shirts and there was Evelyn in a stiff white collar and a bowler hat, carrying a rolled umbrella.'[61] As Harold Acton, who also happened to be in Los Angeles at the time, observed, adaptability was not among Evelyn's traits.

The next day Evelyn went to the vast MGM studios in Culver City, where he was less than elated to learn that their proposed screenwriter was Keith Winter, whom Evelyn 'last knew as Willie Maugham's catamite at Villefranche' as he ominously noted in his diary.[62] On that occasion in 1931 the twenty-four-year-old Winter had been staying at the same hotel as the two Waugh brothers and when Somerset Maugham asked the three young men to dine, Winter ended up spending the night and returned the next day looking very pleased with himself. 'Willie told him how well he used his fingers,' Alec Waugh recalled, 'which made me think of Strickland in the *Moon and Sixpence*, who often despised the people he was enjoying.'[63] Evelyn had taken a strong dislike to Winter then, refusing to speak to him except through the intermediary of Patrick Balfour, and he appeared to like him no better this time around. 'He wore local costume,' Evelyn disdainfully recorded, 'a kind of loose woollen blazer, matelot's vest, buckled shoes. He has been in Hollywood for years and sees *Brideshead* purely as a love story.'

As none of the Americans showed much interest in the book's theological implications the discussions they had over its filming were, as far as Evelyn was concerned, 'futile',[64] although he found 'something a little luxurious in talking in great detail about every implication of a book which the others are paid to know thoroughly'.[65] There was plenty too that was luxurious about MGM's hospitality, which even Evelyn conceded was 'consistently munificent', so he felt 'well content and, as soon as the danger of the film was disposed of, almost serene also'. Laura, meanwhile, 'grew smarter and younger and more popular daily and was serenely happy'.[66]

Besides Harold Acton, who was visiting his American bachelor uncle and benefactor and chanced to meet Evelyn at the Huntington Museum, they also saw Randolph Churchill, who was in the midst of a hectic lecture tour: 'I thought he could never shock me any more but he did,' Evelyn wrote to Peters. 'Brutishly drunk all the time, soliciting respectable women at luncheon parties etc. His lecture, to which we went at Pasadena, was surprisingly good considering the grave condition he was in.'[67]

By March Evelyn was able to tell Peters they were having a surprisingly agreeable time and, contrary to expectations, had been enjoying a 'gay & refined'[68] social life, having befriended Merle Oberon, visited Walt Disney's studios and been taken to supper with Charlie Chaplin by Iris Tree. 'I was thus able to pay my homage to the two artists [Disney and Chaplin] of the place,' Evelyn noted in his diary.[69]

They also saw a lot of the English portrait painter Simon Elwes, an old friend who was visiting Los Angeles with his wife Golly (Peter Rodd's sister). The Elweses' hostess Andrea Cowdin had the Waughs to lunch or dinner every day, took them with her to parties and introduced them to 'all the most agreeable people at her house', Evelyn recorded.[70] Another member of the English colony, Sir Charles Mendl (married to the decorator Elsie de Wolfe) took them to tea with Anna May Wong and lunch with Aldous Huxley, the latter possibly an awkward encounter given that a decade earlier Evelyn had torn into Huxley's novel *Eyeless in Gaza* in a review in *The Tablet*.[71] But they would at least have been able to discuss their shared fascination with Forest Lawn Memorial Park, a cemetery in Glendale that Evelyn had recently discovered and quickly recognised as 'a deep mine of literary gold'.[72]

'I am entirely obsessed with Forest Lawns,' Evelyn wrote to Peters, 'I go there two or three times a week, am on easy terms with the chief embalmer & next week am to lunch with DR HUBERT EATON [the founder] himself. It is an entirely unique place – the only thing in California that is not a copy of something else. It is wonderful literary raw material. Aldous flirted with it in *After Many A Summer* but only with the superficialities. I am at the heart of it. It will be a *very* good story.'[73]

After numerous visits to this extraordinary 300-acre site Evelyn claimed to have become 'something very like friends' with the embalmer, Mr Howells, 'who gives the "personality smile" to the embalmed corpse',[74] each of which was euphemistically referred to at Forest Lawn as 'the loved one'. Evelyn's rapport with the original of Mr Joyboy at Whispering Glades was such that he had 'seen dozens of loved ones half painted before the bereaved family saw them'.[75] With its sentimental sugaring-over of the reality of death, Forest Lawn was for Evelyn the perfect embodiment of the meaningless paganism and general fakery at the heart of the American dream. And while the $140,000 *Brideshead* film deal never materialised, like Dennis Barlow at the end of *The Loved One* he returned from Hollywood carrying 'the artist's load, a great, shapeless chunk of experience'.

But although he had found American society unexpectedly charming, not all of American society had been charmed by him. Among the Waughs' hosts in New York had been two of Evelyn's former American agents with whom he had quarrelled in the 1930s, Carl Brandt and his wife Carol, formerly Carol Hill. Carol, whom Evelyn privately deemed 'a woman of no intellectual interests . . . a secretary raised to its highest power',[76] later told Peters that she had found Evelyn 'delightful, gracious and appreciative in every sense of the word. But I must say we seem to be alone in this land of sunshine.' She was by then MGM's New York story editor and accompanied the Waughs to Los Angeles, so knew all about Evelyn's dealings there: 'I truly think that people here have tried to be friendly and gracious,' she wrote, 'both in terms of the usual dinners and in terms of work, but Evelyn has been so constantly arrogant and rude apparently as to have left a trail of bloody but unbowed heads behind him. Some of this, I gather, has been utter mischief on his part and some of it has been complete misunderstanding of his particular variety of humor and wit.'[77]

Among those immune to Evelyn's charms was Billy Wilder's screenwriting partner Charles Brackett, who met him at a party held in his honour by the director George Cukor (later, incidentally, buried at Forest Lawn). Amid a gathering that included Greta Garbo and Olivia de Havilland, it was perhaps hardly surprising that Brackett found the Waughs 'very unprepossessing' by comparison, describing them as 'a bank clerk and his snuffly wife, an ill-favoured tailor's dummy with halitosis and a blue-eyed Elsa Lanchester part'. Brackett returned later to Cukor's to find that 'in my absence Waugh had sent his wife home, dismissed her in a rude way which impressed everyone unpleasantly'.[78]

If not perhaps in that instance, Evelyn's rudeness often began as a tease to help liven things up, or else it was a bracingly forthright statement of how he actually felt. But it was not always easy to tell which. Igor Stravinsky had lunch with Evelyn in New York in 1949 and remarked afterwards: 'Whether Mr Waugh was disagreeable, or only preposterously arch, I cannot say.' When Stravinsky attempted found some common ground by talking about his own recent sung Mass, Evelyn replied: 'All music is positively painful to me.'[79] Which happened to be true.

Much of Evelyn's humour clearly did get lost in translation; however, even the English colony sometimes failed to appreciate his jokes, David Niven for instance taking strong exception to having his black housekeeper referred to in her presence as 'your native bearer'.[80] Evelyn knew perfectly well that he was rarely at his best with strangers of any nationality, and of how offensive he could be, even to his own wife. When Gilbert Pinfold asks 'Why does everyone except me find it so easy to be nice?',[81] Evelyn was clearly speaking about himself. In Italy Harold Acton recalled his spectacular rudeness in restaurants and his sublime remark to the director of the British Institute, Francis Toye, who had a way of standing too close: 'If you want to kiss me please get it over quickly.' Invited to a tea party as guest of honour, Evelyn spent the entire time handing round the tea and cakes, explaining to his hostess, 'I'd much rather do this than have to talk'. When Baby Jungman told him how much a cousin of hers had enjoyed *Brideshead*, Evelyn thought it best to warn her: 'I am sure you will have fully explained to him how disappointing I am to meet. Writers should be heard and not seen . . . Writers should stay in their burrows. I intend to anyway until the ferrets come for me.'[82]

* * *

When they arrived back in England shortly before Easter, Laura headed straight down to Pixton and the children, while Evelyn, evidently less eager for this family reunion, spent five days in London then went with Simon Elwes to Downside for a four-day retreat before eventually joining Laura, Teresa and Bron at Piers Court on Easter Day. Two weeks later Evelyn recorded: 'Laura is busy and happy with agriculture and has lost all her Californian chic.'[83] Shortly afterwards he went to Ireland, where he had been toying with the idea of buying a castle to escape the socialist regime and his boredom with Gloucestershire social life. 'If only country neighbours would talk like Jane Austen characters about gossip & hobbies,' he wrote to Nancy. 'Instead they all want to know about Molotov & de Gaulle . . . I am anxious to emigrate, Laura to remain & face the century of the common man. She is younger, braver & less imaginative than I. If only they would start blowing the place up with their atoms.'[84] By mid-May he was back again at his writing desk at Piers Court.

The first thing he wrote about his Hollywood experiences was 'an article on Death for *Life*',[85] as he described it, 2,500 words on Forest Lawn and its founder Dr Eaton, 'the first man to offer eternal salvation at an inclusive charge as part of his undertaking service', as Evelyn put it.[86] On 21 May he began work on *The Loved One* and by early September he was able to send a first draft to Peters asking his advice on 'what form it should take in its public appearances in USA and England'.[87]

Uncharacteristically po-faced in this instance, Peters replied that 'being perfectly frank' the question was rather 'whether it should make any public appearance at all'. 'I found parts of it very amusing, of course; but parts were to me revolting, and my over-riding conviction when I had finished the story was that it was not worthy of Evelyn Waugh . . . It seems to be one of those ideas that is extremely amusing in conception [but] it is not possible to be funny about corpses for 25,000 words. The humour begins to putrefy and finally leaves a very bad taste in the mouth.'[88]

Evelyn valued his agent more as a negotiator than as a critic and tactfully suggested that 'the tale should not be read as a satire on morticians but as a study of the Anglo-American cultural impasse with the mortuary as a jolly setting'.[89] Still convinced that *The Loved One* was a work of art, Evelyn approached Cyril Connolly – with whom he had made up after having him and 'his concubine'[90] Lys Lubbock to stay in June – asking if he would be prepared to publish it in its entirety in *Horizon*. Connolly replied: 'Est, est, est! as the bishop said! One of your very best I think. I should be honoured . . .'[91]

The Loved One duly made its first appearance in *Horizon*'s February 1948 issue, with a preface by Connolly commending it as 'a Swiftian satire [which] in its attitude to death, and to death's stand-in, failure . . . exposes a materialistic society at its weakest spot'. It was, he suggested, 'one of the most perfect short novels of the last ten years and the most complete of [Waugh's] creations, a story cast in a kind of light but immensely strong aluminium alloy, like the one-piece chassis of a racing car'.[92]

The magazine sold out overnight but there was then an eight-month interval before the hardback, due to the fact that *Scott-King's Modern Europe* had sold 14,000 copies in the run-up to Christmas and was still doing well. Evelyn was keen to publish *The Loved One* in America to capitalise on his popularity there after *Brideshead*, but publishers on both sides of the Atlantic were concerned that Whispering Glades in the novel was too easily recognisable as Forest Lawn Memorial Park and that Dr Eaton might sue for libel.

To allay such fears Evelyn asked his high-spirited friend Lord Stanley of Alderley to add a codicil to his will stipulating that on his death he wished his body to be transported to Los Angeles for burial at Forest Lawn, as he understood that 'this cemetery bore some resemblance to the beautiful one so movingly described by his friend Mr Evelyn Waugh'.[93] Ed Stanley's letter to his solicitor requesting this, presumably written on House of Lords notepaper, was enough to set publishers' minds at rest and the book appeared in Britain and America in November to generally favourable reviews, although Evelyn's old adversary Edmund Wilson spitefully maintained that the 'patrons and proprietors of Whispering Glades seem more sensible and less absurd than the priest-guided Evelyn Waugh'.[94]

The Loved One was dedicated to Nancy Mitford, who received her advance copy in Paris where she had moved in 1946 in pursuit of her elusive Free French colonel, Gaston Palewski, the great love of her life. 'Do try & laugh a little,' wrote Evelyn. 'It is dedicated to you as the hardest hearted well no toughest is the word girl I know.' Nancy replied: 'The *heaven* of *The Loved One* oh you are kind to dedicate it to me, thank you thank you for it. I've been utterly shrieking over it since it arrived, luckily was lunching alone. I must say I couldn't quite do it and the *foie de veau* together . . . but combined it happily with a banana & am now in despair at having finished it . . . Dined with a young American last night & told him your book was to be called *The Loved One*. "What a beautiful name," he said. Poor him.'[95]

Evelyn greatly missed being able to trade gossip with her at Heywood Hill's bookshop, however if anything they got along even better by letter, their jokes often based upon a shared readiness to be mischievous and cruel about others, unlike Cyril Connolly, the occasional butt of their unkindness, who told Evelyn that he did not regard the suffering of his fellow men as a fit subject of humour. As far as Nancy was concerned, Evelyn was not just a highly entertaining friend and faithful confidant but also a much-valued literary sounding board whose talents as a word-smith and prose stylist she conceded were on an altogether different plain – 'your well known knack of one tap on the nail & in it goes, whereas the rest of us hammer & pound for hours' – yet whose advice on matters such as romance and religion she felt free to disregard.

It was he who had suggested the title of *The Pursuit of Love*, her first bestseller, in 1945, and that Uncle Matthew's home Alconleigh should be dominated by 'stark and real' images of death, however as often as not his suggestions went unheeded. 'I long to read your novel & criticize tho what's the good you never take my advice,'[96] Evelyn wrote to her in 1950 when she was at work on *The Blessing*. He nevertheless remained the writer whom Nancy measured herself against most often in her own mind and whose approval she most craved. At the same time her headstrong determination to stick to her guns served to preserve his great fondness and regard for her.

Several others benefited from Evelyn's generosity with literary advice, among them the Scottish writer Moray McLaren, whom Evelyn helped rescue from alcoholic despair and loss of faith, just as he did with his old Oxford friend Alfred Duggan, whose late-flowering career as a bestselling historical novelist owed a huge debt to Evelyn's help and encouragement.* Another whom Evelyn mentored was the Thomas Merton, the talkative Trappist monk from Kentucky whose autobiography *The Seven Storey Mountain* Evelyn edited and cut by a third for its English edition, *Elected Silence*. 'Americans tend to be very long-winded in conversation,' Evelyn explained to the monk, 'and your method is conversational'; he added: 'it is of course much more laborious to write briefly'.

Evelyn first visited Father Merton at his monastery when he went to America for a second time, in November 1948, the result of a shrewdly aimed proposal that he write about the Catholic Church in America for

---

* Evelyn was also an obliging writer of prefaces to lesser known writers whom he admired, including to Eric Newby's *Short Walk in the Hindu Kush* (1958) and to Christie Lawrence's neglected masterpiece, *Irregular Adventure* (1947), recounting the exploits of this 'highly individualistic' former comrade of Evelyn's in No 8 Commando after he was captured on Crete in 1941. 'No one could ask for a better thriller,' Evelyn declared in his introduction, and Lawrence's adventures 'should bring encouragement to all who may be in danger of doubting whether knight-errantry is still possible in the conditions of modern war'.

Life. The magazine's proprietor, Henry Luce, greeted his idea enthusiastically, not least since his wife, the writer Clare Boothe Luce, was an ardent convert like Evelyn who developed a soft spot for her despite initially thinking her rather self-centred. He would go weak at the knees whenever they subsequently met, and when she came over to London the next year he gave a dinner party at Tom Burns's to introduce her to a selection of distinguished British Catholics. As Lady Pamela Berry observed to Nancy Mitford, Clare regarded Evelyn 'in a quaint Catholic light as a noble gentle person who is capable, oh yes, from time to time of spitefulness, but who is on the whole a saintly, good person healed and beatified by the Church. What do you know about that?'[97]

During the 1948 American trip Evelyn also renewed what was to become a lifelong friendship with Anne Fremantle, another convert and now leading Catholic intellectual whom he had known slightly in the 1920s and was reputedly the only woman his old tutor Mr Cruttwell ever proposed to. After plying Anne with caviar and 'comfortable amounts of Bristol Cream' over Sunday lunch, Evelyn described her to Laura as '*very* nice', yet entirely failed to understand her decision to become an American citizen, 'with full consent deliberately committing this horrid act'.[98] Evelyn's brother Alec, who was by then living apart from Joan and spending much of his time in New York, was himself also on the point of taking this incomprehensible step – he became a US 'resident alien' in 1950 – and when he called on Evelyn at his hotel later the same day Evelyn told Laura he was 'greatly taken up with some woman, dressed with inappropriate gaiety, talking in an unusual & unbecoming drawl. Then I felt so ill & sad I went to bed without any dinner.'[99]

Evelyn returned to America early in 1949, this time with Laura, to give a series of lectures on 'Three Vital Writers', G. K. Chesterton, Ronald Knox and Graham Greene, returning home at the end of March. 'I must say I've seen enough of USA to last me fifty years,' he wrote to Nancy when he got back home. 'It is very degrading to be constantly in the company of people you have to "make allowances for".'[100] But after his 6,000-word article 'The American Epoch in the Catholic Church' eventually appeared in *Life* magazine that autumn, there was yet more demand for Evelyn among American Catholics and in the autumn of 1950 he went there again, his arrival coinciding with the publication of *Helena*, which he had eventually finished that spring, some five years after starting it. Evelyn always maintained that this was by far his best book, yet while he was in New York being lavishly entertained yet again by the Luces, an anonymous reviewer in Henry Luce's *Time* magazine remarked that Evelyn's 'sky-blue prose' had on this occasion gone 'purple with emotion'. The critical reaction was no better in England and Evelyn later told Christopher Sykes that the book's reception was 'the greatest disappointment of his whole literary life'.[101]

21

....

Off My Rocker

Three months earlier, on 11 July 1950, Laura had given birth to their seventh and last child, Septimus. Shortly afterwards Evelyn went to stay at Pixton for the boy's christening but fled as soon as he heard that Laura's brother Auberon was also on his way. 'I think the mixture of all the children & him would be intolerable to you,' wrote Laura after Evelyn had gone, '& even though I know you would be polite to him I know I should be in a fever & miserable, feeling that things were not right.'[1] Alone at Piers Court with nothing much to do after finishing *Helena*, Evelyn soon grew bored and listless. 'I miss you unendurably & go whistling about the house & fields never hearing an answer,' he wrote to Laura. 'Let me know if Auberon looks like going and I will come quick.'[2]

Evelyn missed Laura whenever he was away from her for any length of time, his love constantly underpinned by the feeling that she was perhaps the only person who was entirely unafraid of him and able to call him to order. He may have made occasional sharp remarks about her eccentric housekeeping arrangements or dishevelled dress sense, but on the whole they appeared to be remarkably happy together, so unalike in so many ways yet crucially sharing a very similar sense of humour – 'a very *peculiar* sense of humour,' as Gilbert Pinfold's tormentors described it.

Laura was essentially a very private person, content to see no one beyond her family and a few local farming folk, and equally content to let her more gregarious husband disappear periodically up to London to see his friends. Whenever they were both at Piers Court they did the crossword together (he apparently not minding that she was noticeably better at it than he was) but otherwise got on with their own thing, he writing in the library or pottering in the garden or going for long walks or taking in a matinee at Dursley cinema, she looking after her cows. 'She never had more than six or seven of them,' recalled her son Auberon, 'but she loved them extravagantly, as other women love their dogs or, so I have been told, their children.'[3]

In keeping with his own anarchic tendencies, Evelyn was inclined to let his children do as they pleased when they were young so long as they did not disturb his tranquillity in the library. Much of Bron's early childhood was thus spent prowling about the woods around Piers Court with an assortment of weaponry or conducting chemistry experiments in a 'lab' at the back of the house with explosive substances liberally procured by his father. At Downside, Bron once took a confiscated air pistol from the headmaster's desk and shot another boy in the leg, maintaining afterwards that he had intended only to stir up the gravel by the boy's feet.[4] He held the school record of fourteen beatings in a single term.

When Randolph Churchill asked the Waughs to stay in 1953, Evelyn replied: 'Laura, who, alas, will be busy with farm and children all summer, sends her love and regretfully declines your kind invitation. The boy Auberon Alexander is available for little Winston's entertainment. His chief interest is shooting sitting birds with an airgun and making awful smells with chemicals. He is devoid of culture but cheerful and greedy for highly peppered foods. If not watched closely he smokes and drinks. Shall I bring him for the first weekend of August?'[5]

As soon as they were at boarding school the children were allowed through the green baize doors to have lunch with their parents in the dining room – 'very gloomy occasions', according to Bron[6] – and to mark the end of each school holidays there was also a rather jollier family dinner party, waited on by Ellwood, at which they all gave little speeches beginning 'Unaccustomed as I am to public speaking'. In 1956 Evelyn wrote to Bron at Downside: 'I am delighted to hear that, unaccustomed as you are to public speaking, you have won the debating prize and are going to Sherborne with the team.'[7]

As theatrical as his own father in many respects, Evelyn put on white tie and tails for the end-of-holidays dinners, completing the regalia with a display of his military medals. His own speech, before they all moved through for charades and dumb crambo, was invariably 'some variation on the theme of how delighted he was that the holidays were over and his children were going back to school', as Bron recalled.[8] As it was clear that in this instance he was not being funny, his children could find his remarks quite hurtful, and although their devotion increased as they grew older, in early childhood they felt largely indifferent towards their father: 'We held him in awe, certainly,' wrote Bron, 'but not in much affection at this stage.'[9]

Evelyn made no secret of how bored he often was by his children when they were young, just as he was whenever he encountered anyone unable to respond intelligently or at least humorously to what he had to say. However there was an endearing eccentricity about his letters to them when they were at school, usually gossipy, often subversive but almost always affectionate, if idiosyncratically so. When Meg wrote pointing out that the other girls had all been sent Easter eggs by their parents, Evelyn replied: 'I won't send you an Easter egg. You must nibble bits off the other girls'. Perhaps as a reward for your great unselfishness I will send you a little book of devotion instead.'[10] As Bron prepared to celebrate his fifteenth birthday at Downside in 1954, Evelyn sounded a rare note of censure: 'May your sixteenth year start prudently. Give up this nonsense of drinking beer and smoking with local poachers. Eat heavily. Wash down crumpets and cakes with refreshing cups of tea. Keep good company.'[11]

Of all his children, the one generally reckoned to have come off worst from Evelyn's occasional bullying was his middle son James, who had the misfortune to be continually compared with his brother Septimus, the youngest of the family by four years and thus doted on by both parents. 'Your brother James is home dull as ditchwater,' Evelyn wrote to Teresa in 1964, 'your brother Septimus bright as a button.' At one stage Evelyn made James tell a new joke every day in order to remedy what he saw as his defective sense of humour. 'And now my son will tell an amusing story,' Evelyn would announce if there were guests for dinner. Yet despite such ordeals James remembers his childhood as extremely free and on the whole 'very happy', and he cheerfully confesses to have been left with no lasting sense of maltreatment. The youngest three were always 'less privileged', he recalls, 'but we were part of a tribe so it didn't seem to matter'. Septimus, meanwhile, grew up in awe of his father but 'less from fear than from a desire not appear foolish in front of him'. His abiding impression was of 'a gentle melancholic man whose chief pleasure lay in parodying his condition'. As his father grew older, Septimus felt increasingly protective of him. When the house filled with children, Evelyn would wander around chanting: 'Oh the hell of it, Oh the smell of it, Oh the hell of the family life . . .'[12]

* * *

Evelyn continued to travel far afield during the 1950s, partly as an antidote to the depression that descended on him in winter, particularly at Christmas, which he always found a uniquely dispiriting time of year. In January 1951 he took Christopher Sykes on a tour of the Holy Land under the renewed patronage of Henry Luce, whose wife had enjoyed *Helena* even if most critics had not. As part of the bargain, Evelyn wrote a long article for Luce's *Life* magazine, which later became a short book, *The Holy Places*, published in 1952 by Ian Fleming's Queen Anne Press, with an extra essay on 'St Helena Empress'. By the summer of 1951, Evelyn had returned to fiction and told Graham Greene that he was writing 'an interminable novel about army life, obsessed by memories of military dialogue'.[13]

Greene was about to visit Piers Court with his mistress Catherine Walston, a beautiful and vivacious American-born Catholic convert whom Evelyn had known since before she and Greene became 'chums' (as Evelyn put it) and always liked. Mrs Walston was married with five children and although she told Evelyn that he had 'always been so good to and about us',[14] she had presumably got wind of his occasional splenetic outbursts against adulterers and wrote to Evelyn beforehand to check that her coming to stay would not 'embarrass' him in any way. Evelyn replied: 'Please believe that I am far too depressed by my own odious, if unromantic, sins to have any concern for other people's. For me it would be a delight to welcome you here.'[15] The visit was a great success and it was largely thanks to her that Evelyn saw much more of Greene over the next few years, cementing a close friendship that constantly defied their countless differences and disagreements.

The book that Evelyn was working on at the time of Greene's 1951 visit was *Men at Arms*, the first of his *Sword of Honour* trilogy based on his experiences in the Second World War, more closely autobiographical than any of his work to date and, like *Brideshead Revisited*, having the renewal of Catholic faith as its overall theme. *Sword of Honour* ranks as one of the finest works of fiction produced by the war, however *Men at Arms* had a rather mixed reception on its first publication in September 1952. The most appreciative review appeared in Luce's *Time* magazine, whose anonymous critic compared the experience of reading the novel to 'hearing a full keyboard used by a pianist who has hitherto confined himself to a single octave' and predicted that 'if his trilogy continues as well as it has begun, it will be the best British novel of World War II'.[16]

Evelyn managed to miss the dreaded family Christmas that year by taking himself off on a pilgrimage to Goa, where the relics of the great Jesuit missionary St Francis Xavier were being revealed for the last time on the 400th anniversary of his death: 'One brown stump of toe emerging from white wrapping,' Evelyn noted approvingly. 'Body fully vested, one grey forearm and hand, and grey clay-like skull visible.'[17] If this brings to mind the morticians at Forest Lawn, here Evelyn's attitude was strictly reverential and he postponed his own veneration until he could make it more privately. 'India is very like Stinkers,' he wrote home to Laura, who stayed behind with the children. 'There are cows wandering in all the gardens eating all the flowers. All the lower orders call me "master" which I find very familiar.'[18] When he got back he told Nancy that Goa had been 'heaven', the southern temples 'fascinating and exhilarating', the Indians 'more servile than most foreigners'. 'I can only bear intimacy really,' he added, '& after that formality or servility. The horrible thing is familiarity.'[19]

* * *

In the late spring of 1953, buoyed by the news that *Men at Arms* had won the James Tait Black Memorial Prize, Evelyn published *Love Among the Ruins*, a strange dystopian 'romance of the near future' which he had written the previous year. As usual he sent a special edition of this slim volume to friends, whose opinions he always valued far more than those of professional critics. 'Ta muchly, ole man, for your very generous present,' replied John Betjeman. 'It could not have come at a more appropriate moment, for only last Sunday I visited Stevenage New Town in the rainy afternoon. It was exactly like your book. Three miles of Lionel Brett-style prefabs interrupted by Hugh Casson blocks of flats and two shopping arcades and concrete lampposts throughout and no trees, only muddy

Hertfordshire inclines. I saw through the vast, unprivate ground floor window of a house, a grey-faced woman washing up. My goodness, it was terrifying. And the kiddies' scooters lying out in the rain on the streets and a big vita-glass school on stilts.'[20]

In the same way that their religious differences caused friction between Evelyn and Betjeman, their mutual abhorrence of modern architecture and town planning served as a strong bond, as did their shared liking for Gothic Revival decoration and furniture, although Evelyn's tastes were if anything rather bolder in this regard. For Evelyn's fiftieth birthday in October 1953 Betjeman gave him an elaborate – and as it turned out rather valuable – wash-hand stand that he had found in a junk shop in Lincoln. The stand was designed by William Burges, a follower of Pugin, whose freakish flourishes Betjeman suggested rendered people 'punch-drunk', and he could have been forgiven for thinking that his gift had had just that effect on his friend. 'Well, my dear fellow,' Evelyn wrote thanking him, 'all I can say is I am bowled over. What a present!'[21]*

But Evelyn's dizzy delight soon dissolved when the washstand arrived at Stinchcombe without one of the parts that he so vividly recalled seeing at the home of Patrick Kinross who had stored it temporarily for him in London. 'Sorry to be a bore,' Evelyn wrote to Kinross. 'The Betjeman Benefaction has arrived minus an essential organ – the serpentine bronze pipe which led from the dragon's mouth to the basin. I am making a row with Pickfords. Can you testify that it left your house intact?'[22] He also wrote to Betjeman, including a sketch of what he meant, but Betjeman had not the faintest idea what he was on about. 'Oh no, old boy,' he replied. 'There was never a pipe from the tap to the basin such as you envisaged.'[23] Evelyn wrote back just after New Year: 'I must see an alienist. These delusions are becoming more frequent.'[24]

Friends had for some time noticed that Evelyn was not quite himself. In the spring of 1952 he had asked Christopher Sykes if he would go with him to Sicily, but Sykes this time declined, explaining later: 'I had noticed a change coming over Evelyn lately. He was becoming more arrogant, more quarrelsome, and indulged his horrible delight in needling on sensitive spots more freely than usual ... when we did meet by chance he was

---

* When the young architectural historian Mark Girouard visited Piers Court in 1955 and was shown to his bedroom, he exclaimed 'Burges by God!' when he saw the wash-hand stand. 'Not bad,' wrote Evelyn to Betjeman. EW to IB, 4 July 1955, AWA

invariably unpleasant.'[25] Evelyn had long had a reputation for going a bit far, but now his behaviour seemed somehow even more demonic than before. In November 1952 Barbara Skelton, the celebrated femme fatale then married to Cyril Connolly, recorded Evelyn's wild performance at a party of Ann Fleming's (shortly after her divorce from Lord Rothermere and subsequent marriage to Ian Fleming), 'being rude to everybody, pretending he didn't know who Rosamond Lehmann was when she rushed up to greet him with open arms. Waugh criticised Alan Ross's beard and, when Cecil Beaton approached him when he was sitting on the sofa with Jennifer Ross, Waugh exclaimed, "Here's someone who can tell us all about buggery!" He then had to be carried into a taxi at three in the morning.'[26]

Though capable of periods of abstinence, particularly during Lent, Evelyn continued to drink prodigiously, especially during expeditions to London when even in middle age he was regularly sick before retiring to bed and not infrequently felt obliged to send flowers the next day to hostesses whose guests he had offended, occasionally enlisting the help of friends to atone for his gravest indiscretions. After one spree Evelyn paid a morning call to Diana Cooper, 'portly as an alderman,' as she reported to her son John Julius, 'dressed in loud and shapeless checks. He'd been obstreperous the night before and broken his host's decanters, so I had to dedicate an hour of my brief time to buying *amendes*.'[27]

The hangovers when he finally made it back to Piers Court might last several days, the symptoms invariably 'insomnia, a disordered stomach, weakness at the knees, a trembling hand which becomes evident when I attempt to use a pen'.[28] 'I get so painfully drunk whenever I go there,' he wrote to Nancy after a typical visit to London, '(Champagne, the shortest road out of Welfaria) and nowadays it is not a matter of a headache and an aspirin but of complete collapse, with some clear indications of incipient lunacy. I think I am jolly near being mad & need very careful treatment if I am to survive another decade without the strait straight? jacket.'[29]

All the long lunches and late-night carousing were now taking their toll. Long gone were the days when he felt fit enough to ride to hounds. Shortly after the war, when he went to stay with the Betjemans, he told Penelope he felt too old even to ride any more though he was still in his early forties. Even the various earth-moving operations that used to obsess him in the garden were becoming too strenuous. By 1953 he was spending much of his time in an armchair and feeling increasingly unwell: liverish, lethargic, and suffering intermittently from gout, arthritis, rheumatism and back pain. Like his fictional alter ego Gilbert Pinfold he 'ate less, drank more, and grew corpulent'. He also slept badly. If in the midst of writing something he might 'find the sentences he had written during the day running in his head, the words shifting and changing colour kaleido-scopically, so that he would again and again climb out of bed, pad down to the library, make a minute correction, return to his room, lie in the dark dazzled by the pattern of vocables until obliged once more to descend to the manuscript'.[30]

He developed the habit of getting up in the early hours to shave, having a theory that his smooth face on the smooth pillow induced sleep. But otherwise he relied on a cocktail of chloral and bromide to provide him with the 'six or seven hours of insensibility' he felt he needed to 'face another idle day with something approaching jauntiness'.[31] But the more resistant he became to the sleeping drugs, which he also used as a pain-killer during the day for his rheumatism, the more recklessly he increased the dose, with the result that he began to experience delusions and a memory that even before the Burges washstand episode he told Betjeman was 'not at all hazy – just sharp, detailed and dead wrong'.[32]

During the second half of 1953, Evelyn was also haunted by two inter-views he did for the BBC. The first of these, which according to Auberon Waugh 'eventually drove my father mad',[33] was for broadcast on the Over-seas Service and conducted by a man named Stephen Black in the library at Piers Court in August. Thirteen-year-old Bron listened to it all outside in the recording van and commented afterwards that the interviewer did not seem to like his father very much.[34] In the novel, Gilbert Pinfold has a similarly disagreeable experience at the hands of 'Angel' and his team, and when their BBC van disappears down the drive one of Mr Pinfold's children remarks, 'You didn't like those people much, did you, papa?'[35] But however little Evelyn liked them, for a decent enough fee he was prepared to go through it all again. Hence a few months later he was interviewed for the BBC Home Service's *Frankly Speaking* programme in London, where he was faced by three interviewers, including the same Mr Black. The questions this time were even less friendly, although Evelyn emerged from it with far more credit than his relentlessly po-faced and police-like interrogators. Having been asked about capital punishment and declared that he was in favour of it 'for an enormous number of offences', he was pressed on whether he would be prepared to carry out the executions himself. 'Do you mean actually do the hanging?' asked Evelyn. 'I should think it's very odd to choose a novelist for such tasks.'

Later Evelyn was asked 'in what respect do you as a human being feel that you have primarily failed?', to which he replied: 'I've never learnt French well, and I've never learned any other language at all. I've forgotten most of my classics; I can't often remember people's faces in the streets, and I don't like music. Those are very grave failings.'

'But no others you're conscious of?'

'Those are the ones that worry me most.'[36]

* * *

On New Year's Day 1954 the husband of the woman Evelyn loved more than any other besides Laura died at sea en route to Jamaica. In certain respects, Duff Cooper (who had been created Viscount Norwich in 1952) was quite similar to Evelyn, prone at times to extreme irascibility and uncontrollable rudeness, however as Evelyn had told Diana the previous summer, 'Duff and I have never hit it off.'[37]

There had been some spectacular set-tos over the years, most recently in April 1953 when Evelyn arrived at the Coopers' chateau at Chantilly 'plastered' after drinking a bottle of Burgundy and some brandy on the train, then set about baiting another guest and later said something offensive about Mountbatten at dinner, prompting an explosion from Duff: 'How dare a common little man like you, who happens to have written one or two moderately amusing novels, criticize that great patriot and gentleman? Leave my house at once!'[38]

After some subsequent frank exchanges, the two men eventually made up ('I have apologised to Norwich,' Evelyn told Diana, 'and he has accepted my apology, so that is O.K.')[39] but not before Diana had accused Evelyn of being unable to forgive or forget, and Evelyn had fired off one of his more wounding salvos at her: 'I am very sorry to hear that Duff was surprised and grieved to learn that I have detested him for 23 years. I must have nicer manners than people normally credit me with.'[40]

Duff was already unwell by this time, having suffered his first serious haemorrhage in May, a month after the great row at Chantilly, and the fateful trip at the end of the year had been planned with the idea of completing his convalescence. Even as they boarded Duff was feeling unwell and Diana tried in vain to persuade him that they ought to disembark before leaving Southampton. The next day at noon, New Year's Eve, 'it happened,' as Diana later told Cecil Beaton, 'a rush to the bathroom and a bigger, redder haemorrhage than he'd had before'.[41] He might have survived had he been able to get to a hospital, but on board a ship rolling about in heavy seas it was far more difficult to stem the loss of blood, and he died the following day in Vigo Bay at 3.30 p.m.

'All my prayers are for you and Duff,' Evelyn wrote to Diana when he heard the next day. 'If there is any service anywhere that I can do, command it. If my company would be at all comforting, call for me. Believe in my true, deep love.'[42] Having flown back with Duff's body, Diana could not face the funeral at Belvoir Castle on 6 January, and instead remained in London, where Evelyn spent an hour alone with her, finding her 'wild and witty, full of funny stories',[43] but also hearing a 'detailed account of Cooper's death agonies', as he recorded somewhat coldly in his diary. 'Not such a quick and clean ending as newspapers gave one to think.'[44]

* * *

Evelyn was far from well himself at the time, either physically or mentally, and the next month he set off for what was becoming his annual winter getaway, this time taking ship for Ceylon, the start of the terrifying voyage later chronicled in his avowedly autobiographical novel, *The Ordeal of Gilbert Pinfold*. Before leaving he had told Laura that he thought all the chloral might have caused 'problems with my nut' and it can scarcely have reassured her to get a letter from Cape St Vincent proposing to 'come home & lead a luny bin life for a while'.

'It was at 50 that Rossetti's chloral taking involved him in attempted suicide,' Evelyn added cheerfully, 'part blindness & part paralysis. We will avoid all that . . . To add to my balminess there are intermittent bits of 3rd Programme talks played in private cabin and two mentioned me very faintly and my p.m. [persecution mania] took it for other passengers whispering about me.'[45]

The other passengers had already noticed that Evelyn was behaving peculiarly, talking to the table lamps in the dining room and to the toast rack at breakfast, and repeatedly knocking on the cabin door below his and asking for 'Miss Margaret Black'. During a small dance on board, Evelyn complained that the music was driving him mad, and on another occasion he was seen crouching at the top of a flight of stairs in his pyjamas and then suddenly hurling a stool at an imaginary target. When they reached Port Said the captain persuaded him to disembark, and accompany a fellow passenger by car to Cairo. From there Evelyn wrote to Laura to say that he was 'resolved never to go anywhere without you again', and that he had been the victim of an experiment in telepathy 'real and true. A trick the existentialists invented – half mesmerism – which is most alarming when applied without warning or to a sick man.'[46]

From Cairo Evelyn flew on to Colombo, where he despatched another barking letter to Laura and one to Diana Cooper describing 'a group of psychologists a thousand miles away who read every word I write over my shoulder. As I write this I can hear their odious voices repeating it word for word ... It began with an elaborate series of practical jokes during which I was convinced I was insane. My sufferings were exquisite but now I know that it is merely a trick of telepathy.'[47]

Laura had grown increasingly alarmed by Evelyn's letters and after the one from Cairo she asked their neighbour Jack Donaldson, one of the few locals whom Evelyn got on with, if he would go with her to Colombo to help bring Evelyn home. But before they could get the necessary injections, Evelyn was on his way back and Laura travelled up to the Hyde Park Hotel in London to meet him.

Speaking in a 'high, unrecognizable squeak',[48] Evelyn began telling Laura the whole story of how he had been tormented on the voyage by the same Mr Black from the BBC who had recently interviewed him and chanced to be on board with his whole family, all of whom had used the powers of telepathy described in his letters to persecute him; only the daughter had shown any mercy. Evelyn mentioned to Laura that they both knew this Miss Black, having met her with a neighbour of theirs in Gloucestershire to whom she was engaged. 'But Evelyn,' Laura interrupted, suddenly twigging who he meant, 'her name wasn't Black, it was So-and-So, and she had nothing to do with the BBC man.'[49] Evelyn immediately realised that Laura was right and when she subsequently telephoned the BBC she was able to establish that Mr Black could not have been on Evelyn's voyage either as he had been ill in hospital for some weeks. Partially restored to his senses by this, Evelyn agreed that Laura should now summon their friend Father Philip Caraman, editor of the Jesuit periodical the *Month* for which Evelyn wrote. When Caraman arrived at about 7.30 p.m. he was greeted by Evelyn leaning across the dining-room table and pleading to be exorcised of the devils that were tormenting him. Evelyn also passed on some uncomplimentary remarks the voices had made about Caraman, and when Evelyn briefly left the table, the priest asked Laura whether his behaviour might be part of an elaborate joke of the sort he liked to play. Caraman promptly rang his friend Eric Strauss, an eminent Catholic psychiatrist, who came immediately and concluded that Evelyn had most likely been poisoned by his sleeping drugs, but then told him that the first thing he needed was a good night's sleep. He therefore wrote out a prescription for an alternative sedative, the vinegary-smelling paraldehyde which Evelyn would continue taking for the rest of his life despite lamenting that it gave him only four hours' sleep and 'spoils my zest for wine'.[50] A thorough check-up by a London physician later confirmed that Evelyn's hallucinations were indeed due to bromide poisoning, and after a few good nights' sleep he was back to normal.

Evelyn did not always seem to enjoy being the object of amusement, however in this instance, once the cause had been ascertained, he was eager to tell everyone about his spell of lunacy, retrospectively at least relishing the strangeness of the whole experience. 'I have been quite mad,'[51] he wrote to Diana, explaining his deranged letter to her from Ceylon; to Nancy Mitford, 'I've been suffering from a sharp but brief attack of insanity.'[52]* And to Cyril Connolly: 'I have had my first attack of insanity – quite a sharp one.'[53] When Evelyn met Christopher Hollis at Downside and was asked how he had been keeping, he replied: 'Been mad! Absolutely mad. Clean off my onion!'[54]

Not the least satisfying aspect of the whole episode was that it provided Evelyn with 'a hamper to be unpacked of fresh, rich experiences', from which to write what was to be his last comic novel. He began working on it after finishing *Officers and Gentlemen*, the second in the *Sword of Honour* war trilogy, which also coincided with the death of his mother

---

* Nancy had seen Evelyn's breakdown coming in December, telling Raymond Mortimer: 'He might go mad – madder at least.' (12 December 1953; cited in Selina Hastings, *Evelyn Waugh*, p. 558.)

in December at the age of eighty-four. 'Mrs Yaxley [her maid] found her dead in her chair after tea,' Evelyn wrote to his daughter Meg. 'I am afraid you will always remember her as very old & feeble. I wish you had known her when she was young and active.'[55] To Nancy Mitford he wrote that it was a 'happy release' for his mother who had grown tired of being so dependent 'but it fills me with regret for a lifetime of failure in affection & attention'.[56]

Evelyn began what he was soon calling his 'barmy book' early in the new year while on a restorative trip to Jamaica. He spent the first fortnight writing at a plantation house belonging to his old friend Perry Brownlow, recently widowed, remarried and drinking more than ever. Though indebted to Perry for so much hospitality over the years, Evelyn nevertheless found it 'a great intellectual strain to find words simple enough to converse with them. They are indeed a grisly household, gin from ten-thirty on . . . The women concentrate on a smooth sunburn and hairless bronzed shanks. The men lounge and yawn or play cards . . . There was a lady here who went to sleep on a mattress in a red bathing dress and all the vultures thought she was dead and bloody and tried to eat her.'[57] It was a relief to move on to the Flemings at Goldeneye, where Ian (aka 'Thunderbird') was busy working on *Diamonds are Forever*, 'an inspiring hive of industry & health', Evelyn wrote afterwards to Ann.[58]

Evelyn remained intermittently at work on *The Ordeal of Gilbert Pinfold* for the next two years. 'I am full in the middle of writing an account of my going off my rocker,'[59] he told Daphne Fielding in October 1956. Published in 1957, the novel included some of his most candid passages of self-revelation, but although the self-portrait he drew of 'the Artist in Middle Age' was typically funny, subtle and nuanced it effectively cemented his reputation as a grumpy symbol of reaction who abhors 'plastics, Picasso, sun bathing and jazz – everything, in fact, that had happened in his own lifetime'.

[Mr Pinfold] wished no one ill, but he looked at the world sub specie aeternitatis and he found it flat as a map; except when, rather often, personal annoyance intruded. Then he would come tumbling from his exalted point of observation.

Shocked by a bad bottle of wine, an impertinent stranger or a fault in syntax, his mind like a cinema-camera trucked furiously forward to confront the offending object close-up with glaring lens; with the eyes of a drill sergeant inspecting an awkward squad, bulging with wrath that was half-facetious.

He was neither a scholar nor a regular soldier; the part for which he cast himself was a combination of eccentric don and testy colonel and he acted it strenuously, before his children and his cronies, before it came to dominate his whole outward personality. When he ceased to be alone, when he swung into his club or stumped up the nursery stairs, he left half of himself behind and the other half swelled to fill its place. He offered the world a front of pomposity* mitigated by indiscretion, that was as hard, bright, and antiquated as a cuirass.[60]

Besides a few sharply dissenting voices, most critics considered *The Ordeal of Gilbert Pinfold* to be one of Evelyn's finest works. Writing in the *New Statesman*, John Raymond hailed Evelyn as 'the only major writer in English whose work reveals any genuine signs of development' and said that in reverting to his earliest manner he had 'given us one of his wittiest, most humane entertainments'.[61] Philip Toynbee in *The Observer* confessed to being no great admirer of what he saw as the 'mannered precision' of Evelyn as a stylist, yet concluded that 'these are the self-revelations of a remarkably honest and brave man who has allowed us to see that he is a likeable one'.[62]

---

* 'I have grown stouter and worse tempered and more pompous,' Evelyn told Diana Cooper in 1949. 'Women don't understand pomposity. It is nearly always an absolutely private joke – one against the world. The last line of defense.' 21 December 1949; *MWMS*, p. 105.

Suitably Sequestered

Evelyn had never quite rediscovered his love for Piers Court after return-ing to live there at the end of the war and had lately grown restless. As his grandson observes: 'He enjoyed making, decorating and improving houses, but once these things were done he lost interest.'[1] He was also alarmed by the imminent threat of development around the local town of Dursley, two miles away, but the final straw came in June 1955 when the *Daily Express* journalist Nancy Spain turned up uninvited on his door-step one evening shortly before dinner.

An exuberant early television 'personality' known for her mannish clothes and proudly lesbian love life* – numbering Marlene Dietrich among her various girlfriends – Miss Spain was also 'a lively, if not very literary, book critic',[2] as her obituary put it when she died in a plane crash a decade later, and a 'special' feature writer known for her stunts. She had telephoned Piers Court earlier in the day to ask if she and her companion, Lord Noel-Buxton, might come and see Evelyn and been firmly told by Laura that her husband was 'not at home to the *Daily Express*'.[3] They came nonetheless, and when Evelyn asked why they had ignored the sign at the gate stipulating 'No Admittance on Business', Lord Noel-Buxton, a tall, timid eccentric briefly on the staff of *Farmers' Weekly* and occasionally in the news for attempting to wade across rivers, spluttered: 'I'm not on business. I'm a member of the House of Lords.'[4]

Shortly afterwards, Evelyn wrote a piece for *The Spectator* in which he ruminated on the dotty peer's 'moving and rather mysterious words': 'In

---

* In the more innocent early 1960s, when the *News of the World* hired Nancy Spain as a columnist, the paper proclaimed: 'She's gay, she's provocative . . . she's going places.'

Lord Noel-Buxton we see the lord predatory. He seems to think that his barony gives him the right to a seat at the dinner-table in any private house in the kingdom.'[5]

Privately, Evelyn had been 'tremulous with rage' all evening after the intrusion, as he recorded in his diary. 'And all next day.'[6] Within two weeks he had put the 'polluted' Piers Court on the market, although not before opening his doors to an American television crew under the misapprehension that they would pay him $100 for his trouble. As Evelyn recalled, it was an 'excruciating' day: 'The impresario kept producing notes from his pocket: "Mr Waugh it says here that you are irascible and reactionary. Will you please say something offensive?"'[7]

On 4 July Evelyn wrote to the estate agents Knight Frank & Rutley: 'You may remember that you came here about nine years ago when I had the idea of moving to Ireland. Now I have the idea of moving anywhere. I am sick of the district . . . I don't want the house advertised. But if you happen to meet a lunatic who wants to live in this ghastly area, please tell him.'[8] Another year passed before they found what they were looking for, a 'cosy, sequestered' house in 'very pretty truly rural surroundings' at Combe Florey, seven miles north-west of Taunton, with, as Evelyn told Nancy Mitford 'possibilities of beautification'. 'If only I were a pansy without family cares I could make it a jewel.'[9]

He regarded Combe Florey as 'a suitable place to end my days'. Among its attractions, he told Ann Fleming, was 'a lunatic asylum bang next door which is valuable (a) for me if I get another go of barminess (b) in providing indefatigable gardeners at slave wages (c) husband for Harriet [Waugh]'.[10] He sold Piers Court for £9,500 in June and three months later paid £7,500 for Combe Florey.

The much-needed surplus which he had earmarked for all the planned improvements was doubled in February 1957, four months after their move, by a tax-free award of £2,000 libel damages. Soon after her visit, Nancy Spain had conveniently published an article suggesting Evelyn was an embittered and unsuccessful writer whose total first edition sales were 'dwarfed' by those of his brother's recent novel *Island in the Sun*, which had sold 60,000 copies 'as a direct result of my *Daily Express* notice', maintained Miss Spain – 'rather overstating the case,' as the judge later remarked. But, as the judge also said in his summing-up, some of her other assertions were 'hopelessly inaccurate',[11] Evelyn's books having sold well over four million copies in Britain and America and his total first edition sales amounting to 180,000. Evelyn nevertheless neurotically convinced himself that he would lose the case and his fears were intensified while the jury was out when his counsel, his old Oxford friend Gerald Gardiner, apologised for 'letting him into a mess' and disconcertingly hinted that he might have to pay costs of £5,000.

'At the end of the first day I would have settled for a fiver,' Evelyn later told Nancy Mitford. 'But I had taken the precaution of telling the Dursley parish priest that he should have 10% of the damages. His prayers were answered in dramatic, Old Testament style. A series of Egyptian plagues fell on Sir Hartley Shawcross from the moment he took up the case, culminating in a well-nigh fatal motor accident to his mother-in-law at the very moment when he had me under cross-examination & was making me feel rather an ass. He had to chuck the case and leave it to an understrapper ... I had a fine solid jury who were out to fine the Express for their impertinence to the Royal Family, quite irrespective of any rights or wrongs.'[12] The defendant, he told Diana Cooper, had 'perjured herself frequently but behaved in a gentlemanly way afterwards, gripping my hand and saying "better man won"'.[13]

Alec had flown over from Tangier, where he now lived for much of the year, to bolster his brother's case: 'You flitted out of court like a rare tropical butterfly,' Evelyn wrote to him afterwards, '& I assumed you were off to your exotic pleasures. Else I should have sought you out to thank you for your startling loyalty in coming to my chilly island to give evidence on my behalf.'[14]

Evelyn's Combe Florey beautification budget received another valuable boost in April with a further £3,000 damages from the Beaverbrook press, this time over its review of a new edition of *The Meaning of Treason* by Beaverbrook's old flame and Evelyn's old friend Rebecca West, in which she had accused him and Graham Greene of having 'created a climate of cackbrained confusion between virtues and vices ... a climate in which the traitor flourishes' – a view endorsed by the *Daily Express*'s literary editor in his review. Evelyn's earlier suit against Rebecca West's publishers had resulted in the withdrawal of her book, an outcome for which she never forgave him even though he had mercifully not pressed for damages, and besides which she was scarcely in a position to complain, having herself recently suppressed the autobiographical novel by her illegitimate son with H. G. Wells because of its unflattering portrayal of his parents.*

The libel victories were immensely gratifying for Evelyn, not least since the Beaverbrook press appeared to have been waging a vendetta against him for many years, culminating in various recent sneering profiles and some particularly hostile reviews of *Love Among the Ruins* in 1953. Evelyn's association with Lord Beaverbrook stretched back to his inglorious stint as a cub reporter on the *Daily Express* in 1927 and he first portrayed the power-crazed press baron as Lord Monomark in *Vile Bodies* (his original name, Ottercreek, in the manuscript gave a fairly strong hint as to whom Evelyn had in mind) and more memorably as Lord Copper in *Scoop*, at which point Beaverbrook took Evelyn's publishers to court over the original cover claiming (with good reason) that the lettering the *Daily Beast*'s masthead immediately brought to mind the *Daily Express*. The cover was changed to omit the offending masthead but thereafter Evelyn could not help thinking that his treatment by the Beaverbrook papers was somewhat less than friendly.

The tax-free £5,000 damages were very welcome too, counterbalancing Evelyn's customary extravagance in decorating his new house. 'I have been buying objects like a drunken sailor – candelabra, carpets, fireplaces,' he told Ann Fleming shortly before the first libel award. 'The prodigious sideboard which I bought at Ston Easton has been erected with an infinity of skilled labour.'[15] He had also set aside some of winnings for a luxurious holiday in Monte Carlo with Laura, but his old friend Monsignor Ronald Knox was dying of liver cancer and instead Evelyn agreed that they would accompany him on a depressing trip to the south Devon seaside. Evelyn had known Ronnie Knox as an illustrious and inspirational fellow Catholic convert (and fellow castle creeper, their detractors might add) since the early 1920s and a decade later Knox had been instrumental in persuading Mary Herbert of Evelyn's merits as a potential son-in-law. Their friendship had deepened after the war, when Knox moved from being private chaplain to the Actons at Aldenham Park in Shropshire, where he did the first of his famous Bible translations, to the Asquiths at Mells and became a regular visitor to Piers Court. In 1950 Knox had asked Evelyn to be his literary executor. Evelyn tried to persuade him to come to Monte

---

* *Heritage*, by Anthony West, was published in America in 1955 but Rebecca West's threat to sue anyone who published the book in Britain meant that it only appeared there in 1984, after her death.

Carlo, and failing that Brighton, but Knox was too unwell to travel far so Torquay it had to be. 'Torquay is absolute hell,'[16] Evelyn wrote to Jack Donaldson soon after arriving. 'Poor Ronnie is very infirm & fretful,' he told Ann Fleming, 'can't eat, drink or read. All that gives him any relief is laborious crossword puzzles ... [he] talks as though he will be on my hands for a month. I love and revere him, but oh dear –.'[17] After a week Laura excused herself in order to greet some new cows while they moved on to Sidmouth. But Evelyn soon found that 'ghastly' too, so he took Knox back for a fortnight to Combe Florey, where his stricken friend wrote most of the Romanes Lecture he was due to give that summer at Oxford, 'On English Translation'. 'It was an extraordinary feat,' Evelyn recorded. 'He was oppressed with lassitude and nausea. He had only his host's modest library to draw on. But the paper is as sharp and sparkling as any written in his youth.'[18]

Ronald Knox died that August, aged sixty-nine, but not before he had agreed to Evelyn's proposal that he should write his biography and, fortified by powerful drugs, triumphantly delivered his lecture at the Sheldonian, an occasion movingly described by Evelyn in his subsequent book: 'When half-way through, to illustrate a point, he [Knox] recited in full Cory's familiar rendering of the Greek epigram, "They told me Heraclitus, they told me you were dead," most of those present recognised those words as his own farewell to Oxford, and some with whom of old he had "tired the sun with talking" did not restrain their tears. The applause at the end was terrific.'[19]

Evelyn had been quick to knuckle down to his biography. 'Ronnie's death has transformed my life,' he told Diana Cooper that November. 'Instead of sitting about bored and idle I am busy all day long.'[20] It helped that he was already well acquainted with two of the people who knew most about Knox's life, Katharine Asquith and Daphne Acton, and he lost no time in tracking down Knox's surviving sister, Lady Peck, in Edinburgh, his old friend and disciple Laurence Eyres at Ampleforth and his confidant and confessor Dom Hubert van Zeller at Downside. Evelyn admitted that he felt out of his depth when it came to tackling Knox's spirituality, however Dom Hubert was reassuring. 'I am sure you are right about keeping off Ronald's religious life,' a relieved Evelyn wrote to him in January 1958, after their talk. 'He knew I knew nothing about it, but he wrote to Daphne that he could think of no one more suitable than me to write his biography. So he plainly wanted to be treated as a man of letters rather than of prayer. But of course a lot of people will say that I miss his essential point and of course they will be right.'[21]

In February 1958 Evelyn went out to stay with the Actons in Rhodesia, where they had emigrated after the war to farm at M'Bebi. There Lady Acton freely told him all about her intense platonic love affair with Knox while he had been preparing her for her conversion to Roman Catholicism in 1937, six years after her marriage to the 3rd Lord Acton, whose family had been Catholics for centuries. She sent Evelyn several bundles of their correspondence and urged him to write the biography 'as if I were dead',[22] despite admitting that while Knox had behaved 'with effortless chastity' throughout their relationship she had 'found it more of a strain'.[23] Evelyn greatly admired Daphne's beauty, intelligence and above all perhaps her candour. Her chaotic household (containing ten children) was 'everything that normally makes Hell,' he told Ann Fleming, except for 'Daphne's serene sanctity radiating supernatural peace'. She was, he added, 'the most remarkable woman I know'.[24]

Arriving back in England after his three-week trip, Evelyn got straight down to work and by June he had completed more than half of his manuscript, doing more research as he went along. 'It is a work of pietas,' he told Harold Acton, 'and I enjoy doing it.'[25] But then came the shocking news that Bron was fighting for his life in Cyprus after inadvertently letting off a machine-gun into his own chest while examining it in the turret of his armoured car. Laura flew out the next day, 11 June, and wrote to Evelyn:

Bron has lost one lung and his spleen. He has a shot through the shoulder and his left hand was badly wounded. The Blues doctor who is very nice and who met me when I arrived said his courage was really wonderful. He is an old Downside boy and he said that Bron's resignation and the way he quietly prayed on the way into the hospital had been an inspiring thing to witness and his bravery through it all. They say the next 48 hours are still very critical but he won't be off the danger list for at least another 10 days as there remains the danger of infection. Originally they thought he had no chance at all of surviving. I went and saw him for about 10 minutes tonight and he was clearly in a good deal of pain, particularly breathing – completely uncomplaining but finding hard to speak owing to lack of breath.[26]

Bron had joined the Royal Horse Guards the previous year, aged only seventeen, after choosing to do his National Service before going up to Oxford, a decision he had come to rue well before his horrific accident. When his parents sent him cakes and books to Caterham, Bron replied: 'I cannot tell you how comforting it is to think that there are benevolent agencies working somewhere outside this wilderness of malice and violence and stupidity.'[27]

But soldiering had seemed a good deal more agreeable since arriving on Cyprus: 'So much happens here that I cannot think where to begin,' he wrote to his parents. 'Life is immensely exciting and unbelievably comfortable.'[28] More ominously, he added: 'I cannot hit a human sized target at 10 yards with 20 shots once with my assured pistol, which I am constantly in fear of losing.'[29] On the day of Bron's accident, Evelyn wrote proudly to Diana Cooper: 'My boy is a cornet of the horse. I hope he has some fighting.'[30] A few days later he replied to her letter of sympathy: 'Details are wanting, but it sounds to me as though he will never completely recover. I shall go out to travel home with Laura if he dies.'[31]

Laura sent regular bulletins home and nine days after the accident Evelyn wrote to Ann Fleming: 'It has been an anxious week, but today the news from Cyprus makes it seem probable that Bron will survive. He stopped six bullets and has had a lung, his spleen, two ribs and part of a hand removed. Few people can have lived after such a fusillade. All done by the unaided and independent action of a new-fangled machine gun. I have known many good soldiers hit by their own side (including a posthumous VC)* and several rather moderate soldiers who shot themselves. This is the first time I have known the weapon take control.'[32]

Evelyn's reaction to Bron's plight was in some ways reminiscent of the striking detachment he had displayed all those years ago when his baby daughter Mary died the day after she had been born. His decision not to accompany Laura to Cyprus to see Bron struck some people as odd, however he seems to have decided that his going would make no difference to his son's recovery. 'Prayer is the only thing,' he told Diana. 'The one good result of newspaper reports is that monks and nuns and priests all over the country are praying for him.'[33]

---

* Evelyn probably had in mind his fellow commando Geoffrey Keyes, VC, killed during the Rommel raid in 1941.

Laura Herbert: 'I love her very much,' Evelyn told Baby Jungman, 'and I think there is as good a chance of our marriage being a success as any I know.'

Laura's family home, Pixton Park, whose Irish shabbiness inspired Evelyn's portrait of Boot Magna Hall in *Scoop*.

Evelyn and Laura leaving the church after their wedding in 1936.

Piers Court in Gloucestershire a wedding present from Laura's grandmother.

Evelyn with the infant Teresa; and (*far right*) Laura, at Piers Court shortly before the outbreak of war.

The drawing room at Piers Court.

Evelyn in the Royal Marines, with 'as
smart a little moustache as Errol Flynn',
as Diana Cooper described it.

Bob Laycock: 'That every man in arms
should wish to be'.

Evelyn and Randolph Churchill in Croatia, on the British Military Mission to Tito's
partisans.

Hollywood, 1947: Evelyn and Laura with Sir Charles Mendl and Anna May Wong.

Above: The Piers Court household, 1947. Middle row, from left: Gladys Attwood (cleaning lady), Hatty, Laura, James, Evelyn, Evelyn's mother, Meg and old Mrs Attwood. Teresa and Bron are sitting in the foreground. Directly behind Evelyn stands the butler, Ellwood. Behind Meg is their nanny, Vera, next to the cowman, Norman Attwood.

Left: Evelyn and Laura returning to Plymouth from New York in the *Ile de France*, November 1950.

Evelyn in the library at Combe Florey.

Combe Florey, 1959. From left: Bron, Meg, Evelyn, Septimus, Teresa, James, Giovanni Manfredi, Hatty, Laura, Maria Manfredi.

Evelyn at the front of Combe Florey. The sign reads 'No Admittance on Business'.

Evelyn, Laura, James and the gardener, Walter Coggan – 'my rival Coggins', as Evelyn called him.

Evelyn and Meg on their trip to British Guiana in 1961.

Evelyn with Maimie Lygon and the newly-married Meg and Giles FitzHerbert.

Interviewed by John Freeman in the *Face to Face* television series, June 1960.

At Combe Florey in 1965. Back row, left to right: James, Bron (holding Alexander and Sophia), Laura, Evelyn, Teresa (with her son Justin), Margaret (with her daughter Claudia). Kneeling in front are Hatty and Septimus, with Emily FitzHerbert in the foreground.

Besides, by staying behind and holding the fort he was able pass on all Laura's farming instructions: 'Will you tell Giovanni* to give one spoonful of cake daily to Magdalen and Desdemona this week and two spoonfuls daily to them from next Monday. Also if Lucy is still giving 40lbs a day of milk she had better be artificially inseminated the next time she comes bulling with the Aberdeen Angus bull. If she is not giving as much as 40lbs I do not want her served at all.'[34]

The same letter carried news that Bron would shortly be coming off the danger list. But Evelyn rightly suspected that his son's recovery would still be long and complicated. Hence he wrote to Bron's old housemaster at Downside, Father Aelred: 'Please continue to pray for him. I am sure it is prayer which has saved him so far.'[35] Similarly to Father Caraman: 'Please don't let any of the kind people who have been praying for him turn to other topics.'[36] Whenever Bron suffered a setback, Evelyn suspected all the nuns and monks and clergy and laity who had been 'praying like mad' of suddenly slackening off. When he made progress, the reverse was assumed to be the case. 'The Novena has worked,' Evelyn wrote to Daphne Acton in August. 'My son has taken a turn for the better. Thanks awfully. It was most obliging of you.'[37]

Bron was eventually flown back to the Queen Alexandra Military Hospital at Millbank in early July. 'Welcome home,' wrote Evelyn. 'I am delighted that you have escaped from the torrid and treacherous island of Cyprus. I wish I could come and greet you but I have a long-standing and very tedious engagement in Germany. It started as a treat for your mother, who now can't come with me. I am being paid to stand up in a theatre in Munich and read aloud for an hour to an audience of Huns who think that such a performance will somehow help celebrate the 800th anniversary of the foundation of their city. I am sure neither the Huns nor I will enjoy it.'[38]

Evelyn finally saw Bron a week later and promptly resolved to have him transferred to the more comfortable King Edward VII's Hospital for Officers (Sister Agnes) in Marylebone. But an abscess on Bron's back promptly developed into a chronic infection of his chest cavity, and he was instead moved to the Westminster Hospital to be cared for by Sir

---

* Giovanni Manfredi was employed at Combe Florey to wait at table as well as acting as cowman; his wife Maria did the cooking.

Clement Price Thomas, 'a noted chest surgeon,' as Bron later recorded, 'who had chiefly distinguished himself by his unsuccessful operation on the late King George VI for lung cancer'.[39]

Desperately ill and afraid once again that he might die, Bron scribbled a letter to his father: 'Dear Papa, Just a line to tell you what for some reason I was never able to show you in my lifetime, that I admire, revere and love you more than any other man in the world. My possessions belong to you in any case, and will obviously be retained, divided or jumble-sold at your discretion, but I should very much like my collection of gramophone records to be given to the Grothiers (that is Vera [the Waughs' nanny] and her husband). Love Bron.'[40] He sent this to his bank in a sealed envelope with instructions that it was to go to his father in the event of his pre-deceasing him.

By early August, Bron was still too weak for the major operation that Sir Clement had planned and so the surgeon suggested that he go to King Edward VII's Hospital after all. 'He is now fattening up in Sister Agnes's home for butchery and is greatly enjoying himself being much pampered by all,' Evelyn told Daphne Acton. 'This is primarily to say stop praying for Bron. I am sure there are more urgent cases waiting for your attention.'[41] As a serving officer Bron was admitted free and Evelyn now informed his son that he was stopping the £25 a month allowance he had been paying him as he was short of money and Bron would not need it in hospital, a decision that caused Bron to weep 'bitter tears of rage' by his own account, although naturally he did not say so in his next letter to his father: 'Far from being upset by your action,' Bron replied, 'I am enormously grateful that you should have been so generous as to continue my allowance up to this moment. I hope that you soon overcome your financial difficulties. Mushroom growing is said to be remunerative or you could open a lodging house.'[42]

But his condition continued to fluctuate: 'The news of him is in-decisive,' Evelyn wrote to Father Aelred in October. 'He has been moved back and forth between three hospitals and is now at the Westminster. Sir Somebody Something can't make up his mind when to operate.' He added that the 'pampering' Bron was getting was 'inevitable but regrettable, just when the regiment was making a man of him. Please include in your prayers for his physical welfare prayers for his strength of character, when you are so good as to pray for him.'[43] Evelyn wrote along similar lines to Bron's godmother Maimie Lygon, saying that his character was being undermined by 'well disposed people sitting round his bed and satisfying his every whim . . . Perhaps you will go & beat him & rob him and undo all the bad work of others.'[44]

When Bron turned twenty that November, Evelyn wrote to him: 'Many happier returns of the day. It has been a year of triumph and disaster, has it not? I am sure you feel very much more than a year older. To have looked into the throat of death at 19 is an experience not to be sneered at.' In the same letter he encouraged him to give up the idea of reading English at Oxford: 'It is a fatal school for anyone who may, as I hope you will, become a writer . . . But you are master of your fate and captain of your soul now you are out of your teens.'[45]

Bron finally left hospital the following March. 'At about this time,' he later wrote, 'I began to be quite fond of my father, never having liked him much in childhood or early youth. As I prepared to leave home and set up my own establishments elsewhere he became more tolerant of my various failings, and in the last five years of his life we enjoyed a distinct cordiality.'[46]

If Evelyn's relations with his eldest son had been strained at times, those with his middle daughter Margaret occasionally bordered on a love affair. Known in the family as Meg, and by Evelyn variously as 'pig', 'disgusting hog' and 'sweet swine', Margaret had been his 'eye-apple' ever since she was about five and prematurely allowed to eat in the dining room to save her from a violent nanny. Before sending her to boarding school aged nine, Evelyn described her to the headmistress as 'very pretty, very stupid, with abounding charm'.[47] She was soon homesick and it was while spending the summer term of 1953 being educated at home by Evelyn that she became 'his official favourite', as she later recalled, 'a position neither resented nor sought by my siblings and one which carried with it the risks of disproportionate disfavour as well as the advantages of privilege'.[48]

The previous year Evelyn had written to Ann Fleming: 'My sexual passion for my ten year old daughter is obsessive, I wonder if you'll come to feel this way about your son. I can't keep my hands off her.'[49] If this was most likely a provocative joke, designed to shock his proudly unshockable friend, Evelyn's bond with Meg was clearly intense and became increasingly so as a result of her unhappiness at school. 'When we meet you must tell me whether you are really unhappy or merely giving way to a silly

mood. I love you & will not let you be really unhappy if I can prevent it
... darling little girl.'[50]

Defiant, capricious and intermittently lazy as a teenager, Meg was often
in trouble at St Mary's Ascot. Evelyn was invariably reassuring, if not un-
critically so. 'Darling Meg,' he wrote shortly before her fifteenth birthday,
'I am sorry you are in hot water. You do not have to tell me that you have
not done anything really wicked. I know my pig. I am absolutely confident that you will never be dishonourable, impure or cruel ... the part
of your letter I don't like at all is when you say the nuns "hate" you. That
is rubbish. And when you run down girls who behave better than you.
That is mean. Chuck it, Meg ... You are loved far beyond your deserts,
especially by your Papa.'[51]

Eventually Meg and the school had decided they had enough of one
another and in 1958, aged 15, a few months before Bron's accident, she had
returned home again to be taught by Evelyn. 'Bron has got his commission in the Blues,' Evelyn wrote to Diana Cooper at the time, '– many sons
of old Blues failed. He must have some guts. He succeeds. Scholarship at
the House [Christ Church, Oxford] and now this. But he's a queer morose
boy, sloping round the woods with a gun alone or playing light opera on
his gramophone. Teresa has had a dazzling term academically. But Meg
for me anytime though she's jolly fat at the moment and eats an abnormal
amount.'[52]

To Maime Lygon later that year Evelyn described Meg as 'the joy of my
heart, perhaps what you were to Boom only she does not bring me cocktails in my bath'.[53] That Christmas, with Bron still in hospital in London,
Evelyn seized the opportunity to spend three days at the Hyde Park Hotel
with Meg. 'Our ostensible reason,' he told Ann Fleming, 'is to protect
Bron from the worst of the Welfare festivities when he fears a Saturnalia
when all the nurses dress up as surgeons and the surgeons as nurses and
sing carols. My motive is to escape the Saturnalia at home, Margaret's to
visit the theatre and the Cathedral. It will be easier to keep her sober when
I have my eye directly on her.'[54]

* * *

Evelyn finally finished his Knox biography in early January 1959 and a
few weeks later set off for his annual winter holiday, this year comprising

a two-month tour of Central and East Africa. 'I have let myself in for crossing the whole of Darkers,' he wrote to Diana Cooper, 'and writing a sickening account of it when I get home. Damn.'[55] He returned in April feeling greatly rejuvenated and was soon 'half heartedly writing a travel book of ineffable tedium and triviality'[56] to pay for his trip. *A Tourist in Africa* (1960) is as elegantly written as one might expect and has several very funny passages, however it was fair to say, as Cyril Connolly did, that it was 'quite the thinnest piece of book-making that Mr Waugh has undertaken'.[57]

Of far more importance to Evelyn was the reception of his latest magnum opus, *Ronald Knox*, which was published by Chapman & Hall in the autumn of 1959. Just before publication his agent Peters had told Evelyn that he would value his copy of *Knox* above all his books 'because I suspect that you have put into it more care, thought, time and slogging hard work than into anything else you have written. Certainly it is the most difficult task you have ever undertaken. And certainly it is triumphantly achieved.'[58] The critics on the whole agreed, even Graham Greene, who admitted to finding the subject at times 'repellent', and the sales greatly exceeded expectations, surpassing 12,000 copies within a month.

The book was not without inaccuracies, as detailed in a 2,500-word letter to the author from the Archbishop of Westminster, but Evelyn accepted the corrections with good grace and promised to amend the next edition. Rather more embarrassing for him was the identification of someone both he and Knox had carefully disguised in their books as 'C', a young Etonian whom Knox had fallen platonically in love with while tutoring him for an Oxford scholarship. 'The question you asked me about the identity of "C" in *Knox*,' Evelyn wrote to Maurice Bowra, 'has been answered in the newspapers by prize shit Muggeridge, who bluffed the truth out of my aged mother-in-law.'[59] The mystery person was none other than the then Prime Minister, Harold Macmillan, quite a scoop for Malcolm Muggeridge in his *New Statesman* diary and perhaps doubly satisfying (or revenge even) given that two years earlier Evelyn had ostentatiously discarded his ear-trumpet during a speech Muggeridge made at a Foyles' luncheon given in Evelyn's honour.

In January 1960 he set off on another winter jaunt, enjoying 'a ripping time at the expense of the *Daily Mail*'[60] in Venice and Monte Carlo with

Laura, followed almost immediately by a trip with Margaret to Athens to visit his old friend Coote Lygon, who was living there at the time (her family formed a theory that she was a spy), and then Rome, returning to Combe Florey in early March. Two weeks later, for a £250 fee he agreed to appear on *Face to Face*, the TV interview series which had begun the previous year and already featured an array of luminaries ranging from Carl Jung to King Hussein of Jordan.

'Please make it a condition that all letters addressed to me at BBC are returned to senders marked "address unknown",' Evelyn wrote to Peters beforehand. 'I have been greatly annoyed by readers of *Pinfold* who wish to compare their hallucinations with mine.'[61] As his grilling drew nearer he contacted Tom Driberg: 'I have let myself in for cross-examination on Television by a man named Major Freeman who I am told was a colleague of yours in the Working Class Movement. Do you know anything damaging about him that I can introduce into our conversation if he becomes insolent?'[62] But he need not have feared. John Freeman may have been a far shrewder and more penetrating interviewer than Stephen Black, but Evelyn again comfortably had the upper hand, his sharp responses as calm as they were clever and delivered with a gleam in his eyes that suggested only mild bemusement at all the impertinent questions he was being asked to answer. Freeman later described it as his most disappointing interview, perhaps because he was so consistently outmanoeuvred during their exchanges:

'Are you a snob at all?'

'I don't think.'

'Irritability with your family, with strangers?'

'Absolutely everything. Inanimate objects and people, animals, everything.'

'Have you ever brooded on what appeared to you to be unjust or adverse criticism?'

'No. I'm afraid if someone praises me I think "What an ass", and if they abuse me I think "What an ass".'

'And if they say nothing about you at all and take no notice of you?'

'That's the best I can hope for.'

'You like that when it happens?'

'Yes.'

'Why are you appearing in this programme?'

'Poverty. We've both been hired to talk in this deliriously happy way.'

Having spent so much time for so little reward (his advance was £3,000) on the *Knox* biography, Evelyn had good reason to be worried about money. Beset by punitive taxation and with his *Brideshead* royalties having long since virtually dried up, he struggled to maintain the standard of living that he had enjoyed before the war. He had let go of Ellwood, the butler, when they moved to Combe Florey and after Giovanni and Maria Manfredi finally left in early 1961 they had only daily help in the house; later that year they acquired 'an engine for washing plates' which quickly became 'an object of worship like a tractor in an early Bolshevist film'.[63]

Evelyn was in some ways quite relieved to see the Manfredis go. Besides the fact that Laura no longer had to contend with the 'nervous annoyances of their tantrums and avarice',[64] as Evelyn saw it, she also had less to occupy her after selling all her beloved cows, another consequence of their reduced circumstances. 'Laura has at last had to give up her herd of cows and mourns them,' Evelyn told Diana Cooper that Christmas Eve just past. 'They cost as much to keep as a troupe of ballet girls and the horrible politicians made a law that one can no longer charge them against income tax.'[65]

Evelyn was at the time hard at work on *Unconditional Surrender*, the final novel in his war trilogy, which he had begun in April 1960 and would take a year to write. His expected earnings from the book were modest, however he still had his artistic vocation to fulfil, as he explained to his publisher: 'Soon I shall have to jump at every chance of writing the history of insurance companies or prefaces to school text-books. Squire and Belloc warn us of the horrors of longevity. But meanwhile, while I have any vestige of imagination left, I must write novels.'[66]

To add to his expenses, between finishing his book in the spring and publishing it in the autumn of 1961, his two eldest children were married. In her last year at Oxford Teresa had met and fallen in love with a postgraduate Classics scholar from Princeton called John D'Arms, whom she first brought to Combe Florey in the spring of 1959. After a subsequent visit that summer, Evelyn wrote to Bron: 'He is not superficially very American (his father, too, was at Oxford), dresses somberly, parts his hair

and speaks in low tones. But he has the basic earnestness of his compa-
triots which I should find unendurable. However that is Teresa's business,
not mine. I am sure he would be a kind and conscientious husband and
I shall not have to talk to him.'[67] After receiving John's formal request to
marry Teresa in November 1960, Evelyn wrote to congratulate his future
son-in-law 'on your successful courtship of my daughter' and 'still more
on your resolution to become a Catholic'. 'I am sending you her pedigree,'
he added. 'It is not illustrious on my side but it will demonstrate that she
has no unacceptable taints in her blood.'[68]

Bron, meanwhile, had lately been seeing a lot of a bright young brunette
called Teresa Onslow and in early 1961 they too agreed to marry, a decision
which Evelyn feared they had come to 'in a mood of irresponsible high
spirits which reminds me painfully of my marriage to Evelyn [Gardner],'*
as he told Pansy Lamb.[69] Bron and Teresa were both only twenty-one at
the time and she declined to convert to Catholicism, however on the plus
side she was the daughter of the 6th Earl of Onslow and descended from
more British monarchs than George VI, the king at the time of her birth.[70]
'It is very distressing that my son should think of marriage at an age when
he should give himself to the education of a *femme du monde de quarante
ans*,' Evelyn wrote to Jack Donaldson, 'but, as you remark, in this age of
miscegenation it is agreeable that he should have chosen a consort of his
own class.'[71] And to his brother Alec: 'Your nephew Auberon Alexander
has imprudently become engaged . . . a Protestant alas, but pretty & sharp.
I don't know her well but I think he is fortunate.'[72]

The prospect of both weddings filled Evelyn with a mixture of gloom
and anxiety. 'My life at the moment is hideously overshadowed & agitated
by weddings,' he wrote to Daphne Fielding in May. 'I have a daughter
marrying a studious & penniless yank in a fortnight and hard on that
a son marrying a pretty, well endowed English girl. But the turmoil &
expense are damnable.'[73]

Teresa and John D'Arms were married by Father D'Arcy at a Catholic
church in Taunton at the beginning of June, with the reception held at
Combe Florey. Evelyn later confided to a Catholic friend that the ring
had been placed on Teresa's right hand, adding: 'I hope this will provide
grounds for a suit of nullity.'[74] He was not so much against the match

---

* Lady Teresa Onslow was Evelyn Gardner's first cousin twice removed.

as anxious that his daughter should have an escape route (rather in the same way that some nervous parents nowadays insist on a 'prenup') in case anything went wrong – bearing in mind of course the problems he had had disentangling himself from Evelyn Gardner. Evelyn found the prolonged wedding celebrations 'extremely painful', although John's parents, who came over from Massachusetts, turned out to be 'rather a jolly couple and quite indefatigable', their remarkable stamina over several days staying with the Waughs leaving Evelyn 'prostrated',[75] he told Ann Fleming. When they had all gone, he wrote tenderly to his 'dear first-born' daughter: 'I think you have found an exceptionally nice husband and am confident of your happiness.'

By way of a postscript he added: 'Yesterday's *Sunday Times* had an article on paternity by Mr. Mathew M.P. He said it was essential to the happy relations of fathers and children that they should congregate at bath-time. The children should stand around their father's bath. The spectacle of his nakedness and wetness while they are clothed and dry establishes confidence and equality. I am sorry I failed you in this.'[76]

Bron and Teresa's wedding was to take place a month later in London, in the same Warwick Street church where Evelyn and Laura had married, but as the day loomed Evelyn began to look for ways he might possibly wriggle out of it. Bron was alive to the danger, having previously failed to entice Evelyn to either his passing out parade or his twenty-first birthday party at the Hyde Park Hotel, the latter paid for by Chapman & Hall and combined with a book celebration for Bron's first novel *The Foxglove Saga*, which had quickly sold 14,000 copies in hardback. As Alexander Waugh records: 'The party was crowded with important people – the Prime Minister, the Duke and Duchess of Devonshire, Sir Isaiah Berlin and many of Evelyn's closest and oldest friends – but Evelyn and Laura stayed at home.'[77] A week prior to the wedding, Bron wrote to Evelyn: 'I hope you will have the fortitude to remain throughout the reception – at any rate until the hand shaking and photographing are over.'[78] A few days later Evelyn wrote back: 'Your sister Margaret has the grippe [flu]. I may have to stay and nurse her while your mother attends your nuptials.'[79] But Laura made sure he went in the end.

Four days later Evelyn told Meg that he had 'nearly' recovered from the wedding. 'What I have not recovered from is the photograph of myself in the *Sunday Express*. I had no idea how old & gross I had become. As I eat nothing it must be drink. Not a drop of wine, whisky or gin has passed my lips since Sunday. I hope when we next meet you will notice a great change.'[80] Evelyn had lately been getting through half a bottle of spirits and a bottle of wine a day. Once on his austere regime, on which he was soon claiming to have 'shrunk to a little wizened monkey',[81] he found he did not miss it, although as so often when he stopped drinking he became rather silent and depressed. Only this time the gloom would prove harder to dislodge.

Decline and Fall

'Only when one has lost all curiosity about the future has one reached the age to write an autobiography.'[1] So begins *A Little Learning*, the first of a projected three-part autobiography which Evelyn started shortly after the two weddings, in July 1961. Assured by Peters that the three volumes should bring in 'over £29,000 – say £5,000 a year for six years',[2] Evelyn began by reading a draft of *The Early Years of Alec Waugh*, his brother's memoir which was due out the next year, and afterwards thanked Alec for 'the kind things you say about me'. He tactfully told his brother what 'a deep interest & pleasure' it was to read his book,[3] but later confided to his daughter Meg that it was actually '*not very nice* – a great deal of boasting about his sexual adventures,'[4] and to Diana Mosley that he considered it 'embarrassingly revealing'.[5]

Still on his post-wedding slimming regime, Evelyn was intrigued to learn that Alec was in the habit of 'spending one day in ten in bed totally fasting and so preserves his monkey-like figure'.[6] 'Twice a day I drink a small glass of cider,' he told Ann Fleming the next month. 'I have halved my consumption of cigars. I have become totally silent. Sometimes I sally out with a scythe and after an hour totter back exhausted.'[7]

Towards the end of the summer, knowing that Evelyn would again want to escape the English winter, Peters arranged for him to retrace his steps of twenty-nine years ago in British Guiana, which became a self-governing country after elections that August, five years prior to gaining full independence. The *Daily Mail* agreed to pay £2,000 (to include travel expenses) in return for five articles, and also to cover the expenses of a 'secretary', in which capacity Evelyn proposed taking along his nineteen-year-old daughter Margaret. 'I am taking Meg with me partly for the pleasure of her company,' he told Teresa, by then living in Rome, 'but chiefly to detach her from the young men she spends her evenings with in London.'[8]

After failing to get into Oxford, Margaret had spent the past six months writing pamphlets about martyrs for the Jesuits at Farm Street ('My daughter is a hagiographer by trade,' her father told friends)[9] where Evelyn's old friend Father Philip Caraman quickly became infatuated with her. He assured Evelyn that in her reserve and soundness of judgement, Margaret was 'mature beyond her years'. 'She has an independence and sound sense that owes much to her deep devotion to you.'[10] But Evelyn worried that away from work his daughter led a life of reckless dissipation, 'pub crawling and *smoking* in Notting Hill Gate'.[11] The previous year he had opposed her plan to rent a room off Bron, telling her, 'You are no more ready for "independence" than the Congo,' and after she had an unsettling experience of drunkenness he advised her to 'go straight off & confess it,' and thereafter to be very careful: 'Don't on any account get tight or even noticeably jolly for a long time. What we don't want is for people to say, "There's that Waugh girl drunk again".'[12] On another occasion he wrote to her: 'I am told you drive recklessly. Don't do that, it's vulgar.'[13] When Meg proposed spending the weekend with a boyfriend at a cottage, Evelyn wrote to her: 'I know jolly well that no amount of chaperoning ever prevents those who want to fornicate from doing so. It is a matter of manners not morals. Well born, well brought up girls do not stay away with young men and well born, well brought up young men don't expect them to or respect them if they do.'[14] But the keeping of bad company persisted, in Evelyn's eyes at least, and in the spring of 1961 he told Ann Fleming: 'Meg is making herself obnoxious in London by moving about with a train of riff-raff who break into people's houses & eat all the food in their larders & drink all their whisky.'[15]

Meg often returned to Combe Florey for weekends, but Evelyn could never get enough of her company as she arrived late on Friday, slept all day Saturday and left again on Sunday. Occasionally he sounded needy: 'I gave you good warning that I should lose interest in you if you neglected me,' he wrote to Meg shortly before Teresa's wedding. 'A generous nature wishes to give, not always to take. A prudent nature seeks to keep in favour with those on whom it is dependent. An honourable nature keeps promises.'[16] Subsequently he reminded her: 'When Alec Waugh was your age he wrote to his father every day.'¹⁷ Yet as Evelyn suggested, Meg was as devoted to him as he was to her. 'You know I love you more than anyone else in the world,' she wrote after one slightly cross letter. 'Please don't stop loving me I couldn't bear it . . . Papa I'll give up living in London and come home for good if you like. I don't love any of my friends here one quarter as much as I love you.'¹⁸

Between the two weddings, with his younger daughter Harriet due to leave school that summer and in need of somewhere to live in London, Evelyn wrote to Diana Cooper enquiring about the basement of her newly acquired house in Little Venice: 'I am anxious to find rooms in London which my daughters Meg & Hatty could share this autumn, where a trusted friend could keep an eye on them. They could, when required, do devoted duty as ladies in waiting.' Diana replied enthusiastically, whereupon Evelyn sent her 'the essential data about the little girls':

<u>Harriet</u>. Aged 17. Low mentality, high character. She has inherited her father's deep love of you. She regards you as a lady of the theatre rather than of fashion or letters or high politics. She is pretty when she smiles which is often; sometimes she lapses into blank sullenness. She has no pleasure in rural life and no knowledge of the town. Strong theatrical interests. Strong sense of humour. Chaste, sober, wants to get married but has exaggerated ideas of her market value thinking only elder sons of old nobility suitable. Clean & economical. She leaves school this term without learning one word of any foreign language and is therefore unsuitable for finishing abroad. She goes with a school-friend whose father is on post there at our embassy, to Beirut for August and first three weeks of September. After that she will be a problem. I believe you might find her quite amusing and useful as understrapper. Can't spell at all. No secretarial qualities.

<u>Meg</u> aged 19 'works' all day with Jesuits at Farm Street. Drinks all night with impecunious young men. Expensive tastes. Snob. Chaste but self-indulgent. Smokes when I am not near. Loving but grasping. Has also inherited her father's love of you. Filthy in habits. Always in debt. At present she lives with her cousin Anne Fraser (60 Drayton Gardens, S.W.10. Fremantle 9000) who now has two babies & wants to be rid of her. I will not let her live alone. She can't find any suitable friend to share with. It would be no good setting her up with Hatty. She would not look after Hatty & Hatty would have nothing to do all day. Meg would enter with enthusiasm

into all your undertakings of house arrangement, talk engagingly while others toiled and do nothing herself. I find her company so bright that it compensates for her deplorable failings.[19]

The plan was postponed due to Diana's delayed return to London and eventually came to nothing, but by that time Evelyn had already conceived the idea of taking Meg with him to Guiana, an idea which Father Caraman fell in with, agreeing 'she is not sufficiently robust to work here during the day and then go to parties four or five evenings during the week, staying up till midnight and after. A long rest is just what she needs.'[20] To Ann Fleming Evelyn wrote: 'It will be good for her [Meg] to switch to rum for a bit. Port is inflaming her nose.'[21]

The final volume of Evelyn's war trilogy *Unconditional Surrender* was published shortly before they left, dedicated 'To my daughter Margaret, Child of the Locust Years'. As ever, Evelyn was more interested in the views of his friends and family than those of the critics, and most seemed to think that it was 'as good as anything you have ever written'.[22] Maurice Bowra rhapsodised about the 'endless variety in the use of words, the shape of the sentences, the adroit vocabulary. How I envy you . . .'.[23] Evelyn's mother-in-law Mary Herbert thought 'the wonderful chapter on Guy's father's death & funeral says all the central things about the heart of Catholic life & also the heart of the passing relationships of country life and squirearchy without any over emphasis'.

Among the published reviews, none was more glowing than Cyril Connolly's in *The Sunday Times*, acclaiming the trilogy as 'unquestionably the finest novel to have come out of the war',[24] a remarkably generous tribute given that Ann Fleming had convinced Connolly that Everard Spruce and *Survival* magazine was an unkind caricature of himself and *Horizon*. 'It is not very like him but sufficiently like him to be offensive,' wrote Bowra to Mrs Fleming. 'It is sad that Evelyn has such an urge to torture him. It must be a form of love.'[25] Fearing that Mrs Fleming's mischievous intervention had endangered what he termed 'a very long, the always slightly precarious, friendship,'[26] Evelyn did his best to mend fences: 'There are of course asses in London, who don't understand the processes of the imagination, whose hobby is to treat fiction as a gossip column,' he wrote to Connolly. 'But what distresses me (if true) is that you should suppose I would publicly caricature a cherished friend.'[27] Connolly remained sceptical: 'I do not think posterity will ever believe in our friendship any more than someone who looked me up in the index to your biography!'[28] As he prepared to set sail for British Guiana at the end of November, Evelyn made one final bid to soothe his half-hated friend with the news 'that the vampire bats of Amazonas are now infected with rabies, so we may not meet again'.[29]

By strange coincidence the ship on which Evelyn and Meg sailed out to the Caribbean was the same *Stella Polaris* on which he and his first wife had voyaged in the Mediterranean in 1929. This trip was far happier: 'Little Meg proved a good travelling companion,' Evelyn wrote to Diana Cooper on their return, 'never sea sick in the smallest ships in the worst storms, never complaining of discomfort but jolly appreciative of occasional bits of luxury. We came back in a lovely frog steamer full of decaying literary gents. Now her pecker is down & she wants to circumnavigate the globe.'[30] To Teresa he wrote: 'Meg met no one under 50 during her travels and is developing a pretty manner with the senile.'[31]

Among their hosts had been the sixty-year-old Lord Hailes, Churchill's former private secretary and by then Governor-General of the soon-to-be defunct Federation of the West Indies. Having stayed happily and luxuriously with the Haileses in Trinidad, Evelyn was taken aback to learn from Ann Fleming that 'the Haileses found Evelyn a great bore', gossip she had gleaned from Clarissa Avon. 'Well I mean to say,'[32] Evelyn wrote to Diana Cooper, convinced at first that Lady Avon must have got the wrong end of the stick. Later, as the reality sunk in, he wrote to Nancy:

I must explain about boring the Haileses because it has been what young people call 'traumatic'. Hailes was a pretty young politician you may have known as Patrick Buchan-Hepburn. I knew him slightly years ago . . . I had never met his wife but took a liking to her, and they were jolly hospitable to Meg & me. The crucial point is that I was confident they both enjoyed my visit. It made a lovely change, I thought, from most of their official visitors. When I briefly returned to Trinidad they sent ADCs to drag me back. I talked loud & long & they laughed like anything. Now I find I bored them. Well of course everyone is a bore to someone. One recognizes that. But it is a ghastly thing if one loses the consciousness of being a bore. You do see it means I can never go out again.[33]

Evelyn's self-esteem suffered another blow a week or so later after an encounter at White's: 'I was sitting in the hall at 7 p.m. being no trouble to anyone, when a man I know by sight but not by name – older than I, the same build, better dressed, commoner – came up & said: "Why are you alone?" "Because no one wants to speak to me." "I can tell you exactly why. Because you sit there on your arse looking like a stuck pig."'[34]

Nancy was quick to reassure Evelyn that 'whatever else you may be *you are not a bore*' and that he was 'wasted on people like Buchan-Hepburn with whom one would sooner have been seen dead than dancing, in my recollection of old ballroom days'.[35] However she also told him that her sister Debo Devonshire, whom Evelyn had always adored but also managed to alienate recently with some drunken rudeness, had 'cause to be offended judging by the things I've heard you say (which I did not pass on but others have)'.[36] The result of all this was to 'produce strong Pinfold feelings of persecution' and although he attempted to get back to work tinkering with his autobiography,* in April he admitted to Meg that he was 'in low spirits and in low water'.[37]

Meg's own spirits had risen considerably since their return from the Caribbean, not least due to the fact that by the time she received Evelyn's gloomy letter she had fallen deeply in love. Her new boyfriend was an Irishman called Giles FitzHerbert, who had first met her as a young girl at Pixton in the 1950s but only really registered her when he went to watch the Grand National in March 1962 at the flat she shared with friends Evelyn called 'the scoffers'. Margaret appeared 'quite shy and awkward' at the time but FitzHerbert remembered being struck by her unusual intelligence, even among the scoffers, who included the future Lord Chief Justice Tom Bingham. She was 'incredibly quick with a clear way of talking,' he recalled. 'Everyone noticed. She didn't gush and there was no small talk.'[38] In early August, Margaret and Giles drove down to Combe Florey to ask Evelyn's permission to marry, and afterwards Giles wrote to thank them 'for giving up such a treasure with such rare grace'.[39]

'Well, she has fallen head over heels in love and I can't find it in my heart to forbid consummation,' wrote Evelyn to Nancy. 'He is a penniless Irish stock broker's clerk named FitzHerbert of good family but rather caddish

---

* 'I have reached myself in my autobiography,' he wrote to Ann Fleming in May, 'and you know how boring that is.'

& raffish appearance. 27 years old and has not done a hands turn – his stock-broker's clerkship began on the day of his engagement. A Catholic of not very pious disposition, father killed honorably in the war, a brother I haven't been allowed to see, whom I suspect is a skeleton in cupboard (as is mine, and also Laura's for that matter). She had a number of suitors of the kind an old fashioned father would have preferred, but she must have FitzHerbert, & *so* she shall. She wants children & that is a thing I can't decently provide for her. I expect that in ten years' time she will be back on my doorstep with a brood.'[40]

Ann Fleming commiserated with Evelyn 'because you will miss her dreadfully' and Diana Cooper wrote that it was a time that 'I have so often dreaded for you – a time that I have known myself [her only son John Julius had married aged twenty-two] when one must deliver one's treasure to another with a generous show of approval'.[41] It was indeed 'a bitter pill and ungilded,' Evelyn admitted. 'I would forbid the marriage if I had any other cause than jealousy & snobbery. As it is, I pretend to be complaisant. Little Meg is ripe for the kind of love I can't give her. So I am surrendering with the honours of war – without war indeed . . . You see I feel that with Meg I have exhausted my capacity for finding objects of love. How does one exist without them? I haven't got the gaiety euphoria that makes old men chase tarts.'[42]

The day before writing to Diana Evelyn had begun what would be his last work of fiction, *Basil Seal Rides Again*, a final outing for the hero of *Black Mischief* (1932) and *Put Out More Flags* (1942) who had always contained elements of Evelyn but now, at the age of sixty, came closer than ever to being a self-portrait. Friends could scarcely fail to spot the parallels between Basil's jealousy over his daughter's plan to marry and Evelyn's own feelings about giving up Margaret, nor perhaps the incestuous undertone in the fictional father-daughter relationship: 'Two arms embraced his neck and drew him down, an agile figure inclined over the protuberance of his starched shirt, a cheek was pressed to his and teeth tenderly nibbled the lobe of his ear . . . He disengaged himself and slapped her loudly on the behind.'[43]

Margaret and Giles were married on 20 October at the Catholic Church of St Elizabeth of Portugal in Richmond, with the reception held at the house of their friend John Chancellor in Kew. Meg wore a tea gown from the dressing-up cupboard originally belonging to her great-grandmother

Evelyn de Vesci and 'looked jolly pretty in it,' Evelyn told Daphne Fielding, 'and jolly funny going away in a black velvet hat & red boots'.[44] From honeymoon in Italy Meg wrote to thank Evelyn for 'behaving so beautifully' at the wedding, having earlier thanked him for 'being so kind about my engagement'. 'You are the best father anyone can ever have had in the history of the world – really no flattery or sucking up, I think that. And there need be no divorce between us – I will come home just as often for week ends – Giles won't mind.'[45]

Evelyn's life had been 'much disturbed by the superabundance of weddings,' he told friends, and the marriages of his three eldest children in such quick succession seemed scarcely compensated for by his younger ones still being at home. 'There is another six days of James & Septimus's holidays,' he wrote to Ann Fleming in September. 'Oh the Hell of it.'[46] The birth of his first granddaughter, Sophia Waugh, that summer, appeared to spell potential disruption as much as anything else. 'Bron speaks in a sinister way of quartering his daughter here,' Evelyn wrote to Teresa.[47]

That autumn was spent working on a first draft of his autobiography. 'I am toiling & tinkering away,' he told Daphne Acton. 'The trouble is that I am (genuinely) not interested in myself & that while my friends are alive I can't write candidly about them.'[48] To Nancy Mitford he wrote that he had been contacting 'various men who were at school with me and asking whether they object to revelations of their delinquencies. I think it may have caused a seasonable chill in some reformed breasts. There is a pompous ass called Hot-lunch Molson who I don't suppose you ever met. I have a full diary of his iniquities in 1921–2. Perhaps he will fly the country.'[49]

When Evelyn wrote to ask Lord Molson whether he minded his mentioning that he had been 'tight' on Ascension day at school, Molson replied that he did not want to be a spoilsport but in view of the fact that 'that weakness of mine has never been wholly overcome' it would 'not only upset my wife very much but also faithful friends in the High Peak' – the Derbyshire constituency which he had represented as an MP before he was made a peer in 1961.[50]

Evelyn's reminiscences of Molson eventually went well beyond Ascension Day, and although he omitted his real name, the use of the nicknames 'Preters' and 'Hot Lunch' meant that plenty of people, if not perhaps his Derbyshire constituents, knew perfectly well who he was. When the book was eventually published, in 1964, John Betjeman wrote to congratulate Evelyn on 'how lovably ridiculous appears Hot Lunch Molson'.[51]

Molson's alarm was shared by his fellow peer, Matthew (by then Lord) Ponsonby, who as a magistrate hardly relished having his drunken arrest in 1925 dredged up. Others, though, seemed remarkably relaxed, none more so than Evelyn's pederastic one-legged colleague at Arnold House, Dick Young, whom Evelyn traced to an almshouse in Winchester: 'By all means "publish-and-be-damned" so far as I am concerned,' Young replied cheerfully. 'I always flatter myself that I was the original Capt. Grimes.'[52] A few days later he wrote again:

> Incidentally, when I say 'publish and be damned', I trust you will mention no scandal that could remotely connect me – in the mind of the Master of St Cross, the 'local vicar' – to you. True, no man is entitled to a better reputation than he has earned. But one is at St. Cross in some slight degree on the word of 'Referees', and it might be extremely awkward to have any 'suspicions' about oneself floating around, tho' I imagine that several of our old Brothers may have incidents in their past to which they would not purposely draw attention![53]

That all said, Young had no objection to having his misdeeds fully recounted in Evelyn's autobiography under the pseudonym 'Captain Grimes', and when he eventually read the book wrote to tell Evelyn that he found it all rather 'nostalgic'.[54]

Snowbound for much of January 1963 at Combe Florey, in February Evelyn and Laura escaped to Menton in the South of France, but returned early so that Evelyn could fulfill a $5,000 commission to write an obituary of the ailing Pope John XXIII, who died in June. That spring both Margaret and Bron's wife Teresa announced they were expecting babies: 'I hope at least some of these grandchildren will be a source of delight to you in your old age,' wrote Bron. 'Will you let them pull your beard?'[55] Just short of his sixtieth birthday in October, Evelyn heard that his daughter Teresa, too, was pregnant and wrote to congratulate her: 'Does John feel strongly that his offspring should be born on American soil?' he asked. If not he offered to pay Teresa's air fare 'so that it might be a subject of our good queen'. 'It could always renounce allegiance on coming of age if it feels strong republican sentiments.'[56]

At the age of fifty-nine, Evelyn already felt like a geriatric, 'very lame,' he told Ann Fleming. 'Carrying too much weight. Can't get down the weight walking because of the lameness. A vicious circle.'[57] As he became increasingly decrepit, the gardener 'Coggins' (real name Walter Coggan) seemed to spend more and more time deferentially imparting his rural wisdom to Laura in the kitchen garden to the point where Evelyn began referring to him as 'my rival, Mr Coggins'. 'Coggins has become complete master of this property,' Evelyn reported at the end of August.[58] In September, feeling increasingly seedy, as he told Meg, Evelyn booked himself into a health clinic in the New Forest: 'Well, Madam,' Coggins was heard to say to Laura when he heard Evelyn was to be away for a fortnight, 'we shall really be able to get down to it then?'[59] Midway through his stint at the health farm, Evelyn wrote to Ann Fleming: 'I have lost 13 lbs and all my good spirits.'[60]

Once past his sixtieth birthday, however, Evelyn began to cheer up, 'content to be old,' he told a cousin. 'No one can now expect me to carry anything.'[61] He was equally content to see no one outside his close family, not even old friends, and he found the fortieth anniversary meeting of the Oxford University Railway Club that November 'ghastly', despite the intriguing presence of Terence Greenidge, who announced that he had had a large part of his brain removed, rendering him 'very cheerful', Evelyn told Alfred Duggan, but devoid of 'most of the idiosyncrasies which used to endear him'.[62]* Christmas at Combe Florey was as usual 'Hell', Evelyn told Meg, but he was at least 'glad to have a grandson in the male line', Bron's wife Teresa having given birth to a son on 30 December 1963, later christened Alexander Evelyn Michael.

A Little Learning was eventually finished at the end of 1963 and published in the autumn of 1964. The critics were largely complimentary, although some found it a little reticent. V. S. Pritchett in the *New Statesman* called Evelyn 'a thoughtful rather than intimate autobiographer . . . He keeps the lid on',[63] a view that Evelyn effectively endorsed in his later admission to Diana Mosley: 'It is truthful in the sense of stating nothing false but, of course, it omits a good deal.'[64] Anthony Burgess delighted in the book's 'Gibbonian classicism' but was convinced 'it is an act, a

---

* Even on that trip he surrounded himself with family, taking along with him Bron and his son-in-law Giles FitzHerbert.

posture, and it derives from the father's more Dickensian histrionics as much as the fictional gift itself'.[65] Alec Waugh, perhaps relieved to be treated so gently, called it 'an important book because it presents and interprets the seedtime of one of the most important writers of our day'.[66] Among Evelyn's friends, Katharine Asquith was predictably dismayed by the passages about Captain Grimes but overall found the book 'of absorbing interest . . . some of it sounded so happy – some so terribly sad, some so funny & all so beautifully told'.[67]

The most unhappy reader was Evelyn's old Lancing sidekick Dudley Carew, whom he had not named but unkindly portrayed in the book as 'a boy in another house' whom he had 'fascinated and dominated'. 'Why on earth you should deliberately spit in the eye of one who has always wished you well passes my comprehension,' Carew wrote to him after reading the book. 'I have long letters of yours over a period of years which give a very different picture of an old friendship from the contemptuous squiggle of a caricature you have drawn of our relationship which relegates me to the position of a half-witted hanger-on you tolerantly patronized for a term or two . . . Many people whose opinion of me I value will have little difficulty, thanks to your gratuitous clues, in identifying me with the grotesque figure of the "boy in another house". As for my private feelings, you have hurt them most damnably.'[68]

In a bid to set the record straight, ten years later Carew published his own memoir (*A Fragment of Friendship: A Memory of Evelyn Waugh When Young*), which described *A Little Learning* as 'the worst book Evelyn ever wrote' yet whose bitter tone only served to strengthen the impression created by Evelyn in his rather savage pen portrait. In any event, by the time *A Little Learning* came out, Evelyn was fast losing his teeth, literally as well as metaphorically. 'When the last go I shall harden my gums with salt and eat soft foods,' he told Diana Cooper in October.[69] But in December he announced: 'I may buy a lot of new teeth in the new year and see if they help. Most of my lack of appetite comes from the boredom of chewing with my few, loose teeth. Not eating drives me to the bottle – both spirits & drugs. One can't sleep hungry.'[70]

'I own a toothbrush but since I have no teeth it is a superfluous possession,' he wrote to Ann Fleming in the new year, 'like the tiaras of ladies who are never asked out.'[71] In March 1965 he had his few remaining wobbly teeth drawn in order to make room for a new set, insisting on going through with the procedure without an anaesthetic as his father had done. 'It would be inconvenient for Laura if I kicked the bucket,' he acknowledged to Nancy Mitford beforehand, 'otherwise no apprehensions.'[72] Two months after the operation he told her: 'Honks [Diana Cooper] tells everyone I am dying. I don't think it's true. But I suffer in dignity & pleasure from my new snappers and I do no work.'[73]

But although they initially pleased him, his new teeth were never entirely successful and some months later he announced: 'I have lost the art of eating.'[74] All in all, the past twelve months had been rather grim for him, beset by death as well as dentistry, beginning with that of Alfred Duggan, followed by Baby Jungman's son Richard Cuthbertson, killed in a car accident, then Harry Ilchester (formerly Stavordale) and Phil Dunne. 'There has not been a fortnight without a funeral,' Evelyn told Nancy in May. 'Ian Fleming [who had died in August 1964] is being posthumously canonized by the intelligentsia. Very rum.'[75]

After going to see Edward Albee's play *Who's Afraid of Virginia Woolf?* in September, Evelyn confessed to Nancy: 'I find I can't follow the plot of any plays or films nowadays, whether it is my decay or theirs I don't know.'[76] By far the greatest of his woes, though, was his dismay at the conclusion of the Second Vatican Council, which had radically reformed the Latin Mass, demystifying the priest's role and replacing Latin with the vernacular, to the point at which Evelyn now hated going to church. 'The buggering up of the Church is a deep sorrow to me and to all I know,' he told Nancy. 'We write letters to the papers. A fat lot of good that does.'[77] 'No one minds more than I,' he wrote to Ann Fleming, '& no one can do less.'[78]

His deepening gloom began to worry friends and family. 'I've never seen you so low as before I went away,' wrote Meg at the beginning of December. 'It seemed a more abiding settled depression than ever before. Darling Papa please don't be unhappy – you may think this an impertinence but it is written in love – I think your trouble is that you don't go to the sacraments often enough. You can't expect your faith to suffer these onslaughts unless you sustain it.'[79]

Evelyn replied: 'You must not worry about my condition. I am growing old and old men suffer from aberrations of one kind of another. Dope is less harmful and less sinful than, say, drink or chasing young girls or boys. It would of course be better to be a saint. God chooses his own. The awful prospect is that I may have more than 20 years ahead. Pray that I "make my soul" in this period. I shall just become more and more boring I fear. Don't let me in my dotage oppress you.'[80]

Margaret now feared that he really was trying to kill himself: 'Please, please Papa see a doctor – a proper specialist. Your stomach has probably shrunk or certainly will & you are growing physically weaker under one's eyes . . . If there is no eternity then life is precious & if there is life is just as precious – eternity is forever & ever there is no point in prolonging it.'[81]

Evelyn rallied slightly in the new year of 1966, but responded despairingly when nagged by a publisher about the delivery of a book on the Crusades he had promised the previous year. 'Tell them I have temporarily lost my reason as the result of the Vatican Council,' Evelyn pleaded with Peters. 'Tell them anything. Get them to release me from my foolhardy promise.'[82] He intended instead to concentrate on the second volume of his autobiography; however he gave a fairly clear hint to Christopher Sykes (who was afraid of what it might say about him) that it would never be finished: 'My life is roughly speaking over. I sleep badly except occasionally in the morning. I get up late. I try to read my letters. I try to read the paper. I have some gin. I try to read the paper again. I have some more gin. I try to think about my autobiography. Then I have some more gin and it's lunch time. That's my life. It's ghastly.'[83] His correspondence with friends was littered with oblique references to death: 'Maurice [Bowra] has sent me (unsolicited) the extract from his memoirs that deals with me,' Evelyn told Ann Fleming. 'It is as respectful & affectionate as an obituary.'[84]

On Easter Sunday, 10 April 1966, Evelyn attended a Latin Mass in the Catholic chapel in the small market town of Wiveliscombe, five miles from Combe Florey, accompanied by Laura, Hatty, James, Septimus, and all the FitzHerberts – Margaret, Giles and their two little girls, Emily and Claudia. The service was conducted by Father Philip Caraman, who was staying at Pixton. Evelyn appeared surprisingly cheerful, benign and friendly to everyone, even to Auberon Herbert, who was also in the congregation, along with his mother Mary and sister Bridget. Afterwards they all drove back to Combe Florey, where again Evelyn was in high spirits as they all gathered in the morning room. At some point he left the room to go to the library where a postcard was later found, dated 10 April, addressed to a Catholic academic called Professor Robin Anderson:

'Many thanks for your interesting sympathetic letter. We live in a dark age. I cannot hope to live to see it lighter.'[85]

It was almost certainly the last thing Evelyn wrote. When he failed to reappear for lunch, a search was begun during which Septimus, fifteen at the time, eventually knocked on the door of the downstairs lavatory, which was locked from the inside. Getting no answer, he fetched a ladder so that he could peer in through a high window and saw his father slumped on the floor having suffered a heart attack. In shock he called out to his nineteen-year-old brother James, who managed to climb in through the window and unlock the door. Evelyn was then dragged out into the passageway, where the FitzHerberts' Irish nanny, Maureen Regan (henceforth 'Nurse Regan') attempted mouth-to-mouth resuscitation. Father Caraman, to whom Evelyn had given a cheque that morning for ten guineas for his Mass, administered conditional absolution – 'Si vivis, ego te absolvo a peccatis tuis. In nomine Patris et Filii et Spiritus Sancti, amen'* – before summoning the priest at Wiveliscombe, Father Formosa, to bring his oils to anoint the dead man. Bron and Teresa were living at Hungerford at the time and had been out to a long lunch with friends, leaving their two young children, Sophia and Alexander, at home with their nanny. When they arrived back that evening to find a policeman on their doorstep Bron immediately feared something terrible had happened to his children and it came as a 'conscious relief' to hear that instead his father had died suddenly in Somerset.

On further reflection, he wrote: 'To die on Easter Sunday, after communion, among friends, with no lingering deterioration of the faculties, must be reckoned a merciful death.'[86] Margaret, too, although devastated saw some cause for comfort: 'Don't be too upset about Papa,' she wrote to his great friend Diana Cooper. 'You know how he longed to die and dying as he did on Easter Sunday, when all the liturgy is about death and resurrection, after a Latin mass and holy communion, would be exactly what he wanted. I am sure he had prayed for death at Mass. I am very, very happy for him.'[87]

---

* 'If you are living, I absolve you from your sins. In the name of the Father and of the Son and of the Holy Ghost, amen.'

Epilogue

Evelyn was buried on the Friday after Easter in a special plot on the edge of the Combe Florey garden adjoining the Anglican churchyard of St Peter and St Paul. The funeral at the Catholic church of St Teresa of Lisieux in Taunton was conducted by Father Caraman, who also gave the address at a full Requiem Mass held six days later at Westminster Cathedral, where special dispensation was obtained for the Mass to be said in Latin. The congregation sang six verses of Evelyn's favourite hymn, 'O God, Our Help in Ages Past', which he used to hum to himself while working in the library.

The obituaries paid tribute to the precision of his prose, his wildly comic invention and unique satiric stance, while also recording his deep aversion to the modern world, his staunch Catholic apologetics and his reputation for misanthropy and snobbery. Bron thought the notices 'with few exceptions, extraordinarily grudging',* and indeed they mostly overlooked the more humane side of Evelyn's character, which was left to his friends to record in their letters of condolence to Laura. When news of his death reached Graham Greene in Paris late on Easter Day he promptly sent a note saying he was 'shocked more than I can find it possible to write'. 'As a writer I admired him more than any other living novelist & as a man I loved him. He was a very loyal and patient friend to me. What I loved most in him was that rare quality that he would only say the kind things behind one's back.'†

---

* Responding to the obituaries in an article in *The Spectator* that May, Bron wrote: 'The main point about my father, which might be of interest . . . is not that he was interested in pedigree – it was the tiniest part of his interests. It is not that he was a conservative – politics bored him . . . it is simply that he was the funniest man of his generation.'

† A few days later in *The Times*, Greene described Evelyn as 'the greatest novelist of my generation' and wrote: 'We were deeply divided politically, we were divided even in our conception of the same church, and there were times when certain popular journalists tried

Among the many letters that followed was one from Diana Mosley, who had been estranged from Evelyn for more than thirty years until they were reconciled a few weeks before he died. 'Evelyn was such an extraordinarily gifted, clever and really good person,' she wrote to Laura, 'so unusual – unique – that your loss does not bear thinking about. He is the sort of person one would miss more and more. Even I, who never had the joy of seeing him, feel so sad today.'[2] Her sister Nancy (Mitford) said that she 'loved Evelyn I really think the best of all my friends . . . he was far the best living writer of English without a doubt. For him one can only say he did hate the modern world, which does not become more liveable every day.'[3]

Evelyn's agent Peters called it 'a literary tragedy' that he had not completed his autobiography, and remembered his client as 'unfailingly kind & generous to me during the whole of the forty years that I knew him – never a harsh word or a rebuke, even when I deserved them. The world who did not know him had, I'm afraid, a distorted picture of him which he himself took some trouble to paint. But the real Evelyn was a very fine man. I loved him and I shall miss him for the rest of my life.'[4]

There was much mention in the letters of Evelyn's strength and singularity. For Patrick Kinross, he stood out as 'the most alive, the most consistently his personal self' among his friends. 'Even in his poses he was simply burlesquing some part of himself. What a joy he was to be with, & to hear from and to talk about! Whatever mood he was in, gay or morose, benign or angry – he was always thoroughly positive and in the whollest sense human. What a strong and alive personality. No one so dominated a room by simply being in it. His affections were constant & he was the staunchest of friends & the most outspoken too. His friendship was not only a solace and stimulus, but a challenge. This made him the ideal literary mentor, not only encouraging and praising but criticising sharply.'[5]

Several writers recalled Evelyn's generosity, including P. G. Wodehouse, whom he had long championed as 'the Master' and whose reputation he had staunchly defended after Wodehouse came under attack for broadcasting from Germany during the war. Although they had only met once,

---

to push us into what Indonesians would call a confrontation, but Evelyn had an unshakable loyalty to his friends, even if he may have detested their opinions and sometimes their actions. One could never rely on him for an easy approval or a warm weak complaisance, but when one felt the need of him he was always there.' *The Times*, 15 April 1966.

in New York, Wodehouse had 'always looked on him as one of my dearest friends,' he told Laura, 'and I can never forget all he did for me'.[6] Angus Wilson described Evelyn's praise for his first published short story in 1947 as 'the most exciting thing I can remember to do with my writing' and was equally appreciative of his reviews of his early novels when he felt misunderstood by other critics. 'That this encouragement should have come from someone who differed from me in all social and political questions was only what one had come to expected from somebody who cared so completely about writing for itself. But for me that it should have come from our finest novelist was everything.'[7] Robert Henriques was another who, reading back over the letters Evelyn had written to him over the years, felt 'overwhelmingly what a deeply <u>kind</u> person he was' although he also admitted that he had always been rather afraid of him. 'To me he was a superior kind of person, not just intellectually, and as the best writer of our generation, but morally and in ways I can't define. Yet, while feeling more diffident with him than with anyone else I have ever known, I was always keenly aware of his great concern for his friends. Very few people have seemed to mind as much as he did about how his friends were faring. That, and his generosity and his intense loyalties, were qualities as important to his friends as his wit and brilliance.'[8]

Many sought comfort from the timing of his death and from the fact that, as Daphne Acton wrote, he 'didn't like the way things were going, so he will be happy seeing them from another angle'.[9] Dorothy Lygon remembered Evelyn as 'so much part of our youth & was a focusing point of endless fun & happiness [but] it does seem to have been the sort of end one would wish for oneself & perhaps what he would have chosen too'.[10] Diana Cooper suggested to Laura that Evelyn had died 'too young for you but perhaps right for him who never was closely held by the world & its illusions'. He would mind leaving 'You above all things,' she added, 'for you have loved & served & arranged for him & lived for him as no other woman could have done.'[11]

For John Betjeman, too, it was at least 'a joy to think of how perfectly you [Laura] and he were suited to each other, and that Bron has inherited the family genius'.[12] Penelope said 'what a marvellous wife you have been to him',[13] as did Daphne Acton, who ventured that Evelyn 'must have been a whole-time job for you, which you carried out with all heart'.[14]

With the main focus gone from her life, Laura took increasingly to the sherry and passed the time with crosswords and her cows. Barely three months after Evelyn's death, she put Combe Florey up for sale but later changed her mind and continued to live there until Bron and his family took the house over in 1971, whereupon she moved into a wing at the back. Some years before his death, Evelyn had discussed selling his papers to the University of Texas to help fund his retirement. Laura was wrongly advised that she had been left short of money and agreed to the sale of his entire library, bookshelves and all. Some years later she sold the rights to his diaries to *The Observer* without her or any member of the family having read them. When they were published, first in 1973 as extracts in the newspaper and three years later as a book, the countless disobliging references caused a furore and were widely seen as providing corroboration for those who had come to regard Evelyn as an ogre. Laura was at least spared much of the outcry, having died suddenly from pneumonia shortly after the first extracts appeared. She was buried on her fifty-seventh birthday: 'more deeply mourned,' Bron later wrote, 'than her modest nature would ever have understood.'

Notes

Page references to works cited are to the editions listed in the Bibliography unless otherwise stated.

AWA	Alexander Waugh Archive
BL	British Library
BU	Boston University Library
CU	Columbia University
EAR	*The Essays, Articles and Reviews of Evelyn Waugh*, edited by Donat Gallagher
EWCH	*Evelyn Waugh: The Critical Heritage*, edited by Martin Stannard
EWD	*The Diaries of Evelyn Waugh*, edited by Michael Davie
EWL	*The Letters of Evelyn Waugh*, edited by Mark Amory
GU	Georgetown Univerity
HRC	The Harry Ransom Center, University of Texas at Austin
IWM	Imperial War Museum
LHC	Liddell Hart Centre for Military Archives, King's College, London
LNMEW	*Letters of Nancy Mitford and Evelyn Waugh*, edited by Charlotte Mosley
MWMS	*Mr Wu & Mrs Stitch: the Letters of Evelyn Waugh and Diana Cooper*, edited by Artemis Cooper

1 Second Son

1. *A Little Learning*, p. 28.
2. Ibid.
3. Ibid., p.63.
4. See John Howard Wilson, *Evelyn Waugh: A Literary Biography 1903–1924*, pp. 18 and 180; quoted in Alexander Waugh, *Fathers and Sons*, p. 77.

5. Ibid., p. 77; Alec Waugh, *My Brother Evelyn*, p. 164.

6. Christopher Sykes, *Evelyn Waugh*, p. 7.

7. Alexander Waugh, *Fathers and Sons*, p. 79; Alec Waugh, *My Brother Evelyn*, p. 164.

8. It is not recorded who came up with the nickname. Alexander Waugh suspects it was either Evelyn or his mother.

9. *A Little Learning*, p. 22; Alexander Waugh, *Fathers and Sons*, p. 25.

10. Alec Waugh, The Early *Years of Alec Waugh*, pp. 7–8; Alexander Waugh, *Fathers and Sons*, pp. 24–8; *A Little Learning*, pp. 20–23.

11. *A Little Learning*, p. 22.

12. Arthur Waugh, *One Man's Road*, p. 34.

13. Alexander Waugh, *Fathers and Sons*, p. 24.

14. Alec Waugh, *Early Years*, p. 7.

15. *A Little Learning*, p. 22.

16. Alexander Waugh, *Fathers and Sons*, p. 24.

17. Arthur Waugh, *One Man's Road*, p. 61.

18. Alexander Waugh, *Fathers and Sons*, pp. 90–91; Arthur Waugh, *One Man's Road*, p. 63.

19. Sykes, *Evelyn Waugh*, p. 4.

20. As an example, Evelyn records his 'signally humourless' intended wording (never used) for his planned memorial in the church. See *A Little Learning*, pp. 18 and 20.

21. Auberon Waugh, *Will This Do?*, p. 19.

22. *A Little Learning*, p. 21.

23. Ibid., p. 9.

24. Arthur Waugh, *One Man's Road*, pp. 12–13.

25. *A Little Learning*, p. 21.

26. Alec Waugh, *Early Years*, p. 7.

27. *A Little Learning*, p. 49.

28. Ibid.

29. Ibid., p. 47.

30. Ibid., pp. 44–7.

31. Ibid., p. 48.

32. Arthur Waugh, *One Man's Road*, p. 23.

33. Quoted in Alec Waugh, *Early Years*, p. 9.

34. Alexander Waugh, *Fathers and Sons*, p. 32.

35. *A Little Learning*, p. 69.

36. Alexander Waugh, *Fathers and Sons*, p. 41.

37. Quoted in ibid., p. 42.

38. Arthur Waugh, *One Man's Road*, p. 159.

39. *Nash's Pall Mall Magazine*, March 1937, p. 8.

40. Arthur Waugh, *One Man's Road*, p. 208; *The Times*, 20 October 1892, p. 7: 'Mr Waugh's discriminating judgments have evidently cost time and thought, and proceed from a critical faculty of no mean order.'

41. Arthur Waugh, *One Man's Road*, pp. 217–18.

42. *A Little Learning*, p. 4.

43. Sykes, *Evelyn Waugh*, p. 5.

44. *A Little Learning*, p. 31.

45. Arthur Waugh, *One Man's Road*, p. 218.

46. Selina Hastings, *Evelyn Waugh*, pp. 6–7.

47. *A Little Learning*, p. 31.
48. Alexander Waugh, *Fathers and Sons*, p. 75.
49. Arthur Waugh, *One Man's Road*, p. 218.
50. Arthur Waugh to Alec Waugh, 20 May 1914; BU.
51. Arthur Waugh to Catherine Waugh, 10 July 1993, AWA; quoted in Alexander Waugh, *Fathers and Sons*, p. 116.
52. Ibid., p. 116.
53. *A Little Learning*, p. 31.
54. Ibid., p. 32.
55. Arthur Waugh, *One Man's Road*, pp. 257–9.
56. Alec Waugh, *Early Years*, p. 12.
57. Margot Strickland, Notes on *Catherine Waugh's Diary*, p. 7; AWA
58. Alec Waugh *The Early Years of Alec Waugh*, pp. 13-14.
59. Michael Holroyd, *Bernard Shaw*, Vol. 1, p. 267.
60. Alexander Waugh, *Fathers and Sons*, pp. 50–51.
61. Alec Waugh, *Early Years*, pp. 14–15.
62. Arthur Waugh, *One Man's Road*, p. 290.
63. Ibid., p. 321.
64. Alec Waugh, *My Brother Evelyn*, p. 163.
65. Alexander Waugh, *Fathers and Sons*, pp. 74–5.
66. *A Little Learning*, p. 27.

2 The Sadism of Youth

1. Hugh Petrie, *Hendon and Golders Green Past* (Historical Publications, 2005), p. 54.
2. *A Little Learning*, p. 34.
3. Ibid.
4. Ibid., p. 42.
5. Ibid., p. 44.
6. Ibid., p. 78.
7. Ibid., p. 71.
8. Ibid., p. 72.
9. Alec Waugh interview with Michael Davie, December 1972, AWA.
10. *A Little Learning*, p. 43.
11. Ibid., p. 36.
12. Jean Fleming to Selina Hastings, interview transcript, p. 2, AWA.
13. *A Little Learning*, p. 44.
14. Ibid., pp. 47–8.
15. Stella Rhys to Christopher Sykes, 19 April 1974, copy in AWA.
16. *A Little Learning*, p. 41.
17. Ibid.
18. Ibid., p. 30.
19. Stella Rhys to Christopher Sykes, 19 April 1974; Sykes Papers, GU.
20. Jean Fleming to Selina Hastings, 17 March 1991, AWA.
21. *A Little Learning*, p. 43.
22. Diary, Summer 1912; HRC.
23. *A Little Learning*, p. 59.
24. Alec Waugh, *Early Years*, pp. 20–22.

25. J. S. Granville Grenfell to Catherine Waugh, 31 October 1910, BL.
26. *A Little Learning*, p. 81.
27. Ibid.
28. Article entitled 'My Father', *The Sunday Telegraph*, 2 December 1962.
29. September 1911; *EWD*, p. 5.
30. *A Little Learning*, p. 63.
31. Mr Stebbing, Evelyn's form master.
32. Diary, [September–October 1914]; HRC.
33. Mr Hynchcliffe, the Classics master.
34. *A Little Learning*, p. 84.
35. Cecil Beaton, *The Wandering Years*, p. 173.
36. Hugh Burnett (ed.), *Face to Face*, Jonathan Cape (1964), p. 38.
37. *The Spectator*, 21 July 1961.
38. Stella Rhys to Christopher Sykes, 19 April 1974; Sykes Papers, GU.
39. *The Spectator*, 21 July 1961.
40. Alec Waugh, *My Brother Evelyn*, p. 166.
41. Alexander Waugh, *Fathers and Sons*, p. 79.
42. Arthur Waugh to Andrew Waugh, 1933, quoted in Selina Hastings, *Evelyn Waugh*, p. 25.
43. 'My Childhood' by Alec Waugh copy in AWA.
44. Alec Waugh to Evelyn Waugh, 29 March 1908 and 21 March 1909; BL.
45. Alec Waugh, *My Brother Evelyn*, pp. 163–5.
46. Ibid., p. 168.
47. *A Little Learning*, p. 86.
48. Catherine Waugh Diary, 16 June 1912, 17 June 1912, 18 June 1912; BU.
49. *A Little Learning*, pp. 55–6; Catherine Waugh Diary, 7 July 1912; BU.
50. Catherine Waugh Diary, 11 July 1912 to 22 August 1912; BU.
51. *A Little Learning*, pp. 56–7.
52. Ibid., p. 58.
53. Ibid., p. 60.
54. Arthur Waugh, *One Man's Road*, p. 333.
55. *A Little Learning*, p. 60.
56. Arthur Waugh, *One Man's Road*, p. 334.
57. Ibid., p. 338.
58. *A Little Learning*, p. 60.
59. Ibid., pp. 60–61.
60. Ibid., p. 61.
61. 12–13 June 1912; *EWD*, p. 6.
62. *A Little Learning*, p. 91.
63. 'Come Inside' in John A. O'Brien (ed.), *The Road to Damascus*, 1949; *EAR*, pp. 366–8.
64. *A Little Learning*, p. 52.
65. Ibid., pp. 92–3.
66. Ibid., p. 93; *EWD*, p. 9.
67. Jane Ridley, *The Architect and His Wife: A Life of Edwin Lutyens*, pp. 175–6.
68. 'Charles Ryder's Schooldays', in *Work Suspended and Other Stories*, p. 305.
69. Alec Waugh, Notes on Christopher Sykes's Biography of Evelyn Waugh, HRC.
70. *A Little Learning*, p. 92.

71. Aubrey Ensor, notes on proof copy of *A Little Learning*, p. 92, in author's possession.

72. *A Little Learning*, p. 92.

73. Email from Father Alan Walker, Vicar of St Jude's, 16 January 2013. In 1914 Bourchier had gone out to Belgium as a chaplain to the Red Cross, until he was captured by Germans and sentenced to be shot at dawn as a suspected spy, 'the greatest thrill of my life,' he recalled. He was reprieved, though, and instead held prisoner until he returned to the suburb and to St Jude's in March 1916, shortly before Evelyn's confirmation.

74. Alec Waugh, *Early Years*, pp. 43–4.

75. *A Little Learning*, p. 68; Alec Waugh's notes on Christopher Sykes's biography of Evelyn Waugh, attached to Alec's letter to Auberon Waugh, 6 March 1976; AWA. In *Charles Ryder's Schooldays*, Charles's was 'not a God-fearing home' but his father nevertheless 'read family prayers every morning; on the outbreak of war he abruptly stopped the practice, explaining, when asked, that there was now nothing left to pray for'.

76. Arthur Waugh to Kenneth McMaster, 24 August 1916, HRC, quoted Hastings, p.40.

77. Alec Waugh, *My Brother Evelyn*, p. 168.

78. *A Little Learning*, p. 94.

3 Serving Lord Kitchener

1. Arthur Waugh to Kenneth McMaster, 25 August 1914, HRC.

2. *A Little Learning*, p. 87; Aubrey Ensor notes on proof copy of *A Little Learning*, in author's possession.

3. *A Little Learning*, p. 87.

4. Ibid., pp. 87–8.

5. Arthur Waugh to Kenneth McMaster, New Year's Day 1915, HRC.

6. *A Little Learning*, p. 89.

7. Ibid., pp. 94–5.

8. Diary, [*c.* 8–18 October 1914], HRC.

9. Ibid.

10. Ibid., [*c.*12 September–1 October 1914], HRC.

11. *A Little Learning*, p. 88.

12. Diary, [mid-June 1915], HRC.

13. Ibid., [early November 1914]; *EWD*, p. 8.

14. Alec Waugh, *My Brother Evelyn*, p. 168.

15. *The Times*, 26 January 1926.

16. Hugo Vickers, *Cecil Beaton*, p. 15.

17. Aubrey Ensor notes on proof copy of *A Little Learning*, in author's possession.

18. Ibid.

19. Alec Waugh, *My Brother Evelyn*, p. 169.

20. Aubrey Ensor notes on proof copy of *A Little Learning*, in author's possession.

21. Ibid.

22. Ibid.

23. *A Little Learning*, p. 90; Diary, [November–December 1915], HRC.

24. *A Little Learning*, p. 90.

25. Vickers, *Cecil Beaton*, p. 15.

26. *The Times*, 20 July 1925, p. 11.
27. *A Little Learning*, p. 90.
28. Diary, *c.* 2 January 1916, HRC.
29. Ibid., late January 1916.
30. *A Little Learning*, p. 94.
31. Alexander Waugh, *Fathers and Sons*, p. 53.
32. Arthur Waugh to Kenneth McMaster, 13 December 1913, HRC.
33. *A Little Learning*, p. 95.
34. Arthur Waugh to Alec Waugh, 20 May 1914; BU.
35. Arthur Waugh, *One Man's Road*, p. 332.
36. Alexander Waugh, *Fathers and Sons*, p. 76.
37. Catherine Waugh to Alec Waugh, 25 May 1915; BU.
38. Arthur Waugh to Alec Waugh, 19 October 1916; BU.
39. *A Little Learning*, p. 95.
40. Alec Waugh to Hugh Mackintosh, 25 February 1915; BU.
41. Alec Waugh to Hugh Mackintosh, 29 October 1915; BU.
42. Arthur Waugh to Alec Waugh, 5 June 1915, quoted in Alexander Waugh, *Fathers and Sons*, p.69; BU.
43. Catherine Waugh to Alec Waugh, 24 June 1915; BU.
44. Arthur Waugh to Alec Waugh, 21 January 1916; BU.
45. Arthur Waugh to Alec Waugh, 1 February 1917; BU.
46. *A Little Learning*, p. 141.
47. Arthur Waugh, *One Man's Road*, p. 367.

4 A Lesser Place than Eton

1. *A Little Learning*, p. 163.
2. Ibid., pp. 99–100.
3. B. W. T. Handford *Lancing 1848–1930*, p. 247.
4. Dudley Carew, *A Fragment of Friendship*, p. 38.
5. *A Little Learning*, p. 99.
6. Undated note by Roger Fulford; AWA.
7. Handford, *Lancing*, p. 263.
8. *A Little Learning*, p. 99.
9. Transcript of Basil Handford interview with Selina Hastings; AWA.
10. Obituary in *The Times*, 9 February 1940.
11. *A Little Learning*, p. 99.
12. *Daily Express*, 20 March 1929.
13. *Evelyn Waugh in Letters by Terence Greenidge*, p. 24.
14. Arthur Waugh to Kenneth McMaster, 6 January 1927, HRC.
15. *A Little Learning*, p. 101.
16. Undated note by Roger Fulford in AWA.
17. David Pryce-Jones (ed.), *Evelyn Waugh and His World*, p. 17.
18. Alec Waugh to Hugh Mackintosh, 13 October 1917; BU, quoted in Hastings, p. 57.
19. Pryce-Jones, *Evelyn Waugh and His World*, p. 17.
20. *A Little Learning*, p. 107.
21. Catherine Waugh to Alec Waugh, 19 May 1918; BU, quoted in Hastings, p. 57.
22. *A Little Learning*, p. 109.

23. Ibid.
24. Ibid., p. 110.
25. Ibid., p. 113.
26. Transcript of C. L. Chamberlin interview with Selina Hastings, p. 5; AWA.
27. Arthur Waugh, *One Man's Road*, p. 358.
28. *A Little Learning*, p. 120.
29. Alec Waugh to Hugh Mackintosh, 31 January 1919; BU.
30. *A Little Learning*, p. 117.
31. Hastings, *Evelyn Waugh*, p. 54.
32. *A Little Learning*, p. 122.
33. Ibid., p.117.
34. Arthur Waugh to Evelyn Waugh, 6 February 1919; dedicatory letter printed in *Tradition and Change* (1919).
35. Arthur Waugh to Jean Fleming, 14 April 1918; private collection, quoted in Hastings, p. 55; copy in AWA.
36. *A Little Learning*, p. 124.
37. Ibid., p. 125.
38. Ibid.
39. Ibid., p. 130.
40. Ibid., p. 131; Evelyn Waugh to Randolph Churchill, 5 September 1963, *Encounter*, Vol. 31, p. 17.
41. *A Little Learning*, p. 131.
42. Ibid.
43. Ibid., p. 126; 23 September 1919; *EWD*, p. 19.
44. *A Little Learning*, p. 146.
45. Preface to Francis Crease's *Decorative Designs* (1927); *EAR*, p. 23.
46. *A Little Learning*, p. 147.
47. *EWD*, pp. 53 and 54; EW to Arthur Waugh, 29 January 1920, quoted in Alexander Waugh, *Fathers and Sons*, pp. 140–41; AWA.
48. 8 May 1920; *EWD*, p. 74.
49. 29 January 1929; *EWD*, pp. 53–4 and *A Little Learning*, p. 148.
50. Thus billed on Amazon.
51. 5 February 1920; *EWD*, p. 55.
52. Preface . . . *Essays Articles*, p. 24.
53. 25 March 1920, quoted in Hastings, p. 67; copy in AWA.
54. March 1920; *EWD*, pp. 65–6.
55. Introduction by Arthur Waugh to Ian Mackenzie, *The Darkened Ways* (Chapman & Hall, 1919).
56. Philippa Codrington to Selina Hastings, 27 January 1991; AWA.
57. *A Little Learning*, p. 69.
58. Ibid., p. 153.
59. Ibid, p. 150.
60. *EWD*, p. 78.
61. 19 July 1921; *EWD*, p. 132.
62. *A Little Learning*, p. 162.

5 Watertight Compartments

1. Noel Annan, *Roxburgh of Stowe*, p. 47.
2. 26 September 1919; *EWD*, p. 20.
3. Evelyn Waugh's review of Annan's *Roxburgh of Stowe*, *The Observer*, 17 October 1965; *EAR* pp. 638–9.
4. 19–25 October 1920; *EWD*, p. 107.
5. Diary, 23 April 1921; edited version at request of Alec in *EWD*, p. 125.
6. *A Little Learning*, p. 158; EW to Nancy Mitford, 6 January [1951], *EWL*, p. 343.
7. *A Little Learning*, pp. 159–60.
8. 11 October 1921; *EWD*, p. 141 (with Macdonald's name deleted).
9. *A Little Learning*, p. 160.
10. Ibid., p. 161.
11. 25 October 1920; *EWD*, p. 107.
12. Robert Murray Davis, *Evelyn Waugh, Apprentice*, p. 63.
13. Ibid., p. 68.
14. 21 December 1920; *EWD*, p. 108.
15. *A Little Learning*, p. 161.
16. 29 October 1921; *EWD*, p. 144.
17. EW to Arthur Waugh, 13 June [1921]; *EWL*, p. 3.
18. *A Little Learning*, p. 132.
19. 31 March 1921; *EWD*, p. 122; *A Little Learning*, pp. 134–5.
20. 19 July 1921; *EWD*, p. 131.
21. Arthur Waugh to EW, 1 June 1921; BL; *A Little Learning*, p. 136.
22. 3 June 1921; *EWD*, p. 127.
23. *Evelyn Waugh, Apprentice*, p. 114.
24. Arthur Waugh to EW, 17 May 1921; BL.
25. 26 June 1921; *EWD*, p. 129.
26. James Lees-Milne diary, 29 July 1973, *Ancient as the Hills*, p. 66.
27. Christopher Chamberlin to Selina Hastings, interview transcript, AWA
28. Henrietta McCall, *The Life of Max Mallowan*, p. 15.
29. Max Mallowan, *Mallowan's Memoirs*, pp. 19-20.
30. Richard Ollard (ed.), *The Diaries of A. L. Rowse*, p. 414, 'Evelyn had a nasty nature (though also charm when he chose).'
31. EW to Nancy Mitford, [28 December] 1962; LNMEW, p. 471.
32. 2 October 1919; *EWD*, p. 23.
33. 6 May 1921; *EWD*, p. 126.
34. Ollard, *Rowse Diaries*, p. 414.
35. 2 October 1919; *EWD*, p. 23.
36. *A Little Learning*, p. 128.
37. 17 October 1919; *EWD*, p. 23, rating one of his efforts a 'terrible effusion'.
38. 23 October 1919; *EWD*, p. 31.
39. 2 May 1921; *EWD*, p. 126.
40. 27 February 1921; *EWD*, p. 114 (with name deleted).
41. Francis Wheen, *Tom Driberg*, p. 27.
42. 7 November 1919; *EWD*, p. 35.
43. *A Little Learning*, pp. 143–4.
44. Tom Driberg, *Ruling Passions*, p. 49.
45. 13 June 1921; *EWD*, p. 127.

46. Wheen, *Tom Driberg*, pp. 29 and 32–3.
47. Driberg, *Ruling Passions*, p. 49.
48. 15 October 1920; *EWD*, p. 106.
49. *A Little Learning*, p. 135.
50. Luned Hamilton-Jenkins (née Jacobs) to Selina Hastings, December 1991; AWA.
51. Alec Waugh to Hugh Mackintosh, 31 January 1919; BU.
52. 27 September 1919; *EWD*, p. 21.
53. 24 January 1921; *EWD*, p. 109.
54. Luned Hamilton-Jenkins (née Jacobs) to Selina Hastings, December 1991; AWA.
55. 12 August 1920; *EWD*, p. 95.
56. 22–3 April and 31 August 1920; *EWD*, pp. 69, 99.
57. Dudley Carew Diary, 21 August 1921, HRC.
58. 24 January 1921; *EWD*, p. 109.
59. Dudley Carew Diary, 21 August 1921; HRC.
60. Dudley Carew Diary, 12 May 1921; HRC.
61. 27 June 1920; *EWD*, p. 87.
62. Note to Dudley Carew interview with Michael Davie, 17 November 1972; AWA.
63. Dudley Carew Diary, 15 August 1921, HRC.
64. Alec Waugh, *Early Years*, p. 152.
65. Ibid., p. 160.
66. Alec Waugh, *Early Years*, pp. 155–6.
67. Andrew Waugh to Selina Hastings, transcript of interview, p. 7; AWA.
68. Alexander Waugh, *Fathers and Sons*, p. 147.
69. Ibid.
70. Andrew Waugh to Selina Hastings; AWA.
71. *A Little Learning*, p. 138.
72. 16 October 1921; *EWD*, p. 141.
73. *A Little Learning*, p. 138.
74. 16 and 19 October 1921; *EWD*, pp. 141–2.
75. 19 October 1921; *EWD*, p. 142.
76. 29 October 1921; *EWD*, p. 144.
77. 6 December 1921; *EWD*, p. 150.
78. C. R. M. F. Cruttwell to Evelyn Waugh, 14 December 1921; BL.
79. 16 December 1921; *EWD*, p. 154.

6 *All That One Dreams*

1. Arthur Waugh to EW, 15 December 1921; BL.
2. *A Little Learning*, p. 137.
3. Lancing College report, Christmas Term 1921, AWA.
4. Roxburgh to EW, 12 March 1922; BL.
5. EW to Dudley Carew, undated (*c*.New Year 1922), HRC.
6. *A Little Learning*, p. 163.
7. Ibid., p. 166.
8. [Early 1922]; *EWL*, p.4.
9. 13 February [1922]; *EWL*, p. 7.
10. *Evelyn Waugh in Letters by Terence Greenidge*, p. 43.
11. *A Little Learning*, p. 191.

12. [1922]; *EWL*, p. 10.
13. EW to Dudley Carew [March 1922], *EWL*, p. 8.
14. Claud Cockburn, 'Evelyn Waugh's Lost Rabbit', *Atlantic Monthly*, December 1973.
15. EW to Dudley Carew, undated (spring 1922), HRC.
16. Christopher Hollis, *Oxford in the Twenties*, p. 76.
17. Martin Stannard, *Evelyn Waugh: The Early Years: 1903–1939*, p. 74.
18. *The Isis*, 8 February 1922, p. 12.
19. *Oxford Magazine*, 23 February 1922, p. 246; 30 November 1922, p. 123; and *The Isis*, 29 November 1922.
20. *A Little Learning*, pp. 180–81.
21. Quoted in Noel Annan, *Our Age*, p. 113.
22. Terence Greenidge, *Degenerate Oxford?*, p. 91.
23. Driberg, *Ruling Passions*, p. 55.
24. Sykes, *Evelyn Waugh*, p. 48.
25. EW to Dudley Carew, 10 March 1922; *EWL*, p. 8.
26. EW to Tom Driberg, 21 May 1922, Christ Church, Oxford; *EWL*, p. 10.
27. EW to Tom Driberg, late May 1922, Christ Church, Oxford.
28. Transcript of Selina Hastings's interview with A. L. Rowse, 17 March 1990; AWA.
29. Cited in Clive Fisher, *Cyril Connolly* (Macmillan, 1995), p. 58.
30. EW to Nancy Mitford, 18 December 1954; *EWL*, p. 435.
31. Christopher Hollis to Cyril Connolly, quoted in Jeremy Lewis, *Cyril Connolly*, p. 111.
32. A. L. Rowse to Selina Hastings, 4 June 1991; AWA.
33. Transcript of Selina Hastings's interview with A. L. Rowse, 17 March 1990; AWA.
34. Richard Pares to EW, undated; BL.
35. Ibid.
36. Ollard, *Rowse Diaries*, p. 414.
37. Isaiah Berlin, *Personal Impressions*, (Hogarth, 1980), p. 92.
38. *A Little Learning*, pp. 191–2.
39. *The Isis*, 3 December 1924.
40. Richard Pares to EW, undated [December/January 1923]; BL.
41. Quoted in David Pryce Jones, *Cyril Connolly: Journal and Memoir*, p. 63.
42. Transcript of *Arena* interview with Anthony Bushell; AWA.
43. Hollis, *Oxford in the Twenties*, p. 79.
44. Stannard, *Evelyn Waugh: The Early Years*, pp. 82–3.
45. EW to Dudley Carew, two undated letters, from spring 1923 and spring/summer 1924.
46. *Brideshead Revisited*, p. 25.
47. Transcript of BBC *Arena* interview with Anthony Bushell, p. 250 (although earlier in the interview, on p. 249, he said the incident was 'pure invention'); copy in AWA.
48. Ibid.
49. Anthony Powell, *Infants of the Spring*, p. 154.
50. James Knox, *Robert Byron*, p. 43.
51. Powell, *Infants of the Spring*, p. 113.
52. Rowse, *A Cornishman at Oxford*, p. 23; Lucy Butler (ed.) *Robert Byron Letters Home*, p. 16; Emlyn Williams, *George: An Early Autobiography*, pp. 315–16.
53. John Rothenstein, *Summer's Lease*, p. 94.
54. Rowse, *Cornishman at Oxford*, p. 24.

55. Marie-Jacqueline Lancaster (ed.) *Brian Howard: Portrait of a Failure*, p. 126.
56. Harold Acton to EW, 23 September 1923; BL.
57. *The New York Times Magazine*, 30 November 1952; *EAR*, pp. 423–4.
58. Harold Acton, *Memoirs of an Aesthete*, p. 126.
59. Ibid., p. 120.
60. Harold Acton to Evelyn Waugh, undated; BL.
61. *A Little Learning*, p. 198.
62. Ibid.
63. Ibid., p. 204; Stannard, *Evelyn Waugh: The Early Years*, p. 89.
64. *A Little Learning*, p. 204.
65. *Put Out More Flags*, p. 19.
66. Sefton Delmer, *Trail Sinister*, pp. 337–443; Evelyn's cousin and Murray's friend Claud Cockburn countered with a more innocent explanation that the ape had inadvertently bitten her host's jugular vein while attempting to rouse him from sleep. See Claud Cockburn, 'Spying in Spain and Elsewhere', *Grand Street*, Vol.1 No. 2 (1982); Paul Preston, *We Saw Spain Die*, pp. 125–6.
67. Alec Waugh, *My Brother Evelyn*, p. 172.
68. *Hertford College Magazine*, No. 78 (1992), p. 12.
69. Cockburn, 'Evelyn Waugh's Lost Rabbit', *Atlantic Monthly*, December 1973.
70. *A Little Learning*, p. 171.
71. Ibid., p. 171–2.
72. Alexander Waugh, *Fathers and Sons*, pp. 177–9.

7 His Poor Dead Heart

1. EW to Tom Driberg, [May 1922]; *EWL*, p. 9.
2. Alexander Waugh, *Fathers and Sons*, p. 169.
3. Hugh Molson recalling what Christopher Hollis told him, *Arena* interview with Lord Molson; AWA.
4. Alec Waugh, *Early Years*, p. 165.
5. Cockburn, 'Evelyn Waugh's Lost Rabbit', *Atlantic Monthly*, December 1973.
6. Alec Waugh, *My Brother Evelyn*, p. 169.
7. Fragment of Vol. 2 of autobiography, 'A Little Hope', HRC, quoted in ibid., p. 170.
8. See for example Arundel del Re in *The Isis*, 20 June 1923, p. 12.
9. Transcript of interview with Lord Molson for *Arena*, copy in AWA.
10. Harold Acton to Christopher Sykes, 16 October 1972, AWA; Introduction by Ann Pasternak Slater to *The Complete Short Stories of Evelyn Waugh*.
11. *Evelyn Waugh in Letters by Terence Greenidge*, p. 7.
12. *A Little Learning*, p. 192.
13. Selina Hastings interview with Anthony Powell; AWA; Duncan Fallowell, *How to Disappear*, p. 175.
14. Harold Acton to Alastair Graham and EW, 8 April 1924; BL.
15. Humphrey Carpenter, *The Brideshead Generation*, p. 85.
16. Fallowell, *How to Disappear*, p. 178.
17. *A Little Learning*, p. 193.
18. Alastair Graham to Michael Davie, 30 October 1975, Michael Davie Papers; AWA.
19. 'I wrote to my father asking to be taken away and sent to Paris to enjoy the full life of [George du Maurier's] *Trilby*', *A Little Learning*, p. 175.

20. EW to Dudley Carew, undated; *EWL*, p. 12, where the date is estimated as 1924, however the letter also refers to EW speaking at the Union and the only instance recorded in *The Isis* of his doing that was in late 1923.
21. Jessie Graham to Brasenose College, 6 November 1923, Brasenose College Archives, Oxford.
22. *A Little Learning*, p. 192.
23. *Brideshead Revisited* (Penguin Classics edition, 2000), p. 25.
24. Catherine Waugh's Diary, 15 December 1923; BU.
25. Alastair Graham to EW, 5 September 1925; BL.
26. *A Little Learning*, p. 208.

8 Pure as Driven Slush

1. EW to Dudley Carew, *c.* 12 June 1924, HRC.
2. 29 July to 30 August 1924; *EWD*, p. 172.
3. C. R. M. F. Cruttwell to EW, undated; BL.
4. *A Little Learning*, p. 210.
5. EWD, 25 June 1924.
6. Paula Byrne, *Mad World,* p. 63.
7. Transcript of Selina Hastings's interview with Tamara Talbot Rice; AWA.
8. Harman Grisewood to Selina Hastings, interview transcript; AWA.
9. Powell, *Infants of the Spring*, p. 98.
10. *A Little Learning*, p. 210.
11. Anthony Bushell, *Arena* interview; AWA.
12. 29 October 1924; *EWD*, p. 183.
13. Rothenstein, *Summer's Lease*, p. 110.
14. *A Little Learning*, p. 212.
15. Douglas Goldring, *Odd Man Out*, p. 282.
16. Quoted in Kate Summerscale, *Queen of Whale Cay* (Fourth Estate, 1997), p. 76.
17. 3 July 1924; *EWD*, p. 166.
18. 12 July 1924; *EWD*, p. 169.
19. Anthony and Violet Powell to Selina Hastings, interview transcript; AWA.
20. 9 November 1924, *EWD*, p. 186.
21. *A Little Learning*, p. 213.
22. 12 November 1924; *EWD*, p. 187.
23. 18 November 1924; *EWD*, p. 188.
24. 29 October 1924; *EWD*, p. 183.
25. EW to Harold Acton, [*c.* 15 December 1924]; BL; 19 December 1924; *EWD*, p. 192.
26. Acton, *Memoirs of an Aesthete*, p. 146.
27. The only institutional libraries known to hold copies of *Irais* are the Kinsey Institute, Cornell, and the British Library.
28. 24 December 1924; *EWD*, p. 193–4.
29. *A Little Learning*, pp. 217–18.
30. Dorothea Ponsonby Diary, 28 July 1924, quoted in Taylor, *Bright Young People*, p. 56.
31. Note by Harman Grisewood headed 'Olivia Plunket Greene'; AWA.
32. Harman Grisewood to Selina Hastings, interview transcript; AWA.
33. Harman Grisewood to Christopher Sykes, 2 April 1973, GU.
34. 11 January 1925; *EWD*, p. 197.

35. 21 January 1925; *EWD*, p. 199.

36. 25 January 1925; *EWD*, p. 201.

37. *A Little Learning*, p. 221.

38. EW to Catherine Waugh, undated [*c.*23 January 1925]; BL.

39. 5 May 1925; *EWD*, p. 211.

40. Quoted in Sykes, *Evelyn Waugh*, p. 60.

41. Verschoyle, quoted in ibid., p. 60.

42. *A Little Learning*, p. 224.

43. 2 March 1925; *EWD*, p. 203.

44. 29 March 1925; *EWD*, p. 204.

45. *A Little Learning*, p. 225.

46. Georgiana Russell (later Blakiston) to Patrick Balfour, 22 April 1925, Balfour Papers, Huntington Library.

47. Ibid.

48. *The Daily Telegraph*, 16 April 1925.

49. Georgiana Blakiston to Patrick Balfour, 22 April 1925, Huntington Library.

50. Arthur Ponsonby to Dorothea Ponsonby, 7 April 1925, Shulbrede archives, quoted in Raymond A. Jones, *Arthur Ponsonby*, (Christopher Helm, 1985), p. 161.

51. 20 October 1925; *EWD*, p. 229.

52. 24 April 1925; *EWD*, p. 209.

53. *Evelyn Waugh in Letters by Terence Greenidge*, p. 135.

54. 15 April 1925; *EWD*, pp. 207–8 (with name deleted).

55. Ibid.

56. 18 April 1925; *EWD*, p. 208.

57. Ibid.

58. Alexander Waugh *Fathers and Sons*, p. 192.

59. 14 May 1925; *EWD*, p. 211.

60. *Decline and Fall*, p. 45.

61. *A Little Learning*, pp. 227-8; not recorded in his Diary.

62. 3 July 1925; *EWD*, p. 213.

63. 28 May 1925; *EWD*, p. 212.

64. *A Little Learning*, p. 228.

65. Ibid.

66. 1 July 1925; *EWD*, p. 213.

67. *A Little Learning*, p. 230.

9 Becoming a Man of Letters

1. 28 July 1925; *EWD*, p. 241.

2. EW to Harold Acton, [18 February 1925]; *EWL*, pp. 23–4.

3. 26 August 1925; *EWD*, p. 218.

4. Alastair Graham to EW; 1 September 1925; BL.

5. Alastair Graham to EW; 5 September 1925; BL.

6. 16 and 20 August 1925; *EWD*, pp. 216–7.

7. 23 September 1925; *EWD*, p. 223.

8. 1 and 7 August, 1925; *EWD*, pp. 214–15.

9. 22 December 1925; *EWD*, p. 238.

10. Christmas Day 1925; *EWD*, p. 238.

11. 15 November 1925; *EWD*, p. 234.
12. Note headed 'Olivia Plunket Greene' by Harman Grisewood; AWA.
13. Michael Holroyd, *Augustus John*, Vol. 2, pp. 167–8.
14. 29 December 1925; *EWD*, p. 240.
15. Harman Grisewood to Selina Hastings, transcript of interview, p. 9; AWA.
16. 8 October 1925; *EWD*, p. 226.
17. 26 January 1926; *EWD*, p. 244.
18. 25 February 1926; *EWD*, p. 247.
19. 13 March 1926; *EWD*, p. 248.
20. 20 January 1926; *EWD*, p. 243.
21. 26 January 1926; *EWD*, p. 244.
22. 29 January 1926; *EWD*, p. 244.
23. 30 January 1930; *EWD*, p. 245.
24. *Nash's Pall Mall Magazine*, March 1937, *EAR*, p. 191.
25. Stannard, *Evelyn Waugh: The Early Years*, p. 120.
26. 13 March 1926; *EWD*, p. 249.
27. 10 June 1926; *EWD*, p. 254.
28. 1 April 1926; *EWD*, p. 250.
29. *A Little Learning*, p. 229.
30. 11 January 1926; *EWD*, p. 242.
31. 1 April 1926; *EWD*, p. 250.
32. 8 March 1926; *EWD*, p. 248.
33. 24 July 1926; *EWD*, p. 256.
34. Alastair Graham to Michael Davie, November 1975, AWA. 'It must have been a terrible strain on E's nerves being cooped up with a lot of strangers whom he would never have chosen as companions, and no means of escape.'
35. 25 August 1926; *EWD*, p. 263.
36. Postcript to *PRB* (Dalrymple Press edition, 1982), p. 44.
37. 28 September 1925; *EWD*, p. 225.
38. Alec Waugh, *Early Years*, p. 216.
39. *Manchester Guardian*, 29 October 1926.
40. 30 October 1926; *EWD*, p. 268.
41. *Literary Review*, 9 April 1927, quoted in Robert Murray Davis, *Evelyn Waugh, Writer*.
42. EW to Henry Yorke [1926], *EWL*, p. 24; the book was published before Yorke left Oxford without a degree that Christmas.
43. 22 September 1926; *EWD*, p. 265.
44. 2 October 1926; *EWD*, p. 266.
45. 6 December 1926; *EWD*, p. 272.
46. James Knox, *Robert Byron*, p. 101.
47. Fallowell, *How to Disappear*, pp. 177–8.
48. Andrew Sinclair, *Francis Bacon: His Life and Violent Times*, p. 42.
49. 1 January 1927; *EWD*, p. 275.
50. 7 January 1927; *EWD*, p. 277.
51. 4 January 1927; *EWD*, p. 276.
52. Sykes, *Evelyn Waugh*, p. 71.
53. 20 February 1927; *EWD*, p. 281.
54. Ibid.

55. 21 February 1927; *EWD*, p. 281.

56. Edmund to EW [dated from postmark 21 February 1927]; BL.

57. 7 March 1927; *EWD*, p. 282.

58. 28 February 1927; *EWD*, p. 281.

59. Ibid.

60. Bill Egan, *Florence Mills: Harlem Jazz Queen*, (Scarecrow Press, 2004), p. 174.

61. 28 February 1927; *EWD*, p. 281.

62. 15 March 1926; *EWD*, p. 249.

63. Note headed 'Olivia Plunket Greene' by Harman Grisewood; AWA.

10 Shevelyn

1. 23 May 1927; *EWD*, p. 284.

2. Unpublished, untitled manuscript by Evelyn Gardner 'about my marriage to Evelyn Waugh and its break-up'; copy in AWA.

3. *The Times*, 29 September 1933.

4. Note by Lady Mary Clive headed 'Evelyn Gardner' (1987); AWA.

5. 1 July 1927; *EWD*, p. 284–5.

6. 'Careers for our Sons: The Complete Journalist', *Passing Show*, 26 January 1929; *EAR*, p. 48.

7. Alastair Graham to Michael Davie, November 1975; AWA.

8. Evelyn Gardner to John Maxse, 21 November 1927, Columbia University, cited in Selina Hastings, *Evelyn Waugh*, p. 166.

9. Ibid, p. 162.

10. Evelyn Gardner interview with Michael Davie, 24 February 1973; AWA.

11. Evelyn Gardner to John Maxse, November 1927; CU.

12. Lady Pansy Pakenham to John Maxse, 29 December 1927; CU.

13. Ibid.

14. Evelyn Gardner interview with Michael Davie, 24 February 1973; AWA.

15. 3 September 1927; *EWD*, p. 249.

16. Evelyn Gardner to Mrs Arthur Waugh, 28 December 1927; HRC.

17. Evelyn Gardner to John Maxse, November 1927; CU.

18. Alexander Waugh, *Fathers and Sons*, p. 200.

19. EW to Nancy Mitford, 8 January 1952; *EWL*, p. 364.

20. See Donat Gallagher, 'Evelyn Waugh and the Vatican Divorce', in Alain Blayac (ed.), *Evelyn Waugh: New Directions*, p. 73.

21. Evelyn Gardner to John Maxse, 4 May 1928; CU.

22. Pansy Pakenham to John Maxse, 8 May 1928; CU.

23. Evelyn Gardner to John Maxse, 2 May 1928; CU.

24. Pansy Pakenham to John Maxse, 8 May 1928; CU.

25. EW to *TLS*, 17 May 1928; *EWL*, p. 28.

26. *EWCH*, p. 79.

27. Anthony Powell, *Messengers of Day*, p. 22.

28. Carew, *Fragment of Friendship*, pp. 81–2.

29. Evelyn Gardner to John Maxse, 2 February 1928; CU.

30. Evelyn Gardner to John Maxse, 28 March and 18 July 1928; CU.

31. Pansy Pakenham to John Maxse, 19 March 1928; CU.

32. Pansy Pakenham to John Maxse, 12 June 1928; CU.

33. 27 June 1928; *EWD*, p. 295.

11 A Common Experience, I'm Told

1. Unpublished, untitled manuscript by Evelyn Gardner 'about my marriage to Evelyn Waugh and its break-up'; copy in AWA; Evelyn Gardner to John Maxse, 18 July 1928, CU.
2. Acton, *Memoirs of an Aesthete*, p. 202.
3. 25 June 1928, *Robert Byron Letters Home*, p. 103.
4. Catherine Waugh Diary, 27 June 1928; BU.
5. Evelyn Gardner interview with Michael Davie, 24 February 1973; AWA.
6. Nancy Mitford to Heywood Hill, 22 May 1966, *The Bookshop at 10 Curzon Street*, pp. 117–18.
7. Evelyn Gardner to John Maxse, 18 July 1928; CU; 6 July 1928; *EWD*, p. 295.
8. EW to Tom Balston, [*c.* 27 January 1929], copy in AWA.
9. Saturday, 14 July 1928; *EWD*, p. 295.
10. *The Observer*, 23 September 1928; *EWCH*, p. 81.
11. *Evening Standard*, 11 October 1928; *EWCH*, p. 82.
12. Naomi Mitchison to EW, undated letter [autumn 1928]; BL.
13. Derwent May (ed)., *Good Talk: An Anthology from BBC Radio*, p. 15.
14. *Evening News*, 2 November 1928, *EWCH*, p. 84.
15. *New Statesman*, 3 November 1928, *EWCH*, p. 85.
16. Hollis, *Oxford in the Twenties*, pp. 105–6.
17. Hugh Massingberd in The Antony Powell Society Newsletter, Issue 3, Summer 2001.
18. Harold Acton to EW, 18 September 1928; BL.
19. 8 October 1928; *EWD*, p. 295.
20. *Decline and Fall*, p. 120 (Penguin Modern Classics edition).
21. 18 October 1924; *EWD*, p. 295.
22. Wheen, *Tom Driberg*, p. 258.
23. *Decline and Fall*, p. 120 (Penguin Modern Classics edition).
24. EW to Thomas Balston, 1 October 1928; BL.
25. *Good Talk*, p. 16.
26. Acton, *Memoirs of an Aesthete*, p. 204.
27. Unpublished, untitled manuscript by Evelyn Gardner 'about my marriage to Evelyn Waugh and its break-up'; copy in AWA.
28. 8 October 1928; *EWD*, p. 297.
29. 12 October 1928; *EWD*, p. 298.
30. EW to A. D. Peters, undated; *EWL*, p. 30.
31. 25 October 1928; *EWD*, p. 300.
32. See 'Margot, I Presume' by Duncan McLaren, www.evelynwaugh.org.uk.
33. 27 October 1928; *EWD*, p. 300.
34. Note by Lady Mary Clive on Evelyn Gardner (1987); AWA.
35. *Daily Express*, 13 February 1929, p. 19.
36. *Labels*, pp. 45–6.
37. Unpublished, untitled manuscript by Evelyn Gardner 'about my marriage to Evelyn Waugh and its break-up', copy in AWA.
38. EW to Thomas Balston, [*c.* 27 January 1929]; copy in AWA.

39. *Labels*, pp. 29–30.
40. Ibid., p. 69.
41. Evelyn Gardner interview with Michael Davie, 24 February 1973; AWA.
42. EW to Thomas Balston, [*c.* 10 March 1929]; copy in AWA.
43. EW to Harold Acton, [*c.* 7 March 1929]; *EWL*, p. 31.
44. EW to Henry Yorke (the writer Henry Green) [19 March 1929]; AWA.
45. EW to Arthur Waugh, undated; BU.
46. EW to Thomas Balston, 18 March 1929; BL; EW to Arthur Waugh, undated; BU.
47. Evelyn Gardner interview with Michael Davie, 24 February 1973; AWA. NB in that interview and in her written account she said Evelyn's trip had been to Cyprus, but all the other evidence points to his having gone to Cairo.
48. EW to Harold Acton, 31 March 1929; copy in AWA.
49. EW to Henry Yorke, 4 May 1929; *EWL*, pp. 33–4.
50. EW to Harold Acton, *c.* 10 May 1929; copy in AWA.
51. Ibid.
52. Ibid.
53. Evelyn Gardner to John Maxse, 26 May 1929; CU.
54. *Labels*, p. 206.
55. Evelyn Gardner to John Maxse, [May 1929; CU.
56. EW to Henry Yorke, *c.* 2 June 1929; *EWL*, pp. 35–6.
57. Powell, *Messengers of Day*, p. 99.
58. Ibid., p. 101.
59. Ibid., p. 99.
60. Unpublished, untitled manuscript by Evelyn Gardner 'about my marriage to Evelyn Waugh and its break-up', copy in AWA.
61. 'My Friend Evelyn Waugh' in Nancy Mitford, *A Talent to Annoy*, p. 177.
62. *Daily Express*, 12 June 1929.
63. Note of telephone interview between Eleanor Campbell-Orde and Selina Hastings, March 1990; AWA.
64. Unpublished, untitled manuscript by Evelyn Gardner 'about my marriage to Evelyn Waugh and its break-up'; copy in AWA.
65. EW to Henry Yorke, 20 June 1929; copy in AWA.
66. Sir John Heygate to Michael Davie, 11 February 1975; AWA.
67. *The Tatler*, 3 July 1929, p. 46; *Sketch*, 3 July 1929; see also 'Those Parties Again' by Duncan McLaren in www.evelynwaugh.org.uk.
68. Powell, *Messengers of Day*, p. 126.
69. Elizabeth Montagu, *Honourable Rebel*, p. 105.
70. Powell, *Messengers of Day*, p. 128.
71. Ibid.; the telegram was dated about 26 July, Powell remembered. See 'The Tatler's Role in Waugh's Downfall' by Jacqueline McDonnell, *Times Higher Educational Supplement*, 23 June 1989.
72. Sykes, *Evelyn Waugh*, p. 94; Selina Hastings, *Evelyn Waugh*, p. 195.
73. Evelyn Waugh Petition for Divorce, copy in AWA.
74. Alec Waugh, *My Brother Evelyn*, p. 191.
75. *Bystander*, 17 July 1929.
76. Margaret Wyndham to John Maxse, 30 July 1929; CU.
77. Sir John Heygate to Mark Amory, 25 February 1976; AWA.
78. Selina Hastings interview with Eleanor Campbell Orde, 1991; AWA.

79. EW to Tom Balston, undated, copy in AWA.
80. Alec Waugh, *My Brother Evelyn*, p. 191.
81. Ibid., p. 192.
82. EW to Catherine and Arthur Waugh [5 August 1929]; BU.
83. Ibid.
84. Note by Lady Mary Clive on Evelyn Gardner (1987); AWA.
85. EW to Harold Acton, 4 August 1929; *EWL*, pp. 38–9.
86. Harold Acton to EW, 5 August 1929; BL.
87. EW to Henry Yorke, [*c*. 13 September 1929]; *EWL*, p. 40.
88. See note of Selina Hastings's interview with Eleanor Campbell-Orde, 1991; copy in AWA. In a letter Eleanor wrote to John Heygate, she remembered it slightly differently, recalling that she told him that she would 'wait and see'.

12 Perversion to Rome

1. Henry Lamb to EW, 14 August 1929; BL.
2. Lady Pansy Lamb to J. H. Maxse, 26 September 1929; CU.
3. Note by Lady Mary Clive on Evelyn Gardner (1987); AWA.
4. 'My Friend Evelyn Waugh' in Nancy Mitford, *A Talent to Annoy*, p. 234; see also Nancy Mitford to Christopher Sykes, undated; Christopher Sykes Papers, Georgetown University.
5. Evelyn Nightingale to Michael Davie, 13 October 1975.
6. Nancy Mitford interview with Christopher Sykes; Sykes Papers, GU.
7. Jessica Mitford, *Hons and Rebels*, p. 34.
8. 18 June 1930; *EWD*, pp. 315–16.
9. Nancy Mitford to Mark Ogilvie-Grant, 1930, quoted in Laura Thompson, *Life in a Cold Climate*, p. 93.
10. *The Independent*, 13 August 2003.
11. EW to Henry Yorke [*c*. 13 September 1929]; *EWL*, p. 39.
12. 30 December 1929, *Love From Nancy: The Letters of Nancy Mitford*, p. 34.
13. Diana Mosley to Christopher Sykes, 30 September 1975, Sykes Papers, GU.
14. EW to Diana Mosley, 30 March 1966, *EWL*, pp. 638–9.
15. Diana Mosley to Christopher Sykes, 30 September 1975, Sykes Papers, GU.
16. Catherine Waugh Diary, 24 December 1929; BU.
17. EW to Bryan and Diana Guinness, 4 January 1930, copy in AWA.
18. *Evening Standard*, 30 January 1930.
19. *Paris Review*, Vol. 30 (1963), p. 77.
20. BBC TV *Face to Face* interview with John Freeman, June 1960.
21. *Daily Mirror*, 7 February 1931.
22. J. F. Roxburgh to EW, 11 July 1930; BL.
23. 26 May 1930; *EWD*, p. 311.
24. EW to Lionel Fielden, 7 July 1930; copy in AWA.
25. Lionel Fielden to EW, 10 July 1930; BL.
26. 5 July 1930; *EWD*, p. 320.
27. EW to Diana Guinness, 17 July 1930; copy in AWA.
28. Bryan Guinness to EW, 23 July 1930.
29. EW to Diana Mosley, 9 March 1966; copy in AWA.
30. Cited in Hastings, *Evelyn Waugh*, p. 219.

31. Diana Mosley, *Loved Ones*, p. 54.
32. Alec Waugh, *The Best Wine Last*, p.45; Alec Waugh to Michael Davie, 1972; AWA.
33. Arthur Waugh Diary, 29 April 1930; BU.
34. 29 May 1930; *EWD*, p. 312.
35. 12 June 1930; *EWD*, p. 314.
36. 19 June 1930; *EWD*, p. 316.
37. *John Bull*, 23 August 1930; *EAR*, pp. 94–5.
38. Alec Waugh, *My Brother Evelyn*, pp. 191–2.
39. *Face to Face* interview, 1960.
40. Quoted in Sykes, *Evelyn Waugh*, p. 107.
41. Pryce-Jones, *Evelyn Waugh and His World*, p. 62.
42. 'Come Inside', in John A. O'Brien (ed.), *The Road to Damascus* (1962); *EAR*, p. 367.
43. *Face to Face* interview, 1960.
44. EW to Martin D'Arcy [21 August 1930]; AWA.
45. Pryce-Jones, *Evelyn Waugh and His World*, p. 64.
46. Alexander Waugh, *Fathers and Sons*, p. 217.
47. *Evelyn Waugh in Letters to Terence Greenidge*.

13 The Dutch Girl

1. Loelia, Duchess of Westminster, *Grace and Favour*, p. 117.
2. *The Times*, 16 August 1935.
3. *Grace and Favour*, p. 117.
4. Cecil Beaton, *Book of Beauty* (Duckworth, 1930), p. 35.
5. Teresa Cuthbertson obituary in *The Times*, 15 June 2010.
6. Jacqueline Mcdonnell, *Waugh on Women*, p. 21.
7. Interview with Jacqueline Mcdonnell in 1984, cited in ibid., p. 23.
8. Hastings, *Evelyn Waugh*, p. 222.
9. 1 June 1930; *EWD*, p. 313.
10. *Daily Mail*, 14 June 1930; *EAR*, pp. 78–80.
11. Teresa Jungman to EW, undated; BL.
12. Lord Longford to Selina Hastings, undated interview transcript; AWA.
13. Sarah Bradford, *Sacheverell Sitwell*, p. 217.
14. *Daily Mail*, 12 July 1930, cited in Hastings, *Evelyn Waugh*, p. 213.
15. [2–12 September 1930]; *EWD*, p. 328.
16. Christine Longford, unpublished memoirs, cited in Bevis Hillier, *Young Betjeman*, p. 309.
17. Elizabeth Longford, *The Pebbled Shore*, pp. 105–6.
18. EWD [2–12 September 1930]; *EWD*, p. 328 (omitting the sentence about Frank and Elizabeth).
19. Bradford, *Sacheverell Sitwell*, p. 201.
20. Elizabeth Longford later recalled: 'I rarely saw Evelyn on this visit except in the company of Alastair.' *Pebbled Shore*, p. 105.
21. EW to Patrick Balfour, 25 September 1931; Balfour Papers, Huntington Library.
22. Alastair Graham to Michael Davie, undated; AWA.
23. Fallowell, *How to Disappear*, p. 218.
24. Ibid., p. 202.
25. David N. Thomas, *Dylan Thomas: A Farm, Two Mansions and a Bungalow*, p. 86.

26. Paul Ferris, *Dylan Thomas: The Collected Letters*, (Dent, 2000) p. 603.

27. Fallowell, *How to Disappear*, p. 165.

28. Ibid., pp. 170–73.

29. EW to Catherine and Arthur Waugh, 16 November 1930; AWA.

30. EW to Teresa Jungman [1 February 1931]; private collection, copy in AWA.

31. Alec Waugh, *A Year to Remember*, p. 95.

32. Ibid., p. 96.

33. Arthur Waugh, *One Man's Road*, p. 372.

34. Alexander Waugh, *Fathers and Sons*, p. 216.

35. Alec Waugh, *A Year to Remember*, p. 190.

36. John Farrar to Bernice Baumgarten, 9 October 1931, HRC, cited in Hastings, *Evelyn Waugh*, p. 247.

37. Alec Waugh to Patrick Balfour, 15 July 1931, Huntington Library.

38. Alec Waugh, *A Year to Remember*, p. 123.

39. EW to Patrick Balfour [26 July 1931], Huntington Library.

40. Alec Waugh, *A Year to Remember*, p. 123.

41. Ibid., p. 124.

42. EW to Patrick Balfour [3 August 1931], Huntington Library.

43. Cited in Paula Byrne, *Mad World*, p. 144.

44. Alec Waugh, *A Year to Remember*, p. 106.

45. Jane Mulvagh, *Madresfield*, p. 23.

46. Pryce-Jones, *Evelyn Waugh and His World*, p. 50.

47. *A Little Learning*, pp. 205–6.

48. EW to Teresa Jungman [c. 24 October 1931]; private collection, copy in AWA.

49. EW to Patrick Balfour, [27 October 1931]; Balfour Papers, Huntington Library.

50. EW to Lady Sibell, Lady Mary and Lady Dorothy Lygon, 5 November [1931]; *EWL*, p. 59.

51. EW to Mary and Dorothy Lygon, 14/15 November 1931; copy in AWA.

52. EW to Teresa Jungman, 11 November 1931; private collection, copy in AWA.

53. EW to Teresa Jungman [c. 13 November 1931]; private collection, copy in AWA.

54. EW to Teresa Jungman, 3 December 1931; private collection, copy in AWA.

55. EW to Teresa Jungman, [c. 6 January 1932]; private collection, copy in AWA.

56. EW to Arthur Windham Baldwin, 14 January [1932]; *EWL*, p. 61.

57. *EWL*, p. 649.

58. EW to Teresa Jungman, 29 February 1932; private collection, copy in AWA.

59. EW to Teresa Jungman, [c. 7 March 1932]; private collection, copy in AWA.

60. EW to Teresa Jungman, 16 April 1932; private collection, copy in AWA.

61. EW to Arthur Windham Baldwin [16 April 1932]; *EWL*, p. 63.

62. EW to W. N. Roughead [c. 8 May 1932]; copy in AWA.

63. EW to Lady Dorothy Lygon [April 1932]; copy in AWA.

64. Referred to in his open letter to Archbishop Francis Bourne, 15 May 1933.

65. See James Fox, *White Mischief*, (Cape, 1982), p. 50; the de Traffords' eventual divorce was recorded in *The Times*, 26 October 1937.

66. EW to Lady Dorothy Lygon [c. 20 April 1932]; *EWL*, p. 64.

67. EW to Teresa Jungman, 23 May 1932; private collection, copy in AWA.

68. Cited in Byrne, *Mad World*, p. 192.

69. *Brideshead Revisited*, p. 92.

70. Philip Ziegler, *Diana Cooper*, p. 150.

71. Ibid., p. 160.
72. Diana Cooper, *The Light of Common Day*, p. 112
73. Ziegler, *Diana Cooper*, p. 150.
74. *The Spectator*, 1 October 1932.
75. *The Listener*, 19 October 1932.
76. *Bookman*, November 1932.
77. Eileen Agar, *A Look at My Life*, pp. 103–5.
78. Clare Mackenzie to EW, undated; BL.
79. Joyce Gill to EW, undated; BL.
80. EW to Teresa Jungman, 28 September 1932; private collection, copy in AWA.
81. EW to Teresa Jungman, 23 October 1932; private collection, copy in AWA.
82. EW to Teresa Jungman, 20 November 1932; private collection, copy in AWA.
83. EW to Lady Diana Cooper [2 December 1932]; *MWMS*, p. 20.

14 *Off to the Forest*

1. EW to Lady Diana Cooper, [8 November 1932]; *MWMS*, p. 19.
2. EW to Teresa Jungman, 4–8 December 1932; private collection, copy in AWA.
3. *Ninety-Two Days*, pp. 3, 5.
4. 4 December 1932; *EWD*, p. 355.
5. Ibid.
6. Pryce-Jones, *Evelyn Waugh and His World*, p. 89.
7. EW to Lady Mary Lygon. [*c.* 20 December]; copy in AWA.
8. 4 December 1932; *EWD*, p. 356.
9. EW to Lady Mary Lygon, [*c.* 20 December]; copy in AWA.
10. EW to Teresa Jungman, 1 December 1932; private collection, copy in AWA.
11. EW to Teresa Jungman, 2 December 1932; private collection, copy in AWA.
12. EW to Teresa Jungman, 4–8 December 1932; private collection, copy in AWA.
13. *Ninety-Two Days*, p. 20 (Serif edition, 2007).
14. 20 December 1932; *EWD*, p. 359.
15. Ibid.
16. 20 December 1932; *EWD*, p. 359–60.
17. 20 December 1932; *EWD*, p. 360.
18. Christmas Day 1932; *EWD*, p. 360.
19. EW to Teresa Jungman, 31 December 1932; private collection, copy in AWA.
20. EW to Lady Diana Cooper [2 January 1933]; *MWMS*, p. 19.
21. *Ninety-Two Days*, p. 30 (Serif edition, 2007).
22. *Ninety-Two Days*, p. 50 (Serif edition 2007)
23. 11 January 1933; *EWD*, p. 364.
24. *Ninety-Two Days*, p. 61.
25. EW to Lady Diana Cooper, 28 January [1933]; *MWMS*, p. 23.
26. *Ninety-Two Days*, pp. 71–2.
27. Ibid., p. 67.
28. Ibid., p. 74.
29. Ibid., p. 88.
30. Ibid., p. 87.
31. EW to Lady Diana Cooper, 10 February 1933; *MWMS*, pp. 25–6.

32. EW to Teresa Jungman, Ash Wednesday [1 March 1933]; private collection, copy in AWA.
33. EW to Lady Diana Cooper, 2 March [1933]; *MWMS*, p. 27.
34. EW to Teresa Jungman, Ash Wednesday [1 March 1933]; private collection, copy in AWA.
35. EW to Teresa Jungman, 7 April 1933; private collection, copy in AWA.
36. EW to Teresa Jungman [c. 8 May 1933]; private collection, copy in AWA.
37. Ibid.
38. EW to Teresa Jungman [c. 21 May 1933]; private collection, copy in AWA.
39. Ibid.
40. EW to Teresa Jungman, 23 July 1933; private collection, copy in AWA.
41. EW to Lady Diana Cooper [c. 29 July 1933]; *MWMS*, p. 38.
42. EW to Teresa Jungman, 31 July 1933; private collection, copy in AWA.
43. Teresa Jungman to EW, undated [c. July 1933]; BL.
44. Teresa Jungman to EW, undated [c. July 1933]; BL.
45. EW to Teresa Jungman, 2 August 1933; private collection, copy in AWA.
46. EW to Teresa Jungman, 31 July 1933, private collection, copy in AWA
47. EW to Teresa Jungman, 2 August 1933; private collection, copy in AWA.
48. EW to Nancy Mitford [4 August 1933]; copy in AWA.
49. Teresa Jungman to EW [c. 7 August 1933]; BL.
50. EW to Teresa Jungman, 16 August 1933; private collection, copy in AWA.
51. Ibid.
52. EW to Lady Diana Cooper, [September/October 1933]; *MWMS*, p. 35.
53. Diary of Katharine Asquith, quoted in Hastings, *Evelyn Waugh*, p. 286.
54. EW to Lady Diana Cooper, [September/October 1933]; *MWMS*, p. 35.
55. EW to Teresa Jungman, 1 September 1933 [and c. 28 August 1933]; private collection, copy in AWA.
56. EW to Teresa Jungman, 1 September 1933; private collection, copy in AWA.
57. Hollis, *Oxford in the Twenties*, p. 84.
58. EW to Teresa Jungman [c. 3 July 1933]; private collection, copy in AWA.
59. Unpublished, untitled manuscript by Evelyn Gardner 'about my marriage to Evelyn Waugh and its break-up'; copy in AWA.
60. EW to Lady Dorothy Lygon, [c. 20 Oct 1933]; copy in AWA.
61. Unpublished, untitled manuscript by Evelyn Gardner 'about my marriage to Evelyn Waugh and its break-up'; copy in AWA.
62. See Gallagher, 'Evelyn Waugh and the Vatican Divorce' in Blayac (ed.), *Evelyn Waugh: New Directions*, pp. 62–84.
63. Ibid. pp. 73–4.
64. Ibid., p. 74.
65. EW to Lady Mary Lygon [October 1933]; *EWL*, p. 81.

15 *I Can't Advise You in My Favour*

1. EW to Teresa, [c. 16 November 1933]; private collection, copy in AWA.
2. EW to Lady Dorothy Lygon, [c. 19 October 1933]; copy in AWA.
3. EW to Lady Mary Lygon [31 October 1933]; copy in AWA.
4. EW to Teresa Jungman, 6 November 1933; private collection, copy in AWA.
5. EW to Teresa Jungman, 3 December 1933; private collection, copy in AWA.

6. EW to Teresa Jungman, 24 December 1933; private collection, copy in AWA.
7. EW to Teresa Jungman, 29 December 1933; private collection, copy in AWA.
8. EW to Katharine Asquith [January 1934]; *EWL*, pp. 83–4.
9. EW to Lady Mary and Lady Dorothy Lygon [*c.* 4 January 1934]; *EWL*, p. 82.
10. EW to Lady Mary Lygon [*c.* 20 January 1934]; *EWL*, p. 82.
11. 'Fan-Fare', *Life* magazine, 8 April 1946; *EAR*, p. 303.
12. EW to Katharine Asquith [January 1934]; *EWL*, pp. 83–4.
13. EW to Katharine Asquith, [*c.* 9 February 1934]; *EWL*, p. 85.
14. Henry Yorke to EW, 2 September 1934; BL.
15. EW to Henry Yorke, [*c.* 3 September 1934]; *EWL*, p. 88.
16. EW to Lady Diana Cooper [*c.* 11 February 1934]; *MWMS*, p. 43.
17. EW to A. D. Peters [*c.* 30 April 1934]; HRC, copy in AWA.
18. 6 July 1934; *EWD*, p. 386.
19. EW to Teresa Jungman, 7 July 1934; private collection, copy in AWA.
20. 9 July 1934; *EWD*, p. 388.
21. EW to Lady Diana Cooper, [13 July 1934]; *MWMS*, p. 45.
22. 17 July 1934; *EWD*, p. 390.
23. 'The First Time I Went To The North: Fiasco in The Arctic', published in the anthology *The First Time I* . . . ed. by Theodora Benson (1935); *EAR*, p. 146.
24. 'The First Time I Went To The North'; *EAR*, pp. 144–9.
25. The First Time I Went To The North'; *EAR*, p. 148.
26. Sir Alexander Glen to Selina Hastings, Hastings, *Evelyn Waugh*, p. 306.
27. EW to Tom Driberg [late August 1934], Christ Church, Oxford; copy in AWA.
28. *NYTBR*, 27 May 1934; *EWCH*, pp. 146–8.
29. *New Statesman*, 15 September 1934; *EWCH*, pp. 154–7.
30. EW to Lady Mary Lygon [*c.* 8 September 1934]; *EWL*, p. 89.
31. EW to Lady Dorothy Lygon [*c.* 26 October 1934]; *EWL*, pp. 90–91.
32. Nicola Beauman, *Cynthia Asquith*, (Hamish Hamilton, 1987), p. 314.
33. EW to Lady Mary Lygon [*c.* 10 January 1935]; *EWL*, p. 92.
34. James Lees-Milne, *Ancestral Voices*, p. 184.
35. A. N. Wilson, *Hilaire Belloc* (Hamish Hamilton, 1984), p. 325.
36. EW to Lady Mary Lygon [*c.* 8 February 1935]; *EWL*, p. 93.
37. EW to Laura Herbert [3 May 1935]; *EWL*, p. 94.
38. EW to Katharine Asquith [24 June 1935]; *EWL*, p. 95.
39. EW to Laura Herbert [*c.* late July 1935?]
40. Laura Herbert to EW [8 August 1935]; BL.
41. EW to Laura Herbert [*c.* 9 August 1935]; *EWL*, p. 95.
42. *Evening Standard*, 13 February 1935; *EAR*, p. 163.
43. *Waugh in Abyssinia*, (Penguin Modern Classics edition, 2000), p. 41.
44. W. F. Deedes, *At War With Waugh*, p. 116.
45. Ibid., pp. 90–91.
46. Ibid., p. 35.
47. *Waugh in Abyssinia*, pp. 44–5.
48. EW to Diana Cooper, 13 September [1935]; *MWMS*, p. 52.
49. EW to Laura Herbert, 24 August [1935]; *EWL*, p. 97–8.
50. EW to Laura Waugh 26 October [1935]; AWA.
51. Arthur Waugh Diary, 3 February 1936; BU.
52. Laura Herbert to EW, 28 January 1936; BL.

53. EW to Lady Mary Lygon, 15 April 1936; *EWL*, p. 105.
54. EW to Laura Herbert, 28 April 1936; *EWL*, p. 104.

16 *Goodness She is a Decent Girl*

1. EW to Diana Cooper [June 1936]; *MWMS*, p. 60.
2. *The Spectator*, 1 November 1935; *EWCH*, p. 165.
3. Henry Yorke to EW, 18 June 1936; BL.
4. EW to Henry Yorke, 20 June 1936; copy in AWA.
5. *The Spectator*, 10 July 1936, *EWCH*, pp. 183–4.
6. EW to Katharine Asquith, 4 August 1936; copy in AWA.
7. 18 August 1936; *EWD*, p. 398.
8. *Waugh in Abyssinia*, p. 167.
9. EW to Laura Herbert, 4 August 1936; *EWL*, p. 109.
10. EW to Laura Herbert, 5 August 1936; *EWL*, p. 110.
11. EW to Lady Mary Lygon, 6 August 1936; copy in AWA.
12. 10 September 1936; *EWD*, p. 405.
13. Laura Herbert to EW, August 1936; BL.
14. *The Times*, 20 August 1936.
15. EW to Lady Mary Lygon, 12 September 1936; *EWL*, pp. 110–11.
16. Arthur Waugh Diary, 23 September 1936; BU.
17. EW to Arthur Waugh, 29 September 1936; AWA.
18. Arthur Waugh Diary, 6 October 1936; BU.
19. Arthur Waugh Diary, 7 October 1936; BU.
20. EW to Teresa Jungman, 1 October 1936; private collection, copy in AWA.
21. 15 October 1936; *EWD*, p. 409.
22. 5 November 1936; *EWD*, p. 412.
23. 21 December 1936; *EWD*, p. 417.
24. EW to Lady Diana Cooper [*c.* 21 December 1936]; *MWMS*, p. 62.
25. EW to Laura Herbert [February 1937]; AWA.
26. 21 December 1936; *EWD*, p. 417.
27. 'General Conversation Myself', *Nash's Pall Mall Magazine*, March 1937; *EAR*, p. 190; the fire itself is recorded in Arthur Waugh Diary, 29 January 1935; BU.
28. Arthur Waugh Diary, 31 December 1936; BU.
29. Arthur Waugh Diary, 26 February 1936; BU.
30. Alec Waugh, *The Best Wine Last*, p. 48.
31. Alexander Waugh, *Fathers and Sons*, p. 242.
32. EW to Laura Herbert, February 1937; AWA.
33. EW to Laura Herbert, February 1937; AWA.
34. 4 February 1937; *EWD*, p. 420.
35. EW to Diana Cooper [*c.* 18 July 1937]; *MWMS*, p. 64.
36. Hastings, *Evelyn Waugh*, p. 364.
37. Arthur Waugh Diary, 17 April 1937; BU.
38. 18 April 1937; *EWD*, p. 422.
39. EW to Katharine Asquith, May 1937; copy in AWA.
40. EW to W. N. Roughead, 7 July 1937; copy in AWA.
41. Patrick Balfour to Caroline Kinross, 15 December 1937, National Library of Scotland; cited in Hastings, *Evelyn Waugh*, p. 366.

42. EW to Vivien Greene, 8 March [1938]; *EWL*, p. 116.

43. 8 July 1939; *EWD*, p. 432.

44. 27 November 1937; *EWD*, p. 428.

45. 28 June 1939; *EWD*, p. 431.

46. 17 and 24 November 1937; *EWD*, pp. 426–7.

47. 26 November 1937; *EWD*, p. 428.

48. Arthur Waugh Diary, 25 February 1938, BU

49. EW to A. D. Peters, 10 March 1938; HRC.

50. EW to Thomas Balston, 11 March 1938; copy in AWA.

51. EW to Teresa Jungman, 12 March 1938; private collection, copy in AWA.

52. EW to Teresa Jungman, 17 March 1938; private collection, copy in AWA.

53. Introduction to new Penguin paperback edition of *Scoop* (2000).

54. 7 May 1938; *EWCH*, p. 194.

55. 7 May 1938; *EWCH*, p. 195.

56. 13 May 1938; *EWCH*, p. 199.

57. *The Spectator*, 13 May 1938; *EWCH*, pp. 200-202.

58. Arthur Waugh Diary, 7 July 1938; BU.

59. Alec Waugh, *The Best Wine Last*, p. 58.

60. Arthur Waugh Diary, 8 July 1938; BU.

61. EW to A. D. Peters [*c.* 16 May 1938]; HRC.

62. EW to Mary Herbert, 17 August [1938]; copy in AWA.

63. 28 July 1939; *EWCH*, p. 204.

64. 19 November 1939; *EWCH*, p. 207.

65. EW to Teresa Jungman, 1 January 1939.

66. 23 August 1939; *EWD*, p. 437.

67. Diana Cooper to EW [July 1939]; *MWMS*, p. 68.

68. *The Times*, 5 September 1939, p. 1.

17 A War to End Waugh

1. Catherine Waugh to EW, 5 September 1939; BL.

2. 27 August 1939; *EWD*, p. 438.

3. 1 October 1939; *EWD*, p. 444.

4. Henry Yorke to EW, 14 October 1939, BL.

5. 21 October 1939; *EWD*, p. 447.

6. Carol Mather, *When the Grass Stops Growing*, (Leo Cooper, 1997), p. 35.

7. 18 October 1939; *EWD*, p. 447.

8. EW to Laura Waugh, 23 October 1939; AWA.

9. EW to Laura Waugh [*c.* 25 October 1939]; AWA.

10. All Saints [1 November], 1939; *EWD*, p. 448.

11. EW to Mary Lygon [*c.* 18 November 1939].

12. EW to Laura Waugh [*c.* 30 November 1939].

13. 26 October 1939; *EWD*, p. 448.

14. 23 November 1939; *EWD*, p. 451.

15. Ibid.

16. Ibid.

17. EW to Laura Waugh [10 December 1939]; AWA.

18. EW to Laura Waugh, 18 December 1939; AWA.

19. Diana Cooper, *Trumpets from the Steep*, p. 36.
20. John St John, *To the War with Waugh* (The Whittington Press, 1973), p. 6.
21. EW to Helen Asquith, 27 December 1939; copy in AWA.
22. EW to Laura Waugh, 7 January 1940; *EWL*, p. 133.
23. Obituary of Teresa Cuthbertson, *The Daily Telegraph*, 12 June 2010.
24. EW to Teresa Cuthbertson, 1 August 1940, private collection, copy in AWA.
25. EW to Laura Waugh, 14 January 1940; AWA.
26. Major-General R. D. Houghton to Selina Hastings, interview transcript, side 2, page 1; AWA.
27. 15 January 1940; *EWD*, p. 461.
28. EW to Laura Waugh, 25 February 1940; AWA.
29. Evelyn told Laura that Betjeman had been 'registered insane' after the RAF medical exam.
30. EW to John Betjeman, 24 January and 15 February 1940; copies in AWA.
31. EW to Laura Waugh [April 1940]; *EWL*, p. 139.
32. Major-General R. D. Houghton to Selina Hastings, interview transcript, side 1, page 6; copy in AWA.
33. EW to Laura Waugh, 31 March 1940; AWA.
34. EW to Laura Waugh, 2 April 1940; AWA.
35. Admiralty Form S 206 b, signed by Lieutenant-Colonel G. E. Wildman-Lushington (18 May 1940) and Brigadier St Clair-Morford (25 May 1940), cited in Gallagher, *In the Picture*, p. 139.
36. EW to Laura Waugh, 26 September [1940]; *EWL*, p. 141.
37. EW to Arthur Waugh, 5 November 1940; AWA.
38. See Sushila Anand, *Daisy: The Life and Loves of the Countess of Warwick* (Piatkus, 2008).
39. 'Commando Raid On Bardia', *Life* magazine, 17 November 1941; *EAR*, p. 263.
40. David Niven, *The Moon's A Balloon* (Coronet Books, 1972), p. 220.
41. Typed draft of 'A History of the Commandos' by R. E Laycock, Laycock Papers 6/28, Liddell Hart Centre for Military Archives, cited in Gallagher, *In The Picture*, p. 142.
42. Robert Laycock, unpublished memoir, private collection.
43. 13 November 1940; *EWD*, pp. 487–8.
44. EW to Laura Waugh, 21 November 1941; AWA.
45. 'Memorandum on Layforce; July 1940–July 1941', *EWD*, p. 491.
46. EW to Laura Waugh, 15 November 1940; AWA.
47. EW to Laura Waugh, 20 November 1940; AWA.
48. Mather, *When the Grass Stops Growing*, pp. 30–31.
49. EW to Catherine Waugh, 2 December 1940, AWA.
50. Excerpts quoted in a letter from Arthur Waugh to Joan Waugh, 6 December 1940; AWA.
51. Alexander Waugh, *Fathers and Sons*, p. 252.
52. 3 December 1940; *EWD*, p. 437.
53. EW to Laura Waugh [*c.* 8 December 1940]; AWA.
54. EW to Laura Waugh, 25 December 1940; *EWL*, p. 149.
55. Christopher Sykes and Ann Pasternak Slater think it would have been better; Douglas Lane Patey disagrees.
56. 3 February 1941, cited in James Owen, *Commando*, p. 29.

57. EW to Laura Waugh, 8 February 1941; AWA.
58. EW to Laura Waugh, 23 February 1941; *EWL*, p. 150.
59. EW to Laura Waugh, 6 March 1941; AWA.
60. 'I was Evelyn Waugh's Batman', *Punch*, 19 November 1975.
61. Conversation between Dr R. E. S. Tanner and Antony Beevor, 2 December 1990, copy of transcript in AWA.
62. 'I was Evelyn Waugh's Batman', *Punch*, 19 November 1975.
63. 'Memorandum on Layforce; July 1940–July 1941'; *EWD*, p. 494.
64. Ibid.; *EWD*, p. 495.
65. A. D. Peters to EW, 23 September 1941, cited in Douglas Lane Patey, *The life of Evelyn Waugh*, p. 189.
66. 'Memorandum on Layforce; July 1940–July 1941'; *EWD*, p. 496.
67. Ibid., p. 498.
68. Ibid., p. 499.
69. Ibid., p. 500.
70. Account by Laycock; National Archives, DEFE 2/699.
71. 'Memorandum on Layforce; July 1940–July 1941'; *EWD*, p. 502.
72. Ibid., p. 503.
73. Ibid., p. 504.
74. Major F. C. C. Graham, 'Cretan Crazy Week', p. 5, IWM 76/180/1.
75. 'Memorandum on Layforce; July 1940–July 1941'; *EWD*, p. 507.
76. EW's reply, dated 4 July 1955; Mark Amory (ed.), *The Letters of Ann Fleming*, p. 155.
77. 6 July 1955; *EWD*, p. 728.
78. Layforce Diary, National Archives, WO 218/186.
79. Major-General Sir Robert Laycock, unpublished memoir.
80. 'Memorandum on Layforce; July 1940–July 1941'; *EWD*, p. 509.
81. Layforce Diary, National Archives, WO 218/186.
82. Antony Beevor, 'The First Casualty of Waugh', *The Spectator*, 5 April 1991, p. 26.
83. Journal of Major R. W. Madoc, pp. 101–02, IWM, cited in Gallagher, *In the Picture*, p. 207.
84. Letter to Nicholls's mother in Papers of Captain F. R. J Nicholls, IWM 93/17/1.
85. F. C. C. Graham to Michael Davie, 9 June 1976, IWM 76/180/1.
86. Laycock, unpublished memoir, p. 380.
87. Ibid., pp. 380–81.
88. Ibid., p. 388.
89. Ibid.
90. Antony Beevor, *Crete 1941* (Introduction to Penguin edition, 2014), p. xv.
91. Conversation between Dr R. E. S. Tanner and Antony Beevor, 2 December 1990, copy of transcript in AWA.
92. Ibid.
93. Colonel E. E. Rich, 'The Campaign in Crete', National Archives, CAB 44/121; cited in Gallagher, *In the Picture*, p. 86.

18 Head Unbloodied but Bowed

1. EW to Laura Waugh, 28 September 1941; AWA.
2. Arthur Waugh Diary, 27 September 1941; BU.
3. EW to Laura Waugh, 28 September 1941; AWA.

4. Cited in Selina Hastings, *Evelyn Waugh*, p. 422.
5. EW to Laura Waugh, 30 September 1941; AWA.
6. EW to Laura Waugh, 28 September 1941; AWA.
7. EW to Laura Waugh [*c.* November 1941]; AWA.
8. EW to Laura Waugh, 16 November 1941; *EWL*, p. 157.
9. EW to Laura Waugh [January 1942]; AWA.
10. Diary, 5 January–7 February 1942; *EWD*, p. 518.
11. '[H]eroic and chivalrous disguise', *Scott-King's Modern Europe*, p. 5; 'Do you understand . . .', EW to Diana Cooper, [Spring 1942], *MWMS*; 'I wish I were back with you', EW to Laycock, 23 March 1942, copy in AWA; 'It seems unlikely . . .', *EWD*, p. 517; EW to Laura Waugh [May 1942]; AWA.
12. EW to Lady Dorothy Lygon, 17 May 1942; copy in AWA.
13. EW to Laura Waugh, 31 May 1942; *EWL*, p. 161.
14. Arthur Waugh to EW [25 April 1942]; BL.
15. Laycock to EW, 26 June 1942; BL.
16. 26 October 1942; *EWD*, p. 530.
17. EW to Laura Waugh, 27 October [1942]; *EWL*, p. 164.
18. EW to Laura Waugh 27 December 1942; *EWL*, pp. 164–5.
19. 28 October 1942; *EWD*, p. 530.
20. EW to Laura Waugh [28 September 1943]; *EWL*, p. 172.
21. 27 August 1942; *EWD*, p. 525.
22. EW to Laura Waugh, 24 October [1942]; AWA.
23. EW to Laura Waugh [*c.* 10 December 1942]; AWA.
24. EW to Laura Waugh [26 July 1943]; AWA.
25. Lord Lovat, *March Past*, p. 233.
26. EW to Tom Driberg [*c.* 1 July 1943]; Christ Church, Oxford.
27. EW to Alec Waugh, 8 July 1943; BU.
28. EW to Lord Lovat, 12 July 1943, *EWD*, p. 541.
29. Lord Lovat to EW, 13 July 1943, *EWD*, p. 542.
30. Lieutenant-Colonel A. F. Austen to Auberon Waugh, November 1978; AWA.
31. Gen. Haydon to Laycock, 31 July 1943, Laycock Papers 6/20, Liddell Hart Centre.
32. Jakie Astor to Christopher Sykes, cited in Sykes, *Evelyn Waugh*, p. 228.
33. Laycock Papers, Box 6/15, Liddell Hart Centre; cited in Owen, *Commando*, p. 312.
34. Brigadier Antony Head to Laycock, 9 September 1942, Laycock Papers, 6/4, LHC, cited in Gallagher *In the Picture*, p. 227.
35. Laycock to Lovat, 12 September 1942; Laycock Papers, 6/13, LHC, cited in ibid., p. 227.
36. Laura Waugh to Alec Waugh, 3 July 1943, cited in Alexander Waugh, *Fathers and Sons*, p. 265.
37. EW to Brigadier R. E. Laycock, 19 July 1943, *EWD*, p. 543.
38. 10 August 1943; *EWD*, p. 545.
39. 29 August 1943; *EWD*, p. 548.
40. EW to Laura Waugh [6 December 1943]; *EWL*, p. 174.
41. Evelyn Waugh, *Sword of Honour*, p. 533 (Penguin Classics edition).
42. 13 October 1943; *EWD*, pp. 552–3.
43. EW to Colonel A. H. Ferguson, 24 January 1944; copy in AWA.
44. EW to Laura Waugh, 25 January 1944; *EWL*, p. 176.

19 A Book to Bring Tears

1. EW to Laura Waugh, 2 February 1944; *EWL*, p. 176.
2. EW to A. D. Peters, 8 February 1944; *EWL*, p. 177.
3. 13 February 1944; *EWD*, p. 558.
4. 2 March 1944; *EWD*, p. 559.
5. EW to Laura Waugh, 2 March [1944]; *EWL*, p. 179.
6. EW to Lady Dorothy Lygon, 23 March 1944; *EWL*, p. 180.
7. Ibid.
8. EW to Laura Waugh [26 March 1944]; AWA.
9. EW to Laura Waugh, 19 September 1943; *EWL*, p. 169.
10. Auberon Waugh, *Will This Do?*, p. 29.
11. EW to Laura Waugh, 6 December 1941; AWA.
12. EW to Laura Waugh, [*c.* 15 December 1942]; AWA.
13. EW to Laura Waugh, 19 September 1943; *EWL*, p. 170.
14. EW to Laura Waugh [*c.* 13 February 1944]; AWA.
15. EW to Laura Waugh, 2 June 1941; *EWL*, p. 179.
16. 1 April 1944; *EWD*, p. 561.
17. 3 April 1944; *EWD*, p. 561.
18. 16 April 1944; *EWD*, p. 561.
19. 4 May 1944; *EWD*, p. 562.
20. Ibid.; *EWD*, p. 564.
21. 9 March 1944; *EWD*, pp. 564–5.
22. Auberon Waugh, *Will This Do?*, pp. 13–14.
23. Evelyn Waugh to Nancy Mitford, 18 May [1944]; *LNMEW*, p. 4.
24. EW to Lady Dorothy Lygon, 23 March 1944; *EWL*, p. 182.
25. 6 June 1944; *EWD*, pp. 567–8.
26. EW to A. D. Peters, 20 June 1944; HRC.
27. 24 June 1944; *EWD*, p. 568.
28. EW to Laura Waugh, 25 June 1944; AWA.
29. Fitzroy Maclean, 'Captain Waugh', in Pryce-Jones, *Evelyn Waugh and His World*, p. 134.
30. 2 July 1944; *EWD*, pp. 568–9.
31. EW to Laura Waugh, 6 July 1944; AWA.
32. Nicholas Shakespeare, 'A Life Less Ordinary', *The Independent*, 21 September 2011.
33. Diana Cooper, *Trumpets from the Steep*, p. 201. John Julius Norwich, *Trying to Please*, p. 99.
34. 16 July 1944; *EWD*, p. 573.
35. Randoplh Churchill to Laura Waugh, 26 July 1944; AWA.
36. 31 July 1944; Hermione Ranfurly, *To War with Whittaker*, (Heinemann, 1994), p. 260.
37. Pryce-Jones, *Evelyn Waugh and His World*, p. 53.
38. EW to Laura Waugh, 17 August [1944]; *EWL*, p. 182.
39. Stephen Clissold, 'Civil Waugh in Croatia', *The South Slav Journal*, Vol. 3, No. 3, September 1980.
40. 16 September 1944; *EWD*, p. 579.
41. EW to Laura Waugh, 16 September 1944; *EWL*, p. 182.
42. EW to Catherine Waugh, 17 October 1944; AWA.
43. Clissold, 'Civil Waugh in Croatia', *The South Slav Journal*, Vol. 3, No. 3, September 1980.

44. Pryce-Jones, *Evelyn Waugh and His World*, p. 143.
45. The Earl of Birkenhead, 'Fiery Particles', in ibid., p. 152.
46. Clissold, 'Civil Waugh in Croatia', *The South Slav Journal*, Vol. 3, No. 3, September 1980.
47. The Earl of Birkenhead, 'Fiery Particles', in Pryce-Jones, *Evelyn Waugh and His World*, pp. 151–3.
48. 27 October 1944; *EWD*, p. 587.
49. EW to Nancy Mitford, 12 November [194]; *LNMEW*, p. 7.
50. EW to Laura Waugh, 2 November [1944]; *EWL*, p. 192.
51. EW to Laura Waugh, 5 November [1944]; *EWL*, pp. 192–3.
52. The Earl of Birkenhead to Hugh Trevor-Roper, 29 October 1973; *Evelyn Waugh Newsletter*, Vol. 43, No. 3.
53. Clissold, 'Civil Waugh in Croatia', *The South Slav Journal*, Vol. 3, No. 3, September 1980.
54. EW to Laura Waugh, 5 November 1944; *EWL*, p. 192–3.
55. EW to Catherine Waugh, 11 December [1944]; AWA.
56. EW to Laura Waugh, 25 December 1944; AWA.
57. EW to Nancy Mitford, 4 January 1945; AWA.
58. EW to Laura Waugh, 7 January 1945; *EWL*, p. 195.
59. EW to Nancy Mitford, 7 January 1945; *EWL*, p. 196.
60. 12 January 1945; *EWD*, p. 608.
61. EW to Laura Waugh, 5 January 1945; AWA.
62. EW to Laura Waugh, 10 February 1945; *EWL*, p. 201.
63. EW to Laura Waugh, 8 March 1945; *EWL*, p. 202.

20 *The Occupation*

1. EW to Nancy Mitford, 7 January 1945; *LNMEW*, p. 14.
2. Martin D'Arcy to EW, 21 April 1945; BL.
3. Penelope Betjeman to EW, 23 January 1945; BL.
4. Nancy Mitford to EW, 17 January 1945; BL.
5. Henry Yorke to EW, Christmas Day 1944; BL.
6. Nancy Mitford to EW, 17 January 1945; BL.
7. Preface to 1960 edition of *Brideshead Revisited* (Chapman & Hall).
8. Harold Acton to EW, 30 May 1945; BL.
9. *Manchester Guardian*, 1 June 1945; *EWCH*, p. 233.
10. 23 June 1945; *EWCH*, p. 239.
11. 5 January 1946, *EWCH*, p. 245.
12. *EWL*, p. 219n.
13. 12 April 1945; *EWD*, p. 625.
14. EW to Douglas Woodruff, 12 January 1946; copy in AWA.
15. 1 July 1945; *EWD*, p. 608.
16. EW to Alfred Gilbey, 31 October 1945; copy in AWA.
17. *The Daily Telegraph*, 11 November 1947, *EAR*, p. 339.
18. EW to Laura Waugh, 28 July 1945; AWA.
19. 'What To Do With the Upper Classes', *Town and Country*, September 1946, *EAR*, p. 312.
20. Ibid.

21. 28 July 1945; *EWD*, p. 629.
22. EW to Laura Waugh, 28 July 1945; AWA.
23. 28 July 1945; *EWD*, p. 629.
24. EW to Laura Waugh, 25 August 1945; *EWL*, p. 211.
25. 11 September 1945; *EWD*, p. 608.
26. EW to Lady Diana Cooper, 12 January 1947; *MWMS*, p. 93.
27. EW to Catherine Waugh, 19 September 1945; AWA.
28. EW to Lady Mary Lygon, 12 October 1945; copy in AWA.
29. EW to Randolph Churchill, 8 October 1945; *EWL*, p. 213.
30. 26 December 1945; *EWD*, p. 608.
31. EW to Lady Diana Cooper, 3 January 1946; *MWMS*, p. 82.
32. Auberon Waugh, *Will This Do?* p. 65.
33. EW to Penelope Betjeman [August 1935]; edited version in *EWL*, pp. 96–7.
34. Richard Ingrams to Auberon Waugh, January 1987, cited in Bevis Hillier, John Betjeman: New Fame New Love, 2002, p. 661.
35. Penelope Betjeman to Martin Stannard, cited in Stannard, *Evelyn Waugh*, p. 282.
36. Auberon Waugh, *Literary Review*, December 1986.
37. EW to John Betjeman, 27 May 1945; *EWL*, p. 207.
38. EW to Penelope Betjeman, 15 January 1946; *EWL*, pp. 217–18.
39. Penelope Betjeman to EW, 23 January 1946; BL.
40. EW to John Betjeman, 22 December 1946; copy in AWA.
41. Penelope Betjeman to EW, 1 June 1947; BL.
42. EW to Penelope Betjeman, 4 June [1947]; *EWL*, pp. 252–3.
43. Diary, 4 August 1947; edited version in *EWD*, p. 608.
44. EW to Nancy Mitford, 7 August [1946]; *LNMEW*, p. 46.
45. EW to Graham Greene, 21 August 1951; *EWL*, p. 353. EW to Nancy Mitford, 29 October 1951; *LNMEW*, p. 244.
46. *The Tablet*, 3 December 1938, *EAR*, pp. 238–41.
47. *The Tablet*, 10 November 1945, *EAR*, pp. 281–3.
48. EW to Nancy Mitford, 7 January 1945; *LNMEW*, p. 14.
49. 31 March 1946; *EWD*, p. 645.
50. 'Notes on Nuremberg'; EW to Randolph Churchill [April 1946], *EWL*, p. 226.
51. Philip Ziegler, *Diana Cooper*, p. 241.
52. Diana Cooper to Conrad Russell, 7 April 1946, cited in Ziegler, p. 241.
53. 1–2 April 1946; *EWD*, p. 647.
54. EW to Lady Mary Lygon, 4 February 1946; *EWL*, p. 233.
55. 6 March 1946; *EWD*, p. 643.
56. 'Fan-Fare', *Life*, 8 April 1946, *EAR*, pp. 300–304.
57. A. D. Peters to EW, 15 November 1946; HRC.
58. EW to A. D. Peters, 21 November 1946; HRC.
59. Harold Acton, *More Memoirs of an Aesthete*, p. 225.
60. EW to Lady Diana Cooper [c.2 February 1947]; *MWMS*, p. 94.
61. Alec Waugh to Catherine Waugh, 22 February 1948; BU.
62. Diary, 7 February 1947 (omitted from *EWD*).
63. Selina Hastings, *The Secret Lives of Somerset Maugham*, p. 381.
64. EW to A. D. Peters, 19 February 1947; HRC.
65. 7 February 1947; *EWD*, p. 673.
66. 7 April 1947; *EWD*, p. 675.

67. EW to A. D. Peters, 6 March [1947]; HRC.
68. Ibid.
69. 7 April 1947; *EWD*, p. 675.
70. Ibid.
71. *The Tablet*, 17 July 1936.
72. 7 April 1947; *EWD*, p. 675.
73. EW to A. D. Peters, 6 March [1947]; HRC.
74. EW to Lady Diana Cooper, 10 May [1947]; *MWMS*, pp. 95–6.
75. EW to A. D. Peters, 6 March [1947]; HRC.
76. 1 February 1947; *EWD*, p. 670.
77. Carol Brandt to A. D. Peters, 18 March 1947, HRC, cited in Hastings, *Evelyn Waugh*, p. 517.
78. Anthony Slide (ed.), *'It's the Pictures That Got Small': Charles Brackett on Billy Wilder and Hollywood's Golden Age* (2014), 16 February 1947, p. 304.
79. Cited in Craig Brown, *One on One*, (Fourth Estate, 2011), p. 53.
80. Hastings, *Evelyn Waugh*, p. 517.
81. *The Ordeal of Gilbert Pinfold*, p. 23 (Penguin Modern Classics edition).
82. EW's remark to Toye is in Michael Swan to Maurice Cranston, 16 July [1952], Cranston Papers, HRC. His warning to Baby is in EW to Teresa Cuthbertson, 4 January 1946; private collection, copy in AWA.
83. 19 April 1947; *EWD*, p. 675.
84. EW to Nancy Mitford, 16 October [1946]; *EWL*, p. 246.
85. EW to Margaret Stephens, 26 May 1947; AWA.
86. 'Half in Love with Easeful Death: An Examination of Californian Burial Customs', *Life*, 29 September 1947, *The Tablet*, 18 October 1947, *EAR*, pp. 331–7.
87. EW to A. D. Peters, 11 September 1947; HRC.
88. A. D. Peters to EW, 13 September 1947; HRC.
89. EW to A. D. Peters, 14 September [1947]; HRC.
90. 29 June 1947; *EWD*, p. 681.
91. Cyril Connolly to EW, [2 September 1947]; BL.
92. *Horizon*, February 1948, pp. 76–7; *EAR*, pp. 299–300.
93. Sykes, *Evelyn Waugh*, p. 312.
94. Cited in Jeffrey Meyers, *Edmund Wilson*, (Houghton Mifflin, 1995), p. 271.
95. Nancy Mitford to EW, 9 February 1948; *LNMEW*, p. 90.
96. EW to Nancy Mitford [December 1950]; *LNMEW*, p. 207.
97. Lady Pamela Berry to Nancy Mitford, 27 November 1949, cited in Hastings, *Evelyn Waugh*, pp. 537–8.
98. *EWL*, pp. 288–9n.
99. EW to Laura Waugh, 9 November [1948]; *EWL*, p. 288.
100. EW to Nancy Mitford, 2 April [1949]; *LNMEW*, p. 121.
101. Sykes, *Evelyn Waugh*, p. 337.

21 *Off My Rocker*

1. Laura Waugh to EW [July 1950]; BL.
2. EW to Laura Waugh, 30 July and 31 July 1950; *EWL*, p. 334 and AWA.
3. Auberon Waugh, *Will This Do?*, p. 46.
4. Alexander Waugh, *Fathers and Sons*, p. 312.

5. Ibid., pp. 312–13.
6. Auberon Waugh, *Will This Do?*, p. 41.
7. EW to Auberon Waugh, 20 February 1956, *EWL*, p. 466.
8. Auberon Waugh, *Will This Do?*, p. 41.
9. Auberon Waugh, *Will This Do?*, p. 41; Auberon Waugh to Nicholas Shakespeare, *Arena* interview.
10. Cited in Alexander Waugh, *Fathers and Sons*, p. 308.
11. Alexander Waugh, *Fathers and Sons*, p. 310.
12. EW to Teresa D'Arms 17 April 1964; AWA; James Waugh to author, February 2016; 'Let Evelyn Waugh back into Combe Florey churchyard' by Septimus Waugh, *The Spectator*, 26 March 2016.
13. EW to Graham Greene, 18 August 1951; *EWL*, p. 353.
14. Catherine Walston to EW [24 August 1951]; BL.
15. EW to Catherine Walston, 25 August 1951; *EWL*, p. 355.
16. *Time*, 27 October 1952, *EWCH*, pp. 341–3.
17. 19 December 1952, *EWD*, p. 705.
18. EW to Laura Waugh, 5 January 1953; *EWL*, p. 389.
19. EW to Nancy Mitford, 10 February 1953; *LNMEW*, p. 300.
20. John Betjeman to EW, 24 May 1953; Candida Lycett Green (ed.)., *John Betjeman Letters*, Vol. 2 (Methuen, 1995), p. 42.
21. Cited in A. N. Wilson, *Betjeman*, p. 209.
22. EW to Lord Kinross [1953]; *EWL*, p. 416.
23. John Betjeman to EW, 31 December 1953, *John Betjeman Letters*, Vol. 2, p. 47.
24. EW to John Betjeman, 2 January 1954; coopy in AWA.
25. Sykes, *Evelyn Waugh*, p. 472.
26. Barbara Skelton, *Tears Before Bedtime* (Hamish Hamilton, 1987), pp. 135–6.
27. John Julius Norwich (ed.), *Darling Monster: The Letters of Lady Diana Cooper to her son John Julius Norwich, 1939–1952*, p. 229.
28. 29 July 1947; *EWD*, p. 682.
29. EW to Nancy Mitford, 5 December [1949]; *LNMEW*, p. 158.
30. *The Ordeal of Gilbert Pinfold*, pp. 11–12.
31. Ibid., p. 12.
32. EW to John Betjeman, 17 September 1953, *EWL*, p. 410.
33. Auberon Waugh to Martin Stannard, 9 February 1989; Stannard, *Evelyn Waugh: The Later Years 1939–1966*, p. 334.
34. Ibid.
35. *The Ordeal of Gilbert Pinfold*, p. 15.
36. *Frankly Speaking*, cited in Appendix to Penguin edition of *The Ordeal of Gilbert Pinfold*.
37. EW to Diana Cooper, 7 August [1953]; *MWMS*, p. 179.
38. Philip Ziegler, *Diana Cooper*, p. 266.
39. EW to Diana Cooper, 19 September [1953]; *MWMS*, p. 183.
40. EW to Diana Cooper, 19 August [1953]; *MWMS*, p. 178.
41. Ziegler, *Diana Cooper*, p. 277.
42. EW to Diana Cooper, 2 January 1954; *MWMS*, p. 186.
43. 6 January 1954; *EWD*, p. 724.
44. 6 January 1954; ibid.
45. EW to Laura Waugh, 3 February [1954]; *EWL*, p. 418.

46. EW to Laura Waugh, 8 February [1954]; ibid.

47. EW to Diana Cooper, 18 February [1954]; *MWMS*, p. 187–8.

48. Frances Donaldson, *Evelyn Waugh: Portrait of a Country Neighbour*, p. 59.

49. Ibid., p. 60.

50. EW to Cyril Connolly, 13 March 1954; copy in AWA.

51. EW to Diana Cooper, 6 March 1954; *MWMS*, p. 189.

52. EW to Nancy Mitford, 5 March 1954; *LNMEW*, p. 332.

53. EW to Cyril Connolly, 13 March 1954; copy in AWA.

54. Hollis, *Oxford in the Twenties*, p. 82.

55. EW to Margaret Waugh, 11 December 1954; *EWL*, p. 434.

56. EW to Nancy Mitford, 18 December 1954; *LNMEW*, p. 332.

57. EW to Ann Fleming, 1955; quoted in Matthew Parker, *Goldeneye* (Hutchinson, 2014), p. 188.

58. EW to Ann Fleming, 6 March [1955]; copy in AWA.

59. EW to Daphne Fielding, 2 October [1956]; *EWL*, p. 476.

60. *The Ordeal of Gilbert Pinfold*, pp. 9–10 (Penguin Modern Classics edition, 2006).

61. 20 July 1957, *EWCH*, pp. 384–6.

62. 21 July 1957, *EWCH*, pp. 386–7.

22 Suitably Sequestered

1. Alexander Waugh, *Fathers and Sons*, p. 338.

2. *The Times*, 23 March 1964.

3. Nancy Spain, 'My Pilgrimage to See Mr Waugh', *Daily Express*, 23 June 1955.

4. 'Awake My Soul! It Is A Lord', *The Spectator*, 8 July 1955.

5. Ibid.

6. 21 and 22 June 1955; *EWD*, p. 725.

7. Diary, 30 June 1955; *EWD*, p. 726.

8. EW to Oldfield, 4 July 1955, *EWL*, p. 443.

9. EW to Nancy Mitford, 14 October 1956; *LNMEW*, p. 397.

10. EW to Ann Fleming, 13 September [1956], Amory (ed.), *Letters of Ann Fleming*, pp. 186–7.

11. *The Times*, 20 and 21 February 1957.

12. EW to Nancy Mitford [5 March] 1957, *LNMEW*, p. 405.

13. EW to Diana Cooper, 24 February [1957]; *MWMS*, p. 237.

14. EW to Alec Waugh, 23 February 1957; BU.

15. EW to Ann Fleming, 28 January 1957, *EWL*, p. 484.

16. EW to Jack Donaldson, 12 March [1957]; copy in AWA.

17. Cited in Sykes, *Evelyn Waugh*, pp. 390–91.

18. *Ronald Knox*, p. 286.

19. Ibid., p. 329.

20. EW to Diana Cooper, 20 November [1957], *MWMS*, p. 245.

21. EW to Dom Hubert van Zeller, 23 January 1958; copy in AWA.

22. Daphne Acton to EW, 25 August 1958; BL.

23. Ibid.

24. EW to Ann Fleming, 10 March 1958, *EWL*, p. 505.

25. EW to Harold Acton, 4 December 1958; copy in AWA.

26. Laura Waugh to EW, 11 June 1958; BL.

27. Cited in Alexander Waugh, *Fathers and Sons*, p. 353.
28. Auberon Waugh to EW, 27 April, 1958; ibid., p. 354.
29. Auberon Waugh to EW, May 1958, ibid., p. 356.
30. EW to Diana Cooper, 9 June 1958, *MWMS*, p. 254.
31. EW to Diana Cooper, 13 June [1958], ibid., p. 255.
32. EW to Ann Fleming, 18 June 1958; private collection, copy in AWA.
33. EW to Diana Cooper, 13 June [1958], *MWMS*, p. 255.
34. Laura Waugh to EW, 18 June 1958; AWA.
35. EW to Father Aelred Watkin, 17 June 1958; copy in AWA.
36. EW to Father Philip Caraman, 29 June 1958; copy in AWA.
37. EW to Daphne Acton, 21 August 1958; *EWL*, p. 512.
38. EW to Auberon Waugh, 8 July 1958; *EWL*, p. 510.
39. Auberon Waugh, *Will This Do?*, p. 109.
40. Auberon Waugh, to EW, 21 July 1958; BL.
41. EW to Daphne Acton, 21 August 1958; copy in AWA.
42. Auberon Waugh to EW [September] 1958; BL.
43. EW to Father Aelred [*c.* 8 October 1958]; copy in AWA.
44. EW to Lady Mary Lygon, 26 August 1958; copy in AWA.
45. EW to Auberon Waugh, 14 November 1958, Alexander Waugh, *Fathers and Sons*, p. 373.
46. Auberon Waugh, *Will This Do?*, p. 112.
47. EW to Mother Ignatius, 2 August 1950, *EWL*, p. 334.
48. Christopher Sykes, *Evelyn Waugh*, p. 452.
49. EW to Ann Fleming, 1 September [1952]; *EWL*, p. 380.
50. EW to Margaret Waugh, Whitsun 1953; AWA.
51. EW to Margaret Waugh, 3 June [1957], *EWL* pp. 489–490.
52. EW to Diana Cooper, 29 March 1958, *MWMS*, p. 250.
53. EW to Mary Lygon, 26 August 1958; copy in AWA.
54. EW to Ann Fleming, 3 December 1958; Amory (ed.) *Letters of Ann Fleming*, p. 224.
55. EW to Diana Cooper, 14 January 1959, *MWMS*, p. 262.
56. EW to Ann Fremantle, 31 July 1959, copy in AWA.
57. *The Sunday Times*, 25 September 1960, *EWCH*, p. 415.
58. A. D. Peters to EW, 7 October 1959; BL.
59. EW to Maurice Bowra, 22 October 1959, *EWL*, p. 530.
60. EW to Ann Fleming, 17 February 1960, *EWL*, p. 533.
61. EW to A. D. Peters, 17 March 1960, HRC.
62. EW to Tom Driberg, 11 June 1960, Christ Church, Oxford.
63. EW to Teresa D'Arms, 16 September 1961; AWA.
64. EW to Margaret Waugh, 20 February 1961; AWA.
65. EW to Diana Cooper, 24 December 1960, *MWMS*, p. 282.
66. EW to Jack MacDougall, 18 April 1958, *EWL*, p. 507.
67. EW to Auberon Waugh, 28 July 1959; AWA.
68. EW to John D'Arms, 11 November 1960; copy in AWA.
69. EW to Pansy Lamb, 18 July 1961; copy in AWA.
70. Alexander Waugh, *Fathers and Sons*, p. 394.
71. EW to John Donaldson [24 April 1961], copy in AWA.
72. EW to Alec Waugh, 22 March 1961; BU.
73. EW to Daphne Fielding, 22 May 1961; *EWL*, p. 566.

74. EW to Christopher Sykes, 5 June 1961, Sykes Papers, GU.

75. EW to Ann Fleming, 13 June 1961; copy in AWA.

76. EW to Teresa D'Arms, 5 June 1961; copy in AWA.

77. Alexander Waugh, *Fathers and Sons*, p. 399.

78. Auberon Waugh to EW, 24 June 1961; BL.

79. EW to Auberon Waugh, 29 June 1961; AWA.

80. EW to Margaret Waugh, 5 July [1961]; AWA.

81. EW to Ann Fleming, 17 July 1961; copy in AWA.

23 *Decline and Fall*

1. *A Little Learning*, p. 1.

2. A. D. Peters to EW, 27 April 1961; HRC.

3. EW to Alec Waugh, 19 July 1961; BU.

4. EW to Margaret Waugh, 20 July 1961; AWA.

5. EW to Diana Mosley, 9 March 1966; *EWL*, p. 638.

6. EW to Margaret Waugh, 20 July 1961; AWA.

7. EW to Ann Fleming, 8 August 1961; copy in AWA.

8. EW to Teresa D'Arms, 16 September 1961; copy in AWA.

9. EW to Pamela Berry, 30 October [1961]; copy in AWA.

10. Philip Caraman to EW, 21 April 1961; BL.

11. EW to Ann Fleming, 19 October [1960]; copy in AWA.

12. EW to Margaret Waugh, 7 December 1960; AWA.

13. EW to Margaret Waugh, 20 July 1961; AWA.

14. EW to Margaret Waugh, 12 March 1961; AWA.

15. EW to Ann Fleming, 27 March 1961; *EWL*, p. 563.

16. EW to Margaret Waugh, 24 May 1961; AWA.

17. EW to Margaret Waugh, 20 July 1961; AWA.

18. Margaret Waugh to EW, 6 April 1961; BL.

19. EW to Diana Cooper, 22 June 1961, *MWMS*, p. 288.

20. Philip Caraman to EW, 15 September 1961; BL.

21. EW to Ann Fleming, 30 August 1961; copy in AWA.

22. Christopher Sykes to EW, 21 October 1961; BL.

23. Maurice Bowra to EW, 15 October 1961; BL.

24. *The Sunday Times*, 29 October 1961; *EWCH*, p. 430.

25. Amory (ed.), *Letters of Ann Fleming*, p. 295.

26. EW to Teresa D'Arms, 28 October 1961; copy in AWA.

27. EW to Cyril Connolly, 23 October 1961; copy in AWA.

28. Cyril Connolly to EW, 30 October 1961; BL.

29. EW to Cyril Connolly, 20 November 1961; copy in AWA.

30. EW to Diana Cooper, 30 June 1962, *MWMS*, p. 291.

31. EW to Teresa D'Arms, 19 February 1962; copy in AWA.

32. EW to Diana Cooper, 30 March 1962; *MWMS*, p. 291.

33. EW to Nancy Mitford, 1 April 1962, *LNMEW*, pp. 449–50.

34. EW to Nancy Mitford, 27 March 1962; ibid., p. 447.

35. Nancy Mitford to EW, 10 April 1962; ibid., p. 450.

36. Nancy Mitford to EW, 29 March 1962; ibid., p. 449.

37. EW to Margaret Waugh, 12 April [1962]; copy in AWA.

38. Giles FitzHerbert to the author, December 2013.
39. Giles FitzHerbert to EW, 6 August 1962; BL.
40. EW to Nancy Mitford [*c.* 22 August 1962]; *LNMEW*, p. 457.
41. Diana Cooper to EW [25 August 1962]; *MWMS*, p. 293.
42. EW to Diana Cooper, 28 August 1962; ibid., p. 293.
43. *Basil Seal Rides Again*, p. 13.
44. EW to Daphne Fielding, 25 October 1962; copy in AWA.
45. Margaret Waugh to EW, 7 August 1962; BL.
46. EW to Ann Fleming, 19 September 1962; copy in AWA.
47. EW to Teresa D'Arms, 27 June 1962; copy in AWA.
48. EW to Daphne Acton, 10 June 1963; copy in AWA.
49. EW to Nancy Mitford, 28 December 1962; *LNMEW*, p. 471.
50. Hugh Molson to EW, 2 January 1962; BL.
51. John Betjeman to EW, September 1964; Lycett Green (ed.), *John Betjeman Letters*, Vol. 2, p. 279.
52. W. R. B. Young to EW, 21 November 1963; BL.
53. W. R B Young to EW, 27 November 1963; BL.
54. EW to Teresa D'Arms, 29 October 1964; copy in AWA.
55. Auberon Waugh to EW, 8 June 1963; BL.
56. EW to Teresa D'Arms, 14 October 1963; copy in AWA.
57. EW to Ann Fleming, 13 March 1963; *EWL*, p. 601.
58. EW to Teresa D'Arms, 28 August 1963; copy in AWA.
59. EW to Margaret FitzHerbert, 22 September 1963; copy in AWA.
60. EW to Ann Fleming, 10 October 1963; copy in AWA.
61. EW to Zarita Mattay, 20 November 1963; copy in AWA.
62. EW to Alfred Duggan, 18 November 1963; copy in AWA.
63. *New Statesman*, September 1964; *EWCH*, p. 461.
64. EW to Diana Mosley, 9 March 1966; *EWL*, p. 638.
65. *Encounter*, December 1964; *EWCH*, p. 471.
66. *Cosmopolitan*, November 1964; *EWCH*, pp. 469–70.
67. Katherine Asquith to EW, 9 September 1964; BL.
68. Dudley Carew to EW, 4 September 1964; BL.
69. EW to Diana Cooper, 24 October [1964]; *MWMS*, p. 311.
70. EW to Diana Cooper, 20 December 1964, ibid., p. 315.
71. EW to Ann Fleming, 27 January 1965, *EWL*, p. 630.
72. EW to Nancy Mitford, [2 March] 1965, *LNMEW*, p. 497.
73. EW to Nancy Mitford, 29 May 1965; *EWL*, p. 631.
74. EW to Nancy Mitford, 25 January 1966; *LNMEW*, p. 503.
75. EW to Nancy Mitford, 29 May 1965; *EWL*, p. 631.
76. EW to Nancy Mitford 5 September 1965; *EWL*, p. 633.
77. Ibid.
78. EW to Ann Fleming, 3 January 1966; copy in AWA.
79. Margaret FitzHerbert to EW [4 December 1965]; BL.
80. EW to Margaret FitzHerbert, 6 December 1965; *EWL*, p. 635.
81. Margaret FitzHerbert to EW, 19 December 1965; copy in AWA.
82. EW to A. D. Peters, 29 January 1966; HRC.
83. Sykes, *Evelyn Waugh*, p. 445.
84. EW to Ann Fleming [31 January 1966]; copy in AWA.

85. EW to Professor Robin Anderson, 10 April 1966; copy in AWA.
86. Auberon Waugh, *Will This Do?*, pp. 184–5.
87. Margaret FitzHerbert to Diana Cooper, [April 1966]; *MWMS*, p. 326.

Epilogue

1. Graham Greene to Laura Waugh, 10 April 1966; BL.
2. Diana Mosley to Laura Waugh, 11 April 1966; BL.
3. Nancy Mitford to Laura Waugh, 11 April 1966; BL.
4. A. D. Peters to Laura Waugh, 12 April 1966; BL.
5. Patrick Kinross to Laura Waugh, 17 April 1966; BL.
6. P. G. Wodehouse to Laura Waugh, 11 April 1966; BL.
7. Angus Wilson to Laura Waugh, 13 April 1966; BL.
8. Robert Henriques to Laura Waugh, 12 August 1966; BL.
9. Daphne Acton to Laura Waugh, 13 April 1966; BL.
10. Lady Dorothy Lygon to Laura Waugh, 12 April 1966; BL.
11. Diana Cooper to Laura Waugh, 12 April 1966; BL.
12. John Betjeman to Laura Waugh, 16 April 196; BL.
13. Penelope Betjeman to Laura Waugh, 18 April 1966; BL.
14. Daphne Acton to Laura Waugh, 13 April 1966; BL.

Select Bibliography

Works by Evelyn Waugh

PRB: An Essay on the Pre-Raphaelite Brotherhood, 1847–54, privately
    printed, 1926.
Rossetti: His Life and Works, Duckworth, 1928.
Decline and Fall: An Illustrated Novelette, Chapman & Hall, 1928.
Vile Bodies, Chapman & Hall, 1930.
Labels, A Mediterranean Journey, Duckworth, 1930; US edition: *A
    Bachelor Abroad*, J. Cape & H. Smith, 1930.
Remote People, Duckworth, 1931; US edition: *They Were Still Dancing*,
    Farrar & Rinehart, 1932.
Black Mischief, Chapman & Hall, 1932.
Ninety-Two Days, Duckworth, 1934.
A Handful of Dust, Chapman & Hall, 1934.
Edmund Campion, Longman, 1935.
Mr Loveday's Little Outing and Other Sad Stories, Chapman & Hall, 1936.
Waugh in Abyssinia, Longman Green & Co, 1936.
Scoop: A Novel About Journalists, Chapman & Hall, 1938.
Robbery Under Law, Chapman & Hall, 1939; US edition: *Mexico: An
    Object Lesson*, Little, Brown, 1939.
Put Out More Flags, Chapman & Hall, 1942.
Work Suspended, Chapman & Hall, 1942.
*Brideshead Revisited: The Sacred and Profane Memories of Captain
    Charles Ryder*, Chapman & Hall, 1945.
Scott-King's Modern Europe, Chapman & Hall, 1947.
The Loved One, Chapman & Hall, 1948.
Helena, Chapman & Hall, 1950.
The Holy Places, Queen Anne Press, 1952.

Men at Arms, Chapman & Hall, 1952.

Love Among the Ruins: A Romance of the Near Future, Chapman & Hall, 1953.

Officers and Gentlemen, Chapman & Hall, 1955.

The Ordeal of Gilbert Pinfold, Chapman & Hall, 1957.

The Life of the Right Reverend Ronald Knox, Chapman & Hall, 1959.

A Tourist in Africa, Chapman & Hall, 1960.

Unconditional Surrender, Chapman & Hall, 1961.

Basil Seal Rides Again, Chapman & Hall, 1963.

A Little Learning: The First Volume of An Autobiography, Chapman & Hall, 1964.

Sword of Honour (his final version of the war trilogy *Men at Arms, Officers and Gentlemen* and *Unconditional Surrender*), Chapman & Hall, 1965.

Collected Editions

The Diaries of Evelyn Waugh, edited by Michael Davie, Weidenfeld & Nicolson, 1976 (NB: the 2009 Phoenix paperback edition has a greatly improved index).

The Letters of Evelyn Waugh, edited by Mark Amory, Weidenfeld & Nicolson, 1980.

Evelyn Waugh, A Little Order: A Selection from his Journalism, edited by Donat Gallagher, Eyre Methuen, 1977.

The Essays, Articles and Reviews of Evelyn Waugh, edited by Donat Gallagher, Methuen, 1983.

Mr Wu & Mrs Stitch: The Letters of Evelyn Waugh and Diana Cooper, edited by Artemis Cooper, Hodder & Stoughton, 1991.

The Letters of Nancy Mitford & Evelyn Waugh, edited by Charlotte Mosley, Hodder & Stoughton, 1996.

The Complete Short Stories of Evelyn Waugh, edited by Ann Pasternak Slater, Everyman, 1998.

Other Sources

Acton, Harold, *Memoirs of An Aesthete*, Methuen, 1948.

Acton, Harold, *More Memoirs of An Aesthete*, Methuen, 1970.

Acton, Harold, *Nancy Mitford*, Hamish Hamilton, 1975.

Agar, Eileen, *A Look at My Life*, Methuen, 1988.

Amory, Mark (ed.), *The Letters of Ann Fleming*, Collins Harvill, 1985.

Amory, Mark, *Lord Berners*, Chatto & Windus, 1998.

Annan, Noel, *Roxburgh of Stowe*, Longman, 1964.

Annan, Noel, *Our Age*, Weidenfeld & Nicolson, 1990.

Barber, Michael, *Anthony Powell*, Duckworth, 2004.

Barber, Michael, *Evelyn Waugh*, Hesperus Press, 2013.

Beaton, Cecil, *The Wandering Years: Diaries 1922–1939*, Weidenfeld & Nicolson, 1966.

Beevor, Antony, *Crete: The Battle and the Resistance*, John Murray, 1991; rev. edition: Penguin, 2014.

Blayac, Alain (ed.), *Evelyn Waugh: New Directions*, Macmillan, 1992.

Blondel, Nathalie, *Mary Butts: Scenes from Life*, Kingston, NY, 1998.

Bowra, C. M., *Memories*, Weidenfeld & Nicolson, 1966.

Boyd, William, *Bamboo*, Hamish Hamilton, 2005.

Bradbury, Malcolm, *Evelyn Waugh*, Oliver & Boyd, 1964.

Bradford, Sarah, *Sacheverell Sitwell*, Sinclair-Stevenson, 1993.

Butler, Lucy (ed.), *Robert Byron: Letters Home*, John Murray, 1991.

Byrne, Paula, *Mad World: Evelyn Waugh and the Secrets of Brideshead*, Harper Press, 2009.

Carew, Dudley, *A Fragment of Friendship: A Memory of Evelyn Waugh When Young*, Everest Books, 1974.

Carpenter, Humphrey, *The Brideshead Generation*, Weidenfeld & Nicolson, 1989.

Charteris, Evan (ed.), *The Life and Letters of Edmund Gosse*, William Heinemann, 1931.

Cooper, Diana, *The Rainbow Comes and Goes*, Rupert Hart-Davis, 1958.

Cooper, Diana, *The Light of Common Day*, Rupert Hart-Davis, 1959.

Cooper, Diana, *Trumpets from the Steep*, Rupert Hart-Davis, 1960.

Davis, Robert Murray, *Evelyn Waugh: A Checklist of Primary and Secondary Material*, Whitston, 1972.

Davis, Robert Murray, *A Catalogue of the Evelyn Waugh Collection at the Humanities Research Center, The University of Texas at Austin*, Whitston, 1981.

Davis, Robert Murray, *Evelyn Waugh, Writer*, Pilgrim Books, 1981.

Davis, Robert Murray, *Evelyn Waugh, Apprentice*, Pilgrim Books, 1985.

Davis, Robert Murray et al., *A Bibliography of Evelyn Waugh*, Whitston, 1986.

Deedes, W. F., *At War with Waugh: The Real Story of Scoop*, Macmillan, 2003.

Delmer, Sefton, *Trail Sinister*, Secker & Warburg, 1961.

Donaldson, Frances, *Evelyn Waugh: Portrait of a Country Neighbour*, Weidenfeld & Nicolson, 1967.

Driberg, Tom, *Ruling Passions*, Quartet Books, 1978.

Fallowell, Duncan, *How to Disappear: A Memoir for Misfits*, Ditto Press, 2011.

Fussell, Paul, *Abroad: British Literary Traveling Between the Wars*, Oxford University Press, 1980.

Gale, Iain, *Waugh's World: A Guide to the Novels of Evelyn Waugh*, Sidgwick & Jackson, 1990.

Gallagher, Donat, *In the Picture: The Facts Behind the Fiction in Evelyn Waugh's Sword of Honour*, Rodopi, 2014.

Gallagher, Donat, Ann Pasternak Slater and John Howard Wilson (eds), *A Handful of Mischief: New Essays on Evelyn Waugh*, Farleigh Dickinson University Press, 2011.

Goldring, Douglas, *Odd Man Out*, Chapman & Hall, 1935.

Green, Henry (Henry Yorke), *Pack My Bag: a Self-Portrait*, Hogarth Press, 1979.

Green, Martin, *Children of the Sun: A Narrative of 'Decadence' in England After 1918*, Constable, 1977.

Greenidge, Terence, *Degenerate Oxford?*, Chapman & Hall, 1930.

Grisewood, Harman, *One Thing at a Time: An Autobiography*, Hutchinson, 1968.

Handford, B. W. T., *Lancing 1848–1930*, Blackwell, 1933.

Hastings, Selina, *Nancy Mitford*, Hamish Hamilton, 1985.

Hastings, Selina, *Evelyn Waugh: A Biography*, Sinclair-Stevenson, 1994.

Hastings, Selina, *The Secret Lives of Somerset Maugham*, John Murray, 2009.

Heath, Jeffrey, *The Picturesque Prison*, Weidenfeld & Nicolson, 1982.

Hillier, Bevis, *Young Betjeman*, John Murray, 1988.

Hillier, Bevis, *New Fame, New Love*, John Murray, 2002.

Hillier, Bevis, *The Bonus of Laughter*, John Murray, 2004.

Hollis, Christopher, *Evelyn Waugh*, Longman, 1966.

Hollis, Christopher, *The Seven Ages*, Heinemann, 1974.

Hollis, Christopher, *Oxford in the Twenties: Recollections of Five Friends*, Heinemann, 1976.

Holman-Hunt, Diana, *My Grandfather, His Wives & Loves*, Hamish Hamilton, 1969.

Holroyd, Michael, *Augustus John, Vol. 2*, Heinemann, 1975.

Holroyd, Michael, *Bernard Shaw, Vol. 1*, Chatto & Windus, 1989.

Ker, Ian, *The Catholic Revival in English Literature, 1845–1961*, University of Notre Dame Press, 2003.

Knox, James, *Robert Byron*, John Murray, 2003.

Lancaster, Marie-Jacqueline (ed.), *Brian Howard: Portrait of a Failure*, Antony Blond, 1968.

Lees-Milne, James, *Ancestral Voices*, Chatto & Windus, 1975.

Lees-Milne, James, *Ancient as the Hills: Diaries 1973–1974*, John Murray, 1997.

Lewis, Jeremy, *Cyril Connolly*, Jonathan Cape, 1997.

Linck, Charles E., *The Development of Evelyn Waugh's Career*, unpublished PhD thesis, 1962.

Linck, Charles E., *Evelyn Waugh in Letters by Terence Greenidge*, Cow Hill Press, 1994.

Longford, Elizabeth, *The Pebbled Shore*, Weidenfeld & Nicolson, 1986.

Lovat, Lord, *March Past*, Weidenfeld & Nicolson, 1978.

Lycett, Andrew, *Ian Fleming*, Weidenfeld & Nicolson, 1995.

Lycett, Andrew, *Dylan Thomas: A New Life*, Weidenfeld & Nicolson, 2003.

McCall, Henrietta, *The Life of Max Mallowan*, British Museum Press, 2001.

Maclean, Fitzroy, *Eastern Approaches*, Cape 1949.

McDonnell, Jacqueline, *Waugh on Women*, Duckworth, 1986.

McLaren, Duncan, *Evelyn! Rhapsody for an Obsessive Love*, Harbour, 2015; see also his website www.evelynwaugh.org.uk

Mallowan, Max, *Mallowan's Memoirs*, Collins, 1977.

May, Derwent (ed.), *Good Talk: An Anthology from BBC Radio*, Victor Gollancz, 1968.

Mead, Richard, *Commando General: The Life of Major General Sir Robert Laycock*, Pen & Sword, 2016.

Mitford, Jessica, *Hons and Rebels*, Victor Gollancz, 1960.

Mitford, Nancy, *A Talent to Annoy: Essays, Articles and Reviews, 1929–1968*, Hamish Hamilton, 1986.

Montagu, Elizabeth, *Honourable Rebel*, Montagu Ventures, 2003.

Morriss, Margaret and D. J., Dooley, *Evelyn Waugh: A Reference Guide*, G. K. Hall & Co, 1984.

Mosley, Charlotte (ed.), *Love from Nancy: The Letters of Nancy Mitford*, Hodder & Stoughton, 1993.

Mosley, Diana, *A Life of Contrasts*, Hamish Hamilton, 1977.

Mosley, Diana, *Loved Ones*, Sidgwick & Jackson, 1977.

Mosley, Diana, *The Pursuit of Laughter*, Gibson Square, 2009.

Mulvagh, Jane, *Madresfield: The Real Brideshead*, Doubleday, 2008.

Norwich, John Julius, *Trying to Please*, Dovecote, 2008.

Norwich, John Julius, (ed.) *Darling Monster: The Letters of Lady Diana Cooper to her son John Julius Norwich, 1939–1962*, Chatto & Windus, 2013.

Ollard, Richard, *A Man of Contradictions: A Life of A.L. Rowse*, Allen Lane, 1999.

Ollard, Richard (ed.), *The Diaries of A. L. Rowse, 1903–1997*, Allen Lane, 2003.

Owen, James, *Commando: Winning WW2 Behind Enemy Lines*, Little, Brown, 2012.

Pakenham, Frank, *Born to Believe*, Cape, 1953.

Patey, Douglas Lane, *The Life of Evelyn Waugh: A Critical Biography*, Blackwell, 1998.

Powell, Anthony, *Infants of the Spring*, Heinemann, 1976.

Powell, Anthony, *Messengers of Day*, Heinemann, 1978.

Powell, Anthony, *Faces in My Time*, Heinemann, 1980.

Powell, Anthony, *The Strangers All Are Gone*, Heinemann, 1982.

Powell, Anthony, *Journals 1982–1986*, Heinemann, 1995.

Preston, Paul, *We Saw Spain Die: Foreign Correspondents in the Spanish Civil War*, Constable, 2008.

Pryce-Jones, David, *Cyril Connolly: Journal and Memoir*, Collins, 1983.

Pryce-Jones, David (ed.), *Evelyn Waugh and His World*, Weidenfeld & Nicolson, 1973.

Rothenstein, John, *Summer's Lease: Autobiography 1901–1938*, Hamish Hamilton, 1965.

Ridley, Jane, *The Architect and His Wife: A Life of Edwin Lutyens*, Chatto & Windus, 2002.

Rowse, A. L., *A Cornishman at Oxford*, Jonathan Cape, 1965.

Rowse, A. L., *A Cornishman Abroad*, Jonathan Cape, 1976.

Rowse, A. L., *A Man of the Thirties*, Jonathan Cape, 1979.

St John, John, *To the War with Waugh*, Leo Cooper, 1973.

Saumarez Smith, John (ed.), *The Bookshop at 10 Curzon Street: Letters between Nancy Mitford and Heywood Hill, 1952–1973*, Francis Lincoln, 2004.

Shakespeare, Nicholas, *Priscilla: The Hidden Life of an Englishwoman in Wartime France*, Harvill Secker, 2013.

Stannard, Martin, *Evelyn Waugh: The Critical Heritage*, Routledge & Kegan Paul, 1984.

Stannard, Martin, *Evelyn Waugh: The Early Years 1903–1939*, JM Dent & Sons, 1986.

Stannard, Martin, *Evelyn Waugh: No Abiding City 1939–1966*, JM Dent & Sons, 1992.

Stopp, Frederick, *Evelyn Waugh: Portrait of an Artist*, Chapman & Hall, 1958.

Taylor, D. J., *Bright Young People*, Chatto & Windus, 2007.

Thomas, David N., *Dylan Thomas: A Farm, Two Mansions and a Bungalow*, Seren, 2000.

Thompson, Laura, *Love in a Cold Climate: Nancy Mitford – A Portrait of a Contradictory Woman*, Review, 2003.

Thwaite, Ann, *Glimpses of the Wonderful: The Life of Philip Henry Gosse*, Faber & Faber, 2002.

Thwaite, Ann (ed.), *My Oxford*, Robson Books, 1977.

Treglown, Jeremy, *Romancing: The Life and Work of Henry Green*, Faber & Faber, 2000.

Sieveking, Paul (ed.), *Airborne: Scenes from the Life of Lance Sieveking*, Strange Attractor Press, 2013.

Sinclair, Andrew, *Francis Bacon: His Life and Violent Times*, Sinclair-Stevenson, 1993.

Sykes, Christopher, *Evelyn Waugh: A Biography*, William Collins, 1975.

Vickers, Hugo, *Cecil Beaton*, Weidenfeld & Nicolson, 1985.

Vickers, Hugo, *The Unexpurgated Beaton: The Cecil Beaton Diaries as He Wrote Them*, Weidenfeld & Nicolson, 2002.

Waugh, Alec, *The Early Years of Alec Waugh*, Cassell, 1962.

Waugh, Alec, *My Brother Evelyn & Other Profiles*, Cassell, 1967.

Waugh, Alec, *The Fatal Gift*, WH Allen, 1973.

Waugh, Alec, *A Year to Remember: A Reminiscence of 1931*, WH Allen, 1975.

Waugh, Alec, *The Best Wine Last*, WH Allen, 1978.

Waugh, Alexander, *Fathers and Sons: The Autobiography of a Family*, Headline, 2004.

Waugh, Arthur, *Alfred Lord Tennyson*, William Heineman, 1894.

Waugh, Arthur, *One Man's Road*, Chapman & Hall, 1931.

Waugh, Auberon, *Will This Do? The First Fifty Years of Auberon Waugh: An Autobiography*, Century, 1991.

Westminster, Loelia, *Grace and Favour*, Weidenfeld & Nicolson, 1961.

Wheen, Francis, *Tom Driberg: His Life and Indiscretions*, Chatto & Windus, 1990.

Williams, Emlyn, *George: An Early Autobiography*, Hamish Hamilton, 1961.

Wilson, A. N., *Betjeman*, Hutchinson, 2006.

Wilson, John Howard, *Evelyn Waugh: A Literary Biography 1903–1924*, Associated University Presses, 1996.

Wilson, John Howard, *Evelyn A Literary Biography 1924–1966*, Associated University Presses, 2001.

Wykes, David, *Evelyn Waugh: A Literary Life*, Macmillan, 1999.

Ziegler, Philip, *Diana Cooper*, Hamish Hamilton, 1981.

Zinovieff, Sofka, *The Mad Boy, Lord Berners, My Grandmother and Me*, Jonathan Cape, 2014.

Index